9.04
Desktop
Handbook

To my niece,

Larisa

Ubuntu 9.04 Desktop Handbook

Richard Petersen

Surfing Turtle Press

Alameda, CA

www.surfingturtlepress.com

Please send inquires to: editor@surfingturtlepress.com

ISBN 0-9820998-4-3

ISBN-13   978-0-9820998-4-1

Library of Congress Control Number: 2009928329

Copyright Richard Petersen, 2009

Trademark Acknowledgements

UNIX is a trademark of The Open Group

Microsoft and MS-DOS are registered trademarks of Microsoft Corporation

IBM and PC are registered trademarks of the International Business Machines Corporation

UNIX is a trademark of Canonical

Fedora is a trademark of Red Hat, Inc.

Ubuntu is a trademark of Cannonical, inc.

 are trademarks of Ubuntu, Cannonical, inc.

See **www.ubuntu.com** for more information

 is a trademark of Surfing Turtle Press

Preface

The Ubuntu 9.04 desktop covers the latest Ubuntu 9.04 (Jaunty Jackalope) features of interest to users. The emphasis here is on what users will face when using Ubuntu, covering topics like installation, applications, software management, the GNOME and KDE4 desktops, shell commands, and both the Ubuntu 9.04 administration and network tools. Office, multimedia, mail, and Web applications are reviewed. Desktops are examined in detail including features like the GNOME file manager capability to directly eject both removable media and network shared directories. The KDE4 desktop provides a completely different KDE desktop with a new panel, menu, desktop, configuration tools, and plasmoid applets, as well as the Zoom User Interface (ZUI). Though administrative topics are covered, the emphasis is on what a user would need to know to perform tasks. Desktop effects as implemented by GNOME's Compiz-fusion and KDE's KWin with 3D workspace and windows switching are examined. Certain new tools are covered in detail like Network Manager which now supports both wireless 3G and Ethernet connections and Computer Janitor which removes unused software. The Printing configuration tool provides support for online access to printer drivers. Gufw provides a user interface for managing ufw firewall, the default firewall. Advanced components of Ubuntu 9.04 are also examined such as Dynamic Kernel Module Support (DKMS) now used for vendor graphics drivers, Private Encrypted Directories, and the creation of Ubuntu Live and Netbook USB drives, as well as MID installs discs. Numerous smaller enhancements are also discussed like the Synaptic Package Manager quick searches and sample screenshots, the PulseAudio Device Chooser applet for accessing all Pulse Audio tools, GNOME's file manager support for tabs, and the combined user switcher and quit applet, as well as the new notification windows. Alternate multimedia releases like Ubuntu Studio and Mythbuntu are also referenced.

Part 1 focuses on getting started, covering Ubuntu information and resources, using Ubuntu Live CD/DVD/USB discs, installing and setting up Ubuntu, upgrading Ubuntu from 8.10, basic use of the desktop interface, and connecting to wired and wireless networks.

Part 2 keys in on applications and software management. Repositories and their use are covered in detail, including the third-party Medibuntu repository that holds popular multimedia codecs and applications that have licensing issues. Then office, multimedia, mail, and Web applications are examined such as the Evolution and Thunderbird email applications, the Totem media player, the Brasero disc burner, and the OpenOffice.org office suite. The section includes coverage of the PulseAudio sound interface, the new volume control applet, Firefox and Epiphany Web browsers, and VoIP applications like Skype and Ekiga. Ubuntu Studio graphics release and Mythbuntu multimedia release are also discussed.

Part 3 covers the two major desktops, GNOME and KDE, in detail discussing features like panels, desktop effects, applets, and file managers. GNOME also includes discussion of Compiz-fusion and its popular desktop effects. KDE is implemented as KDE 4.2 which provides and entirely different interface with new desktop features, panels, and menus, along with its own KWin desktop effects. KDE also features a new software management tool called KPackageKit. In addition, the shell interface is also explored, with its command editing, directory navigation, and shell file and directory management capabilities.

Part 4 deals with administration topics, first discussing system tools like the GNOME system monitor, the Disk Usage Analyzer, and Computer Janitor. Then a detailed chapter on Ubuntu system administration tools for managing users and file systems is presented, along with service management and the Wine Windows emulator for running Windows applications directly. The network connections chapter covers a variety of network tasks, including manual configuration of network connections, wireless connections, and firewalls, including the Gufw firewall tool. Printers are handled in their own chapter, featuring the numerous interface features.

Overview

Contents

Part 1

Getting Started

Part 2

Applications

Part 3

Interfaces

10. The K Desktop Environment: KUbuntu 297

Part 4

Administration

Appendices

Part 1: Getting Started

Introduction

Installation

Usage Basics

1. Ubuntu 9.04 Introduction

Ubuntu releases

Linux

Open Source Software

Ubuntu Editions

Ubuntu 9.04

Ubuntu Live CD/DVD

Ubuntu Live USB drive

Ubuntu Software

Ubuntu Linux Help and Documentation

History of Linux and Unix

Ubuntu Linux is currently one of the most popular end-user Linux distributions (**www.ubuntu.com**). Ubuntu Linux is managed by the Ubuntu foundation, which is sponsored by Cannonical, Ltd (**www.cannonical.com**), a commercial organization that supports and promotes open source projects. Ubuntu is based on Debian Linux, one of the oldest Linux distributions dedicated to incorporating cutting edge developments and features (**www.debian.org**). The Ubuntu project was initiated by Mark Shuttleworth, a South African and Debian Linux developer. Debian Linux is primarily a development Linux project, trying out new features. Ubuntu provides a Debian based Linux distribution that is stable, reliable, and easy to use.

Ubuntu is designed as a Linux operating system that can be used easily by everyone. The name Ubuntu means "humanity to others". As the Ubuntu project describes it: "Ubuntu is an African word meaning 'Humanity to others', or 'I am what I am because of who we all are'. The Ubuntu distribution brings the spirit of Ubuntu to the software world."

The official Ubuntu philosophy lists the following principles.

1. Every computer user should have the freedom to download, run, copy, distribute study, share, change, and improve their software for any purpose, without paying licensing fees.

2. Every computer user should be able to use their software in the language of their choice.

3. Every computer user should be given every opportunity to use software, even if they work under a disability.

The emphasis on language reflects Ubuntu's international scope. It is meant to be a global distribution, not focused on any one market. Language support has been integrated into Linux in general by its internationalization projects, denoted by the term i18n. These include sites like **www.li18nux.net** and **www.openi18n.org**.

Making software available to all users involves both full accessibility supports for disabled users as well as seamless integration of software access using online repositories, making massive amounts of software available to all users at the touch of a button. Ubuntu also makes full use of recent developments in automatic device detection, greatly simplifying installation as well as access to removable devices and attached storage.

Ubuntu aims to provide a fully supported and reliable, open source and free, easy to use and modify, Linux operating system. Ubuntu makes these promises about its distribution.

➢ Ubuntu will always be free of charge, including enterprise releases and security updates.

➢ Ubuntu comes with full commercial support from Canonical and hundreds of companies around the world.

➢ Ubuntu includes the very best translations and accessibility infrastructure that the free software community has to offer.

➢ Ubuntu CDs contain only free software applications; we encourage you to use free and open source software, improve it and pass it on.

Ubuntu releases

Ubuntu provides both long term and short term releases. Long term support releases (LTS) are released every two years. Ubuntu 8.04 is a long term release. Short term releases are provided every six months between the LTS versions. These are designed to make available the latest application and support for the newest hardware. Each has its own nickname, like Jaunty Jackalope for the 9.04 release. The long term releases are supported for three years for the desktop and five years for the servers, whereas short term releases are supported for 18 months. Canonical also provides limited commercial support for companies that purchase it.

Installing Ubuntu has been significantly simplified. A core set of applications are installed, and you add to them as you wish. Following installation, added software is taken from online repositories. Install screens have been reduced to just a few screens, moving quickly through default partitioning, user setup, and time settings. The hardware like graphics cards and network connections are now configured and detected automatically.

The Ubuntu distribution of Linux is available online at numerous sites. Ubuntu maintains its own site at **www.ubuntu.com/getubuntu** where you can download the current release of Ubuntu Linux.

Linux

Linux is an fast, stable, and open source operating system for PC computers and workstations that features professional-level Internet services, extensive development tools, fully functional graphical user interfaces (GUIs), and a massive number of applications ranging from office suites to multimedia applications. Linux was developed in the early 1990s by Linus Torvalds, along with other programmers around the world. As an operating system, Linux performs many of the same functions as UNIX, Macintosh, Windows, and Windows NT. However, Linux is distinguished by its power and flexibility, along with being freely available. Most PC operating systems, such as Windows, began their development within the confines of small, restricted personal computers, which have only recently become more versatile machines. Such operating systems are constantly being upgraded to keep up with the ever-changing capabilities of PC hardware. Linux, on the other hand, was developed in a different context. Linux is a PC version of the UNIX operating system that has been used for decades on mainframes and minicomputers and is currently the system of choice for network servers and workstations. Linux brings the speed, efficiency, scalability, and flexibility of UNIX to your PC, taking advantage of all the capabilities that personal computers can now provide.

Technically, Linux consists of the operating system program, referred to as the *kernel,* which is the part originally developed by Linus Torvalds. But it has always been distributed with a massive number of software applications, ranging from network servers and security programs to office applications and development tools. Linux has evolved as part of the open source software movement, in which independent programmers joined together to provide free quality software to any user. Linux has become the premier platform for open source software, much of it developed by the Free Software Foundation's GNU project. Many of these applications are bundled as part of standard Linux distributions. Most of these applications are also incorporated into the Ubuntu repository, using packages that are Debian compliant.

Linux's operating system capabilities include powerful networking features, including support for Internet, intranets, and Windows networking. As a norm, Linux distributions include fast, efficient, and stable Internet servers, such as the Web, FTP, and DNS servers, along with proxy, news, and mail servers. In other words, Linux has everything you need to set up, support, and maintain a fully functional network.

With the both GNOME and K Desktop, Linux also provides GUI interfaces with that same level of flexibility and power. Linux enables you to choose the interface you want and then customize it further, adding panels, applets, virtual desktops, and menus, all with full drag-and-drop capabilities and Internet-aware tools.

Linux does all this at the right price. Linux is free, including the network servers and GUI desktops. Unlike the official UNIX operating system, Linux is distributed freely under a GNU General Public License as specified by the Free Software Foundation, making it available to anyone who wants to use it. GNU (the acronym stands for "GNU's Not Unix") is a project initiated and managed by the Free Software Foundation to provide free software to users, programmers, and developers. Linux is copyrighted, not public domain. However, a GNU public license has much the same effect as the software's being in the public domain. The GNU general public license is designed to ensure Linux remains free and, at the same time, standardized. Linux is technically the operating system kernel—the core operations—and only one official Linux kernel exists. People sometimes have the mistaken impression that Linux is somehow less than a professional operating system because it is free. Linux is, in fact, a PC, workstation, and server version of UNIX. Many consider it far more stable and much more powerful than Windows. This power and stability have made Linux an operating system of choice as a network server.

Open Source Software

Linux is developed as a cooperative Open Source effort over the Internet, so no company or institution controls Linux. Software developed for Linux reflects this background. Development often takes place when Linux users decide to work on a project together. The software is posted at an Internet site, and any Linux user can then access the site and download the software. Linux software development has always operated in an Internet environment and is global in scope, enlisting programmers from around the world. The only thing you need to start a Linux-based software project is a Web site.

Most Linux software is developed as Open Source software. This means that the source code for an application is freely distributed along with the application. Programmers over the Internet can make their own contributions to a software package's development, modifying and correcting the source code. Linux is an open source operating system. Its source code is included in all its distributions and is freely available on the Internet. Many major software development efforts are also open source projects, as are the KDE and GNOME desktops along with most of their applications. The OpenOffice office suite supported by Sun is an open source project based on the StarOffice office suite. You can find more information about the Open Source movement at **www.opensource.org**.

Open source software is protected by public licenses. These prevent commercial companies from taking control of open source software by adding a few modifications of their own, copyrighting those changes, and selling the software as their own product. The most popular public license is the GNU General Public License provided by the Free Software Foundation. This is the license that Linux is distributed under. The GNU General Public License retains the copyright, freely licensing the software with the requirement that the software and any modifications made to it always be freely available. Other public licenses have also been created to support the demands of different kinds of open source projects. The GNU Lesser General Public License (LGPL) lets commercial applications use GNU licensed software libraries. The Qt Public License (QPL) lets open source developers use the Qt libraries essential to the KDE desktop. You can find a complete listing at **www.opensource.org**.

Linux is currently copyrighted under a GNU public license provided by the Free Software Foundation, and it is often referred to as GNU software (see **www.gnu.org**). GNU software is distributed free, provided it is freely distributed to others. GNU software has proved both reliable and effective. Many of the popular Linux utilities, such as C compilers, shells, and editors, are GNU software applications. Provided with your Linux distribution are the GNU C++ and Lisp compilers, Vi and Emacs editors, BASH and TCSH shells, as well as TeX and Ghostscript document formatters. In addition, there are many open source software projects that are licensed under the GNU General Public License (GPL). Most of these applications are available on the Ubuntu software repositories. Chapter 4 describes in detail the process of accessing these repositories to download and install software applications from them on your system.

Under the terms of the GNU General Public License, the original author retains the copyright, although anyone can modify the software and redistribute it, provided the source code is included, made public, and provided free. Also, no restriction exists on selling the software or giving it away free. One distributor could charge for the software, while another one could provide it free of charge. Major software companies are also providing Linux versions of their most popular applications. Oracle provides a Linux version of its Oracle database. (At present, no plans seem in the works for Microsoft applications, though you can use the Wine, the Windows compatibility layer, to run many Microsoft applications on Linux, directly.)

Ubuntu Editions

Ubuntu is released in several editions, each designed for a distinct group of users or functions (see Table 1-1). Editions install different collections of software such as the KDE desktop, the XFce desktop, servers, educational software, and multimedia applications. Table 1-2 lists Web sites where you can download ISO images for these editions. ISO images can be downloaded directly or using a BitTorrent application like Transmission.

The Ubuntu Desktop edition provides standard functionality for end users. The standard Ubuntu release provides a Live CD using the GNOME desktop. Most users would install this edition. This is the CD image that you download from the Get Ubuntu download page at:

`www.ubuntu.com/getubuntu/download`

Those that want to run the Ubuntu Desktop edition on their netbook can download the Ubuntu Netbook Remix (UNR). This is a USB image file that can be copied to a USB drive. The USB drive can operate as an Ubuntu Live USB drive or be used to install Ubuntu Linux on your netbook. You can find out more about the Remix at:

`http://www.canonical.com/projects/ubuntu/unr`

You can download the Ubuntu Netbook Remix image file from:

`http://www.ubuntu.com/getubuntu/download-netbook`

Those that want to run Ubuntu just as a server, providing an Internet service like a Web site, would use the Server edition. The server edition also provides Cloud computer support. The Server edition provided only a simple command line interface; it does not install the desktop. It is designed to primarily run servers. Keep in mind that you could install the desktop first, and later download server software from the Ubuntu repositories, running them from a system that also has a desktop. You do not have to install the Server edition to install and run servers. The Server edition can be downloaded from the Ubuntu download page, like the Desktop edition.

Users that want more enhanced operating system features like RAID arrays, LVM file systems, or file system encryption would use the Alternate edition. The Alternate edition, along with the Desktop and Server editions, can be downloaded directly from.

```
releases.ubuntu.com/jaunty
releases.ubuntu.com/releases/9.04
```

Ubuntu Editions	Description.
Ubuntu Desktop	Live CD using GNOME desktop, **www.ubuntu.com/getubuntu**.
Server Install	Install server software (no desktop) **www.ubuntu.com/getubuntu**.
Alternate Install	Install enhanced features **http://releases.ubuntu.com**.
Netbook Remix	Install a netbook version. The netbooks remix is a Live USB image. **http://www.ubuntu.com/getubuntu/download-netbook**
Kubuntu	Live CD using the KDE desktop, instead of GNOME, **www.kubuntu.org**. kubuntu-desktop
Xubuntu	Uses the Xfce desktop instead of GNOME, **www.xubuntu.org**. Useful for laptops.
Edubuntu	Installs Educational software: Desktop, Server, and Server add-on CDs, **www.edubuntu.org**
goubuntu	Uses only open source software, no access to restricted software of any kind. See the **goubuntu** link at **http://www.ubuntu.com/products/whatisubuntu**
ubuntustudio	Ubuntu desktop with multimedia and graphics production applications, **www.ubuntustudio.org**. **ubuntustudio-desktop** (Meta Packages, universe)
mythbuntu	Ubuntu desktop with MythTV multimedia and DVR applications, **www.mythbuntu.org**. **mythbuntu-desktop** (Meta Packages, multiverse)

Table 1-1: Ubuntu Editions

Other editions use either a different desktop or a specialized collection of software for certain groups of users. Links to the editions are listed on the **http://www.ubuntu.com/products/whatisubuntu** Web page. From there you can download their live/install CDs. The KUbuntu edition used the KDE desktop instead of GNOME. Xubuntu uses the XFce desktop instead of GNOME. This is a stripped down highly efficient desktop, ideal for low power use on laptops and smaller computer. The Edubuntu edition provides educational software. It can also be used with a specialized Edubuntu server to provide educational software on a school network. The Goubuntu edition is a modified version of the standard edition that includes only open source software, with no access to commercial software of any kind, including restricted vendor graphics drivers. Only Xorg open source display drivers are used. The ubuntustudio edition is a new edition that provides a collection of multimedia and image production software. The mythbuntu edition is designed to install and run the MythTV software, letting Ubuntu operate like Multimedia DVR and Video playback system.

The Ubuntu Server, KUbuntu, and Edubuntu are all officially supported by Ubuntu. The Xubuntu, Goubuntu, Mythbuntu, and Ubuntu Studio editions are not supported, but are officially recognized. These are all considered derivatives of the original Ubuntu Desktop. You can find out more about these derivatives at: **http://www.ubuntu.com/products/whatisubuntu/derivatives**.

All these editions can be downloaded from their respective Web sites, as well as from the **http://cdimages.ubuntu.com** site, and from links at **http://www.ubuntu.com/products/whatisubuntu**.

The Kubuntu and Edubuntu editions can be downloaded directly from both:

```
http://releases.ubuntu.com
http://www.ubuntu.com/getubuntu/
```

The Gobuntu, Mythbuntu, Xubuntu, and Ubuntu Studio are all available, along with all the other editions and Ubuntu releases, on the cdimage server, and from the Ubuntu Web site's whatisubuntu page.

```
http://cdimages.ubuntu.com
http://www.ubuntu.com/products/whatisubuntu
```

URL	Internet Site
www.ubuntu.com/getubuntu/download	Primary download site for Desktop and Server CDs
http://releases.ubuntu.com/jaunty	Download site for Desktop, Alternate, and Server CDs: also the Netbook USB (image files, jigdo, and BitTorrent)
http://cdimages.ubuntu.com/releases/jaunty/release/	Download site for Install/Live DVD and for MID USB (image files and BitTorrent).
http://releases.ubuntu.com	Download site for Ubuntu, along with KUbuntu and Edubuntu.
http://cdimages.ubuntu.com	Download site for all Ubuntu editions, including KUbuntu, XUbuntu, Edubuntu, mythbuntu, goubuntu, and ubuntustudio. Check also their respective Web sites.
http://launchpad.net	Ubuntu mirrors
http://torrent.ubuntu.com	Ubuntu BitTorrent site for BitTorrent downloads of Ubuntu distribution ISO images. Bittorrent files also available at **http://releases.ubuntu.com** and **http://cdimages.ubuntu.com**.
http://www.ubuntu.com/getubuntu/download-netbook	Netbook Remix live USB image

Table 1-2: Ubuntu CD ISO Image locations

The **http://releases.ubuntu.com** and **http://cdimages.ubuntu.com** sites hold both BitTorrent and full image files for the editions they provide. The **http://releases.ubuntu.com** site also provides jigdo files for Jigsaw downloads from multiple mirrors.

Keep in mind that most of these editions are released as Live CDs or Live DVD install discs, for which there are two versions, a 32 bit x86 version and a 64 bit x86_64 version. Older computers may only support a 32 bit version, whereas most current computers will support the 64 bit versions. Check your computer hardware specifications to be sure. The 64 bit version should run faster, and most computer software is now available in stable 64 bit packages.

Ubuntu 9.04

Check the Ubuntu Technical Overview for an explanation of changes.

```
https://wiki.ubuntu.com/JauntyJackalope/TechnicalOverview
```

For operational issues and bugs check the Ubuntu Release notes.

```
http://www.ubuntu.com/getubuntu/releasenotes/9.04
```

Ubuntu 9.04 includes the following features.

- For netbooks, Ubuntu 9.04 provides the Ubuntu Netbook Remix (UNR), available as a USB image. See **http://www.canonical.com/projects/ubuntu/unr** for more information. Download from either **http://www.ubuntu.com/getubuntu/download-netbook** or **http://releases.ubuntu.com/jaunty/**. You can use the UNR to install Ubuntu on most netbooks, using a USB drive.

- The installation program (Ubiquity) has been reworked, with a new time zone selection screen supporting graphical map time zone selection. For the keyboard there is a detected default selected for you, and an added option for selecting the keyboard type yourself. There are also graphical representations for hard disk partition configuration. It also features an option for automatically logging in to the main user account.

- The default Ubuntu login screen, though functionally the same, has been redesigned with new artwork.

- The recovery menu adds options for fixing the GRUB boot loader and entering a root shell with networking.

- You use the User Switcher/Quit menu to shut down, logout, restart, suspend, and hibernate. Pressing your computer power button opens the Shut Down dialog with Shutdown, Restart, Hibernate, and Suspend options. The System menu no longer has Log Out and Shut Down entries.

- KUbuntu now uses KDE 4.2 with its new desktop including the Plasma desktop and panel, Dolphin file manager, Kickoff application launcher, and the Zoom User Interface (ZUI).

- The Synaptic Package Manager features a "Get Screenshot" capability, allowing you download a screenshot of the application and display it in the package description pane. Screen shots are not available for all packages.

- There is now a unified notification system that all messages use. The notification messages have been redesigned with a black background.

- Brasero is the integrated GNOME DVD/CD burner used to perform all disc burning tasks, including create, copy, erase, and check. To burn files to a CD/DVD disc, you still use the same Nautilus CD/DVD Creator interface, but the Write to operation will use Brasero to perform the disc writing. For copy, erase, and check operations on an existing CD/DVD disc, right-click on a CD/DVD desktop icon to list Copy Disc, Blank Disc, and Check Disc entries. You can also burn CD/DVD image files directly from the desktop.

- Startup Applications Preferences has replaced the Sessions tool.

- Computer Janitor detects unused packages and lets you remove them. It can also perform configuration fixes, like those to your GRUB **menu.lst** file, reflecting any changes.

- Volume control features a tab for selecting PulseAudio sound themes. You can also choose to have no sound for your alerts.

- There are three new GNOME desktop themes for Ubuntu: Dust, Dust Sand, and New Wave.

- GNOME archiving and compression (File Roller, named Archive Manager), now supports LZMA compression which is more efficient and faster.

- The Ubuntu server edition provides support for Cloud computing. You can set up your own cloud with Ubuntu Enterprise Cloud, or use the public cloud provided by Amazon with Ubuntu on Amazon with EC2. The Amazon cloud is a commercial/fee service provided by Amazon.

Ubuntu 8.10

Feature introduced previously with Ubuntu 8.10.

- The User Switcher (Fast User Switcher Applet, FUSA) supports a Guest login, so temporary users can login without having to use an existing account (like your personal one). Select "Guest session". Also with Pidgen and Empathy IM applications, online, away, busy, and offline entries are displayed, with an image showing the current state.

- The new version of NetworkManager is now used for configuring all network connections, even manually. The older GNOME network-admin has been dropped. You can also use NetworkManager to configure 3G wireless networks.

- The user switcher and Quit button on the desktop panel have been combined, displaying options for both other users to switch to, and entries to logout, restart, and shutdown.

- For users, Ubuntu provides a Private encrypted directory (**ecryptfs**). The Private directory is not accessible to other users or groups. Furthermore the directory remain unmount until you decide to access it. The **encryptfs-setup-private** command implements the Private directory.

- You can more easily create a USB install drive, letting you install Ubuntu using just a USB drive instead of a CD/DVD ROM disc. The tool to use is **usb-creator**.

- An improved hardware driver install tool (jockey) better locates and installs restricted (third party) drivers.

- Synaptic supports Quick searches, displaying results as you type in your query.

- GNOME Nautilus file manager supports tabs for displaying multiple folders in the same window, as well as a new compact view for listing files.

- Gufw provides a user interface for configuring the UFW default firewall on the GNOME desktop.

- GNOME Nautilus file manager provides an Eject button for removable media like USB drives and CD/DVD discs (similar to KDE 4). The Places view on the sidebar will display an Eject icon next to the mounted removable media. Just click the button to eject the media (or unmount in the case of USB drives so you can then remove it).

- The GNOME Archive Mounter allows you to access archives, displaying or extracting their contents. Works also on CD/DVD disc images (does not mount them as file systems).

- Adobe FLASH is included

- The GNOME Archive Manager (fileroller) supports additions archiving formats, ALZ, CAB, RZIP, and TAR.7Z. These are based on the p7zip archiving format.

- GNOME Archive Manager can now encrypt archives (password accessible)

- CompizFusion is fully integrated with the GNOME desktop with plugins like cube deformation (cylinder and sphere) and window thumbnails. KDE4's KWin provides similar desktop effects for workspace switching and window selection.

- OpenOffice 3.0 features support for MS Office 2007 files.

- Open Java 6 JRE and JDK are included as part of the main Ubuntu repository.

Ubuntu 8.04

Features introduced previously with Ubuntu 8.04.

- PolicyKit authorization for users, allowing limited controlled administrative access to users for administration tools, and for storage and media devices.

- Brasero GNOME CD/DVD burner

- Kernel-based Virtualization Machine (KVM) support is included with the kernel. KVM uses hardware virtualization enabled processors. Use the Virtual Machine Manager to manage and install both KVM and Xen virtual machines.

- Applications like Transmission BitTorrent client, Vinagre Virtual Network Client, and the World Clock applet with weather around the world.

- Features automatic detection of removable devices like USB printers, digital cameras, and card readers. CD/DVD discs are treated as removable devices, automatically displayed and accessed when inserted.

- GNOME supports GUI access to all removable devices and shared directories on networked hosts, including Windows folders, using the GNOME Virtual File System, **gvfs**. Gvfs replaces gnomevfs.

- Any NTFS Windows file systems on your computer are automatically detected and mounted using **ntfs-3g**. Mounted file systems are located in the **/media** directory.

- The Update Manager automatically updates your Ubuntu system and all its installed applications, from the Ubuntu online repositories.

- Software management (Synaptic Package Manager) accesses and installs software directly from all your configured online Ubuntu repositories.

- Wine Windows Compatibility Layer lets you run most popular Windows applications directly on your Ubuntu desktop.

Ubuntu Live CD/DVD/USB

With the Ubuntu Desktop install CD and DVDs for most editions, will operate as Live CD/DVDs, letting you run Ubuntu from any CD-ROM drive. You can also install the Live CD image to a USB drive. In effect, you can carry your operating system with you on just a CD/DVD-ROM or a USB drive. New users could also use the Live-CD/USB to check out Ubuntu to see if they like it. The standard Ubuntu Desktop CD and the Install DVD both can operate as Live CDs (Server and Alternate editions do not). The Ubuntu Desktop CD will run as a Live CD automatically, with the Install DVD it is a start up option. Both run GNOME as the desktop. If you want to use the KDE desktop instead, you would use the KUbuntu CD. For Live USB, you have to first install the Live CD image to a USB drive using the Ubuntu USB creator software.

In addition to the standard Live CD/DVDs, Ubuntu also provides Live USB images for specialized small computers, both the Netbook PCs (UNR) and handhelds using Intel Atom or A1xx processors. These are available as IMG images that use a different tool to burn to a USB drive, USB ImageWriter.

Ubuntu Live CD

Keep in mind that all the Live CD/DVDs also function as install discs for Ubuntu, providing its limited collection of software on a system, but installing a full fledged Ubuntu operating system that can be expanded and updated from Ubuntu online repositories. From the Live CD desktop, double-click on the "Install" icon on the desktop to start the installation.

The Live CD provided by Ubuntu includes a limited set of software packages. On the Ubuntu Desktop CD, for desktop support you use GNOME. Other than these limitations, you have a fully operational Ubuntu desktop. You have the full set of administrative tools, with which you can add users, change configuration settings, and even add software, while the Live CD is running. When you shut down, the configuration information is lost, including any software you have added.

Files and data can be written to removable devices like USB drives and CD/DVD write discs, letting you save your data during a Live CD session.

When you start up the Ubuntu Desktop CD/DVD, the GNOME desktop is automatically displayed (see Figure 1-1). You are logged in as the live session user. The top panel will display menus followed by application icons for a Web browser (Firefox) and mail. To the right is a network connection icon for NetworkManager, which you can configure (right-click) for wireless access. See Chapter 3 for information on basic desktop usage. At the right side of the top panel is a

User switcher/Quit button for shutting down your system. It is important to use the shut down button to unmount any removable devices safely.

Figure 1-1: Ubuntu Live CD

On the desk an icon is displayed for an Examples directory. Here you will find example files for OpenOffice.org (Productivity), ogg video and spx/ogg sound files (Multimedia), and gimp xcf and image png files (Graphics). OpenOffice.org files begin with the prefix **oo-** and include word-processing (odt), spreadsheets (xls), presentation (odp), and drawing (odg). Check the **oo-welcome.odt** file for information about Ubuntu, and the **oo-about-these-files.odt** file for information about the example files. Also included are png image files of the official Ubuntu logos for Ubuntu, Kubuntu, and Edubuntu.

The Computer window, accessible from the Places menu, will display icons for all partitions on your current computer. These will be automatically mounted as read only, including Windows file systems. The File System icon will let you peruse the configuration files, but these are located on a Read Only File System (rofs) which you can access but not change. These folders and files will show a lock emblem on their icons

You can save files to your home directory, but they are only temporary and will disappear at the end of the session. Copy them to a DVD, USB drive, or other removable device to save them.

There is also an Install icon to let you install Ubuntu on your computer, performing a standard installation to your hard drive.

Ubuntu Live USB drive

With the **usb-creator** utility you can now create an install and Live disk on a USB drive. The USB Live/install drive is generated using the CD/DVD iso images that you first have to download. First download and install the **usb-creator** package (Ubuntu main repository). From the System | Administration menu select" Create a USB startup disk", or enter **usb-creator** on the command line. An **-s** option will create the disk with safer options, but may slow down booting. ,

The Make USB Startup Disk window opens with an entry at the top to select an ISO image, and an entry below to select the USB drive to use. Click the Other button to locate a specific disk image to use (see Figure 1.2).

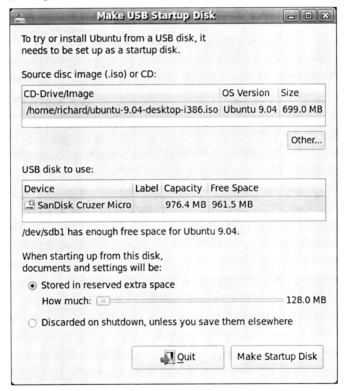

Figure 1-2: USB Creator

The make operation will not erase any data already on your USB drive. You can still access it, even Windows data. The Ubuntu Live OS will coexist with your current data, occupying available free space.

To boot from the Live USB, be sure to modify your BIOS to boot from the USB drive. The Live USB drive will then start up just like the Live CD, displaying the install screen with options to try Ubuntu or directly install.

When you create the Live USB drive you have the option to specify writable memory. This will allow you to save files to your USB drive as part of the Ubuntu Live operating system. You can save files to your Document or Pictures directory and then access them later. You can also create new users, and give those users administrative permission, just as you would on a normally installed OS. With the Login Window tool you could even have the new user be the automatic login, instead of the ubuntu users. In effect the Ubuntu Live USB drive becomes a portable Ubuntu OS. Still, even with these changes, the Ubuntu Live USB still remains the equivalent of a Live CD, just one that you can write to. There is not GRUB boot loader. You still use the install start up screen. And you cannot update the kernel. One advantage of this approach is that your other data can coexist on the USB drive, accessible by other operating systems.

If you want a truly portable Ubuntu OS, just perform a standard installation to a USB drive, instead of to a hard drive. You will, though, have to create a new clean partition on the USB drive to install to. You would either reduce the size of the current partition, preserving data or simple delete it, and opening up the entire drive for use by the new Ubuntu OS.

Ubuntu Netbook Remix (UNR) Live USB drive

The Ubuntu Netbook Remix (UNR) USB is a version Ubuntu designed for use on small Ultra-mobile PCs with 10 inch screens and 256MB RAM. The UNR can operate like a Live USB image or install Ubuntu on your Netbook.

The UNR images arise available either as a torrent files or full USB image file (**.img**) at **http://releases.ubuntu.com/jaunty** as **ubuntu-9.04-netbook-remix-i386.img**. You can also download it from **http://www.ubuntu.com/getubuntu/download-netbook**. You can also access it with the following URL.

```
http://releases.ubuntu.com/jaunty/ubuntu-9.04-netbook-remix-i386.img
```

This is an IMG file, not an ISO file. You use USB ImageWriter (**usb-imagewriter**) to burn it, not usb-creator. You can also use a **dd** command in a terminal window to burn the image. You will have to unmount the device first. You can find detailed information about burning the IMG image at:

```
https://help.ubuntu.com/community/Installation/FromImgFiles
```

You can even burn the image file on Windows and OSX. On Windows use the Disk Imager to burn the IMG file. On OSX you use a command line **dd** operation in a terminal window.

Ubuntu Mobile Internet Device (MID) USB Live drive

Ubuntu now supports MID USB Live drives, designed for use on handhelds with 4x7 touch screens. Like a Live CD, the MID USB Live drive can boot Ubuntu to your handheld from a USB drive, without affecting the installed OS on your handheld. It runs just like any Ubuntu Live CD or USB drive.

Currently there is only a version available for the Low-Power Intel Architecture (LPIA), handhelds using the Intel Atom and A1xx processors. This is a Live CD image that can be burned to a USB drive, which can then be run on the handheld directly from the USB drive. The MID USB image is available from **http://cdimages.ubuntu.com/releases/jaunty/release/**as **ubuntu-9.04-mid-lpia.img**. At least 128MB RAM is required on the handheld. This is an IMG file, not an ISO file. You use USB ImageWriter to burn it, not usb-creator. You can also access it with the following URL.

```
http://cdimages.ubuntu.com/releases/jaunty/release/ubuntu-9.04-mid-lpia.img
```

You use USB ImageWriter (**usb-imagewriter**) to burn it, not usb-creator. This is available on the Ubuntu Universe repository. Install it with apt-get or the Synaptic Package manager. You can also install it from Windows and OSX. See the following site for details on burning USB img files.

```
https://help.ubuntu.com/community/installation/FromImgFiles
```

The Ubuntu 9.04 release notes states a warning that MID can only finish an installation if connected to a network.

USB ImageWriter

Both the MID USB and UNR USB images are IMG files, not ISO files. You cannot use usb-creator to write them to a USB drive. The usb-creator tool only works on ISO image files or CD discs.

To burn the MID or UNR USB img files to a USB drive, you use the **usb-imagewriter** tool, USB Imagewriter. Check the Imagewriter documentation at:

```
https://launchpad.net/usb-imagewriter
https://help.ubuntu.com/community/Installation/FromImgFiles
```

The usb-imagewriter software package is available on the Ubuntu repository (Universe). You can download and install it using the Synaptic Package Manager. The package name is **usb-imagewriter**.

From the Applications | Accessories | Image Writer menu entry you can start up the USB Imagewriter, select the USB image to install and the USB drive to install to (see Figure 1-3).

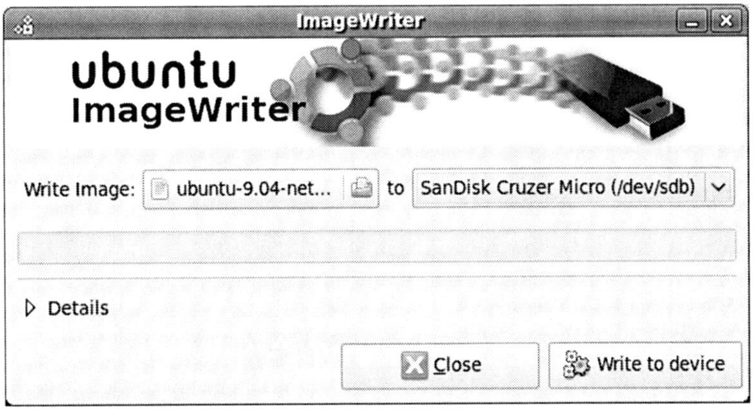

Figure 1-3: USB ImageWriter

Ubuntu Software

For Ubuntu, you can update to the latest software from the Ubuntu repository using the update manager. The Ubuntu distribution provides an initial selection of desktop software. Additional applications can be downloaded and installed from online repositories, ranging from office and multimedia applications to Internet servers and administration services. Many popular applications are included in separate sections of the repository. During installation, your system is configured to access Ubuntu repositories.

All Linux software for Ubuntu is currently available from online repositories. You can download applications for desktops, Internet servers, office suites, and programming packages, among others. Software packages are primarily distributed in through Debian-enabled repositories, the largest of which is the official Ubuntu repository. Downloads and updates are handled automatically by your desktop software manager and updater.

A complete listing of software packages for the Ubuntu distribution, along with a search capability is located at.

```
http://packages.ubuntu.com
```

In addition, you could download from third-party sources software that is in the form of compressed archives or in DEB packages. DEB packages are those archived using the Debian Package Manager. Compressed archives have an extension such as **.tar.gz**, whereas Debian packages have a **.deb** extension. You could also download the source version and compile it directly on your system. This has become a simple process, almost as simple as installing the compiled DEB versions.

Due to licensing restrictions, multimedia support for popular operations like MP3, DVD, and DivX are included with Ubuntu in a separate section of the repository called multiverse. Ubuntu does include on its restricted repository Nvidia and ATI vendor graphics drivers. Ubuntu also provides as part of its standard installation, the generic X.org which will enable your graphics cards to work.

All software packages in different sections and Ubuntu repositories are accessible directly with the Install/Remove Applications and the Synaptic Package Manager.

Due to further licensing issues, added multimedia support for popular operations like DVD Video, as well as popular applications like Google Earth, Skype, and Adobe reader are provide by the **medibuntu.org** repository. This is a third party repository which does not have repository support initially configured. You have to implement repository support manually before you can access the software packages with the Synaptic Package Manager. See Chapters 4 and 6 for details on how to configure medibuntu.org repository access for your system.

Ubuntu Linux Help and Documentation

A great deal of help and documentation is available online for Ubuntu, ranging from detailed install procedures to beginners questions (see Table 1-3). The two major sites for documentation are help.ubuntu.com and the Ubuntu forums at **http://ubuntuforums.org**. In additions there are blog and news sites as well as the standard Linux documentation. Also helpful is the Ubuntu Guide Wiki at **www.ubuntuguide.org**. Links to Ubuntu documentation, support, blogs, and news are listed at **www.ubuntu.com/community**. Here you will also find links for the Ubuntu community structure including the code of conduct. A Contribute section links to sites where you can make contributions in development, artwork, documentation, support.

For mailing lists, check **http://lists.ubuntu.com**. There are lists for categories like Ubuntu announcements, community support for specific editions, and development for areas like the desktop, servers, or mobile implementation. For more specialized tasks like Samba support and LAMP server installation check **www.ubuntugeek.com**.

Site	Description
http://help.ubuntu.com	Help pages
http://packages.ubuntu.com	Ubuntu software package list and search
http://ubuntuforums.org	Ubuntu forums
www.ubuntuguide.org	Guide to Ubuntu
http://fridge.ubuntu.com	News and developments
http://planet.ubuntu.com	Member and developer blogs
http://blog.canonical.com	Latest Canonical news
www.tldp.org	Linux Documentation Project Web site
www.ubuntuguide.org	All purpose guide to Ubuntu topics
www.ubuntugeek.com	Specialized Ubuntu modifications
www.ubuntu.com/community	Links to Documentation, Support, News, and Blogs
http://lists.ubuntu.com	Ubuntu mailing lists
www.ubuntugeek.com	Tutorials and guides for specialized tasks

Table 1-3: Ubuntu help and documentation

help.ubuntu.com

Ubuntu-specific documentation is available at **help.ubuntu.com**. Here on tabbed pages you can find specific documentation for different releases. Always check the release help page first for documentation. The documentation though may be sparse. It covers mainly changed areas. The Ubuntu LTS release usually includes desktop, installation, server guides. The guides are very complete and will cover most topics. For 9.04 Documentation section will cover key desktop topics like software management, music and video applications, Internet application including mail and instant messaging, office applications, security topics, and a guide for new users

The short term support releases tend to have just a few detailed documentation topics like software management, desktop customization, security, multimedia and Internet applications, and printing. These will vary depending on what new features are included in the release.

One of the most helpful pages is the last, Community Docs page. Here you will find detailed documentation on installation of all Ubuntu releases, using the desktop, installing software, and configuring devices. Always check the page for your Ubuntu release first. The page has these main sections:

➢   Getting Help: links to documentation and FAQs. The official documentation link displays the tabbed page for that release on **http://help.ubuntu.com**.

➢   Getting Ubuntu: Link to Install page with sections on desktop, server, and alternate installation. Also information on how to move from using other operating systems like Windows or Mac.

➢   Using and Customizing your System: Sections on managing and installing software, Internet access, configuring multimedia applications, and setting up accessibility, the desktop appearance (eye candy), server configuration, and development tools (programming).

➢   Maintain your Computer: Links to system administration, security, and trouble shooting pages. System administration cover topics like adding users, configuring the GRUB boot loader, setting the time and date, and installing software. The Security page covers lower level issues like IPtables for firewalls and how GPG security works.

➢   Connecting and Configuring Hardware: Links to pages on drives and partitions, input devices, wireless configuration, printers, sound, video, and laptops.

ubuntuforums.org

Ubuntu forums provide detailed online support and discussion for users. An Absolute Beginner section provides an area where new users can obtain answers to questions. Sticky threads include both quick and complete guides to installation for the current Ubuntu release. You can use the search feature to find discussions on your topic of interest.

The main support categories section covers specific support areas like networking, multimedia, laptops, security, and 64 bit support.

Other community discussions cover ongoing work such as virtualization, art and design, gaming, education and science, Wine, assistive technology, and even testimonials. Here you will also find community announcements and news. Of particular interest are third party projects that include projects like Mythbuntu (MythTV on Ubuntu), Ubuntu Podcast forum, Ubuntu Women, and Ubuntu Gamers.

The forum community discussion is where you talk about anything else. The **http://ubuntuforums.org/** site also provides a gallery page for posted screenshots as well as RSS feeds for specific forums.

ubuntuguide.org

The Ubuntu Guide is a kind of all purpose HowTo for frequently asked questions. It is independent of the official Ubuntu site and can deal with topics like how to get DVD-video to work (**www.ubuntuguide.org**. Areas cover topics like popular add-on applications like Flash, Adobe Reader, and MPlayer. The Hardware section deals with specific hardware like Nvidia drivers and Logitech mice. Emulators like Wine and VMWare are also discussed.

Ubuntu news and blog sites

Several news and blog sites are accessible from the News pop-up menu on the **www.ubuntu.com** site.

- **http://fridge.ubuntu.com** The Fridge site lists the latest news and developments for Ubuntu. It features the Weekly newsletter, latest announcements, and upcoming events.

- **http://planet.ubuntu.com** Ubuntu blog for members and developers

- **http://blog.canonical.com** Canonical news

Linux documentation

Linux documentation has also been developed over the Internet. Much of the documentation currently available for Linux can be downloaded from Internet FTP sites. A special Linux project called the Linux Documentation Project (LDP), headed by Matt Welsh, has developed a complete set of Linux manuals. The documentation is available at the LDP home site at **www.tldp.org**. The Linux documentation for your installed software will be available at your **/usr/share/doc** directory.

History of Linux and Unix

As a version of UNIX, the history of Linux naturally begins with UNIX. The story begins in the late 1960s, when a concerted effort to develop new operating system techniques occurred. In 1968, a consortium of researchers from General Electric, AT&T Bell Laboratories, and the Massachusetts Institute of Technology carried out a special operating system research project called MULTICS (the Multiplexed Information and Computing Service). MULTICS incorporated many new concepts in multitasking, file management, and user interaction.

UNIX

In 1969, Ken Thompson, Dennis Ritchie, and the researchers at AT&T Bell Laboratories developed the UNIX operating system, incorporating many of the features of the MULTICS research project. They tailored the system for the needs of a research environment, designing it to run on minicomputers. From its inception, UNIX was an affordable and efficient multi-user and multitasking operating system.

The UNIX system became popular at Bell Labs as more and more researchers started using the system. In 1973, Dennis Ritchie collaborated with Ken Thompson to rewrite the programming code for the UNIX system in the C programming language. UNIX gradually grew from one person's tailored design to a standard software product distributed by many different vendors, such as Novell and IBM. Initially, UNIX was treated as a research product. The first versions of UNIX were distributed free to the computer science departments of many noted universities. Throughout the 1970s, Bell Labs began issuing official versions of UNIX and licensing the systems to different users. One of these users was the Computer Science department of the University of California, Berkeley. Berkeley added many new features to the system that later became standard. In 1975, Berkeley released its own version of UNIX, known by its distribution arm, Berkeley Software Distribution (BSD). This BSD version of UNIX became a major contender to the AT&T Bell Labs version. AT&T developed several research versions of UNIX, and in 1983, it released the first commercial version, called System 3. This was later followed by System V, which became a supported commercial software product.

At the same time, the BSD version of UNIX was developing through several releases. In the late 1970s, BSD Unix became the basis of a research project by the Department of Defense's

Advanced Research Projects Agency (DARPA). As a result, in 1983, Berkeley released a powerful version of UNIX called BSD release 4.2. This release included sophisticated file management as well as networking features based on Internet network protocols—the same protocols now used for the Internet. BSD release 4.2 was widely distributed and adopted by many vendors, such as Sun Microsystems.

In the mid-1980s, two competing standards emerged, one based on the AT&T version of UNIX and the other based on the BSD version. AT&T's Unix System Laboratories developed System V release 4. Several other companies, such as IBM and Hewlett-Packard, established the Open Software Foundation (OSF) to create their own standard version of UNIX. Two commercial standard versions of UNIX existed then—the OSF version and System V release 4.

Linux

Originally designed specifically for Intel-based personal computers, Linux started out as a personal project of a computer science student named Linus Torvalds at the University of Helsinki. At that time, students were making use of a program called *Minix,* which highlighted different UNIX features. Minix was created by Professor Andrew Tanenbaum and widely distributed over the Internet to students around the world. Linus' intention was to create an effective PC version of UNIX for Minix users. It was named Linux, and in 1991, Linus released version 0.11. Linux was widely distributed over the Internet, and in the following years, other programmers refined and added to it, incorporating most of the applications and features now found in standard UNIX systems. All the major window managers have been ported to Linux. Linux has all the networking tools, such as FTP file transfer support, Web browsers, and the whole range of network services such as e-mail, the domain name service, and dynamic host configuration, along with FTP, Web, and print servers. It also has a full set of program development utilities, such as C++ compilers and debuggers. Given all its features, the Linux operating system remains small, stable, and fast. In its simplest format, Linux can run effectively on only 2MB of memory.

Although Linux has developed in the free and open environment of the Internet, it adheres to official UNIX standards. Because of the proliferation of UNIX versions in the previous decades, the Institute of Electrical and Electronics Engineers (IEEE) developed an independent UNIX standard for the American National Standards Institute (ANSI). This new ANSI-standard UNIX is called the Portable Operating System Interface for Computer Environments (POSIX). The standard defines how a Unix-like system needs to operate, specifying details such as system calls and interfaces. POSIX defines a universal standard to which all UNIX versions must adhere. Most popular versions of UNIX are now POSIX-compliant. Linux was developed from the beginning according to the POSIX standard. Linux also adheres to the Linux file system hierarchy standard (FHS), which specifies the location of files and directories in the Linux file structure. See **www.pathname.com/fhs** for more details.

Linux development is now overseen by The Linux Foundation (**www.linux-foundation.org**), which is a merger of The Free Standards Group and Open Source Development Labs (OSDL). This is the group that Linux Torvalds works with to develop new Linux versions. Actual Linux kernels are released at **www.kernel.org**.

2. Installing Ubuntu

Install CD and DVDs

Hardware, Software, and Information Requirements

Installing Ubuntu

Installation

Start Up Issues

Login and Logout

Initial Configuration Tasks

Recovery

Re-Installing the Boot Loader

Alternate Install

Automating Installation with Kickstart

Wubi: Windows-based installer

Installing Ubuntu Linux has become a very simple procedure with just a few screens with default entries for easy installation. A pre-selected collection of software is installed. Most of your devices, like your monitory and network connection, are detected automatically. The most difficult part would be a manual partitioning of the hard drive, but you can use a Guided partitioning for installs that use an entire hard disk, as is usually the case. As an alternative, you can now install Ubuntu on a virtual hard disk on your Windows system, avoiding any partition issues.

Install CD and DVDs

In most cases, installation is performed using an Ubuntu LiveCD that will install the GNOME desktop along with a pre-selected set of software packages for multimedia players, office applications, and games. The Ubuntu LiveCD is designed to run from the CD, while providing the option to install Ubuntu on your hard drive. This is the disc you will download from the Ubuntu download site. The CD has both 32 and 64 bit versions. If you are want to use the 64 bit version, be sure you have CPU that is 64 bit compatible (all current CPUs are).

`http://www.ubuntu.com/getubuntu/download`

You can also download CD and DVD images directly from:

`http://releases.ubuntu.com`

Installation choices

Ubuntu tailors its installs by providing different CD/DVD install disc for different releases and versions. The LiveCD/DVD is not the only Ubuntu installation available. Ubuntu provides two other CDs, one designed for servers and the other provides specialized features like LVM and RAID. Alternate install also supports small installs with less than 320MB RAM, automated installs, customized OEM systems, and upgrading older releases that have no network access. The Wubi installation option will install a fully functional Ubuntu system on a virtual hard disk on Windows system. This is the easiest installation of Ubuntu and requires no hard disk partitioning.

➢ **Desktop CD** Run as Live CD or install GNOME desktop with standard set of applications.

➢ **Desktop USB** Run as Live USB or install GNOME desktop with standard set of applications, uses Desktop CD image installed on USB drive.

➢ **Server install CD** Install Ubuntu with set of standard servers

➢ **Alternate CD** Installs specialized features like LVM, RAID, encrypted file systems, small systems, and OEM configurations.

➢ **Wubi**, Windows install on virtual hard disk.

➢ **Ubuntu Netbook Remix (UNR) USB**. A Live USB for use on Netbooks. You can also use it to install Ubuntu on a netbook. Supports screens up to 10 inches, and requires at least 256MB RAM.

➢ **Install/Live DVD** Install GNOME desktop with a more extensive set of applications. The Text Mode Install also allows you install servers as well as just a command line system without the desktop.

> ➢ **MID USB** Run as Live or install on a handheld device with 4x7 touch screen and 128MB RAM, one Low-Power Intel Architecture version available (Atom and A1xx processors).

The Desktop CD, Alternate CD, Server CD, and Ubuntu Netbook Remix (UNR) USB are available at:

`http://releases.ubuntu.com/9.04`

The Install/Live DVD and the MID USB are available at:

`http://cdimages.ubuntu.com/releases/jaunty/release/`

Ubuntu releases	Description
Ubuntu Desktop Live/Install CD/USB	Primary Ubuntu release, GNOME desktop, can be burned to either CD disc or USB drive.
Ubuntu Desktop CD/Wubi	Insert Ubuntu Desktop CD in Windows system, and you can perform a Wubi installation.
Ubuntu Alternate CD	Support for specialized features like LVM, RAID, encrypted file systems, OEM distributions, and small memory.
Ubuntu Server CD	Server only installation, no desktop, command line interface
Ubuntu Netbook Remix UNR	Live USB image for use on Netbooks, can also use it to install Ubuntu on your netbook.
Ubuntu Install/Live DVD	Installation DVD, primarily for installs, large software collection on disc, can operate as a Live DVD
Ubuntu Live/Install MID USB	Install USB image for use on handhelds
Ubuntu Editions	
KUbuntu	Installs the KDE desktop and software instead of GNOME, **www.kubuntu.org**.
Edubuntu	Installs Educational software: Desktop, Server, and Server add-on CDs, **www.edubuntu.org**
XUbuntu	Installs XFce desktop, **www.xubuntu.org**
Ubuntu Studio	Install Ubuntu multimedia and graphics applications, **www.ubuntustudio.org**.
Mythbuntu	MythTV multimedia software selection for Ubuntu, **www.mythbuntu.org**

Table 2-1: Ubuntu releases and versions

The Install/Live DVD is meant to primarily install Ubuntu, and provides a large selection of software, though it can also serve as a Live DVD. It has the advantage of providing a large collection of installable software without needing network access to a repository. It also includes all the servers, all those also found on the Server CD. If you choose a Text Mode install, you can choose servers to install (F4, Modes) during the install procedure. The DVD Text Mode Install also allows you option to install just a command line interface without a desktop. This is useful for server dedicated systems or those with little graphics support. All releases have 32 and 64 bit versions.

Other Ubuntu editions include KUbuntu, Edubuntu, and Goubuntu (see Table 2-1). The KUbuntu LiveCD installs KDE as the desktop instead of GNOME, along with KDE software. You could also install KUbuntu later on a GNOME install by selecting the KUbuntu-desktop meta-package for software installation. KUbuntu can then become an option in your login window sessions menu. You should download these editions from their Web sites directly. They are also available from the Ubuntu download sites. For KUbuntu you can use:

```
http://releases.ubuntu.com/kubuntu/jaunty/
```

Edubuntu is installs a collection of educational software, instead of the standard GNOME office and multimedia applications. The Edubuntu version provides three CDs, a desktop, server, and server add-on. The server add-on provides additional educational applications.

```
http://cdimages.ubuntu.com/edubuntu/releases/9.04/release/
```

You can also download the different editions, including Mythbuntu and Ubuntu Studio, from:

```
http://cdimages.ubuntu.com/
```

Using BitTorrent: Transmission

Most current Linux and Windows systems support BitTorrent for downloading. BitTorrent provides an efficient, safe, and fast method for downloading large files. Various BirTorrent clients are available, including one from the original BitTorrent developer. Most Linux systems now use Transmission, the GNOME BitTorrent client, also the preferred BitTorrent client for Ubuntu 9.04. When downloading a new release, just when it comes out, BitTorrent is often the only practical solution. Also, it is much faster for the DVD, at any time. One exception is if you have a slow Internet connection. BitTorrent relies on making multiple connections that can use up bandwith quickly. For slow connections, especially just for the LiveCD, you may want to just download directly from the Ubuntu site or one of its mirrors.

The Ubuntu BitTorrent site is located at:

```
http://bittorrent.ubuntu.com
```

The BitTorrent files can also be found at the following site, including DVD and CD BitTorrent files for all versions (LiveCD, DVD, Alternate, and Server), along with direct downloads:

```
http://releases.ubuntu.com/releases/9.04
```

Jigdo (Jigsaw Download)

The preferred method for downloading large DVD ISO images is Jigdo (Jigsaw Download). Jigdo combines the best of both direct downloads and Bittorrent, while maximizing use of the download data for constructing various spins. In effect, Jigdo sets up a bittorrent download operation using just the Ubuntu mirror sites (no uploading). Jigdo automatically detects the mirror sites that currently provide the fastest download speeds and downloads your image from them. Mirror sites accessed are switched as download speeds change. If you previously downloaded directly from mirrors, with Jigdo you no longer have to go searching for a fast download mirror site. Jigdo finds them for you.

See the JigdoDownloadHowto page at **http://help.ubuntu.com** for more details.

```
https://help.ubuntu.com/community/JigdoDownloadHowto
```

Jigdo is available for the server and alternate CD/DVDs. It is not used for the desktop versions (32 or 64 bit). First install the **jigdo-file** package and then run the **jigdo-lite** command in a terminal window. The **jigdo-lite** command uses **wget** to perform the actual download operations. You will be prompted for a **.jigdo** file. You can provide the URL for the **.jigdo** file for the ISO image you want, or download the .jigdo file first and provide its path name. At the **http://releases.ubuntu.com** site you will find jigdo files for each ISO image, along with **.torrent** and **.iso** files. The jigdo file for an i386 server is:

```
ubuntu-9.04-alternate-i386.jigdo
```

Its full URL would be:

```
http://releases.ubuntu.com/releases/jaunty/ubuntu-9.04-alternate-i386.jigdo
```

Jigdo organizes the download into central repository that can be combined into different spins. If you download the Ubuntu desktop CD, and then later the server CD, the data already downloaded for the desktop CD can be used to build the server CD, reducing the actual downloaded data significantly. You will be prompted to provide the location of any mounted CD or CD image.

You can also use jigit (**jigit** package) and jigdo (**jigdo** package) applications to perform jigdo downloads. The jigit application can update images already downloaded with jigdo. Use the **jigit** command.

The jigdo package provides a beta version of a jigdo GNOME interface for using jigdo to perform downloads. Enter the **jigdo** command in a terminal window. In the URL textbox enter the URL for the jigdo file for the image file you want to download. In the Save to text box enter the download location. Click Start to start the download.

Installing Dual-Boot Systems

The GRUB boot loader already supports dual-booting. Should you have both Linux and Windows systems installed on your hard disks; GRUB will let you choose to boot either the Linux system or a Windows system. During installation GRUB will automatically detect any other operating systems installed on your computer and configure your boot loader menu to let you access them. You do not have to perform any configuration yourself.

If you want a Windows system on your computer, you should install it first if it is not already installed. Windows would overwrite the boot loader that a previous Linux system installed, cutting off access to the Linux system.

To install Windows after Ubuntu, you need to boot from your Ubuntu disk and select the "Boot from hard disk" option. Then run the **grub-install** command with the device name of your hard disk to reinstall the boot loader for GRUB.

Hardware, Software, and Information Requirements

Most hardware today meets the requirements for running Linux. Linux can be installed on a wide variety of systems, ranging from the very weak to the very powerful. The install procedure will detect most of your hardware automatically. You will only need to specify your keyboard, though a default is automatically detected for you.

Hardware Requirements

Listed here are the minimum hardware requirements for installing a standard installation of the Linux system on an Intel-based PC:

➢ A 32-bit or 64-bit Intel- or AMD-based personal computer. At least an Intel or compatible (AMD) microprocessor is required. A 700 MHz processor or more is recommended with 300 MHz minimum. For visual effects support you will need at least a 1.2GZ processor.

➢ For 64-bit systems, be sure to use the 64-bit version of Ubuntu, which includes a supporting kernel.

➢ A CD-ROM or DVD-ROM drive. Should you need to create a bootable DVD/CD-ROM, you will need a DVD/CD-RW drive. For a USB Live drive at least a 1GB drive.

➢ Normally you will need at least 64MB RAM minimum, with 384MB recommended.

See the Ubuntu System Requirements page at **http://help.ubuntu.com** for details:

```
http://help.ubuntu.com/community/Installation/SystemRequirement
```

Hard Drive Configuration

These days, Linux is usually run on its own hard drive, though it can also be run on a hard drive that contains a separate partition for a different operating system such as Windows.

If you have already installed Windows on your hard drive and configured it to take up the entire hard drive, you would resize its partition to free up unused space. The freed space could then be used for a Linux partition. You can use a partition management software package, such as **Parted**; to free up space (GParted and QTParted are Linux versions).

Tip: You can also use the Ubuntu Live CD to start up Linux and perform the needed hard disk partitioning using GParted for QTParted.

Hardware and Device Information

If you are not installing Linux on your entire hard drive, decide how much of your hard drive (in megabytes) you want to dedicate to your Linux system. If you are sharing with Windows, decide how much you want for Windows and how much for Linux. Install Windows first.

Know where you live so that you can select the appropriate time zone.

Mice are now automatically detected. Ubuntu no longer supports serial mice. If you should need to later configure your mouse, you can use the GNOME or KDE mouse configuration tool.

Monitor and graphics cards are detected automatically by the Xorg service. Should you need to tweak or modify your configuration later, you can use either the Vendor configuration tools (ATI or Nvidia) supplied by restricted drivers.

Network connections are automatically detected and configured using NetworkManager. Most network connection use DHCP or IPv6 which will automatically set up your network connection. For dial-up and wireless you may have to later configure access.

Installing Ubuntu

Installing Ubuntu involves several processes, beginning with creating Linux partitions, and then loading the Linux software, selecting a time zone, and creating new user accounts. The installation program used on Ubuntu is a screen-based program that takes you through all these processes, step-by-step, as one continuous procedure. You can use either your mouse or the keyboard to make selections. When you finish with a screen, click the Forward button at the bottom to move to the next screen. If you need to move back to the previous screen, click Back. You can also use TAB, the arrow keys, SPACEBAR, and ENTER to make selections. You have little to do other than make selections and choose options.

Installation Overview

Installation is a straightforward process. A graphical installation is very easy to use, providing full mouse support and explaining each step with detailed instructions on a help pane.

➢ Most systems today already meet hardware requirements and have automatic connections to the Internet (DHCP).

➢ They also support booting a DVD-ROM or CD-ROM disc, though this support may have to be explicitly configured in the system BIOS.

➢ Also, if you know how you want Linux installed on your hard disk partitions, or if you are performing a simple update that uses the same partitions, installing Ubuntu is a fairly simple process. Ubuntu features an automatic partitioning function that will perform the partitioning for you.

➢ A preconfigured set of packages are installed, you will not even have to select packages.

For a quick installation you can simply start up the installation process, placing your DVD or CD disc in your optical drive and starting up your system. Graphical installation is a simple matter of following the instructions in each window as you progress. Installation follows seven easy steps:

1. **Welcome and Language Selection**   A default is chosen for you, like English, so you can usually just press Forward.

2. **Where are you?, Time Zone**   Use the map to choose your time zone or select it from the pop-up menu.

3. **Keyboard Layout**   A default is chosen for you; you can usually press Forward.

4. **Prepare Disk Space, Prepare partitions**   For automatic partitioning you have the option of using a Guided partition which will set up your partitions for you. You have the option to perform manual partitioning, setting up partitions yourself.

5.   **Who are you?**   Set up a user and host name for your computer, as well as a password for that user.

6.   **Ready to Install**   At this point nothing has been done to your system. You can opt out of the installation at this point. If you click Forward, then the install process will take place, making actual changes. The system will first be formatted, then packages installed, with installation progress shown.

7.   **Installation Complete** After the install, you will be asked to remove your DVD/CD-ROM and click the Exit button. This will reboot your system (do not reboot yourself).

Starting the Installation Program

If your computer can boot from the DVD/CD-ROM, you can start the installation directly from the CD-ROMs or the DVD-ROM. Just place the CD-ROM in the CD-ROM drive, or the DVD-ROM in the DVD drive, before you start your computer. After you turn on or restart your computer, the installation program will start up.

Ubuntu Live CD

The Ubuntu Live CD (Desktop) is designed for both running Ubuntu from the CD and installing Ubuntu. Most users will also use the Desktop Live CD to install or upgrade Ubuntu. With the Desktop Live CD, you first start up Ubuntu, and then you can initiate an installation. (see Figure 2-2). The installation program will present you with a menu listing the following options (see Figure 2-1):

```
Try Ubuntu without any changes to your computer
Install Ubuntu
Check CD for defects
Test Memory
Boot from first hard disk
```

Tip: To boot from a CD-ROM or DVD-ROM, you may first have to change the boot sequence setting in your computer's BIOS so that the computer will try to boot first from the CD-ROM. This requires some technical ability and knowledge of how to set your motherboard's BIOS configuration.

"Try Ubuntu without any changes to your computer" will start Ubuntu as a Live CD. However, even if you just opt to try Ubuntu without changes (first option), you can still perform an installation, just as you would with a LiveCD.

"Install Ubuntu" will start up the installation Welcome screen immediately, beginning the install process (see the next section).

"Install Ubuntu in text mode" will install without a graphical interface, using text boxes you navigate with keyboard arrow, TAB, and ENTER keys.

"Check CD for defects" will check if your CD burn was faulty.

"Memory Test" will check your memory.

"Boot from first hard disk" will let your LiveCD work as boot loader, starting up an operating system on the first hard disk, if one is installed. Use it to boot a system that the boot loader is not accessing for some reason.

Figure 2-1: Install disk start menu for Desktop Live CD

Ubuntu Install/Live DVD

The Install/Live DVD is designed for users who intend to perform an installation, though it also serves as a Live DVD. It is a full DVD with over 4GB of software on the disc. As with the CD, you will have the option to just try Ubuntu or go directly to the Install procedure. The Install option will install the standard desktop.

The Install/Live DVD adds an "Install Ubuntu in text mode" option which will let you install Ubuntu without the need for any graphics card support. If you are having trouble with your display, you can use this option to install Ubuntu first, and then try to later configure your graphics card and monitor.

"Install Ubuntu in text mode" entry is DVD only. This mode also can be used to install servers during installation, or to just install the command line interface. To choose servers to install, be sure to press F4 and select the Install a server option

```
Try Ubuntu without any changes to your computer
Install Ubuntu
Install Ubuntu in text mode
Check CD for defects
Test Memory
Boot from first hard disk
```

Ubuntu Install Options

Along the bottom of the screen are options you can set for the installation process. These are accessible with the function keys, 1 through 6.

`F1 Help F2 Language F3 Keymap F4 Modes F5 Accessibility F6 Other Options`

A description of these options is listed here:

➢ **Help** Boot parameters and install prerequisites

➢ **Languages** List of languages , pop up menu

➢ **Keymap** Languages for keyboard, pop up menu

➢ **Modes** Lists possible install modes: For the CD there are two modes: Normal and Use driver update disc. For the DVD you have several more: OEM, safe graphics mode, and use of a driver CD. The safe graphics mode uses a low resolution for better compatibility. OEM install is a special kind of install allowing an administrator to first configure an install before turning over access. Install with driver update CD is used for a CD with more current driver updates, particularly for newer hardware. The driver CD allows you to use a CD with and special drivers for your system. For the DVD, the Text Mode Install also allows you to install servers.

➢ **Accessibility**   Contrast setting, Magnifier, On screen keyboard, Braille support, keyboard modifiers, and screen reader

➢ **Other options**, Opens an editable text line labeled Boot Options that lists the options of the current selected menu choice. You can add other options here, or modify or remove existing ones. As you move down the list of menu choices you will see the text listed options change, showing the boot options for that choice. The Other Option menu lists several specialized options like acpi=off, noapic, nolapic, edd=on, and Free Software only. The Free Software only option will install only Open Source software packages. Press ESC to return, or enter to start.

Use the arrow keys to move from one menu entry to the Forward, and then press ENTER to select the entry. Should you need to add options, say to the Install or Upgrade entry, press the TAB key. A command line is displayed where you can enter the options. Current options will already be listed. Use the backspace key to delete and arrow keys to move through the line. Press the ESC key to return to the menu.

Tip: Pressing ESC from the graphics menu places you at the boot prompt, boot, for text mode install.

The OEM install mode (Modes) is used for organizations that will be installing Ubuntu on several machines, but want to later add their own applications and configurations to the install. The OEM install will set up an OEM default user with a password provided by the installer. When the installer is ready to turn over control to a regular user, then can run the **oem-prepare** command that will set up a normal user and password, removing the OEM user.

The DVD's text mode install also has an option to install servers (F4). In this respect, the DVD also doubles as a server install disk, including all the servers found on the Server CD. To be able to install a server during installation, you press the F4 key (Modes) and select the "Install a server" entry. There is also an entry for installing an LSTP server.

Modes (F4) added for DVD "Install ubuntu in text mode"

➤ Install a server

➤ Install a command-line system

➤ Install an LTSP server

Starting up Ubuntu

Your system then detects your hardware, providing any configuration specifications that may be needed. For example, if you have an IDE CD-RW or DVD-RW drive, it will be configured automatically.

If you cannot start the install process and you are using an LCD display, you should press F6 on the Install entry and enter **nofb** (no frame buffer) in the options command line.

```
nofb
```

As each screen appears in the installation, default entries will be already selected, usually by the auto probing capability of the installation program. Selected entries will appear highlighted. If these entries are correct, you can simply click Forward to accept them and go on to the next screen.

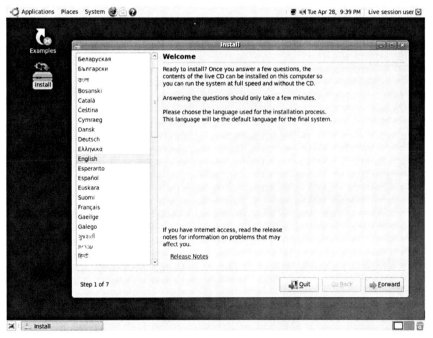

Figure 2-2: Live CD/USB (Desktop) with Install icon.

Installation

If you are installing from the a Live CD/DVD, the Ubuntu operating system will start up in full live CD mode. To install, click on the Install icon on the desktop (see Figure 2-2). If you are using the DVD, installation will begin immediately.

Step 1: Language

A Welcome screen will be displayed, with a Forward button on the lower-right corner. Once finished with a step, you click Forward to move on. In some cases you will be able to click a Back button to return to a previous step. On most screens, a link the lower left will display the Release Notes. On the Welcome screen you select the language to use in the sidebar scroll window. A default language will already be selected, usually English (see Figure 2-3)

Step 2: Where Are You?

On the "Where are you?" screen, you have the option of setting the time by using a map to specify your location (see Figure 2-4). The Time Zone tool uses a new map feature that displays the entire earth, with sections for each time zone. Click on your general location, and the entire time zone for your part of the world will be highlighted in green. The major city closest to your location will be labeled with its current time. The region you selected and the nearest city will appear in the Region and City drop down menus located below the map. You can also select your time zone by region and city from the Region and City drop down menus directly. The corresponding time zone will be highlighted on the map, along with the city time.

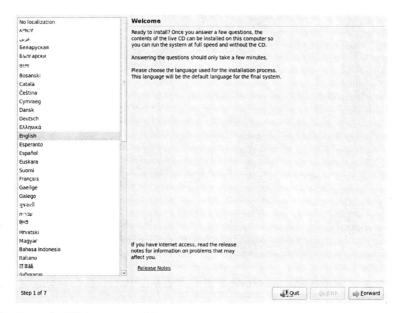

Figure 2-3: Step 1 - Welcome and Language

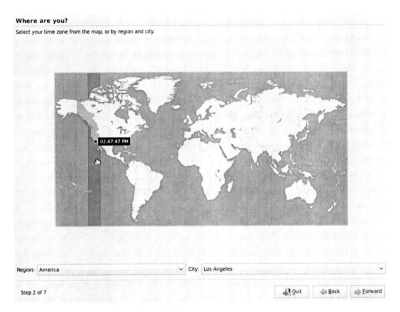

Figure 2-4: Step 2: Where Are You, Time zone

Step 3: Keyboard Layout

You will then be asked to select a keyboard—the default is already selected, such as U.S. English (see Figure 2-5). There are two options at the top of the page; one for Suggested option and another for Choose your own. The Suggested option will be selected by default listing your recommended key board type. Should the keyboard selection be inaccurate, you can click on the Choose your own option, and then choose the keyboard from the list, first by location, and then by type. If you are unsure of your keyboard layout, you can have it automatically selected by clicking on the test box and pressing keys.

Step 4: Prepare disk space

Then you will be asked to designate the Linux partitions and hard disk configurations you want to use on your hard drives. Ubuntu provides automatic partitioning options if you just want to overwrite your drive or use a blank hard drive to install you system on. Alternatively, to manually configure your hard disks, Ubuntu uses a very simple partitioning interface for setting up standard partitions. Unless you are using the Alternate install; LVM, RAID, and encrypted file systems are not supported during the install process.

No partitions will be changed or formatted until you select your packages later in the install process. You can opt out of the installation at any time until that point, and your original partitions will remain untouched. A default layout sets up a swap partition and a root partition of type ext3 (Linux native) for the kernel and applications.

Warning: The "Use the entire disk" option will wipe out any existing partitions on the
selected hard drive. If you want to preserve any partitions on that drive, like
Windows or other Linux partitions, always choose "Specify partitions manually".

Figure 2-5: Step 3: Keyboard Layout

First a dialog informs you that the partitioner is being started.

The "Prepare disk space" screen is displayed showing the partitions on your current hard
disk, and listing options for creating your Linux partitions. A graphical bar at the top shows the

current state of your hard disk, showing any existing partitions, if any, along with their sizes and labels. A graphical bar at the bottom of the screen shows how space on your hard drive will be used, depending on the option you choose.

If you have several hard disks, they will be listed on the drop down menu located below the "Use the entire disk" option. You can then select the disk on which to install Ubuntu.

The options available will change according to the partitioning of your hard disk. Your hard disk could have several configurations: no partitions, partitions with unused (free) space, and partitions with no unused space but with resizing allowed. You can think of the options as a blank hard drive, a hard drive that uses only part of its space, and a hard drive that uses all of its space.

In all cases you will have the options to "Use the entire disk" and "Specify partitions manually (advanced)". The "Use the entire disk" options will destroy any existing partitions, creating new partitions. Your hard drive will then have only your new Ubuntu system on it, and any data on your old partitions will be lost. The "Specify partitions manually (advanced)" will open a new screen which will let you create, edit, and delete partitions. You can set your own size and type for your partitions. Use this option to preserve or reuse any existing partitions.

If you have another operating system on your disk, like a Windows system, be very careful to first de-select the "Use the entire disk" option by clicking on the "Specify partitions manually" option. The "Use the entire disk" option is selected by default. It will wipe out your Windows partition if you continue directly.

The most common partitioning options are discussed in the following sections. Choose the one that best fits your current configuration.

- ➢ Automatic Partitioning "Use entire disk" Used for blank hard drives and to delete all existing partitions old drives entirely
- ➢ Creating new partitions on a blank hard drive manually "Specify partitions manually (advanced)"
- ➢ Reuse existing Linux partition on a hard drive to install on "Specify partitions manually (advanced)"
- ➢ Installing on a hard drive with a Windows system and free space (dual boot) "Specify partitions manually (advanced)"
- ➢ Side by side install: Installing on a fully partitioned hard drive, where there exists a system that has unused space; resizing the hard drive. "Install them side by side, choosing between them at each startup"

Tip: Some existing Linux systems may use several Linux partitions. Some of these may be used for just the system software, such as the boot and root partitions. These can be formatted. Others may have extensive user files, such as a **/home** partition that normally holds user home directories and all the files they have created. You should *not* format such partitions.

Automatic partitioning: "Use the entire disk"

Automatic partitioning will create partitions for you on your hard drive. It is selected by default as the "Use the entire disk" option. (see Figure 2-6). You can use automatic partitioning on

62 *Part 1: Getting Started*

a new un-partitioned hard drive, or to erase used hard drive. Erasing a hard drive will destroy any partitions already on it, along with any data. It will erase all partitions, including any used of other operating systems. Be very careful when using this option.

Automatic partitioning creates two partitions, a primary partition for your entire file system (a root file system, /), and a swap partition. The swap partition is set up as a logical partition within an extended partition.

Automatic partitioning creates a small swap partition that is smaller than the size of your RAM memory. Normally a swap partition is the same size as RAM memory. A computer with 4 GB of memory would have a swap partition of the same size. Because the default swap partition is so small, the Hibernate function (which used RAM memory) may not work when using an automatic partitioning configuration. Hibernate (suspend-to-disk) uses the swap partition to save the system image. If the swap partition is not large enough, the system image cannot be saved. Should you want to use the hibernate operation, you should choose to set up your partitions manually and make sure you set the size of your swap partition to the same as your computer's memory.

With the "Use the entire disk" option, just click the Forward button. You will be warned that all existing partitions will be destroyed. Just continue.

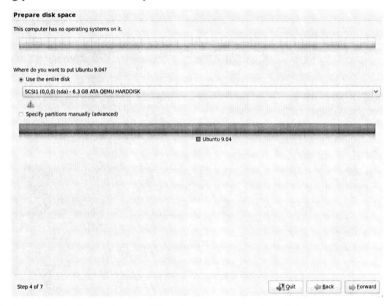

Figure 2-6: Step 4: Automatic partitioning on a new hard drive

Creating new partition on a blank hard drive manually

To create partitions on a blank hard drive manually, choose "Specify partitions manually (advanced)" (see Figure 2-7). The partitioner interface starts up with the "Prepare partitions" screen, listing any existing partitions. A graphical bar at the top will show the partition on your selected hard drive. For a blank hard drive this will be empty.

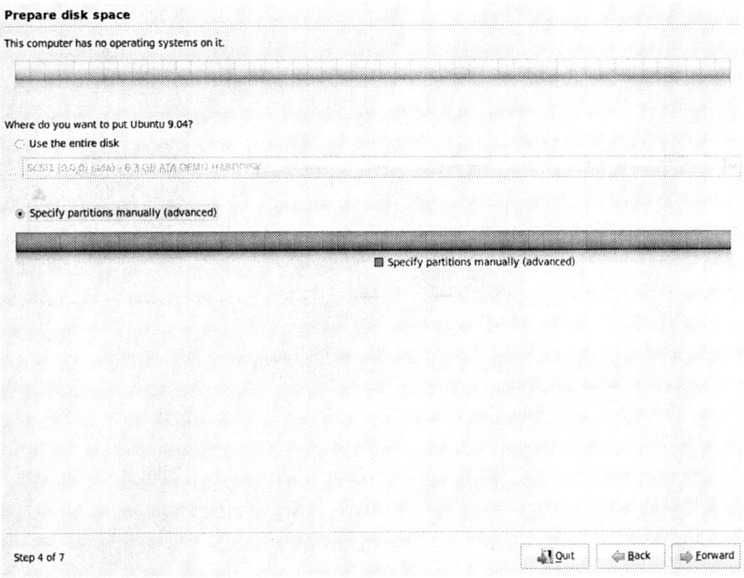

Figure 2-7: Step 4: Manually partitioning a new hard drive

At the bottom of the screen are actions you can perform on partitions and free space: New partition table, New partition, Edit partition, Delete partition, and Undo changes to Partitions.

For a new blank hard drive, you will be first prompted to create the partition table, warning that it will erase any data on the drive. Click Continue. The warning dialog is there in case you accidentally click the New partition table button on a drive that has partitions you want to preserve. In this case you can click Go Back and no partition table is created (see Figure 2-8).

Your hard disk will be listed with the available free space (see Figure 2-8). To create a new partition, select the free space entry for the hard disk and click the New button. A dialog opens with entries for the partition type (Primary or Logical), the size in megabytes, the location (beginning or end), the file system type (Use as), and the Mount point. For the root partition where you will install your system, the file system type would usually be **ext3**, and the root mount point is referenced with the / symbol (see Figure 2-10).

You will have to create at least two partitions, one swap and the other a Linux partition. Click free space and then click New partition. This opens a New partition window where you can choose the file system type (Use as) and the size of your partition. Do this for each partition. You can set the size of the swap partition to the size of your computer's RAM memory (see Figure 2-9).

For the partition type, the Do not use partition entry is initially selected. Choose a partition type from the pop-up menu. The "Ext3 journaling file system" is selected for the root partition and Swap is used for the swap partition. The Linux root partition would have the file system type (Use As) **ext3** and a mount point of /, which is the root directory. The / refers to the root mount point and is used to install your system. The size can be set to the remaining space (see Figure 2-10).

Prepare partitions

Device	Type	Mount point	Format?	Size	Used
/dev/sda					

Create new empty partition table on this devi

You have selected an entire device to partition. If you proceed with creating a new partition table on the device, then all current partitions will be removed.

Note that you will be able to undo this operation later if you wish.

[Go Back] [Continue]

[New partition table] [New partition] [Edit partition] [Delete partition]
[Undo changes to partitions]

Step 4 of 7   [Quit] [Back] [Forward]

Prepare partitions

☐ Free space
5.9 GB

Device	Type	Mount point	Format?	Size	Used
/dev/sda					
free space			☐	6291 MB	

[New partition table] [New partition] [Edit partition] [Delete partition]
[Undo changes to partitions]

Step 4 of 7   [Quit] [Back] [Forward]

Figure 2-8: Create a new partition table on a blank hard drive

If you make a mistake, you can edit a partition by selecting it and clicking the Edit button. This opens an Edit partitions window where you can make changes. You can also delete a partition, returning its space to free space, and then create a new one. Select the partition and click the Delete button. The "Undo changes to partitions button" is always available and undo any changes.

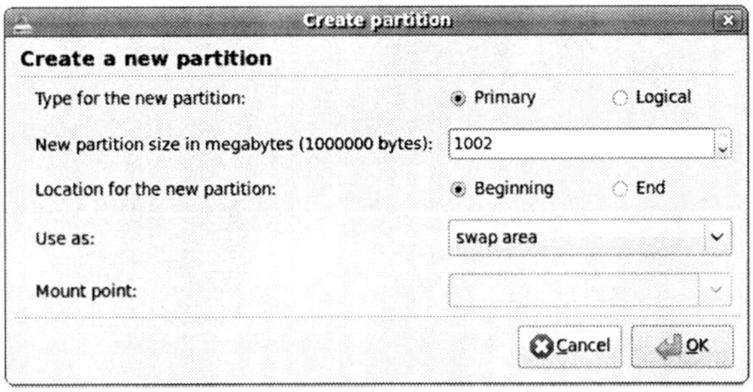

Figure 2-9: Create a new swap a partition

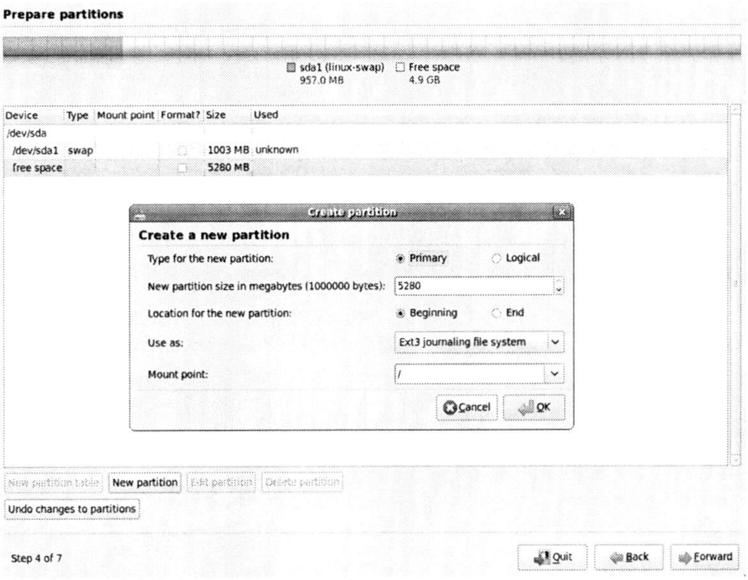

Figure 2-10: Create a new root partition

When you have finish setting up your partitions, you will see entries for them display ad, the graphical bar will show their size and location (see Figure 2-11). Click the Forward button to create the partitions and continue on to Step 5.

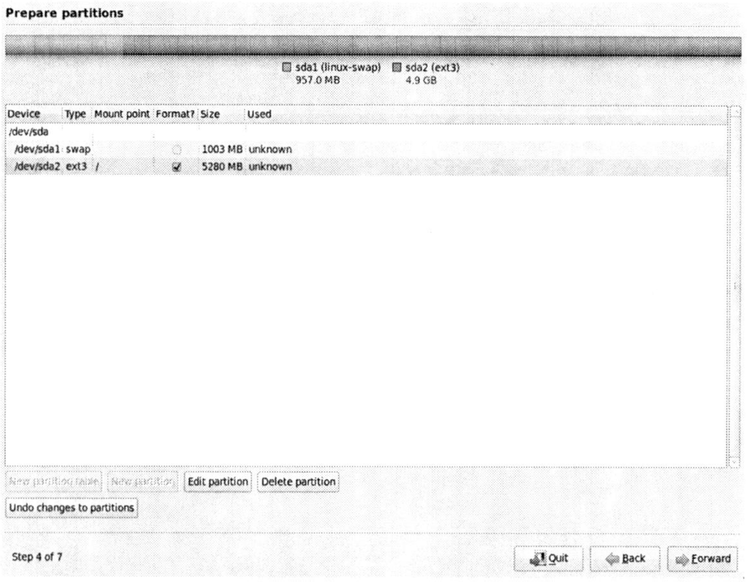

Figure 2-11: New swap and root partitions

Reuse existing Linux partitions on a hard drive to install on

If you already have a hard drive with Linux partitions that you want to reuse, you choose the "Specify partitions manually (advanced)" option on the Prepare Partitions screen. In this case, you have a hard disk you are already using for Linux, with partitions already set up on the hard drive for your Ubuntu systems. But you don' want to keep any of the data on those partitions. In effect, you just want to reuse those partitions for the new release, creating an entirely new install, but with the old partitions. With this action, all current data on those partitions will be destroyed. This procedure avoids having to change the partition table on the hard drive. You just keep the partitions you already have. In this case you wish to overwrite existing partitions, erasing on the data on them.

This procedure is used often for users that have already backed up their data, and just want to create a fresh install on their hard disk with the new release. Also, a Linux system could be configured to save data on a partition separate from the root partition, like a separate partition for the **/home** directories. In this case you would only need to overwrite the root partition, leaving the added Linux partition alone.

This procedure is also useful for a hard disk that may have another operating system on the disk, like Windows, along with existing Linux partitions. Deleting and creating the Linux partitions always runs the risk of deleting your Windows partition accidentally.

The partitioner interface starts up with the "Prepare partitions" screen, listing any existing partitions. The graphical bar at the top will show the partition on your selected hard drive. The depiction changes as you add, delete, or edit your partitions. Each partition device name and label will be displayed. Unused space will be labeled as free space.

Each hard disk is listed by its device name, such as **sda** for the first Serial ATA device. Then underneath the hard disk are its partitions and/or free space available (see Figure 2-7). At the bottom of the screen are actions you can perform on partitions and free space: New partition table, New partition, Edit partition, Delete partition, and Undo changes to Partitions.

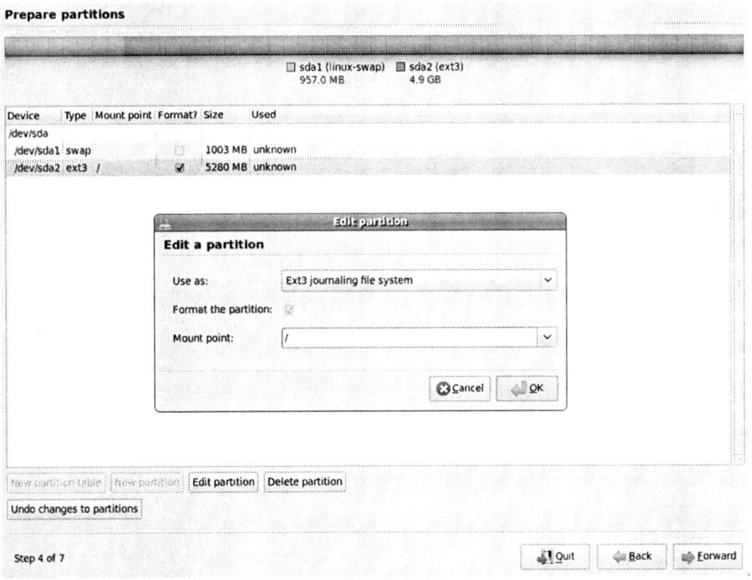

Figure 2-12: Edit existing partitions on a hard drive

Note: The New partition table becomes active whenever the top level hard drive device name is selected instead of a particular partition. This will be initially selected when your Prepare partition screen if first displayed, activating the New partition table button. Do NOT click it. It will wipe out any existing partitions.

To edit an existing partition, click on its entry and click the Edit partition table button. A dialog opens with entries for the partition type (Use as), a format checkbox, and the mount point (see Figure 2-12).

All you have to do is edit your exiting root partition. You will see your partitions listed. You can leave the swap partition alone.

Click on the root partition. This is the partition labeled /. The Edit button will become active. This opens an Edit window. Select the type, which would normally be **ext3**. Then select the mount point, which, for the root partition, is /. The size can remain the same (see Figure 2-13). Once finished, you will see your Windows partition (**ntfs**) if there is one, as well as the swap and Linux root partition (**ext3**).

If you change the partition type of the root partition to **ext4**, you will have to later reinstall the grub boot loader.

Once you have edited the root partition, you can click the Forward button to continue on to Step 5.

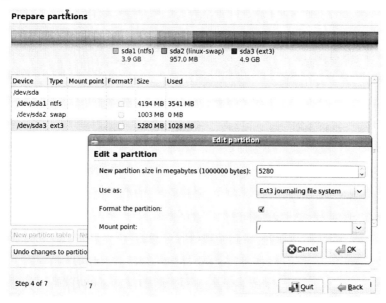

Figure 2-13: Editing an existing partition (Windows partition also exists)

Installing on a hard drive with a Windows system and free space (dual boot)

If you have a Windows system already installed on your hard disk, and the Windows system take up only part of the hard disk, leaving the rest as free space, you would choose "Specify partitions manually (advanced)". You would then create your Linux partitions manually on the remaining free space (see Figure 2-14).

Be very careful NOT to choose the "Use entire disk" option (automatic partitioning). This will destroy you Windows partition.

The partitioner interface starts up with the "Prepare partitions" screen, listing any existing partitions. A graphical bar at the top will show the partition on your selected hard drive. Each partition device name and label will be displayed. Unused space will be labeled as free space. If you delete existing partitions, their space will be labeled free space. A hard disk with an existing Windows partition will show entries for the Windows partition and the remaining free space.

Each hard disk is listed by its device name, such as **sda** for the first Serial ATA device. Then underneath the hard disk are its partitions and/or free space available (see Figure 2-7). At the bottom of the screen are actions you can perform on partitions and free space: New partition table, New partition, Edit partition, Delete partition, and Undo changes to Partitions. When you select free space entry, the New partition button will become available. When you select an existing partition, the Edit partitions and Delete partitions buttons become available, but not the New button. The "Undo changes to partitions button" is always available.

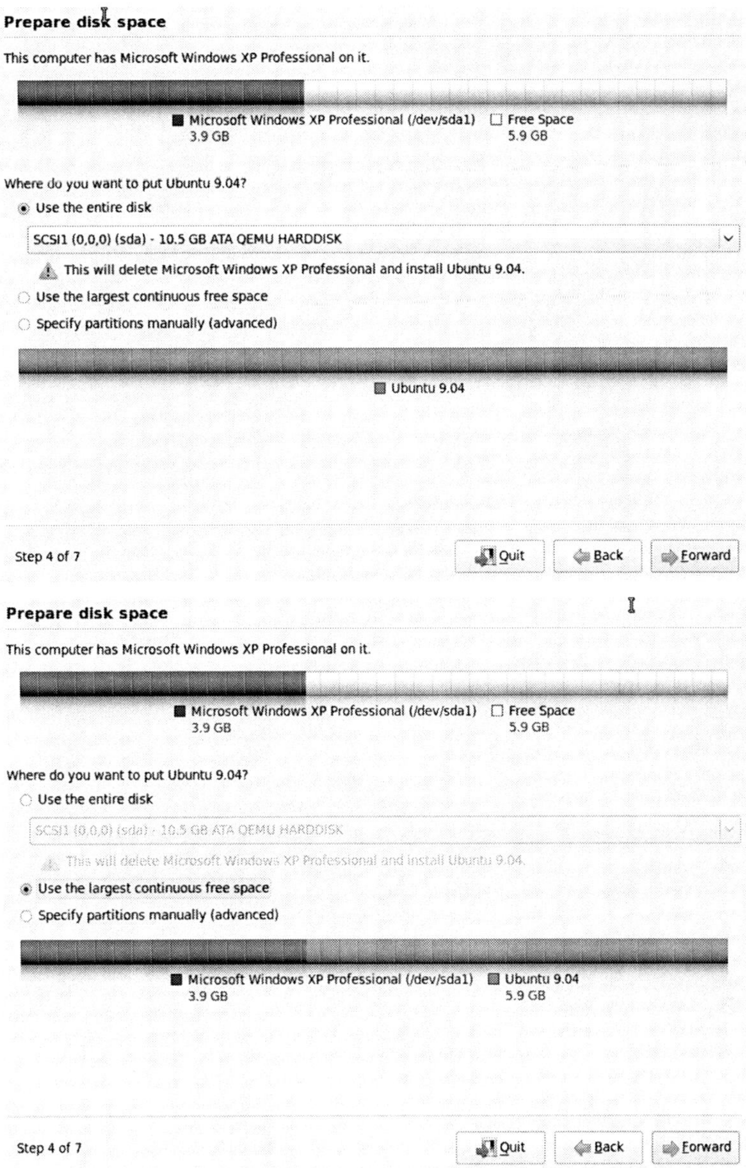

Prepare disk space

This computer has Microsoft Windows XP Professional on it.

■ Microsoft Windows XP Professional (/dev/sda1)   ☐ Free Space
3.9 GB   5.9 GB

Where do you want to put Ubuntu 9.04?

◉ Use the entire disk

SCSI1 (0,0,0) (sda) - 10.5 GB ATA QEMU HARDDISK	⌄

⚠ This will delete Microsoft Windows XP Professional and install Ubuntu 9.04.

○ Use the largest continuous free space

○ Specify partitions manually (advanced)

■ Ubuntu 9.04

Step 4 of 7   Quit   Back   Forward

Prepare disk space

This computer has Microsoft Windows XP Professional on it.

■ Microsoft Windows XP Professional (/dev/sda1)   ☐ Free Space
3.9 GB   5.9 GB

Where do you want to put Ubuntu 9.04?

○ Use the entire disk

SCSI1 (0,0,0) (sda) - 10.5 GB ATA QEMU HARDDISK	⌄

⚠ This will delete Microsoft Windows XP Professional and install Ubuntu 9.04.

◉ Use the largest continuous free space

○ Specify partitions manually (advanced)

■ Microsoft Windows XP Professional (/dev/sda1)   ■ Ubuntu 9.04
3.9 GB   5.9 GB

Step 4 of 7   Quit   Back   Forward

Figure 2-14: Dual boot with windows. The Prepare disk space initially selects "Use the entire disk". Be sure to select instead "Specify partitions manually (advanced)"

The Prepare Partitions screen can be confusing, especially if you are want to preserve a Windows partition. Initially the partitions on your hard drive will be listed, but only the New partition table will be active. This is because you have not selected any partition to edit or any free space entry on which to create a new partition. Once you do this, the New partition and Edit partition buttons be come active, whereas the New partition table be comes inactive. Should you initially click on the New partition button, you would erase your entire hard drive, though you will be given a warning first and a chance to back out.

There will be two partition entries already listed. The first will be for your existing Windows partition. It will have the partition type **ntfs**. The second entry will be free space. This is the entry to select to create new partitions. To preserve any other partitions, like Windows partitions, first click on the free space entry on the list of your hard disk partitions. Use the New partition button to set up your Linux partitions.

To install Ubuntu, you will need two partitions: a swap partition and a root partition. The swap partition is the size of your computer RAM memory (usually 1 to 4 GB). The root partition should be at least 20 GB. You can just set it to the remaining free space on your disk. The root partition will hold your Ubuntu Linux system.

First set up the swap a partition. Select the free space entry. The New partition button will become active. Click it to open a New partition dialog. Set the type to swap and the size to the same size as your computer memory. Click the OK button. An entry for the new swap partition will appear.

Then set up the root partition. Click on the free space entry. The New partition button will become active again. Click it to open a New partition dialog. Set the type to ext3. The size will already be selected to use the remaining disk space. Then choose the mount point from the drop down menu. For the root partition this is the / symbol. Click the OK button. An entry for the new Linux partition will appear (see Figure 2-15).

You can still make any changes to the Linux partitions if you wish. Just select the partition and click the Edit button.

Once finished, click the Forward button to continue on to Step 5.

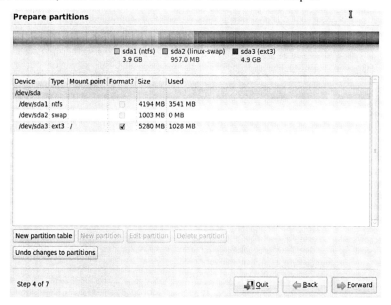

Figure 2-15: Hard drive partitions including Windows (ntfs)

Note: If you select the top level hard drive entry, the New partition table button will become active. Do NOT click it.

Side by side install: Installing on a fully partitioned hard drive, where there exists a system that has unused space; resizing the hard drive.

If your hard disk has operating systems on it that already use the entire hard disk, but the operating systems themselves only use a small portion of their allocated space, you can install Linux by have the existing partitions resized smaller, freeing up space for the new Linux partitions. New partitions would be created in the freed space. For example, a Windows partition could be allocated an entire hard disk, but actually use only a small portion of it for its files. The Windows partition can be reduced in size safely, keeping all its data, and allowing its unused space to be freed up for use by other partitions.

Resizing is time consuming.

On a hard disk completely allocated by one or more existing operating systems, the Ubuntu installer will detect if the existing system can be resized safely, that they have an extensive amount of unused free space. In this case you will be given an option to perform a side by side install. You will be shown how much the existing partitions will be reduced, as well as the size and location of the new Linux partitions. The option "Install them side by side, choosing between them each startup" will be selected, though you still have the options to choose "Use the entire disk" and "Specify partitions manually" (see Figure 2-16).

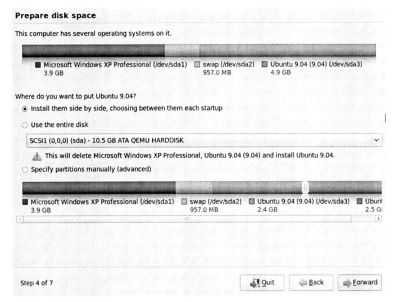

Figure 2-16: Freeing space on a full hard disk, resize

Two graphical bars will be shown. The top one shows the existing partitions, their size and location. The bottom graphical bar show the new partition set up that would exist after a resize. This will include the new Linux partitions. A slider button shows the beginning of the new Linux root partition. This is set to the size recommended by the installer. You can move it to expand or reduce the size of the new Linux partition.

Upon choosing a side by side install, a dialog will prompt with the warning that the resize cannot be undone and it may take a long time (see Figure 2-17). Click Continue to perform the resize, or click Go Back to just return to the Prepare disk space screen.

The side by side option is in effect an automatic partitioning, but one that preserves the existing operating system.

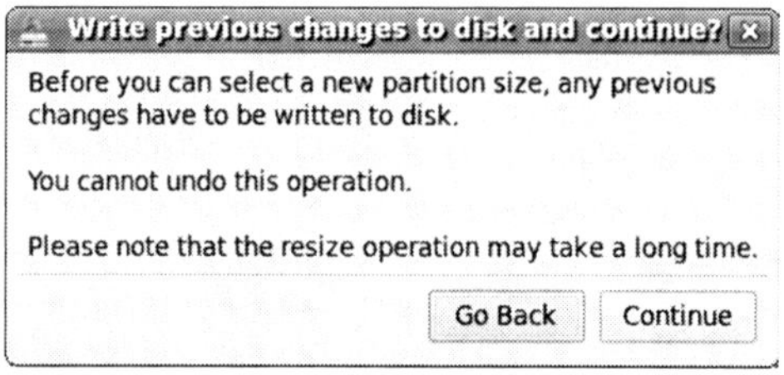

Figure 2-17: Resize warning

Step 5: Who Are You?

On the Who are you? screen you enter your name, your user log in name, that user's password (see Figure 2-18). The user you are creating will have administrative access, allowing you to change your system configuration, add new users and printers, and install new software. The name for the computer is the computer's network host name.

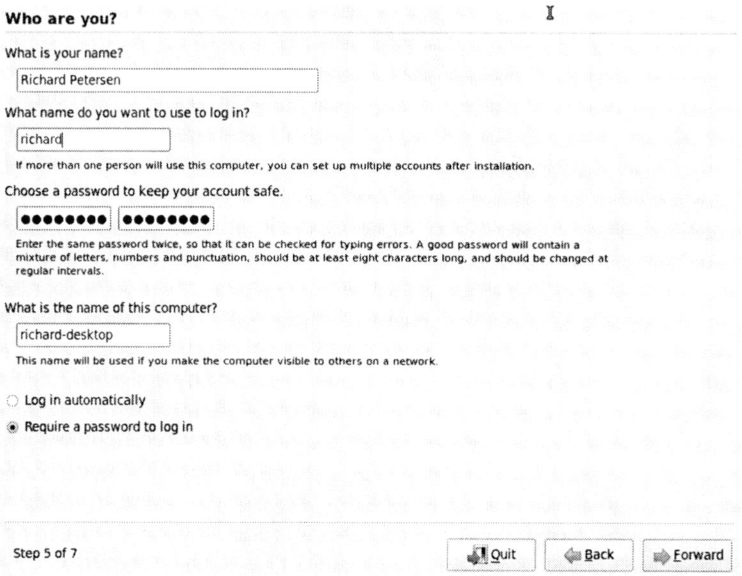

Figure 2-18: Step 5 - Who are you?

At the bottom of the screen, you have an option to login automatically, or Require a password to login. Click this checkbox for "Log in automatically" to have your system login to your account when you start up, instead of stopping at the login screen.

Step 6: Migrate documents and settings

If you have another operating system on your computer, like Windows, a Migrate documents and settings screen will be displays. A list of installed operating systems will be displayed, as an expandable tree, with a checkboxes next to entries (see Figure 2-19). Expand an entry to see a list of possible data you can import directly from that operating system to your Ubuntu system. A Windows entry will show items like Internet Explorer, Wallpaper, My Documents, My Music, and My Pictures. Each will have check boxes. To import all the files in your Windows My Documents folder, check the My Documents entry. The files will be placed your Ubuntu Documents directory. The user account used is the one you specified in the "Who are you screen". To just copy everything, check the checkbox for the operating system, like Windows.

Figure 2-19: Step 6: Migrate documents and settings

Step 7: Ready to install

The Ready to Install window then lets you review the changes that will be made, especially the partitions that will be formatted. Use the scrollbar to move down the page to display the list of partitions to be formatted. You can still cancel and back out at this time. Once you press the Install button, our partitions will be formatted and installation will begin (see Figure 2-20).

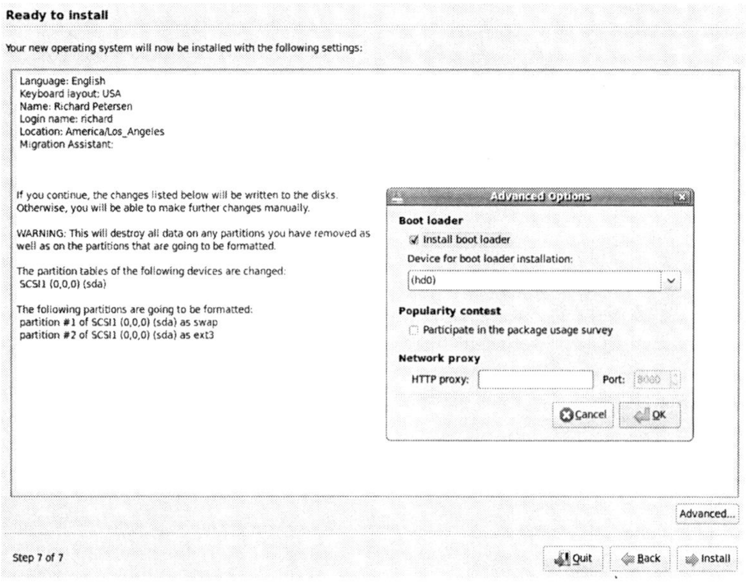

Ready to install

Your new operating system will now be installed with the following settings:

Language: English
Keyboard layout: USA
Name: Richard Petersen
Login name: richard
Location: America/Los_Angeles
Migration Assistant:

If you continue, the changes listed below will be written to the disks.
Otherwise, you will be able to make further changes manually.

WARNING: This will destroy all data on any partitions you have removed as
well as on the partitions that are going to be formatted.

The partition tables of the following devices are changed:
SCSI1 (0,0,0) (sda)

The following partitions are going to be formatted:
partition #1 of SCSI1 (0,0,0) (sda) as swap
partition #2 of SCSI1 (0,0,0) (sda) as ext3

Advanced Options

Boot loader
☑ Install boot loader
Device for boot loader installation:
(hd0)

Popularity contest
☐ Participate in the package usage survey

Network proxy
HTTP proxy: Port: 8080

❌ Cancel   ✅ OK

Advanced...

Step 7 of 7   Quit   Back   Install

Figure 2-20: Step 7: Ready to Install

The advanced option on this window will let you decide where to place the boot loader and whether to install it at all, or allow you to specify an HTTP proxy. The boot loader was automatically configured for you. You can also choose to participate in a package usage survey.

When you click Install, a progress screen is displayed showing install progress (see Figure 2-21). You should not interrupt this for any reason. A standard set of packages from the CD/DVD are being installed.

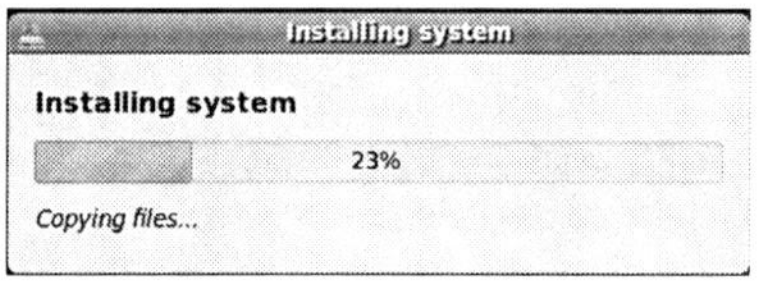

Installing system

Installing system

23%

Copying files...

Figure 2-21: Install progress

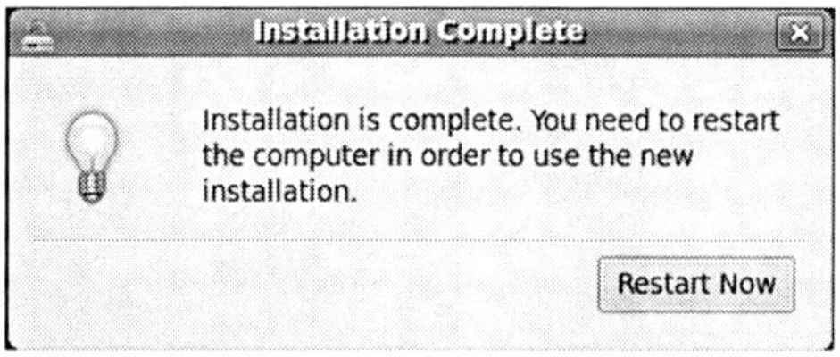

Installation Complete

Installation is complete. You need to restart
the computer in order to use the new
installation.

Restart Now

Figure 2-22: Installation completed

Once finished, the Installation complete dialog appears letting you to continue using the LiveCD to restart and reboot to the new installation (see Figure 2-22). Your CD will be automatically ejected when your reboot. A screen will appear prompting you to remove the CD/DVD disc, and then press ENTER (see Figure 2-23).

Figure 2-23: Remove CD/DVD disc

If you installed from the LiveCD session, you are also given the option to return to the LiveCD session.

Start Up Issues

When your system restarts, the GRUB boot loader will quickly select your default operating system and start up its login screen. If you have just installed Ubuntu, the default operating system will be Ubuntu.

Selecting and editing GRUB

If you have more than one operating system, you can select one using the GRUB menu. You first need to display the GRUB menu at start up. You will have about a 3 second chance to do this. A quick message will be displayed saying that GRUB is starting up your operating system. At this point, press the ESC key. Your GRUB menu will be displayed as shown in Figure 2-24.

The GRUB menu will list Ubuntu and other operating systems you specified, such as Windows. Use the arrow keys to move to the entry you want, if it is not already highlighted, and press ENTER

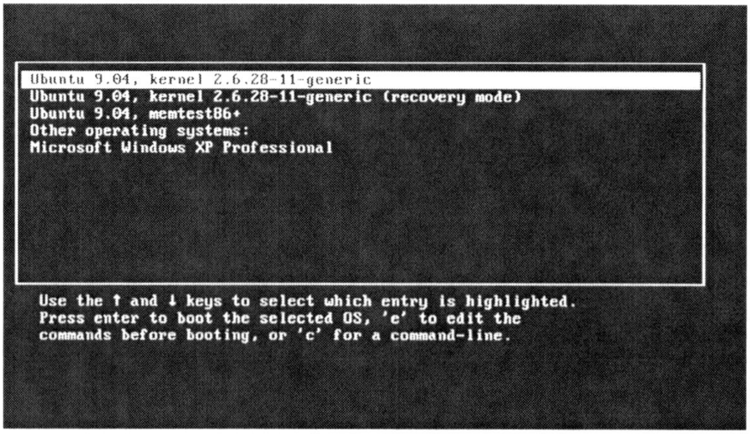

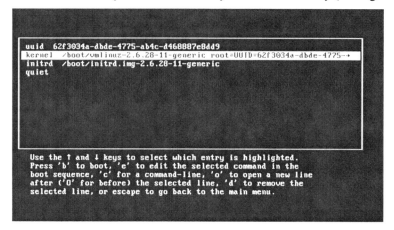

Figure 2-24: Ubuntu GRUB menu

For graphical installations, some displays may have difficulty running the graphical start up display. If you have this problem, you can edit your Linux GRUB entry and remove the **splash** term at the end of the Grub start up line. Press the **e** key to edit a Grub entry (see Figure 2-25).

Figure 2-25: Editing a GRUB menu item

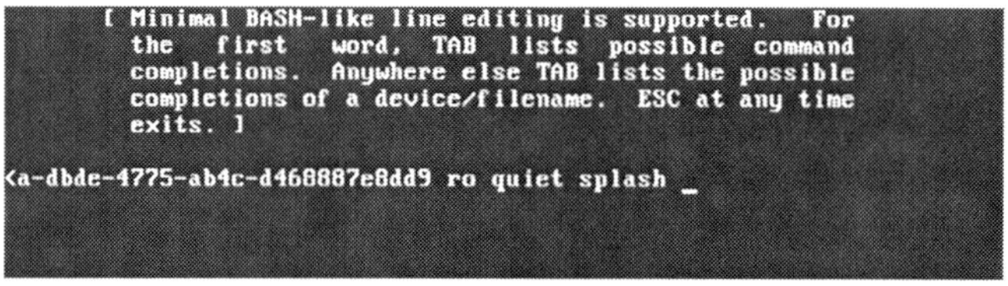

Figure 2-26: Editing a GRUB line

To change a particular line, select it and then press the **e** key. The end of the line is then displayed (see Figure 2-26). You can use the arrow keys to move along the line. The Backspace key will delete characters and simply typing will insert characters. All changes are temporary. Permanent changes can only be made by directly editing the **/boot/grub/menu.lst** file.

Login and Logout

When your Ubuntu operating system starts up, a progress screen appears showing you the startup progress. You can press the ESC key to see the start up messages instead.

The login screen will then appear. You can then log in to your Linux system using a login name and a password for any of the users you have set up. An entry box will be displayed in the middle of the screen and labeled User. Just type in your user name and press ENTER. The label of the box will then change to password and the box will clear. Then enter your password and press ENTER.

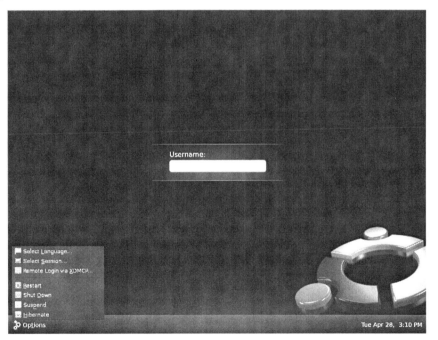

Figure 2-27: Login screen

On the login screen, the Options pop-up menu in the lower left corner lets Shut Down or Restart Linux. The Sessions entry in this menu lets you choose what desktop graphical interface to use, such as KDE or GNOME. The Language entry lets you select a language to use.

When you finish, you can shut down your system. From GNOME, you can click the User switcher/Quit button to display a menu with Shut Down, Log Out, and Restart entries (see Figure 2-27). You can then choose to shut down the entire system. If you log out from either GNOME or KDE and return to the login screen, you can click the Options button to select Shut Down to shut down the system.

If the system should freeze on you for any reason, you can hold down the CTRL and ALT keys and press DEL (CTRL-ALT-DEL) to safely restart it. Never just turn it off. You can also use CTRL-ALT-F3 to shift to a command line prompt and log in to check out your system, shutting down with the **halt** command (the CTRL-A LT-F7 keys would return you to the graphical interface).

Initial Configuration Tasks

There are a few configuration tasks you many want to configure right away. These include:

- The Time and Date - Configure using the world clock applet or the Time and Date configuration tool, date-admin (System | Administration | Time and Date). The world clock applet is on the right side of the top panel. Right-click on it and choose Preferences to configure. System time is set by Time and Date, World clock sets user time.

- Create Users - This is handled by users-admin, System | Administration | Users and Groups.

- Sound Configuration - this is handled by PulseAudio, System | Preferences | Sound

- Firewall and Virus Projection: Use Firestarter (System | Administration | Firestarter) or UFW for your firewall. Firestarter you will have to install with Synaptic, but provides a GNOME Desktop interface. UFW is installed by default, but has to be activated and is managed with commands entered in a terminal window. You can install ClamAV for virus protection and ClamTK for the interface, Applications | System Tools | Virus Scanner.

- Display configuration - If you are using a quality graphics card from Nvidia or ATI (AMD), you may want to install their vendor graphics hardware drivers for Linux. These drivers provide better support for Nvidia and ATI graphics cards. To install these drivers just use the Hardware Drivers utility in the System | Administration window. If you want to configure these drivers yourself, you will also need their configuration interfaces. These you have to download using the Synaptic Package Manager. For Nvidia you would install the **nvidia-settings** package, and for ATI the **fglrx-amdcccle** package. Alternatively, if you want to still use the standard X.org drivers.

Upgrading

You can upgrade a current Ubuntu system to the next release using the APT package manager or an Alternate CD. Upgrading is a simple matter of updating software the new release versions, along with updating your GRUB configuration.

You can only upgrade to Ubuntu 9.04 from Ubuntu 8.10. You cannot upgrade from Ubuntu 8.04 to 9.04 directly. Be sure you have first performed any needed updates for your Ubuntu 8.10 system. Your Ubuntu 8.10 system must be completely up to date before you perform an upgrade to Ubuntu 9.04.

Note: KUbuntu systems can be upgraded directly from KUbuntu 8.04 to KUbuntu 9.04.

To upgrade using KUbuntu, an upgrade notifier icon will appear which you can click to start the upgrade. KUbuntu users can also upgrade from KUbuntu 8.04 directly to KUbuntu 9.04 (the update notifier icon will not appear). KUbuntu upgrades will also have to manually add the KUbuntu NetworkManager applet. It does not appear by default.

Check the following site for upgrade details:

```
http://www.ubuntu.com/getubuntu/upgrading
```

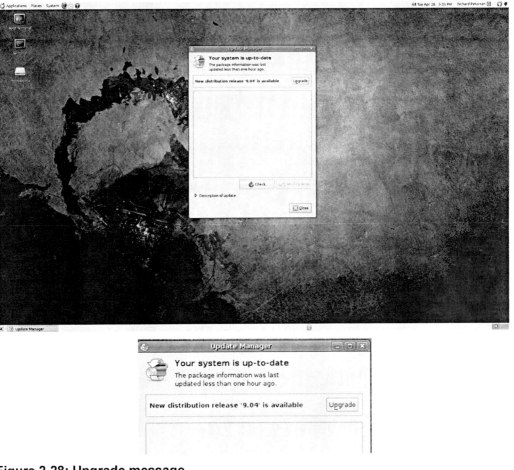

Figure 2-28: Upgrade message

Upgrade over a network from Ubuntu 8.10

To upgrade your system using your Internet connection, you can use the Update Manager. The upgrade will be performed by downloading the latest package versions from the Ubuntu repository, directly. When a new release becomes available, Update Manager will display a message notifying you of the new release. An Upgrade button will be displayed next to the message should you decide to upgrade your system to that release (see Figure 2.28). If you want to stay with the Ubuntu 8.10 release for now, you just ignore the message. Should you want to upgrade to the new release, in this case Ubuntu 9.04, you click the Upgrade button to start the upgrade. Be sure to first update all you current software. An upgrade should be performed from the most recent versions of your current release's software packages.

When you click the Upgrade button a Release Notes message is displayed, with both a Cancel and another Upgrade button (see Figure 2-29). You can check the release notes to see what new features and changes will be made. If you decide not to upgrade at this time, just click the Cancel button. To continue with the upgrade, click the Upgrade button.

Figure 2-29: Release notes window with Cancel and Upgrade buttons

Once you click the Release Notes window Upgrade button, a Distribution Upgrade dialog opens showing the progress of the Upgrade (see Figure 2-30).

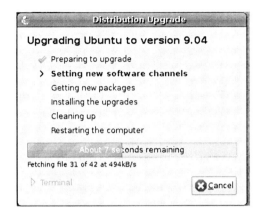

Figure 2-30: Distribution Upgrade dialog

The upgrade procedure will first prepare the upgrade, detecting the collection of software packages that have to be downloaded. A dialog will then open asking if you want to start the upgrade, displaying both a Cancel and Start Upgrade button (see Figure 2-31). You can still cancel the upgrade at this time and nothing will be changed on your system (click the Cancel button). To continue with the Upgrade, click the Start Upgrade button.

Figure 2-31: List of Upgrade packages with Cancel and Start Upgrade buttons

The Distribution Upgrade dialog will again be displayed (see Figure 2-32). Packages will be downloaded (Getting new packages), and then installed on your system (Installing the upgrades). The download process can take some time depending on the speed of your Internet connection.

Figure 2-32: Distribution Upgrade dialog, downloading packages

During the install packages process, you will be prompted about how you want your Grub menu.lst file configured (see Figure 2-33). A dialog will open with the query "What would you like to do about menu.lst?". The **menu.lst** file displays your boot options when you boot up your system. It also determines your default kernel. Several options are available from the drop down menu. The default is to keep your current **menu.lst** file. However, this will use your old Ubuntu kernel from the previous release (the new kernels will be installed; there just won't be any entries for them in your old **menu.lst**).

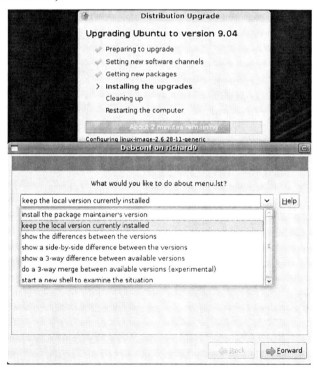

Figure 2-33: The Grub menu.lst install options

To use the new kernel, select the first option, "Install the package maintainer's version". With this option, any added OS entries you may have added to the current menu.lst, will still be included in the new version of **menu.lst**, and displayed when you boot.

You also have the option to examine the differences between your current menu.lst and the new maintainer's version, as well as opening a shell to display the versions.

Keeping you old **menu.lst** version is something you would do if you had set up your own customized version of menu.lst. You can always edit the **/boot/grub/menu.lst** file later to may changes to boot the new release's kernel.

Once the upgrade is completed, a completion message is displayed. Reboot to start your system with the new release and its kernel.

Upgrading you system can still leave unused software packages still on installed on your system, taking up space. This is particularly true for older kernels used in the previous release. It is difficult, though, to tell which software is no longer needed. To remove such software, you can use the Computer Janitor application. After you have upgraded, select System | Administration | Computer janitor. The Computer Janitor application will start up, and automatically detect unused software; even kernels from the previous release (see Figure 2-34). The selected software packages will all be checked. Should there be one you want to keep, like a specialized applications or one from a third party repository, you can uncheck it. Normally though you would just remove them all. Computer Janitor will also perform any required editing of configuration files, like editing the **/boot/grub/menu.lst** file to remove entries for any removed old kernels (it will not modify your default kernel number, if you changed that previously, you might have to change it again manually if the numbering is off due to the removed kernel entries).

When ready click the Cleanup button. A warning dialog will be displayed asking you to really cleanup, just click Yes. The packages will be removed, and Computer Janitor will rescan.

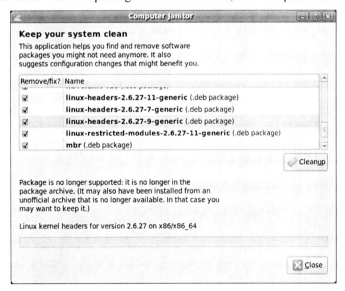

Figure 2-34: Computer Janitor to remove software from previous releases

Upgrade using a CD (Alternate CD)

To upgrade from a CD, you use the Alternate CD, not the standard desktop CD. Download the CD ISO image file from the **http://releases.ubuntu.com/jaunty** site, or use the Alternate CD torrent to download the image using BitTorrent.

```
http://releases.ubuntu.com/jaunty/
```

Keep in mind that upgrading from the CD upgrades to the package versions in the official release, not the latest updated versions available on the Ubuntu repository. You would still have to perform an added update for the 9.04 packages from the Ubuntu repository which could be time consuming, depending on the number of packages that have to be updated.

Then burn the ISO image file to a CD disc and insert it. You can also mount the CD ISO image file directly using the following command, which uses a **mount** command with the **loop** option to mount the ISO image to the **/media/cdrom0** device interface.

```
sudo mount -o loop ~/Desktop/ubuntu-9.04-alternate-i386.iso /media/cdrom0
```

Once inserted or mounted, the Alternate CD will display a dialog prompted you to upgrade using that CD.

If the dialog is not displayed you can manually start it with the following command to run the **cdromupgrade** command on the Alternate CD.

```
gksu "sh /cdrom/cdromupgrade"
```

Upgrading to a new release with apt-get

You can also use the **apt-get** command in a terminal window or on a command line interface to upgrade your system. To upgrade to an entirely new release you use the **dist-upgrade** option. A **dist-upgrade** would install a new release; say 9.04 on a 8.10 system, preserving your original configuration and data. This option will also remove obsolete software packages.

```
sudo apt-get update
sudo apt-get dist-upgrade
```

Recovery

If for some reason you are not able to boot or access your system, it may be due to conflicting configurations, libraries, or applications. To enter the recovery mode, press the ESC key on start up to display the GRUB boot menu. Then select the recovery mode entry, the ubuntu kernel entry with the (recover Mode) label attached to the end.

Ubuntu 9.04, kernel 2.6.28-11-generic (recovery mode)

This will start up a menu where you can use the arrow and ENTER keys to select from several recovery options (see Figure 2-35) These include Resume, clean, dpkg, fsck, grub, netroot, root, and xfix. Short descriptions for each are shown in Figure 2-20.

The root option will start up Ubuntu as the root user with a command line shell prompt. In this case, you can boot your Linux system in a recovery mode and then edit configuration files with a text editor such as Vi, remove the suspect libraries, or reinstall damaged software with DEB.

The xfix entry will try to automatically detect and configure your X server. Use this if you are having hardware problems running your Xorg drivers on your graphics card and monitor. The fsck entry will run fsck to check all your file systems, prompting you to repair those that may be damaged. dpkg will use the dpkg tool to check your software packages and repair any broken installs. Use clean to open up free space, in case you run out. The grub entry will let you edit your Grub bootloader.

The resume entry will start up Ubuntu normally.

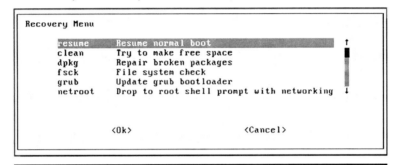

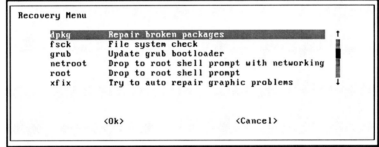

Figure 2-35: Recover options

If you are not able to start up your system from your hard disk install, you can run the Live CD/DVD and choose Restore broken system from the Start up menu.

Re-Installing the Boot Loader

If you have a dual-boot system, where you are running both Windows and Linux on the same machine, you may run into a situation where you have to re-install your GRUB boot loader. This problem occurs if your Windows system completely crashes beyond repair and you have to install a new version of Windows, or you are adding Windows to your machine after having installed Linux. Windows will automatically overwrite your boot loader (alternatively, you could install your boot loader on your Linux partition instead of the MBR). You will no longer be able to access your Linux system.

All you need to do is to reinstall your boot loader. First boot from your Linux DVD/CD-ROM installation disk, and at the menu select Rescue Installed System.

As noted in the preceding section, this boots your system in rescue mode. Then use **grub-install** and the device name of your first partition to install the boot loader. Windows normally wants to be on the first partition with the MBR, the master boot record. You would specify this partition. At the prompt enter

```
grub-install /dev/sda1
```

This will re-install your current GRUB boot loader, assuming that Windows is included in the GRUB configuration. You can then reboot, and the GRUB boot loader will start up. If you are adding Windows for the first time, you will have to add an entry for it in the **/boot/grub/menu.lst** file to have it accessible from the boot loader.

Alternate Install

Ubuntu also provides an Alternate CD to support specialized features like LVM, RAID, and encrypted file systems. The Alternate CD use a text based installation interface. You use the TAB key to move between entries, and the arrow and spacebar keys to select and choose items in a menu. Installation tasks are very similar to the LiveCD and Install DVD. The Alternate CD will provide you with the option to set up LVM partitions (see Figure 2-36).

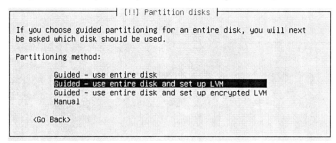

Figure 2-36: Alternate partition choices

A default LVM partition will create a separate boot partitions and then an LVM Group partitions with volumes for the swap and root partitions. You can specify your own.

You are then informed of the changes partitions to be formatted. You then create a new user, and the software is installed.

Automating Installation with Kickstart

Kickstart is a method for providing a predetermined installation configuration for installing Ubuntu. Instead of having a user enter responses on the install screens, the responses can be listed in a kickstart file the install process can read from. You will need to create a kickstart configuration file on a working Ubuntu system. (Kickstart configuration files have the extension **.cfg**.) A kickstart file is created for every Ubuntu system that holds the install responses used for that installation. It is located in the root directory at

```
/root/anaconda-ks.cfg
```

If you plan to perform the same kind of install on computers that would be configured in the same way, say on a local network with hosts that have the same hardware, you could use this kickstart file as a model for performing installations. It is a text file that you can edit, with entries for each install response, like the following for keyboard and time zone:

```
keyboard us
timezone America/LosAngeles
```

More complex responses may take options such as **network**, which uses **--device** for the device interface and **bootproto** for the boot client.

```
network --device eth0 --bootproto dhcp
```

Display configuration is more complex, specifying a video card and monitor type, which could vary. You can have the system skip this with **xskip**.

The first entry is the install source. This will be **cdrom** for a CD/DVD-ROM install. If you want to use an NFS or Web install instead, you could place that here, specifying the server name or Web site.

You can also use the **system-config-kickstart** file to create your kickstart file. This provides a graphical interface for each install screen. First install it. Then to start it select Applications | System Tools | Kickstart. The help manual provides a detailed description on how to use this tool.

The name of the configuration file should be **ks.cfg**. Once you have created your kickstart file, you can copy it to CD/DVD or to a floppy disk. You could also place the file on a local hard disk partition (such as a Windows or Linux partition), if you already have one. For a network, you could place the file on an NFS server, provided your network is running a DHCP server to enable automatic network configuration on the install computer.

When you start the installation, at the boot prompt you specify the kickstart file and its location. In the following example, the kickstart file will be located on a floppy disk as **/dev/fd0**.

```
linux ks=floppy
```

You can use **hd:***device* to specify a particular device such as a hard drive or second CD-ROM drive. For an NFS site, you would use **nfs**.

Wubi: Windows-based installer

Wubi is a very simple, safe, and painless way to install Linux for users that want to preserve their Windows system, without having to perform any potentially hazardous hard disk partition operations to free up space and create new hardware partitions for Ubuntu.

Wubi is an Ubuntu installer that lets you install and run Ubuntu from Windows. Wubi is already integrated into the Ubuntu 9.04 Desktop CD. With Wubi you do not have to create a separate partition for Ubuntu. A file created on your Window system that functions as a virtual disk. Ubuntu is installed on this virtual disk, which operates like a hard disk with a Linux file system on it. The Windows boot loader is modified to list a choice for Ubuntu. When Windows starts up, you have the choice to start Ubuntu instead. The Wubi installation of Ubuntu is fully functional in every way. Though it uses a virtual hard disk, it is not a virtual system. When you start Ubuntu, you are only running Ubuntu. The only differences from a standard install is that the system is installed on a file, rather than an actual hard disk partition, and the original Windows boot loader is used instead of the GRUB boot loader. As far as usage is concerned, operations are the same, though with slightly slower disk access. You can find out more about Wubi at **www.wubi-installer.org**.

Check the Ubuntu Wubi Guide for detailed information about install and management issues like boot problems, virtual disk creation, and details of the Wubi installation for Ubuntu.

`http://wiki.ubuntu.com/WubiGuide`

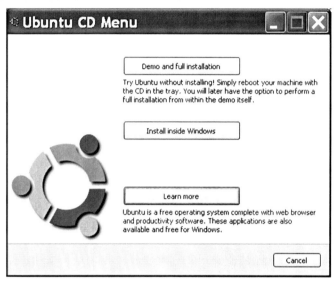

Figure 2-37: Ubuntu CD Menu on Windows

To install Ubuntu with Wubi, just insert the Ubuntu Desktop CD into you CD/DVD drive. The Ubuntu CD Menu automatically starts up, giving you the option to perform the standard install (restart and possibly partition your drive), or Install inside Windows (use a Wubi virtual hard disk file on Windows), see Figure 2-37. The Learn more option opens the Ubuntu Web site.

The install screen will prompt you for the drive to install the virtual disk file on, the install size which is the size for the virtual disk file, the desktop environment (Ubuntu), the language to use, and a username and password. You then click the Install button to download and install Ubuntu (see Figure 2-38). The Accessibility button opens a dialog where you can specify accessibility install options like contrast, magnifier, Braille, and on-screen keyboard.

Wubi then installs the standard Ubuntu desktop. Your language, keyboard, partitions, and user login have already been determined from the setup window. Wubi will first copy over files from the Desktop install disk, and then prompt you to reboot. When you reboot, your Windows boot menu is displayed with an entry for Ubuntu. Use the arrow keys to select the Ubuntu entry and press ENTER. Ubuntu will then start up. The first time it will complete the installation showing just a progress bar on the desktop, formatting, installing software, detecting hardware, and configuring your system. You do not have to do anything. Once finished you reboot and select Ubuntu again. Ubuntu will start up.

Ubuntu is fully functional. You can configure your system, install hardware drivers, and set preferences just as you do for any Ubuntu system.

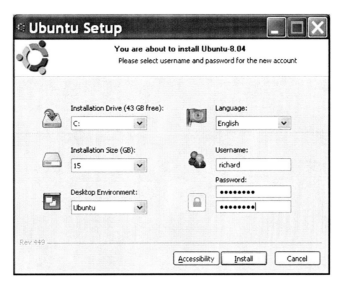

Figure 2-38: Ubuntu Setup window for Wubi

Wubi sets up an **ubuntu** directory on the hard drive partition you decided to install Ubuntu on, usually the **c:** drive. Here you will find boot and disks subdirectory. In the disks subdirectory is your virtual hard disk where Ubuntu is installed. You will also find another virtual hard disk file for your swap disk. Your Ubuntu virtual disk will be named, **root.disk**, as in **c:\ubuntu\disks\root.disk**. Keep in mind that Ubuntu is installed as a file on your Windows system. Be careful not to accidentally delete the ubuntu directory. Should you reformat your Windows partition for any reason, you, of course, loose you Ubuntu system also.

You can uninstall a Wubi installed Ubuntu system by simple remove it using Window's Add/Remove Software.

3. Usage Basics: Login, Desktop, Network, and Help

User Accounts

Accessing Your Linux System

Guest login

Important Laptop Features

The GNOME Desktop

Network Connections: wired and wireless

Desktop Operations

Display Configuration

Help Resources

Accessing Linux from the Command Line Interface

Command Line Interface

Running Windows Software on Linux: Wine

Using Linux has become an almost intuitive process, with easy-to-use interfaces, including graphical logins and graphical user interfaces (GUIs) like GNOME and KDE. Even the standard Linux command line interface has become more user-friendly with editable commands, history lists, and cursor-based tools. To start using Linux, you have to know how to access your Linux system and, once you are on the system, how to execute commands and run applications. Access is supported through a graphical login. A simple window appears with menus for selecting login options and a text box for entering your username and password. Once you access your system, you can then interact with it using the windows, menus, and icons.

Linux is noted for providing easy access to extensive help documentation. It's easy to obtain information quickly about any Linux command and utility while logged in to the system. You can access an online manual that describes each command or obtain help that provides more detailed explanations of different Linux features. A complete set of manuals provided by the Linux Documentation Project is on your system and available for you to browse through or print. Both the GNOME and KDE desktops provide help systems that give you easy access to desktop, system, and application help files.

Important Laptop Features

For working on a laptop, you will need two important operations: power management and support for multiple network connection, including wireless and LAN. Both are configured automatically.

For power management, Ubuntu uses the GNOME Power Manager (later in this chapter), gnome-power-manager, which is configured with the Power Management Preferences window (gnome-power-preferences), accessible from System | Preferences | System | Power Management. On a Laptop, the battery icon displayed on the panel will show how much power you have left, as well as when the battery become critical. It will also indicate an AC connection, as well as when the battery has recharged.

For network connections, Ubuntu uses Network Manager. Network Manager will automatically detect available network connections. Click on the Network Manager icon in the upper panel to the right. This displays a pop-up menu showing all possible wireless networks, as well as any wired networks. You can then choose the one you want to use. The name and strength of each wireless connection will be listed. When you try to connect to an encrypted wireless network, you will be prompted for the security method and the password. Wireless networks that you successfully connect to will be added to your Network Manager configuration. You also have the option to connect to a hidden wireless network as well as create a connection of your own.

To configure your wireless connection you would open the Network Connections window and select the Wireless tab. To open the Network Connections window, right-click on the Network Manager icon and select Edit Connections from the pop-up menu. Then, on the Wireless tab, you will see listed any network connections you have accessed. Use the Edit button to open an Editing Wireless connection window configure a connection, setting up passphrase, encryption methods, and domain addressing. You can also use Network Manager to manually configure a wired network connection (see Chapter 14).

Accessing Your Ubuntu System

If you have installed the boot loader GRUB, when you turn on or reset your computer, the boot loader first decides what operating system to load and run. The boot loader then loads the default operating system, which will be Ubuntu. Ubuntu will use a graphical interface by default, presenting you with a graphical login window at which you enter your username and password.

If other operating systems, like Windows, are already installed on your computer, then you can press the spacebar at start up to display a boot loader menu showing those systems as boot options. If a Windows system is listed, you can choose to start that instead.

The Display Manager: GDM

With the graphical login, your GUI interface starts up immediately and displays a login window with box for your username. When you enter your username, press ENTER, and then enter your password in the same box. Upon pressing ENTER, your default GUI starts up. On Ubuntu, this is GNOME by default.

For Ubuntu, graphical logins are handled by the GNOME Display Manager (GDM). The GDM manages the login interface along with authenticating a user password and username, and then starting up a selected desktop. (the CTRL-ALT-BACKSPACE keys for restarting the X server is disabled by default, use the **dontzap --disable** command to enable it). From the GDM, you can shift to the command line interface with the CTRL-ALT-F1 keys, and then shift back to the GUI with the CTRL-ALT-F7 keys.

Figure 3-1: GDM Login Window

When the GDM starts up, it shows a login window with a box for login (see Figure 3-1). Various GDM themes are available, which you can select using the GDM configuration tool. The default theme currently used is the Ubuntu Human theme. An Options pop-up menu at the lower left of the screen shows the entries Shut Down, Restart, Suspend, and Hibernate. In addition there are Language and Session entries that display dialogs for selecting the language or user interface you want to use like GNOME or KDE.

Tip: You can also force your system to reboot at the login prompt, by holding down the CTRL and ALT keys and then pressing the DEL key (CTRL-ALT-DEL). Your system will go through the standard shutdown procedure and then reboot your computer.

To log in, enter your username in the entry box labeled Username and press ENTER. You are then prompted to enter your password. Do so, and press ENTER. By default, the GNOME desktop is then started up.

Tip: You can configure your GDM login window with different features like background images and user icons. The GDM even has its own selection of themes to choose from. Select Login Window entry on the System | Administration menu to configure your login window.

When you log out from the desktop, you return to the GDM login window. To shut down your Linux system, select the Shut Down entry in the Options menu. To restart, select Restart from the Options menu. Alternatively, you can also shut down from GNOME. Click the User switcher button on the top panel to the right. A menu is displayed with entries for Log lout, Suspend, Hibernate, Restart, and Shut Down (The Shut Down and Log Out entries are no longer listed in the System menu).

From the Select Sessions entry in the Options menu, you can select the desktop or window manager you want to start up. A dialog box is displayed showing all installed possible user interfaces. Here you can select KDE to start up the K Desktop, for example, instead of GNOME. The KDE option will not be shown unless you have already installed it. Failsafe entries for both Gnome and the terminal provide a stripped down interface you could use for troubleshooting. The Run Xclient script lets you run just your X Windows System configuration script. This script will normally start up Gnome or KDE, but it could be specially configured for other desktops or Window managers. Normally you would have the Last session entry selected which starts up the interface you use previously. Once you have selected your interface, click the Change Session button (you can opt out of any change by clicking the Cancel button).

The Select languages entry opens a dialog with a pop-up menu that lists a variety of different languages that Linux supports. Choose one can click the Change Language button to change the language your interface will use.

The Fast User Switcher Applet (FUSA)

The User Switcher (the Fast User Switcher Applet, FUSA) lets you switch to another user, without having to log out or end your current user session. The User Switcher is installed automatically as part of your basic Gnome desktop configuration. The switcher will appear on the right side of the top panel as the name of the currently logged in user. It has been combined with the Quit button, displayed to the right. If you left-click the name, a list of all other users will be displayed (see Figure 3-2), along with quit options to log out, suspend, hibernate, restart and shut down. You will also see a Guest session and Lock screen entries for guest login or blocking access.

Logged in users managed by the User switcher will be listed first. Bold font is used for users that are logged in and running. To switch a user, select the user from this menu. If the user is not already logged in, the login manager (GDM) will appear and you can select the user and enter that user's password. If the user is already logged in, then the login window for the lock screen will appear (you can disable the lock screen). Just enter the user's password. The user's original session will continue with the same open windows and applications running when the user switched off. You can easily switch back and forth between logged-in users, with all users retaining their session from where they left off. When you switch off from a user, that user's running programs will continue in the background.

With IM applications running like Pidgen or Empathy, the user switcher will display IM settings: online, busy, away, and offline, with the current status shown as an associated image (see Chapter 8, Figure 8-7).

Right-clicking the switcher will list several user management items, like configuring the Login screen, managing users, or changing the user's password and personal information. The Preferences item lets you configure how the User Switcher is displayed on your panel. Instead of the user's name, you could use the term Users or a user icon. You can also choose whether to use a lock screen when the user switches. Disabling the lock screen option will let you switch seamlessly between logged-in users.

Figure 3-2: User Switcher

Guest login

Ubuntu now supports a guest account, allow you to let other user use your system, without have to give them a user account of their own or use someone else's. It is designed for situations like letting someone use your laptop to quickly check a Web site. The Guest login is accessible from the User Switcher as the Guest session entry (see Figure 3-2). The guest user is immediately placed on their own desktop, while your account remains locked. Upon logging out from the Guest account, the locked screen dialog is displayed, letting you login to your own account again.

Shut down and Logging out

To shut down the GNOME desktop, click the red log out button on the right side of the top panel. This button has been combined with the User switcher, displaying both logged in users and Shut down options. The Shut down options will be shown at the bottom of the menu: Log out, Suspend, Hibernate, Restart, and Shut down (see Figure 3-2). To add a button for the shut down options to another panel, you can choose the User Switcher panel applet from the Add to Panel window. To just add a button to display a window for just the shut down options, you would use the Shut down applet.

There are several ways to shut down your system.

➢ User switcher menu: select one of the shut down options (see Figure 3-2).

➢ Press the power button on your computer. This opens a menu with shutdown options (see Figure 3-3).

➢ Click the power button applet on your panel: This button is not added by default. You will first have to add it to your panel. Upon clicking the applet icon, the same shut down menu appears as that which appears when pressing your computer power button (see Figure 3-3).

When you select the Shut Down, Restart, Hibernate, or Log Out entry from the User switcher menu, the appropriate dialog is displayed giving you 60 seconds to cancel the operation (See Figure 3-3).

Figure 3-3: Shut Down, Log out, and Restart dialogs

You can just press your computer power button to shut down, restart, suspend, or hibernate your system. When you press the power button on your computer, a shut down dialog is displayed with menu entries for Shut Down, Restart, Suspend and Hibernate (see Figure 3-4). Click the Shut Down entry to shut down the system. The Restart button will shut down and the restart the system. Use Suspend and Hibernate to stop your system temporarily, using little or no power. Press the space key to redisplay the locked login screen where you can access your account and continue your session from where you left off.

Figure 3-4: Shut down dialog

You can also add Shut down and Logout buttons to a panel, using Add To Panel. Once the Shut down button is displayed on your panel, you can just click it to open the Shutdown menu (see Figure 3-3), and then choose to shutdown, restart, suspend, or hibernate.

Note: The Shut Down and Log Out entries are no longer available on the System menu.

To logout, you can use wither the User switcher Log out entry, or a Logout button on your panel (first add the Logout button to your panel; it is not there by default). When you click on the Log out button on the panel, the Log Out dialog is display with options to Log Out or Switch User (see Figure 3-5). Click Log Out to return to the login screen where you login again as a different user. Switch User will keep you logged in while you login to another user. Your active programs will continue to run in the background.

Figure 3-5: Log Out dialog

The GNOME Desktop

Ubuntu supports both the GNOME and KDE desktops. The default Ubuntu live CD will install GNOME, whereas the KUbuntu live CD will install KDE. The Ubuntu DVD lets you install both, and you can later install one or the other using a Synaptic Package Manager meta package, The Ubuntu Desktop or The K Desktop. GNOME uses the Ubuntu Human theme for its interface with the Ubuntu screen background and menu icon as its default (see Figure 3-6).

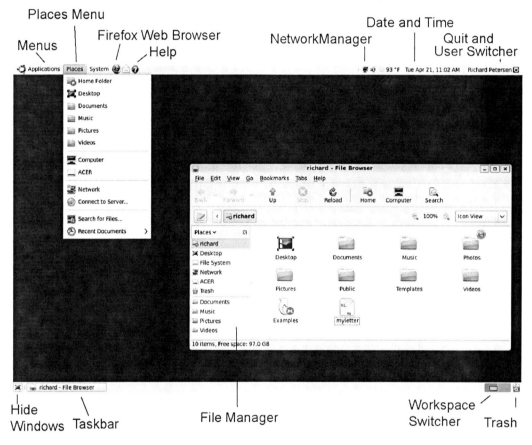

Figure 3-6: Ubuntu GNOME desktop

It is important to keep in mind that though the GNOME and KDE interfaces appear similar, they are really two very different desktop interfaces with separate tools for selecting preferences. The Preferences menus on GNOME and KDE display a very different selection of desktop configuration tools.

GNOME also includes a window manager called compiz-fusion that provides 3-D effects. To use compiz-fusion, select System | Preferences | Appearance, Visual Effects panel. You can select normal, or extras for full effects. When you log in to GNOME again, compiz-fusion will be used with your desktop effects enabled.

The Ubuntu GNOME desktop display, shown in Figure 3-5, initially displays two panels at the top and bottom of the screen, as well as any file manager folder icons for your home directory and for the system. The top panel is used for menus, application icons, and notification tasks like your clock (see Figure 3-7). There are three menus:

- **Applications**   With category entries like Office and Internet, these submenus will list the applications installed on your system. Use this menu to start your applications. The Install/Remove Software entry will start the Add/Remove Applications tool for basic package install operations.

- **Places**   This menu lets you easily access commonly used locations like your home directory, the desktop folder for any files on your desktop, and the Computer window, through which you can access devices and removable disks, and Network for accessing shared file systems. It also has entries for searching for files (Search For Files), accessing recently used documents, and logging in to remote servers, such as NFS and FTP servers. A Recent Documents menu lists all your recently accessed files.

- **System**   This includes Preferences and Administration menus. The Preferences menu is used for configuring your GNOME settings, such as the theme you want to user and the behavior of your mouse. The Administration menu holds all the Ubuntu system configuration tools used to perform administrative tasks like adding users, setting up printers, configuring network connections, and managing network services like a Web server or Samba Windows access. This menu also holds entries for locking the screen (Lock) and logging out of the system (Logout).

Next to the menus are application icons for commonly used applications. These include Firefox (the Fox and World logo), the mail utility, and the help icon. Click one to start that application. You can also start applications using the Applications menu. On the right you will see icons and text for the combined user switcher and quit button (FUSA), the date/time, the sound volume control, and the Network Manager.

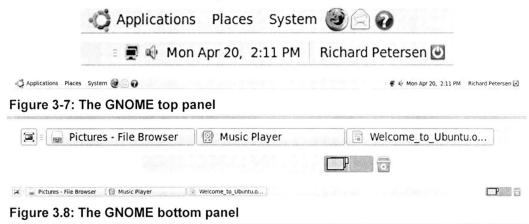

Figure 3-7: The GNOME top panel

Figure 3.8: The GNOME bottom panel

The bottom panel is used for interactive tasks like selecting workspaces and docking applications (see Figure 3-8). The workspace switcher for virtual desktops appears as four squares in the lower-left corner. Clicking a square moves you to that area. To the right of the workspace switcher is the trash space that shows what items you have in your trash. The keyboard shortcut to switch workspace is Ctrl-Alt-arrow, where arrow can be any left, right, up, or down arrow keys. Right-click on the workspace switcher and select Preferences to open a settings window where you can increase then number of workspaces (increment the number of columns or rows) and how the workspace switcher displays them.

To move a window, left-click and drag it's title bar. Each window supports Maximize, Minimize, and Close buttons. Double-clicking the title bar will maximize the window. Each window will have a corresponding button on the bottom panel. You can use this button to minimize and restore the window. The desktop supports full drag-and-drop capabilities (see Table 3-1). You can drag folders, icons, and applications to the desktop or other file manager windows open to other folders. The move operation is the default drag operation (you can also press the SHIFT key while dragging). To copy files, press the CTRL key and then click and drag before releasing the mouse button. To create a link, hold both the CTRL and SHIFT keys while dragging the icon to where you want the link, such as the desktop.

Key press	Action
SHIFT	Move a file or directory, default
CTRL	Copy a file or directory
CTRL-SHIFT	Create a link for a file or directory
CTRL-ALT-Arrow (right, left, up, down)	Move to a different desktop
CTRL-w	Close current window
ALT-spacebar	Open window menu for window operations, including moving window to another workspace
ALT-F2	Open Run command box
ALT-F1	Open Applications menu
F2	Rename selected file or directory
Ctrl-F	Find file

Table 3-1: Desktop Keyboard shortcuts: click-and-drag, workspace, windows

Gnome file manager

You can access your home directory from its entry in the Places menu. A file manager window opens showing your home directory. Your home directory will already have default directories created for commonly used files. These include Pictures, Documents, Music, and Videos. Your office applications will automatically save files to the Documents directory by default. A Pictures directory is where image and photo applications will place images files. The Desktop folder will hold all files and directories saved to your desktop.

Note: For both GNOME and KDE, the file manager is Internet-aware. You can use it to access remote FTP directories and to display or download their files.

The File manager window will display several components, including a browser toolbar, location bar, and side pane commonly found on most traditional file managers. When you open a new directory, the same window is used to display it, and you can use the forward and back arrows to move through previously opened directories. In the location window, you can enter the pathname for a directory to move directly to it. Figure 3-9 shows the file manager window.

The GNOME file manager also supports tabs. You can open up several folders in the same file manager window. To open a tabbed pane, select New Tab from the File menu or press **Ctrl-t**. You can then use the entries in the Tabs menu to move from one tab to another, or to rearrange tabs. You can also use the Ctrl-PageUp and Ctrl-PageDown keys to move from one tab to another. Use the Shift-Ctrl-PageUp and Shift-Ctrl-PageDown keys to rearrange the tabs.

Figure 3-9: File manager for home folder

Note: Your desktop also features a new notification display format. Notifications appear with a large black background. A tool to let you set preferences for your notification messages is under development.

GNOME Applets

GNOME applets are small programs that operate off your panel. It is very easy to add applets. Right-click the panel and select the Add to Panel entry. This lists all available applets (see Figure 3-10). Some helpful applets are dictionary lookup, the current weather, the system monitor, which shows your CPU usage, the CPU Frequency Scaling Monitor for Cool and Quiet processors, and Search for Files, which searches your system for files. For most applets, you will have to perform basic configuration. To do this, right-click on the applet and select Preferences. This will open the Preferences window for that applet.

Figure 3-10: GNOME Add to Panel window to add applets

Figure 3-11 shows some of the more common applets. They are organized into loose categories using separator lines, also available on the Add to Panel window. The first three following the Web and mail buttons, are applications added to the panel by right-clicking on the application entry in the Applications menu and selecting "Add to panel". Shown are the GNOME movie player, Pidgen instant messenger, and OpenOffice word processor. These are followed by applets added from the Add to Panel window. First are buttons for shutdown, logout, and run applications. Deskbar desktop search and Tomboy note taker are next, followed by monitoring buttons: laptop battery, CPU Frequency Monitor, and the System monitor. And finally Eyes that follow your mouse around. After the added applets, the standard GNOME applets are shown starting with the update notification button, Network Manager, Volume Control, Weather-Date-Time (International Clock), and combined User switcher and Log out button (FUSA).

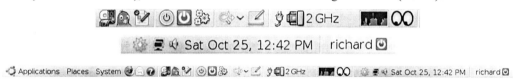

Figure 3-11: GNOME applets added on top panel

Note: The K Desktop Environment (KDE) displays a panel at the bottom of the screen that looks very similar to one displayed on the top of the GNOME desktop. The file manager appears slightly different but operates much the same way as the GNOME file manager.

Network Connections

Network connections will be set up for you by Network Manager which will automatically detect your network connections, both wired and wireless. Network Manager is designed to work in the background, providing status information for your connection and switching from one configured connection to another as needed. For initial configuration, it detects as much information as possible about the new connection. It operates as a GNOME Panel applet, monitoring your connection, and can work on any Linux distribution.

Network Manager is user specific. Wired connections will be started automatically. For wireless connections, when a user logs in, Network Manager selects the connection preferred by that user. The user can choose the wireless connection to use from a menu of detected wireless networks.

Network Manager will display a Network applet icon to the right on the top panel. The Network Manager applet icon will vary according to the type of connection. An Ethernet (wired) connection will display two computer monitors, one in front of the other. A wireless connection will display a staggered bar graph (see Figure 3-12). If the connection is not active, a red x will appear on the icon. When Network Manager is detecting possible wireless connections, it will display a rotating connection image. If you have both a wired and wireless connection, and the wired connection is active, the wired connection image (double monitor) will be used.

Figure 3-12: Network Manager wired, wireless, and detection icons.

Network Manager wired connections

For computers connected to a wired network, like an Ethernet connection, Network Manager will automatically detect the network connection and establish a connection. Most networks use DHCP to provide network information like an IP address and network DNS server automatically. With this kind of connection, Network Manager can automatically connect to your network whenever you start your system. The network connection would be labeled something like Auto eth0, eth0 being the actual Ethernet network device name on your system. When you connect, a connection established message will be displayed, as shown here.

The Network Manager panel icon will display the double monitors, as shown here.

When you left-click on the Network Manager icon, a pop-up menu will display your wired connection, along with a submenu for VPN Connections. Computers with only a wired network device (no wireless) will show only Wired Network connections, as shown here as Auto eth0.

Network Manager wireless connections

With multiple wireless access points for Internet connections, a system could have several different network connections to choose from, instead of a single-line connection like DSL or cable. This is particularly true for notebook computers that could access different wireless connections at different locations. Instead of manually configuring a new connection each time one is encountered, the Network Manager tool can automatically configure and select a connection to use.

Network Manager will scan for wireless connections, checking for Extended Service Set Identifiers (ESSIDs). If an ESSID identifies a previously used connection, then it is automatically selected. If several are found, then the most recently used one is chosen. If only a new connection is available, then Network Manager waits for the user to choose one. A connection is selected only if the user is logged in.

Left-click to see a list of all possible network connections; including all available wireless connections (see Figure 3-13). Wireless entries will display the name of the wireless network and a bar-graph showing the strength of its signal. Password-protected access points will display a lock next to them. Computers with both wired and wireless devices will show entries for both Wired Network and Wireless Networks. Computers with only a wireless device will only show entries for Wireless Networks.

Note: If a computer has both wired (Ethernet or dial-up) and wireless connection devices, as most laptops have, then you will see entries for both Wired and Wireless networks. Should you disable wireless network, then only the wired entry will be displayed.

Figure 3-13: Network Manager connections menu: wired and wireless

To connect to a wireless network, find its network entry in the Network Manager applet's menu and click on it. If this the first time you are trying to connection to that network, you will be prompted to enter connection information: the wireless security and passphrase. The type of wireless security used by the network will be detected and displayed for you. If it is incorrect, you can use the drop-down menu to select the correct method. The entries will change depending on the method chosen. The WPA passphrase is one of the more common methods. Figure 3-14 shows the prompt for the passphrase to a wireless network that uses the WPA security method. A checkbox lets you see the passphrase should you need to check that you are entering it correctly. Click Connect to activate the connection.

Figure 3-14: NetworkManager wireless authentication

Once connected a message will be displayed showing the connection, as shown here.

When you connect to a wireless network for the first time, a configuration entry will be made for the wireless connection in the Wireless tab of the Network Connections tool.

Figure 3-15: KDE NetworkManager connection menu (wired and wireless) and panel icon

The very first time you make a wireless connection, you will be prompted to set up a keyring. The keyring holds your wireless connection passphrase, allowing you to connect to a wireless network without having to re-enter the network passphrase each time. You will be asked to create a keyring password for accessing the keyring. This is a one time operation. Once the keyring is set up, any additional wireless connection passphrases will be added to it. When you first login and try to connect to a wireless network, you will be prompted for your keyring password.

On KDE, the Network Manager menu is displayed by clicking the Network Manager icon on the Plasma panel (see Figure 3-15). The entries are the same, except for an added entry showing the currently connected wireless connection. An enable checkbox next to it lets you disconnect or later connect.

Wireless connection can also be hidden. These are wireless connections that do not broadcast an SSID, making them undetectable to with an automatic scan. To connect to a hidden wireless network, you select "Connect to hidden wireless network" on the Network Manager menu (see Figure 3-16). The Connection drop-down menu will select the New entry. If you have set up any hidden connections previously, they will also be listed in the Connection drop-down menu. For a New connection, enter the wireless network name and select a security method. You will be prompted in either case for your network keyring password.

Figure 3-16: Connect to a Hidden Wireless Network

Network Manager options

Right-click to have the option of editing your connection, shutting   off your connection (Enable Networking and Enable Wireless), or to see information about the connection (see Figure 3-17). A computer with both wired and wireless connections will have entries to Enable Networking and Enable Wireless. Selecting Enable Wireless will disconnected only the wireless connections, leaving the wired connection active. The Enable Wireless checkbox will be come unchecked and a message will be displayed telling you that your wireless connection is disconnected.   Selecting Enable Networking will disable your wired connection, along with any wireless connections. Do this to work offline, without any network access.

Figure 3-17: NetworkManager options

A computer with only a wired network device (no wireless) will only show an Enable Networking entry, as shown here. Selecting it sill disconnect you from any network access, allowing you to work offline.

Desktop Operations

There are several desktop operations that you may want to take advantage of when first setting up your desktop. These include setting up your personal information, burning CD/DVD disks, searching your desktop for files, and using removable media like USB drives, along with access to remote host.

Tip: With very large monitors and their high resolutions becoming more common, one feature users find helpful is the ability to increase the desktop font sizes. To increase the font size, open the Font panel on Appearance preferences located in System | Preferences | Appearance menu. There you can change the font sizes used on your desktop.

GNOME International Clock: Time, Date, and Weather

The international clock applet is located on the top panel to the right. It displays the current time and date for your region, but can be modified to display the weather, as well as the time, date, and weather of any location in the world.

To add a location, right-click on the time and select Preferences from the pop-up menu. The Clock Preferences window will display three tabs: General, Location, and Weather (see Figure 3-18). To add a new location, click on the Add button on the Locations tab. This opens a window where you can enter the name, timezone, and coordinates of the location. To specify a location, just start typing its name in the Location Name box. As you begin typing, a drop down menu appears automatically will possible completions. The listing of possible locations reduces the more you type, narrowing your choices. When the location you want is shown in the drop down menu, select it. The timezone, latitude, and longitude for that location will be added for you.

Figure 3-18: Selecting a location on the international clock

On the Weather panel, you can specify the temperature and wind measures to use. The General panel you can set the clocks display options for the locations, whether to show weather, temperature, date and seconds.

The Time Settings button opens a dialog where a user can manually set the time. A button on this dialog labeled System Time opens a dialog for setting system-wide time.

Note: Ubuntu provides several tools for configuring your GNOME desktop. These are listed in the System | Preferences menu. The Help button on each preference window will display detailed descriptions and examples. Some of the commonly used tools are discussed in the Desktop Operations section later in this chapter.

Once you set the location for your own location, you will see a weather icon appear next to the time on the panel, showing you your current weather (see Figure 3-19).

64 °F Wed Apr 30, 4:54 PM

Figure 3-19: International clock with weather icon

To see the locations you have selected, click on the time displayed on the top panel (see Figure 3-20). This opens a calendar, with Location label with an expandable arrow at the bottom. Click this arrow to display all your locations, their time and weather. You home location will have a house icon next to it. A world map will show all your locations as red dots, with a blue house icon for your current home location. When you click on a location entry, its corresponding dot will blink for a few seconds. Each location will have a small globe weather icon, indicating the general weather, like sun or clouds. To see weather details, move your mouse over the weather icon. A pop-up dialog will display the current weather, temperature, wind speed, and time for sunrise and sunset. The clock icons for each location will be dark, grey, or bright depending on the time of day at that location.

Figure 3-20: International clock, full display

You can easily change your home location, by click the Set button to the right the location you want made your home. You will see the home icon shift to the new location. This is helpful when traveling. Each location has a set button which will be hidden until you move your mouse over it, on the right side of the clock display

To make any changes, you can click the Edit button next to the Locations label. This opens the Clock Preferences window where you can configure the display or add and remove locations.

The calendar will show the current date, but you can move to different months and years using the month and year scroll arrows at the top of the calendar.

To set the time manually, right-click on the time and select Adjust Date & Time (also from the General panel of the Clock Preferences window, click the Time Settings button). This opens a Time Settings window where you can enter the time and set the date. Use the month and year arrows on the calendar to change the month and year. To set the time for the entire system, click the Set System Time button which open **date-admin** (System | Administration | Time and Date).

Configuring your personal information

To set up your personal information, including the icon to be used for your graphical login, you use the About Me preferences tool. On the Ubuntu GNOME desktop, select the About Me entry in the System | Preferences menu (System | Preferences | About Me). The About Me preferences dialog lets you set up personal information to be used with your desktop applications, as well as change your password (see Figure 3-21). Each user can set up their own About Me personal information, including the icon or image they want to use to represent them.

Clicking on the image icon in the top left corner opens a browser where you can select a personal image. The Faces directory is selected by default displaying possible images. The selected image is displayed to the right on the browser. For a personal photograph you can select the Picture folder. This is the Pictures folder on your home directory. Should you place a photograph or image there, you could then select if for your personal image. The image will be use in the login screen when showing your user entry.

Figure 3-21: About Me information: System | Preferences | About Me

Should you want to change your password, you can click on the Change password button at the top right.

There are three panels: Contact, Addresses, and Personal Info. The Contact panel you enter email (home and work), telephone, and instant messaging addresses. On the Address panel you enter your home and work addresses, and on the Person Info panel you list your Web addresses and work information.

Desktop Background

You use the Background panel on the Appearance tool to select or customize background image (see Figure 3-221). To open this panel, you can either right click anywhere on the desktop background and select Change Desktop Background from the pop-up menu, or from the panel menus select System | Preferences | Appearance | and select the Background panel. Installed backgrounds are listed, with the current one selected. To add your own image, either drag and drop the image file to the Background panel tool, or click on the Add button to locate and select the image file. To remove an image, select it and click the Remove button.

Figure 3-22: Choosing a desktop background, System | Preferences | Appearance

The style menu lets you choose different display options like centered, scaled, or tiled. A centered or scaled image will preserve the image proportions. Fill screen may distort it. Any space not filled, such as with a centered or scaled images, will be filled in with the desktop color. You can change the color if you wish, as well as make it a horizontal or vertical gradient (Colors menu). Colors are selected from a color wheel providing an extensive selection of possible colors.

Initially only the Ubuntu backgrounds are listed. Install the **gnome-background** package to add a collection of GNOME backgrounds. You can download more GNOME backgrounds from **www.art.gnome.org** and **www.gnome-look.org**.

TIP: You can set your screen resolution as well as screen orientation using the Monitor Resolution Settings utility accessible from System | Preferences | Screen Resolution. The utility supports RandR screen management features like screen rotation, resolution, and refresh rate.

Using Removable Devices and Media

Removable media such as CD and DVD discs, USB storage disks, digital cameras, and floppy disks will be displayed as icons on your desktop. These icons will not appear until you place the disks into their devices. To open a disk, double-click it to display a file manager window and the files on it.

Ubuntu now supports removable devices and media like digital cameras, PDAs, card readers, and even USB printers. These devices are handled automatically with an appropriate device interface set up on the fly when needed. Such hotplugged devices are identified, and where appropriate, their icons will appear in the file manager window. For example, when you connect a USB drive to your system, it will be detected and displayed as storage device with its own file system. If you copied any files to the disk, be sure to unmount it first before removing it (right-click and select Unmount Volume).

Removable media can now be ejected using Eject buttons in the file manager Places sidebar. The Places sidebar lists all your storage devices, including removable media. Removable media will have an Eject button to the right. Just click the Eject button and the media is ejected or unmounted.

Accessing File Systems, Devices, and Remote Hosts

From the file manager you not only to access removable media, but also to access all your mounted file systems, remote and local, including any Windows shared directories accessible from Samba. You can browse all your file systems directly from GNOME, which implements this capability with the GNOME virtual file system (GVFS) mapping to your drives, storage devices, and removable media. HAL and udev access removable media directly.

You can access your file systems and removable media using the Computer entry Places menu (you can place this on your desktop). This opens a top-level window showing icons for all removable media (mounted CD-ROMs, USB drives, and so on), your local file system, and your network shared resources (see Figure 3-23). Double-click any icon to open a file manager window displaying its contents. The file system icon will open a window showing the top-level directory for your file system. Access will be restricted for system directories, unless you log in as the root user.

File systems on removable media will also appear automatically as icons directly on your desktop. A DVD/CD-ROM is automatically mounted when you insert it into your DVD/CD-ROM drive, displaying an icon for it with its label. The same kind of access is also provided for card readers, digital cameras, and USB drives. Be sure to unmount the USB drives before removing them so that data will be written.

If you have already configured associated applications for audio and video CD/DVD discs, or discs with images, sound, or video files, the disc will be opened with the appropriate application; like Fspot for images, Rhythmbox for audio, and Movie Player for DVD/video. If you have not yet configured these associations you will be prompted to specify what application you want to open it with.

You can access a DVD/CD-ROM disc from the desktop by either by double-clicking it or by right-clicking and selecting the Open entry. A file manager window opens to display the contents of the CD-ROM disc. To eject a CD-ROM, you can right-click its icon and select Eject Volume from the pop-up menu. The same procedure works for floppy disks, using the Floppy Disk or USB drive icon, but with an Umount Volume entry. Be sure you don't remove a mounted floppy disk until you have first unmounted it, selecting the Unmount Volume entry in the pop-up menu.

Tip: Default actions for removable media and drives are now handled by different tools. The GNOME file manager (Nautilus) handles removable media like music CDs and DVD video directly, whereas the Removable Device and Media preferences tool only handles devices like cameras, PDAs, and scanners.

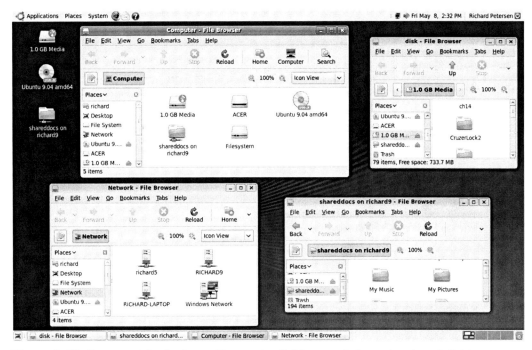

Figure 3-23: Removable devices, Computer folder, and shared network folders

To see network resources, open the Network window using the Network entry in the Places menu (you can also placed this on your desktop). The network window will list your connected network hosts. Opening these will display the shares, such as shared directories, that you can have access to. Drag-and-drop operations are supported for all shared directories, letting you copy files and folders between a shared directory on another host with a directory on your system. To browse Windows systems on GNOME using Samba, you first have to configure your firewall to accept Samba connections (Gufw or Firestarter).

Tip: Nautilus can also burn ISO DVD and CD images using Brasero, as well as DVD Video. Just open the ISO disc image file with Disc Burner.

GNOME will display icons for any removable devices and perform certain default actions on them. For example, cameras will be started up with F-spot photo manager. To set the preferences for how removable devices are treated, you use the Removable Drives and Media preferences tool, accessible with the Removable Drives and Media entry in the System | Preferences menu. Certain settings are already set.

Accessing Archives from GNOME: Archive Mounter

Ubuntu now supports the access of archives directly from GNOME using Archive Mounter. You can select the archive file and then right-click and select Archive Mounter to open the archive. The archive contents are listed in a Nautilus file manager window. You can extract or display the contents.

You can also use Archive Mounter to mount CD/DVD disk images as archives. You can then browse and extract the contents of the CD/DVD. Simply double-click on a disk image file (.iso extension) and the image is automatically mounted as an archive. A disk icon for the CD/DVD will appear on the desktop. It will be read only. You can also right-click on the disk image file and select Archive Mounter (usually the first option). The disk will appear in the Computer folder as a valid disk. To unmount the disk image as an archive, right-click and select Unmount Volume.

Burning DVD/CDs with GNOME (Brasero)

GNOME performs disc burning operation using the Brasero Disc Burner application. Brasero is integrated into GNOME, letting you burn data disc using a GNOME Nautilus file manager window as well as accessing DVD/CD disc operations like copy, erase, and checking from a DVD/CD disc's GNOME desktop menu (right-click on the DVD/CD desktop icon).

File Manager CD/DVD Creator interface

Using the GNOME file manager to burn data to a DVD or CD is a simple matter of dragging files to an open blank CD or DVD and clicking the Write To Disk button. When you insert a blank DVD/CD, a window will open labeled CD/DVD Creator. To burn files, just drag them to that window. All Read/Write discs, even if they are not blank, are also recognized as writable discs and opened up in a DVD/CD Creator window. Click Write To Disc when ready to burn a DVD/CD. A Brasero Disc burning setup dialog will open, which will perform the actual write operation. You can specify the DVD/CD writer to use (if you have more than one), and the disc label (name). Also, click the Properties button to open a dialog with burning options like the burn speed.

Burning ISO images from the file manager

The GNOME file manager also supports burning ISO images using Brasero. Just double-click the ISO image file or right-click the file and select Open with Disc Burner. This opens the Brasero Disc Burning dialog, which prompts you to burn the image. Be sure to first insert a blank CD or DVD into your CD/DVD burner. You can also burn DVD-Video disks.

GNOME desktop CD/DVD disc operations

Disc copy, erasing, and checking uses the Brasero CD/DVD burner directly, which is now integrated into GNOME. Once a disc is inserted, right-click on its CD/DVD desktop icon to display a menu with the Copy Disc, Blank Disc, and Check Disc entries. Selecting the Copy Disc entry will start the Brasero copy dialog (see Figure 3-24). You have the option of writing to an ISO image to another disc. For the ISO image file, the Properties dialog lets you choose the folder to save the file. For copying to another disc, the Properties dialog lets you choose the burning speed and options like using burnproof or performing a simulation first.

The Blank Disc entry works on CD/DVD RW disc, and will erase a disc. Check Disc will check the integrity of the disk, with the option of using the disc's md5 file, if available.

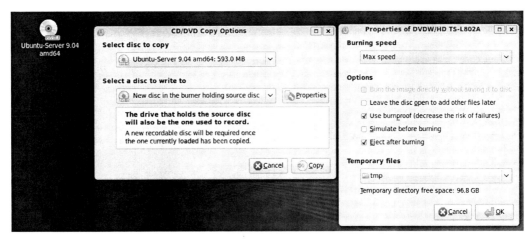

Figure 3-24: Copying CD/DVD discs on GNOME Desktop (Brasero)

Brasero Disc Burner application interface

For more complex DVD/CD burning you can use the Brasero DVD/CD burner application interface (see Figure 3-25), Applications | Sound & Video | Brasero Disc Burner. Brasero supports drag and drop operations for creating Audio CDs. In particular, it can handle CD/DVD read/write discs, erasing discs. It also supports multi-session burns, adding data to DVD/CD disc. Initially Brasero will display a dialog with buttons for the type of project you want to do. You have the choice to create a data or audio project, create a DVD/Video disc, copy a DVD/CD, or burn a DVD/CD image file.

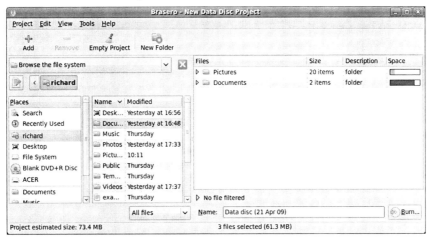

Figure 3-25: Burning DVD/CD with Brasero

For a Data project, the toolbar will display an Add button which you use to select files and directories to be burned to your disc. You can choose to display a side panel (View menu) which will let you select files and directories using the Nautilus Places listing.

Searching files

On Ubuntu, there are two primary search tools available for your desktop, "Search for Files" and Tracker. "Search for Files" is installed by default and will be accessible from Places | Search for Files, and the desktop menu. The Tracker search and desktop indexer is also installed and accessible from its applet icon (magnifying glass) in the top panel to the right. Tracker will actually index your files making access more efficient. The GNOME file manager also provides its own search tool for quickly finding files. As an alternative search applet you can use DeskBar which also makes use of Tracker indexing.

Search for Files

The Search for Files tools performs basic file searching (see Figure 3-26). It is just a GNOME front end for the Linux **grep**, **find**, and **locate** tools. Select Search for Files from the Places menu and enter the pattern to search for. File matching characters (wildcards) will help, like * for file name completion or || to specify a range of possible characters or numbers.

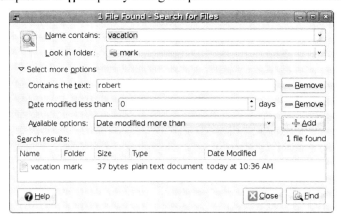

Figure 3-26: Search for Files

Enter the pattern to search in the Name contains box, and then select the folder or file system to search from the Look in Folder pop up menu. The user home folder is selected by default. You can then elect to specify advanced options like the Contain text option for searching the contents of text files (**grep**), or additional file characteristics like the file date, size, or owner type (**find**). You can also use a regular expression to search file names.

GNOME File Manager Search

The GNOME file manager uses a different search tool, with the similar features. You enter a pattern to search, but you can also specify file types. Search begins from the folder opened, but you can specify other folder to search (Location option). Click the + button to add additional location and file type search parameters. In the browser mode, you can click on the Search button on the toolbar to make the URL box a Search box. Popup menus for location and file type will appear in the folder window, with + and - button to add or remove location and file type search parameters.

Tracker: Indexed Search

Tracker is a GNOME desktop indexing search tool **(www.gnome.org/projects/tracker/)**, technically named Meta-Tracker. It is not installed by default. Use Synaptic to install the tracker package. Tracker is turned off by default as its indexing function can be resource intensive. You can enable Tracker by selecting the Search and Indexing item in the System | Preferences menu and checking the Enable Indexing entry on the General tab. If you find that indexing is consuming too many resources, you can turn it off by unchecking the Enable Indexing entry. You can still use Tracker to perform searches if you have Watch directories specified on the Files tab. Your home directory will already be enabled for watching.

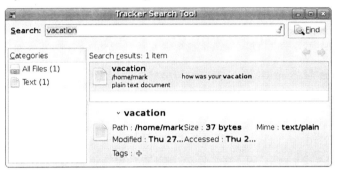

Figure 3-27: Tracker Desktop search and indexing

Once enabled, the Tracker applet is placed on the right side of the top panel using a magnifying glass as its icon. You can right click on the panel icon to display a menu for selecting preferences as well as starting tracker or pausing indexing. Tracker indexes not just by name or location, but also by meta data and content of files and directories. Indexing is performed by the **trackerd** daemon.

To use Tracker, click on its icon in the top panel. This opens a search window where you can enter your search and display the results (see Figure 3-27). You can open this window directly by right-clicking on the icon and choosing Search from the pop-up menu. Search results are organized into categories on a side pane. The results for a selected category or shown in the top right pane. Information about a selected result appears in the lower right pane.

Tracker also has an indexer that can be configure using the Tracker preferences window. Select Preferences from the Tracker applet's pop-up menu, or with Search and Indexing item in the System | Preferences menu. There are General, Files, Ignored Files, Email, and Performance panels. On the General panel you can enable or disable indexing. On the Files panel you can specify what directories to index. Your home directory is already specified. You can also choose to index the contents of files. The Ignored Files panels lets you exclude directories from indexing, as well as files with certain patterns in their names. On the Email panel you can index Email clients like Evolution or Thunderbirds, as well as specify specific mbox files. The Performance panel lets you control the amount of resources indexing will use.

Private Encrypted Directories (ecryptfs)

Ubuntu now provides each user with the capability of setting up a private encrypted directory. Encryption adds a further level of security. Should others gain access to your home directory, they still would not be able to read any information in your private encrypted directory.

Private directory encryption is implemented using the **ecryptfs** utilities, **ecryptfs-utils** on the Ubuntu main repository. You use the **ecryptfs-setup-private** command to set up an encrypted private directory.

```
ecryptfs-setup-private
```

You are prompted to enter your user password, and then your mount password. The mount password is the password set up for the Private directory. Leave blank to have one generated automatically.

A directory named **.Private** is set up which is the actual encrypted directory, holding the encrypted data files. This is a dot file, with a period preceding the name. Then a directory is set up named **Private** which will serve as a mountpoint for the **.Private** directory. For security purposes, your encrypted private directory (**.Private**) remains unmounted until your decide to access it.

To access your encrypted private directory (**.Private**), you first mount it to the **Private** directory. Then you can access it. The **Private** directory is located in your home directory. Initially the directory is unmounted. You can open your file browser to the home directory where you will find an icon for the Private folder. When you click on this icon, the Private folder opens with a message in the folder saying that the directory is not mounted. Click on the message icon to mount the Private directory. The contents of your Private directory are then displayed. On the desktop, an icon will appear labeled Private which you can also use to then access your Private directory.

On the Places sidebar in the file manager window, the Private directory will be listed with an eject button next to it. Click on the eject button to unmount the Private directory, or right-click on the desktop icon and select Umount. The Private desktop icon will disappear and the data in the Private directory becomes inaccessible. What happens is that the **.Private** directory which holds the actual data, become unmounted from the **Private** mount point. The data remains in the **.Private** directory, but can no longer be accessed through the **Private** directory, until you decide to mount it again.

If you are working from the command line interface, attempts to access the contents of the **Private** directory will simply result in a warning message notifying you that the directory is unmounted. You can then mount the Private directory with the **mount.encryptfs_private** command. Do not to run this command from within the **Private** directory.

```
mount.encryptfs_private
```

You can later unmount it with the **umount.ecryptfs_private** command.

During setup an **.ecryptfs** directory is created which holds your encryption keys and manages access.

To create a passphrase for your private directory, you use the ecrypt-manager command. This displays a simple menu for creating passphrases.

GNOME Power Management

For power management, Ubuntu uses the GNOME Power Manager, **gnome-power-manager**, which makes use of ACPI support provided by a computer to manage power use. The GNOME Power manager is configured with the Power Management Preferences window (**gnome-power-preferences**), accessible from System | Preferences | Power Management (see Figure 3-28). Power management can be used to configure both a desktop and a laptop.

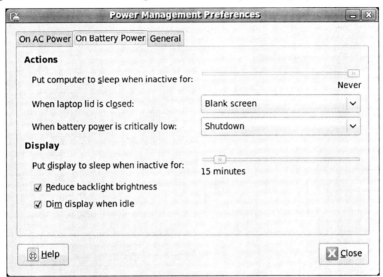

Figure 3-28: GNOME Power Manager

On a Laptop, the battery icon displayed on the panel will show how much power you have left, as well as when the battery become critical. It will also indicate an AC connection, as well as when the battery has recharged.

Tip: With the GNOME Screensaver Preferences you can control when the computer is considered idle and what screen saver to use if any. You can also control whether to lock the screen or not, when idle. Access the Screensaver Preferences from System | Preferences | Screensaver. You can turn off the Screensaver by unchecking the "Activate screensaver when computer is idle" box.

For a desktop there are only two tabs, On AC Power and General. On the On AC Power tab you have two sleep options, one for the computer and one for the screen. You can put each to sleep after a specified interval of inactivity. On the General tab you set desktop features like actions to take when pressing the power button or whether to display the power icon. The AC power icon will show a plug image for desktops and a battery for laptops. The icon is displayed on the top panel.

A laptop will also have an On Battery Power tab where you can set additional option for the battery and display, such as shutting down if the battery is too low, or dimming the display when the system is idle.

To see how your laptop or desktop is performing with power, you can use Power statistics. Right-click on the Power Manager icon and select Power History. This runs the **gnome-power-statistics** tool. You may have to first choose to display the Power Manager icon in its General preferences.

To keep a measure of how much time you have left, you can use the Battery Charge Monitor applet. An icon will appear on your panel showing you how much time is left. The preferences let you specify features like showing time or percentage and when to notify of low charge.

Display Configuration

The GUI interface for your desktop display is implemented by the X Window System. The version used on Ubuntu is X.org (**x.org**). X.org provides its own drivers for various graphics cards and monitors. You can find out more about X.org at `www.x.org`.

X.org will automatically detect most hardware. The **/etc/X11/xorg.conf** file is no longer used for the open source drivers (**nv** and **ati**). It is still used to a limited extent by proprietary drivers, though mouse and keyboard entries are ignored as these are handled directly by HAL and udev. Information such as the monitor used is automatically determined. Should you want to change the screen resolution, use the Screen Resolution tool accessible from System | Preferences | Screen Resolution. If you have an older monitor that is not correctly detected, you may have to specify monitor information by editing the **/etc/X11/xorg.conf** file.

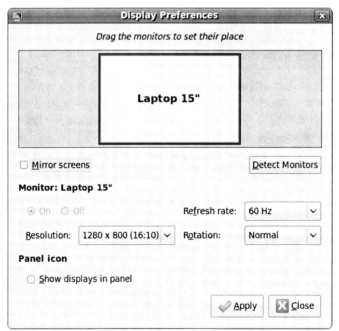

Figure 3-29: Screen Resolution

Resolution Preferences: RandR

The X display drivers for Linux used on Ubuntu now support user level resolution and orientation changes. Any user can specify their own resolution or orientation without affecting the settings of other users. The gnome-display-properties tool provides a simple interface for setting rotation, resolution, and selecting added monitors, allowing for cloned or extended displays across several connected monitors. Open the Monitor Resolution Settings window by selecting Administration | Preferences | Screen Resolution (see Figure 3-29). This is a feature provided by GNOME. From pop-up menus you can set the resolution, refresh rate, and rotation, as well as detect attached displays. After you select a resolution, click Apply. The new resolution is displayed with a dialog with button that asks you whether to keep the new resolution or return to the previous one. You can use the Detect Monitors button to detect any other monitors connected to your system. The Show Displays in Panel checkbox will display a button for each display in the top panel, letting you switch between them easily.

Vendor drivers: restricted hardware

Your display will be detected automatically, configuring both your graphics card and monitor. Normally you should not need to perform any configuration yourself. However, if you have a graphics card that uses Graphics processors from a major Graphics developer and vendor like Nvidia or ATI (AMD) or Nvidia, you have the option of using their driver, instead of the open source X drivers installed with Ubuntu. Some cards may work better with the vendor driver, and provide access to more of the cards features like 3D support.

After you install Ubuntu and login, your graphic card will be detected and you will be notified that you can use a vendor driver instead for better performance. A restricted hardware notification icon will be displayed on the top panel. Click on it or select System | Administration | Hardware Drivers to open the Hardware Drivers window (see Figure 3-30). This invokes the jockey application which will detect and mange the installation of needed hardware drivers.

Select the driver entry and then click on the Activate button to use download and install the driver. Once installed the Activate button will change to a Deactivate button. You are notified to Restart your system. Close the Hardware Drivers window and then restart your system. On restart, your system will then be using the vendor drivers such as ATI or Nvidia. The drives are part of the restricted repository, supported by the vendor but not by Ubuntu. They are not open source, but proprietary. This situation is beginning to change, with AMD (ATI) and Nvidia releasing much of its driver source code as open source.

Once installed, an examination of the Hardware Drivers window will show the selected driver in use (see Figure 3-31). Should you want to remove the driver for any reason, click the Remove button. The driver will be removed and you will have to restart your system. Upon restart the open source Xorg driver will be automatically selected and used.

You no longer have to install a new kernel compatible version of your proprietary graphics driver each time you update to a new kernel. The kernel drivers are automatically generated for you by the DKMS (Dynamic Kernel Module Support) utility. See Chapter 13 for more details on DKMS.

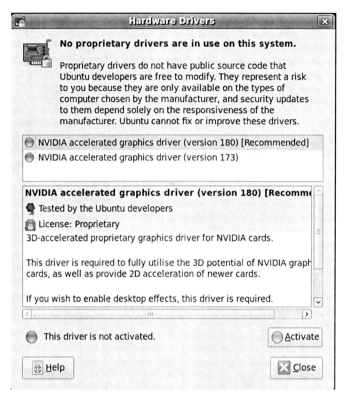

Figure 3-30: Hardware Drivers

When new version of the proprietary drivers becomes available, you will be notified and prompted to select the new version. A note will tell you that a different version is currently in use, and the Activate button will be displayed (see Figure 3-32). Clicking it will download and install the new version.

The graphic vendors also have their own Linux-based configuration tools which are installed with the driver. The Nvidia configuration tool is in the **nvidia-settings** package. Once installed, you will see the Nvidia X Server Settings entry in the Administration menu (System | Administration | Nvidia X Server Settings). This interface provides Nvidia vendor access to many of the features of Nvidia graphics cards like color corrections, video brightness and contrast, and thermal monitoring. You can also set the screen resolution and color depth.

`nvidia-settings`

ATI/AMD provides a Linux version of its Catalyst configuration tool for use on Linux. Much of the ATI video drivers have now become open source, making the ATI video driver much more Linux compatible. The ATI/AMD Catalyst configuration tool for Linux is in the **fglrx-amdcccle** package, which you will have to install with the Synaptic Package Manager.

`fglrx-amdcccle`

If you have problems with the vendor driver, you can always uninstall it. Your original X open source driver will be used instead. The change over will be automatic. To uninstall the vendor driver, use the Hardware Drivers window and un-check the vendor driver entry. After the uninstall process, you will be prompted to reboot.

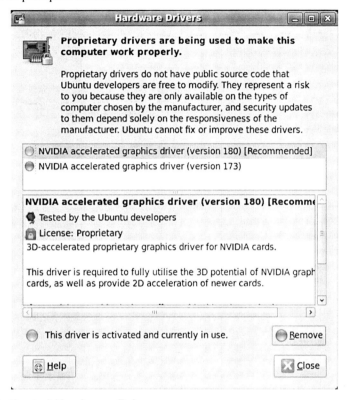

Figure 3-31: Activated Hardware Drivers

Figure 3-32: Update Hardware Drivers

If the problem is more severe, with the display not working, you can use the GRUB display (ESC at start up) and select the recovery kernel. Your system will be started without the graphics driver. You can the use the "drop to shell" to enter the command line mode. From there you can use **apt-get** command-line APT tool to remove the graphics driver. The ATI drivers have the prefix fglrx and Nvidia have **nvidia**. In the following example, the asterisk will match on all the **fglrx** packages (ATI).

```
sudo apt-get remove fglrx*
```

xorg.conf

All configuration tools will generate an X Window System configuration file called **/etc/X11/xorg.conf**. This is the file the X Window System uses to start up. Ubuntu uses the X.org drivers for the X Window System. You can find out more about X.org at **www.x.org**. Whenever you change your settings, your current configuration is saved to **/etc/X11/xorg.backup.conf**. Should need to restore your old settings manually, you can just replace your current **xorg.conf** with the backup file.

It is advisable that you make your own backup of a **xorg.conf** file that works. Should your display configuration become unrecoverable, you can always resort the reliable backup. The following creates a backup file called **xorg-mybackup.conf**.

```
sudo cp /etc/X11/xorg.conf  /etc/X11/xorg.mybackup
```

This way, should the new configuration fail; you can restore the original by copying over the current **xorg.conf** file with the saved version.

```
sudo cp /etc/X11/xorg.mybackup  /etc/X11/xorg.conf
```

Help Resources

A great deal of support documentation is already installed on your system, as well as accessible from online sources. Table 3-2 lists Help tools and resources accessible on your Ubuntu Linux system. Both the GNOME and KDE desktops feature Help systems that use a browser-like interface to display help files. To start the GNOME or KDE Help browser, select the Help entry in the main menu or click help icon on the panel. The Help browsers now support the Ubuntu Help Center, which provides Ubuntu specific help, as well as the GNOME desktop and system man page support.

If you need to ask a question, you can select the Get online help entry in the Help menu to access the Jaunty help support at **http://answers.launchpad.net**. Here you can submit your question, as well as check answered questions.

Ubuntu Help Center

To start the Ubuntu Help Center, click the Help button on the panel (the **?** icon on the top panel). This starts the GNOME help browser (Yelp) which now presents the Ubuntu Help Center (see Figure 3-33). The GNOME Help browser supports bookmarks for pages you want to access directly. The Help Topics button will return you to the start page. For detailed documentation and tutorial on the GNOME help browser, just select Contents from the Help menu or press F1.

The GNOME Help Center display topics geared to Ubuntu. Links range from adding software, managing files and folders, to printing and scanning. A help page will display detailed information on the left, and a sidebar of links for more information on the right. These will include any associated links

As you progress through a document collection, its bookmarks appear at the top of the page. Figure 3-34 shows the import photos from dial camera, with bookmarks for "Music, video and photos" and "Photos and cameras". The sidebar links expand as you progress through the document collection.

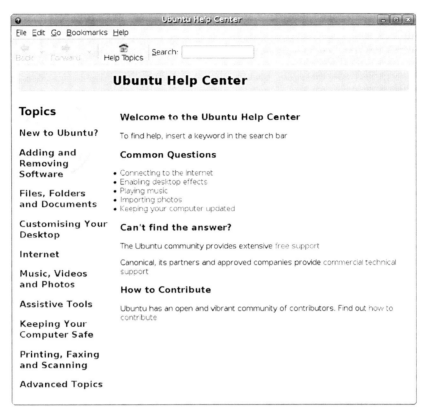

Figure 3-33: Ubuntu Help Center

Figure 3-34: Help Center bookmarks and sidebar

The GNOME help browser contents will also show a sidebar listing direct links to all the major help topics (Help | Contents), rather than the Ubuntu specific links on the Ubuntu Help Center page. These topics include An Introduction to the Desktop, Basic Skills, Desktop Overview, Using the panels, Tools and Utilities, and Configuring your desktop. The Introduction to the Desktop provides a comprehensive set of links to desktop pages. Many of these topics will also appear as links in pages you access through the Ubuntu Help Center (see Figure 3-35).

You can easily bring up documentation and manuals on different applications by performing a search on their names. A search on "archive" will show link to the Archive Manager Manual. A search on "system monitor" will show a link to the System Monitor manual.

The Advanced Topic link will display links for accessing the Man and Info pages.

Figure 3-35: Introduction to desktop

Context-Sensitive Help

Both GNOME and KDE, along with applications, provide context-sensitive help. Each KDE and GNOME application features detailed manuals that are displayed using their respective Help browsers. Also, system administrative tools feature detailed explanations for each task.

Application Documentation

On your system, the **/usr/share/doc** directory contains documentation files installed by each application. Within each directory, you can usually find HOW-TO, README, and INSTALL documents for that application.

The Man Pages

You can also access the Man pages, which are manuals for Linux commands available from the command line interface, using the `man` command. Enter `man` with the command on which you want information. The following example asks for information on the `ls` command:

```
$ man ls
```

Pressing the SPACEBAR key advances you to the next page. Pressing the B key moves you back a page. When you finish, press the Q key to quit the Man utility and return to the command line. You activate a search by pressing either the slash (/) or question mark (?). The / searches forward; the ? searches backward. When you press the /, a line opens at the bottom of your screen, and you then enter a word to search for. Press ENTER to activate the search. You can repeat the same search by pressing the N key. You needn't reenter the pattern.

Tip: You can also use either the GNOME or KDE Help system to display Man and info pages.

The Info Pages

Online documentation for GNU applications, such as the gcc compiler and the Emacs editor, also exist as *info* pages accessible from the GNOME and KDE Help Centers. You can also access this documentation by entering the command **info**. This brings up a special screen listing different GNU applications. The info interface has its own set of commands. You can learn more about it by entering **info info**. Typing **m** opens a line at the bottom of the screen where you can enter the first few letters of the application. Pressing ENTER brings up the info file on that application.

Accessing Linux from the Command Line Interface

For the command line interface, you are initially given a login prompt. On Ubuntu you can access the command-line interface by pressing CTRL-ALT-F1 at any time (ALT-F7 returns to the graphics interface). The login prompt is preceded by the hostname you gave your system. In this example, the hostname is **turtle**. When you finish using Linux, you first log out. Linux then displays exactly the same login prompt, waiting for you or another user to log in again. This is the equivalent of the login window provided by the GDM. You can then log in to another account.

Once you log in to an account, you can enter and execute commands. Logging in to your Linux account involves two steps: entering your username and then entering your password. Type in the username for your user account. If you make a mistake, you can erase characters with the BACKSPACE key. In the next example, the user enters the username **richlp** and is then prompted to enter the password:

```
Ubuntu release 9.04
Kernel 2.6 on an i686

turtle login: richlp
Password:
```

When you type in your password, it does not appear on the screen. This is to protect your password from being seen by others. If you enter either the username or the password incorrectly, the system will respond with the error message "Login incorrect" and will ask for your username again, starting the login process over. You can then reenter your username and password.

Once you enter your username and password correctly, you are logged in to the system. Your command line prompt is displayed, waiting for you to enter a command. Notice the command line prompt is a dollar sign ($), not a number sign (#). The $ is the prompt for regular users, whereas the # is the prompt solely for the root user. In this version of Ubuntu, your prompt is preceded by the hostname and the directory you are in. Both are bounded by a set of brackets.

```
[turtle /home/richlp]$
```

To end your session, issue the `logout` or `exit` command. This returns you to the login prompt, and Linux waits for another user to log in.

```
[turtle /home/richlp]$ logout
```

To, instead, shut down your system from the command line, you enter the `halt` command. This command will log you out and shut down the system.

```
$ halt
```

Command Line Interface

When using the command line interface, you are given a simple prompt at which you type in your command. Even with a GUI, you sometimes need to execute commands on a command line. You can do so in a terminal window. The terminal window is accessed from the Applications | Accessories menu. You can add the terminal window icon to the desktop by right-clicking on the menu entry and selecting Add launcher to the desktop.

Linux commands make extensive use of options and arguments. Be careful to place your arguments and options in their correct order on the command line. The format for a Linux command is the command name followed by options, and then by arguments, as shown here:

```
$ command-name options arguments
```

An *option* is a one-letter code preceded by one or two hyphens, which modifies the type of action the command takes. Options and arguments may or may not be optional, depending on the command. For example, the `ls` command can take an option, `-s`. The `ls` command displays a listing of files in your directory, and the `-s` option adds the size of each file in blocks. You enter the command and its option on the command line as follows:

```
$ ls -s
```

An *argument* is data the command may need to execute its task. In many cases, this is a filename. An argument is entered as a word on the command line after any options. For example, to display the contents of a file, you can use the `more` command with the file's name as its argument. The `less` or `more` command used with the filename **mydata** would be entered on the command line as follows:

```
$ less mydata
```

The command line is actually a buffer of text you can edit. Before you press ENTER, you can perform editing commands on the existing text. The editing capabilities provide a way to correct mistakes you may make when typing in a command and its options. The BACKSPACE and DEL keys let you erase the character you just typed in. With this character-erasing capability, you can BACKSPACE over the entire line if you want, erasing what you entered. CTRL-U erases the whole line and enables you to start over again at the prompt.

Tip: You can use the UP ARROW key to redisplay your last-executed command. You can then re-execute that command, or you can edit it and execute the modified command. This is helpful when you have to repeat certain operations over and over, such as editing the same file. This is also helpful when you've already executed a command you entered incorrectly.

Running Windows Software on Linux: Wine

Wine is a Windows compatibility layer that will allow you to run many Windows applications natively on Linux. Though you could run the Windows OS on it, the actual Windows operating system is not required. Windows applications will run as if they were Linux applications, able to access the entire Linux file system and use Linux-connected devices. Applications that are heavily driver dependent, like graphic intensive games, may not run. Others that do not rely on any specialized drivers, may run very well, including Photoshop, Microsoft Office, and newsreaders like Newsbin. For some applications, you may also need to copy over specific Windows DLLs from a working Windows system to your Wine Windows system32 or system directory. Wine is scheduled for its first full release in the summer of 2008.

To install Wine on your system, search for **wine** on the Synaptic Package Manager. You will a wine package listed, described as the Windows Compatibility Layer.

Once installed, a Wine menu will appear in the Applications menu. The Wine menu holds entries for Wine configuration, the Wine software uninstaller, and Wine file browser, as well as a regedit registry editor, a notepad, and a Wine help tool.

To set up Wine, a user starts the Wine Configuration tool. This opens a window with panels for Applications, Libraries (DLL selection), Audio (sound drivers), Drives, Desktop Integration, and Graphics. On the Applications window you can select which version of Windows an application is designed for. The Drives panel will list your detected partitions, as well as your Windows-emulated drives, such as drive C. The C: drive is really just a directory, **.wine/drive_c**, not a partition of a fixed size. Your actual Linux file system will be listed as the Z drive.

Once configured, Wine will set up a **.wine** directory on the user's home directory (the directory is hidden, so enable Show Hidden Files in the file manager View menu to display it). Within that directory will be the **drive_c** directory, which functions as the C: drive holding your Windows system files and program files in the Windows and Program File subdirectories. The System and System32 directories are located in the Windows directory. Here is where you would place any needed DLL files. The Program Files directory will hold your installed Windows programs, just as they would be installed on a Windows Program Files directory.

To install a Windows application with Wine, you can open a terminal window and run the **wine** command with the Windows application as an argument. Instead of using the terminal window, you can just right-click on the application icon on the desktop, and then choose Open with, selecting Wine. The following example installs the popular newsbin program:

```
$ wine newsbin.exe
```

Icons for installed Windows software will appear on your desktop. Just double-click an icon to start up the application. It will run normally within a Linux window as would any Linux application.

Installing Windows fonts on Wine is a simple matter of copying fonts from a Windows font directory to your Wine **.wine/drive_c/Windows/fonts** directory. You can just copy any Windows **.ttf** file to this directory to install a font.

To install applications that have the **.msi** extension you use the msiexec command with the **/a** option. The following installs the Mobipocket Ebook Reader.

```
msiexec /a mobireadersetup.msi
```

To add books to the Mobipocket reader library, just drag the book to the open Mobipocket window.

Tip: Alternatively, you can use the commercial Windows compatibility layer called CrossoverOffice. This is a commercial product tested to run certain applications like Microsoft Office. Check **www.codeweavers.com** for more details. CrossoverOffice is based on Wine, which CodeWeavers supports directly.

ubuntu

Part 2: Applications

Installing and Updating Software
Office Applications and Editors
Multimedia and Graphics
Mail and News
Internet Applications

4. Installing and Updating Software

Installing Software Packages

Ubuntu Package Management Software

Ubuntu Software Repositories

Updating Ubuntu with Update Manager

Managing Packages with Add/Remove Applications

Synaptic Package Manager

Source code files

Software Package Types

DEB Software Packages

Managing software with apt-get

Command Line Search and Information

Managing non-repository packages with dpkg

Using packages with other software formats

Ubuntu software has grown so large that it no longer makes sense to use discs as the primary means of distribution. Instead distribution is effected using the online Ubuntu software repositories. These repositories contain an extensive collection of Ubuntu-compliant software. Most software is now located on the Internet connected repositories. With the integration of repository access into your Linux system, you can now think of that software as an easily installed extension of your current collection.

For Ubuntu, you can add software to your system by accessing software repositories supporting Debian packages (DEB) and the Advanced Package Tool (APT). Software is packaged into DEB software package files. These files are, in turn, installed and managed by APT.

The Ubuntu software repository is organized into several sections, depending on how the software is supported. Software supported directly is located in the main Ubuntu repository section. Other Linux software that is most likely compatible is placed in the Universe section.

In addition many software applications, particularly multimedia ones, have potential licensing conflicts. Such software is placed in the Multiverse section and is not maintained directly by Ubuntu. Many of the popular multimedia drives and applications such as video and digital music support can be obtained from Ubuntu Multiverse section using the same simple APT commands you would use for Ubuntu sponsored software.

Also, some drivers are entirely proprietary and supplied directly by vendors. This is the case with the Nvidia and ATI vendor provided drivers. Such drivers are placed in a restricted section, noting that there is no open source support. This situation is currently being changed by ATI and, to some extent, Nvidia, who are making part of their drivers open source.

You can also download source code versions of applications and then compile and install them on your system. Where this process once was complex, it has been significantly streamlined with the addition of *configure scripts.* Most current source code, including GNU software, is distributed with a configure script. The configure script automatically detects your system configuration and create a binary file that is compatible with your system.

You can also download Linux software from many online sources directly, but it is always advised that you use the Ubuntu prepared package versions if available. Most software for GNOME and KDE has corresponding Ubuntu compliant packages in the Ubuntu Universe and Multiverse repositories.

Installing Software Packages

Installing software is an administrative function performed by a user with administrative access. Unless you chose to install all your packages during your installation, only some of the many applications and utilities available for users on Linux were installed on your system. On Ubuntu, you can easily install or remove software from your system with the Add/Remove Applications tool, the Synaptic Package Manager, or the **apt** command. Alternatively, you can install software by downloading and compiling its source code.

APT (Advanced Package Tool) is integrated as the primary install packages tool. When you install a package with Package Manager or with Synaptic, APT will be invoked and it will automatically select and download the package from the appropriate online repository. This is a major change that users may not be aware of at first glance. After having installed your system, when you then want to install additional packages, the install packages tool will now use APT to install from an online repository, though it will check your CD or DVD ROM first if you wish. This will include the entire Ubuntu online repository, including the main repository as well as Universe and Multiverse ones.

A DEB software package includes all the files needed for a software application. A Linux software application often consists of several files that must be installed in different directories. The program itself is most likely placed in a directory called **/usr/bin**, online manual files go in another directory, and library files go in yet another directory.

When you select a package for download, APT will install any additional dependent (required) packages. With Ubuntu 9.04, APT will also install all recommended packages by default. Many software applications have additional features that rely on recommended packages.

Note: Be careful not to mix distributions. The distribution segments of all your **sources.list** entries should be the same: jaunty if you are using Ubuntu 9.04, gutsy for 7.10, edgy for 7.05, dapper for 6.06, and so on.

Ubuntu Package Management Software

Though all Ubuntu software packages have the same DEB format, they can be managed and installed using different package management software tools. The primary software management tool is APT.

➤ **Gdebi** Simple package installation for installing single packages. Uses a GNOME interface.

➤ APT (Advanced Package Tool): Synaptic, Package Manager, update-manager, dpkg and apt-get are front ends fro APT.

➤ Synaptic Package Manager: Graphical front end for managing packages, repository info at **/var/cache/apt**, same as APT

➤ Update Manager: Ubuntu graphical front end for updating installed software uses APT.

➤ Add/Remove Applications tool, **gnome-app-install**: GNOME Graphical front end for managing packages, repository info at **/var/cache/apt**, same as APT

➤ KPackageKit: KDE4 software manager, graphical front end for APT.

➤ **dpkg** older command line tool to install, update, remove, and query software packages. Uses own database, **/var/lib/dpkg**, , repository info at **/var/cache/apt**, same as APT

➤ **apt-get** primary command line tool to install, update, and remove software, uses own database, **/var/lib/apt/**, repository info at **/var/cache/apt**

➤ **aptitude** Front end for tools like dpkg or apt-get, cursor based, uses own database, **/var/lib/aptitude**

Gdebi

Gdebi is designed to perform an installation of a single DEB software package. These are usually packages that are downloaded directly from a Web site and have few or no dependent packages. When you use your browser to download a particular package, you will be prompted to open it with Gdebi when the download is finished. Gdebi will install the package for you; displaying information about the package and checking to see if it is compatible with your system (see Figure 4-1). It is advisable to always use Gdebi to install a manually downloaded package.

Figure 4-1: Web browser prompt with Gdebi selected

You could also first download the package, and then later select it from your GNOME nautilus window. Double clicking should open the package with Gdebi. You can also right-click and choose to open it with Gdebi. Gdebi can be started directly from Applications | System Tools | Gdebi Package Installer (this menu item is turned off by default, use System | Preferences | Main Menu to have it displayed).

In Figure 4-2, The Gdebi tool is opened for a download of the **libdvdcss2** library, the codec for DVD Video. The package is part of the Medibuntu.org repository, but if you did not configure access to that repository, you can use your Web browser to download and install packages directly with Gdebi (**http://packages.medibuntu.org/jaunty/**).

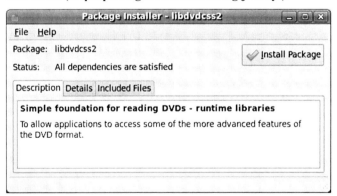

Figure 4-2: Gdebi installer

Once downloaded Gdebi display the package name and status. There are tabs for Description, Details, and Included Files. Status will indicate if any dependent files are needed. You can then click the Install Package button to install the package. The package file will first be downloaded, along with any dependent packages, and then installed (see Figure 4-3). With some packages, like Google Earth, the terminal segment will open and prompt you to access the license. Once installed, the If you did previously configure access to that repository, you will be warned to use that software channel instead, using **apt-get** or the Synaptic Package Manager to install.

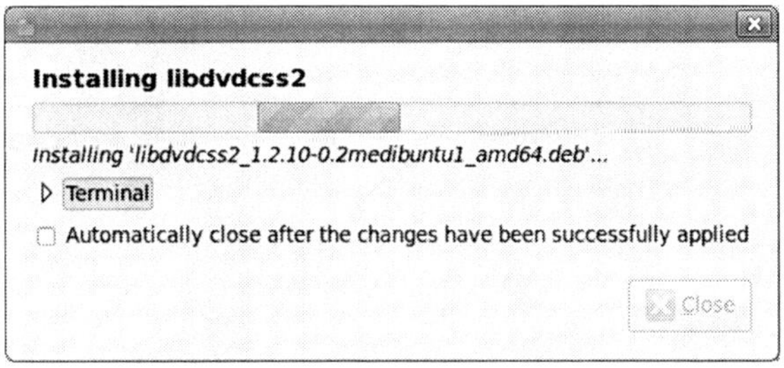

Figure 4-3: Gdebi install progress

Ubuntu Software Repositories

There are four main components or sections to the Ubuntu repository: main, restricted, universe, and multiverse. These components are described in detail at:

`www.ubuntu.com/ubuntu/components`

To see a listing of all packages in the Ubuntu repository see **http://packages.ubuntu.com**. To see available repositories and their sections, open Synaptic, click Repositories from Settings menu.

In addition, there is a third-party repository called **medibuntu.org** which provides several popular codecs and applications like Skype and the DVD Video codec. This repository has to be manually configured, as discussed later in this chapter. It is not configured on your Ubuntu system automatically.

Repository Sections

The repository sections for the main Ubuntu repository are as follows:

- **main**: Officially supported Ubuntu software (canonical), includes gstreamer good.

- **restricted**: Commonly used and required for many applications, but not open source or freely licensed, like proprietary graphics card drivers from Nvidia and ATI. Needed for hardware support, because not open source, they are not guaranteed to work.

- **universe**: All open source Linux software not directly supported by Ubuntu would include Gstreamer bad.

- **multiverse**: Linux software that does not meet licensing requirements. But is not considered essential. It may not necessarily work. For example, the Gstreamer ugly package is in this repository. see **www.ubuntu.com/community/ubuntustory/licensing**.

Repositories

In addition to the main repository, Ubuntu maintains several other repositories, primarily for maintenance and support for existing packages. The updates repository holds updated packages for a release. The security updates repository contains critical security package updates every system will need.

- **Main** repository: Collection of Ubuntu compliant software packages for releases.

- **Updates**: Corresponding updates for packages in the main repository, both main and restricted sections. Universe and Multiverse sections are not updated.

- **Backports**: Software under development for the next Ubuntu release, but packaged for use in the current one. Not guaranteed or fully tested.

- **Security updates**: security fixes for main software.

In addition, the backports repository provides un-finalized or development versions for new or current software. They are not guaranteed to work, but may provide needed features.

There is also a third-party repository called **Medibuntu.org (www.medibuntu.org)** that is commonly used for multimedia and Web applications that have licensing issues, like the DVD Video **libdvdcss** codec for commercial DVD Video, the Adobe Acrobat Reader, and Google Earth. You first have to configure access to this repository. Once setup, packages from this repository will be listed in the Synaptic Packages Manager, which you then use to install them. See the following sections (page 137) for quick configuration instructions, and Chapter 6 for more detailed information.

- **Medibuntu.org**   Third-party repository for software and codecs with licensing issues.

Note: for added repositories be sure your have installed the correct signature key as well as a valid URL for the repository.

TIP: Though it is possible to add the Debian Linux distribution repository, it is not advisable. Packages are designed for specific distributions. Combining them and lead to irresolvable conflicts.

Ubuntu Repository Configuration file: sources.list and sources.list.d

Repository configuration is managed by APT using configuration files in the **/etc/apt** directory. The **/etc/apt/sources.list** file holds repository entries. The main and restricted sections are enabled by default. An entry consists of a single line with the following format:

```
format URI    distribution    component
```

The format is normally **deb**, for Debian package format. The URI (universal resource identifier) provides the location of the repository, such as an FTP or Web URL. The distribution is the official name of a particular Ubuntu distribution like dapper or gutsy. Ubuntu 9.04 has the name jaunty. The component can be one or more terms that identify a section in that distribution repository, like main for the main repository and restricted for the restricted section. You can also list individual packages if you want.

```
deb http://archive.ubuntu.com/ubuntu/    jaunty   main restricted
```

Corresponding source code repositories will have a **deb-src** format.

```
deb-src http://us.archive.ubuntu.com/ubuntu/ jaunty main restricted
```

Update sections of a repository are referenced by the **-updates** suffix, as jaunty-updates.

```
deb http://archive.ubuntu.com/ubuntu/   jaunty-updates   main restricted
```

Security sections for a repository have the suffix **-security**.

```
deb http://archive.ubuntu.com/ubuntu/   jaunty-security   main restricted
```

Both Universe and Multiverse repositories should already be enabled. Each will have an updates repository as well as corresponding source code repositories, like those shown here for Universe.

```
deb http://us.archive.ubuntu.com/ubuntu/ jaunty universe
deb-src http://us.archive.ubuntu.com/ubuntu/ jaunty universe
deb http://us.archive.ubuntu.com/ubuntu/ jaunty-updates universe
deb-src http://us.archive.ubuntu.com/ubuntu/ jaunty-updates universe
```

Comments begin with a # mark. You can add comments of your own if you wish. Commenting an entry effectively disables that component of a repository. Placing a # mark before a repository entry will effectively disable it.

Commented entries are included for the backports and Cannonical partners repositories. Backports holds applications being developed for future Ubuntu releases and may not work. Partners include companies like Vmware and Parallels. To activate these repositories, just edit the **/etc/apt/sources.list** file using any text editor, and then remove the # at the beginning of the line.

```
# deb http://us.archive.ubuntu.com/ubuntu/ jaunty-backports \
    main restricted universe multiverse
```

Certain entries like third-party entries for Ubuntu partners can be managed using Software Sources. Others, like backports, require that you edit the **sources.list** file. You can edit the file directly with the following command.

```
gksu gedit /etc/apt/sources.list
```

Repository information does not have to be added to the **sources.list** file directly. It can also be placed in a file in the **/etc/apt/sources.list.d** directory, which APT will read as if part of the **sources.list** file.

Medibuntu.org repository quick configuration

Medibuntu repository, which holds many non-free multimedia codec and proprietary applications like Skype, requires special operations. A **medibuntu.list** repository file, which holds the Medibuntu repository references, has to be added to the **/etc/apt/sources.list.d** directory. In addition the Medibuntu software key has to be installed on your system. These tasks are usually performed on a command line in a terminal window. See the Medibuntu help page for details:

```
https://help.ubuntu.com/community/Medibuntu
```

To quickly configure access to the Medibuntu repository, you can copy the command line from the Web page and paste it directly to a terminal window, without having to type anything. First, locate the "Adding the Repositories" section on the Web page, and within it the Jaunty section. Then click and drag to select the following line.

```
sudo wget http://www.medibuntu.org/sources.list.d/jaunty.list --output-
document=/etc/apt/sources.list.d/medibuntu.list
```

From the Web browser Edit menu, select Copy.

Open a terminal window, Applications | Accessories | Terminal.

Select the terminal window, then click on the Edit menu for the terminal window and select the Paste entry. The selected text from the Web page will be pasted to the terminal window. Make sure it was copied correctly. Then press the Enter key.

Follow the same copy and paste procedure for the GPG key (further down the Web page). Copy and paste the following to a terminal window and press enter.

```
sudo apt-get update && sudo apt-get install medibuntu-keyring && sudo apt-get
update
```

You can then start up the Synaptic Package Manager. The first time you start after configuring Medibuntu.org, click the Reload button so that Synaptic will scan and load the Medibuntu.org package list. The Synaptic Package Manage to list and install Medibuntu packages like Skype or **libdvdcss** for DVD Video support.

Software Sources managed from Ubuntu Desktop

If you have installed a desktop interface, you can manage your repositories with the Software Sources tool. With the Software Sources you can enable or disable repository sections, as well as add new entries. This tool edits the **/etc/apt/sources.list** file directly. Choose System | Administration | Software Sources entry. This opens the Software Sources window with four tabs: Ubuntu Software, Third-Party Software, Updates, Authentication, and Statistics (see Figure 4-4). The Ubuntu Software tab will list all your current repository section entries. These include the main repository, universe, restricted, and multiverse, as well as source code. Those that are enabled will be checked. All of them, except the source code, will initially be enabled. You can enable or disable a repository section by simply checking or uncheck it entry. From a pop-up menu you can select the server to use. To install from a CD/DVD disc, just insert it.

On the Third-Party Software tab, you can add repositories for third party software. The repository for Ubuntu Software Partners will already be listed, but not checked. Check that entry if you want access software from the Partners. To add a third party repository click the Add button. This opens a dialog window where you enter the complete APT entry, starting with the deb format, followed by the URL, distribution, and components or packages. This is the line as it will appear in the **/etc/apt/sources.list** file. Once entered, click the Add Channel button.

The Updates tab lets you configure how updates are handled (see Figure 4-5). The tab specifies both your update sources and how automatic updates are handled. You have the option to install security (jaunty-security), recommended (jaunty-updates, pre-released (jaunty-proposed), and unsupported (jaunty-backports) updates. The security and recommended updates will already be selected. These cover updates for the entire Ubuntu repository. Pre-released and unsupported updates useful if you have installed any packages from the backports or development repositories.

Your system is already configured to check for updates automatically on a daily basis. You can opt to not check for updates at all by un-checking the Check or updates box. You also have options for how updates are to be handled.

Figure 4-4: Software Sources Ubuntu Software repository sections.

Figure 4-5: Software Sources Update configuration

You can install any security updates automatically, without confirmation. You can download updates in the background. Or you can just be notified of available updates, and then manually choose to install them when you wish. The options are exclusive. The Authentication tab shows the repository software signature keys that are installed on your system (see Figure 4-6). Signature keys will already be installed for Ubuntu repositories, including your CD/DVD-ROM. If you are adding a third party repository, you will need to add its signature key. Click Import Key File button to browse for and locate a downloaded signature key file. Ubuntu requires a signature key for any package that it installs. Signature keys for all the Ubuntu repositories are already installed, and will be listed on this tab. For third party repositories you will have to locate their signature key on their Web site, download it to a file, and then import that file.

Figure 4-6: Software Sources Authentication, package signature keys

Most repositories will provide a signature key file for you to download and import. Click the Import Key File to open a file browser where you can select the downloaded key file. This procedure is the same as the **apt-key add** operation. Both add keys that APT then uses to verify DEB software packages downloaded from repositories before it installs them.

The Statistics package lets you provide Ubuntu with software usage information, letting them know what software is being used.

After you have made changes and click the Close button, the Software Sources tool will notify you that your software package information is out of date, displaying a Reload button. Click on the Reload button to make the new repositories or components available on your package managers like the Synaptic Package Manager. If you do not click Reload, you can run apt-get update or perform the Check operation on the Synaptic Package Manager to reload the repository configuration.

Updating Ubuntu with Update Manager

New updates are continually being prepared for particular software packages as well as system components. These are posted as updates you can download from software repositories and install on your system. These include new versions of applications, servers, and even the kernel.

Figure 4-7: Update Manager with selected packages

Such updates may range from single software packages to whole components. Updating your Ubuntu system has become a very simple procedure, using the Update Manager tool. For Ubuntu, you can update your system by accessing software repositories supporting Apt update methods. To update your packages, you now use the Update Manager. Update Manager is a graphical update interface for Apt, which now performs all updates.

Update Manager makes use of the Update Manager applet on your GNOME panel, which will automatically check for updates whenever you log in. If updates are detected, Update Manager icon will flash its icon on the panel and display a message telling you that updates are available and how many there are. Click the Update Manager button to start Update Manager. You can also select Update Manager manually from its Updater Manager entry in the System | Administration menu, and click the Check button to check current repository package listings for updates.

Figure 4-8: Detailed Update information

With Ubuntu 9.04, you are notified of security updates daily, but for recommended updates you are notified only once a week. You can restore the update notification behavior used in previous Ubuntu releases by turning off the update-notifier auto_launch option.

```
gconftool -s --type bool /apps/update-notifier/auto_launch false
```

All needed updates will be selected automatically when Update Manager starts up (see Figure 4-7). The check boxes for each entry let you deselect any particular packages you may not want to update. Packages are organized according to importance, beginning with Important security updates and followed by Recommended updates. You should always perform the security updates.

Click the Install Updates button to start updating. The packages will be downloaded from their appropriate repository. Once downloaded, the packages are updated. All the Apt-compatible repositories that are configured on your system will be checked.

To see a detailed description of an update, select the update and then click on the "Description of update" arrow at the bottom of the window (see Figure 4-8). Two panes are displayed, Changes and Description. Changes list detailed update information, whereas description provides information about the software.

When downloading and installing, a dialog will first appear that shows the download and install progress (see Figure 4-9). You can choose to show progress for individual files. A window will open up that lists each file and its progress.

Figure 4-9: Download and install updates

Once downloaded, the updates are installed. Click details for see install messages for particular software packages.

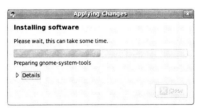

When the download completes, Update Manager will display a message saying that your system is up-to-date.

Managing Packages with Add/Remove Applications

To perform simple install and removal of software you use the Add/Remove Applications tool located in the Applications menu. This is the **gnome-app-install** application designed for simple package installation and removal. For more detailed and extensive installation such as libraries and kernel packages, you would use the Synaptic Package Manager.

Figure 4-10: Add/Remove Applications package manager

To use Add/Remove Applications tool you select the Add/Remove Applications entry from the Applications menu. Add/Remove Applications tool will start up by gathering information on all your packages (see Figure 4-10).

You then have different ways to display applications. A pop-up menu labeled Show will list of applications organized by their kind of source. To access just applications maintained for Ubuntu you would select "Canonical-maintained applications" (see Figure 4-10). Other options are: All open source applications, All available applications, Third party applications, or Installed applications. If you just want to remove a package, you could select Installed applications to narrow your search.

The pane on the left will let you list software for different categories, like Office, Graphics, or Programming, further refining your search.

You can also perform a search using the Search box. If you have selected a category in the left pane, the search will be performed just on application in that category. Clicking on different categories will apply your current search entry to that category automatically. A search on "ink" in Graphics displays Inkscape, but in Accessories it only displays the Tomboy Notetaker.

An uninstalled package will have an empty checkbox to the left of its entry, whereas installed packages will have a check mark in its box. To install a package just click its empty checkbox. The Apply Changes button on the bottom right will become active. Click it to install the selected package. You can check several packages first and then click Apply Changes to install them all at once.

To uninstall a package, click its check box. You will see its check mark disappear. Then click Apply Changes to perform the removal. You can uncheck several before clicking Apply Changes, and the remove them all at once.

APT is integrated as the primary install packages tool. When you install a package with Add/Remove Applications, APT will be invoked and it will automatically select and download the package from the appropriate online repository.

The packages listed in Add/Remove Applications are set up using the app-install-data packages. These are accessibly through the Synaptic Package Manager. The app-install-data and app-install-data-partner packages will already be installed. These list the commonly used packages on the Ubuntu repository. In addition you can install the app-install-data-edubuntu package to list edubuntu educational packages. If you have set up Medibuntu.org repository access, you can install the **app-install-data-medibuntu** package to list software applications on the Medibuntu.org repository.

Synaptic Package Manager

The Synaptic Package Manager provides more control over all your packages. Packages are listed by name and include supporting packages like libraries as well as system critical packages. You can start up Synaptic from System | Administration | Synaptic Package Manager entry.

The Synaptic Package Manager window display three panes, a side pane for listing software categories and buttons, a top pane for listing software packages, and a bottom pane for displaying a selected package's description. When a package is selected, description pane will also display a Get Screenshot button. Clicking this button will download and display an image of the application, if there is one (see Figure 4.11).

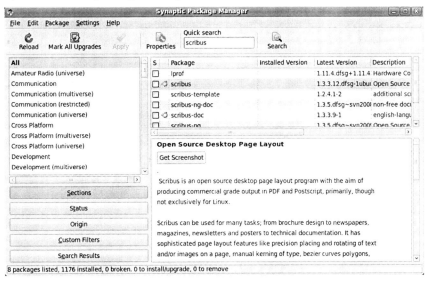

Figure 4-11: Synaptic Package Manager: Quick search

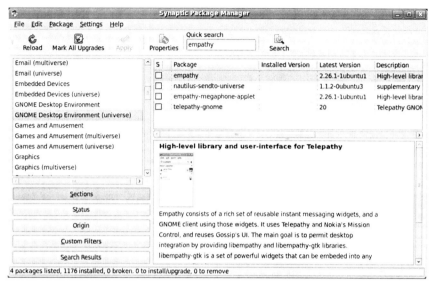

Figure 4-12: Synaptic Package Manager: Sections

Buttons on the lower left of the Synaptic Package Manager window provide options for organizing and refining the list of packages shown (see Figure 4-12). Five options are available: Sections, Status, Origin, Custom Filters, and Search results. The dialog pane above the buttons will change depending on which option you choose. Clicking on the Sections button will list section categories for your software such as Base System, Communications, or Development. The Status button will list options for installed and not installed software. The Origin button shows entries for different repositories, as well as those locally installed (manual or disk based installations). Custom filters lets you choose a filter to use for listing packages. You can create your own filter and use it to display selected packages. Search results will list your current and previous searches, letting you move from one to the other.

Synaptic supports a quick search option. Enter the pattern to be searched for in the Quick search box and the results will appear. In Figure 4-9 the scribus pattern is used to locate the Scribus desktop publishing software.

The Sections option is selected by default. You can choose to list all packages, or refine your listing using categories provided in the pane. The All entry in this pane will list all available packages. Packages are organized into categories like Base System, Cross Platform, and Communications. Each category is in turn subdivided by multiverse, universe, and restricted software.

Quick searches will be performed within selected sections. In Figure 4-12, the empathy instant messenger package is searched for in the GNOME Desktop Environment (Universe) section. Selecting different sections will automatically apply your quick search pattern to the packages in that section. Clicking on the Graphics section with an empathy search pattern would give no results, since empathy is not a graphics package.

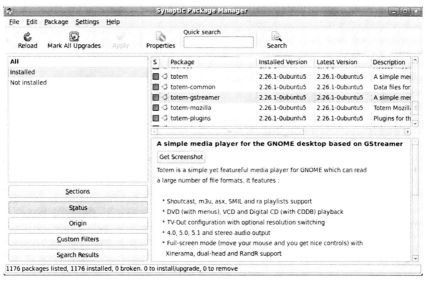

Figure 4-13: Synaptic Package Manager: Status

Status entries further refine installed software as auto-removable or as local or obsolete (see Figure 4-13). Local software consists of packages you download and install manually

With the Origins options, Ubuntu compliant repositories may further refine access according to multiverse, universe, and restricted software. A main entry selects Ubuntu supported software. Both the Ubuntu and Ubuntu security repositories are organized this way.

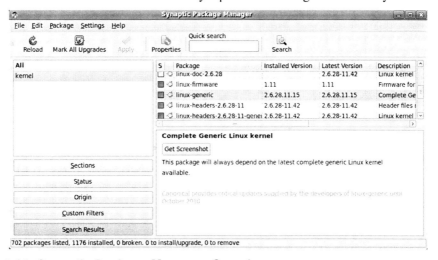

Figure 4-14: Synaptic Package Manager: Search

To perform more detailed searches, you can use the Search tool. To perform a search, click the Search button on the toolbar. This opens a Search dialog with a text box where you can enter your search terms. A pop-up menu lets you specify what features of a package to search. The

"Description and Name" feature is used most commonly. You can search other package features like just the Name, the maintainer name, the package version, packages it may depend on, or provided (associated) packages.

A list of searches will be displayed in Search Results. You can move back and forth between search results by clicking on the search entries in this listing (see Figure 4-14).

Properties

To find out information about a package, select the package and click the properties button. This opens a window with panels for Common, Dependencies, Installed files, Versions, and Description. The Common pane provides section, versions, and maintainer information. The Installed files panel show you exactly what files are installed, useful for finding the exact location and names fro configuration files as well as commands. Description information displays a detailed paragraph about the software. Dependencies will show all dependent software packages needed by this software, usually libraries.

Installing packages

Before installing software, you should press the Reload button to reload to load the most recent package lists from the active repositories

To install a package, click on its entry to display a pop-up menu and select the Mark for installation entry. Should there be any dependent packages, a dialog opens listing those packages. Click the Mark button to also mark those packages for installation. The package entry will then have its checkbox marked.

Once you have selected the packages you want to install, click the Apply button on the toolbar to begin the installation process. A Summary dialog opens up showing all the packages to be installed. You have the option to just download the package files. The number of packages to be installed is listed, along with the size of the download and the amount of disk space used. Click Apply button on the dialog to download and install the packages. A download window will appear showing the progress of your package installations. You can choose to show the progress of individual packages, which opens a terminal window listing each package as it is downloaded and installed.

Once downloaded, the dialog changes to Installing Software label. You can choose to close the dialog automatically when finished.

Sometimes installation requires user input to set up a configuration for the software. You will be prompted to enter the information.

On the submenu that opens when you right-click, you also have the options to Mark Suggested for Installation or Mark Recommended for Installation. These will mark applications that can enhance your selected software, though they are not essential.

Certain software, like desktops or office suites that require a significant number of packages, can be selected all at once using metapackages. A metapackage has configuration files that select, download, and configure the range of packages needed for such complex software like a desktop.

Removing packages

To remove a package, just locate it. Then right-click and select the "Mark package for removal" entry. This will leave configuration files untouched. Alternatively, you can mark a package for complete removal which will also remove any configuration files. Dependent packages will not be removed.

Once you have marked packages fro removal, click the Apply button. A summary dialog will display the packages for removal. Click Apply to remove them.

Synaptic may not remove dependent packages, especially shared libraries that might or might not be used by other applications. This means that your system could eventually have installed packages that are never being used. Their continued presence will not harm anything, but if you want to conserve space, you can clean them out using the **deborphan** tool. **deborphan** will output a listing of packages no longer needed by other packages or no longer used. You can then use this list to remove the packages.

Search filters

You can further refine your search for packages by creating search filters. The Filters window will show two components, a filter list on the left, and a set of three tabbed panels on the right, showing a selected Filter's status, repository section, and properties. To create a new filter, click on the New button located just below the filter listing.

Click on the New Filter 1 entry in the filter list on the left panel. On the Status panel you can refine your search criteria according to a package's status (see Figure 4-15). You can search just uninstalled packages, or include installed ones. Include or exclude those marked for removal. Or just search or those that are new in the repository. Initially all criteria are selected. Uncheck those you do not want included in your search.

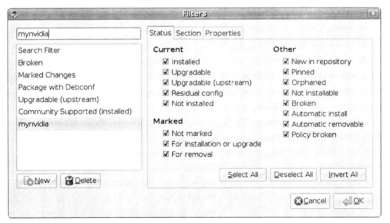

Figure 4-15: Synaptic Package Manager: Search Filter Status

The Section panel lets you include or exclude different repository sections like games, documentation, or administration. If you are just looking for a game, you could choose to just include the game section, excluding everything else.

On the Properties panel you can specify patterns to search on package information like package names, using Boolean operators to further refine your search criteria.

Package search criteria are entered using the two pop-up menus and the text box at the bottom of the panel, along with AND or OR Boolean operators (see Figure 4-16).

Figure 4-16: Synaptic Package Manager: Search Filter Properties

To create search criteria, select the package feature to search from the pop up menu, like Package name. Then select the action to take like includes. In the text box, enter the patterns to be searched. If you have more than one, you can choose either an AND Boolean operation for a small result, or an OR operation for an expanded result. Click on the New button to add the search criteria to the Properties listing. You can create several search criteria, removing old ones with Detect button.

On the Synaptic Package Manager, when you click on the Custom Filters button you will see the custom filters you created. Just click on a filter to automatically perform the package selection based on its search criteria.

Synaptic configuration

To configure the Synaptic Package Manager, select Preferences from the Settings menu. This opens the Preferences dialog with several panels. Some like Columns and Fonts, and Colors, configure the appearance. Preferences applicable to how packages are managed are located on the General panel. Here you can set features for Marking and Applying changes.

Consider recommended packages as dependencies. This will install associated packages that are not necessarily required, but would be normally used with package.

System Upgrade: Will try to identify any associated packages to be installed, updated, or removed when installing or updating a package. Not as effective as apt-get dist-upgrade.

Reload outdated package information. Can automatically keep its package list up to date.

Applying changes in a terminal window. Useful when interactive installation is required.

Note: For KDE4 you can use the KPackageKit to install and update packages.

Source code files

Though you can install source code files directly, the best way to install one is to use **apt-get**. Use the **source** command with the package name. Packages will be downloaded and extracted.

```
sudo apt-get source mplayer
```

The **--download** option lets you just download the source package without extracting it. The **--compile** option will download, extract, compile, and package the source code into a Debian binary package, ready for installation.

No dependent packages will be downloaded. If you have a software packages that requires any dependent packages to run, you will have to download and compile those also. To obtain needed dependent files, you use the **build-dep** option. All your dependent files will be located and downloaded for you automatically.

```
sudo apt-get build-dep mplayer
```

Installing from source code requires that supporting development libraries and source code header files be installed. You can to this separately for each major development platform like GNOME, KDE, or just the kernel. Alternatively you can run the APT metapackage **build-essential** for all the Ubuntu development packages. You will only have to do this once.

```
sudo apt-get install build-essential
```

Extension	File
.deb	A Debian/Ubuntu Linux package
.gz	A **gzip**-compressed file (use **gunzip** to decompress)
.bz2	A **bzip2**-compressed file (use **bunzip2** to decompress; also use the **j** option with **tar**, as in **xvjf**)
.tar	A tar archive file (use **tar** with **xvf** to extract)
.tar.gz	A **gzip**-compressed **tar** archive file (use **gunzip** to decompress and **tar** to extract; use the **z** option with **tar**, as in **xvzf**, to both decompress and extract in one step)
.tar.bz2	A **bzip2**-compressed **tar** archive file (extract with **tar -xvzj**)
.tz	A **tar** archive file compressed with the **compress** command
.Z	A file compressed with the **compress** command (use the **decompress** command to decompress)
.bin	A self-extracting software file
.rpm	A software package created with the Red Hat Software Package Manager, used on Fedora, Red Hat, Centos, and SuSE distributions

Table 4-1: Linux Software Package File Extensions

Software Package Types

Ubuntu uses Debian compliant software packages (DEB) that will have a **.deb** extension. Other packages, such as those in the form of source code that you need to compile, may come in a variety of compressed archives. These commonly have the extension **.tar.gz**, **.tgz**, or **.tar.bz2**. Packages with the **.rpm** extension are Red Hat Package software packages used on Red Hat, Fedora, SuSE and other Linux distributions that use RPM packages. They are not compatible directly with Ubuntu. You can use the alien command to convert most RPM packages to DEB packages that you can then install. Table 4-1 lists several common file extensions that you will find for the great variety of Linux software packages available to you. You can download any Ubuntu compliant deb package as well as the original source code package, as single files, directly from **packages.ubuntu.com**.

DEB Software Packages

A Debian package will automatically resolve dependencies, installing any other needed packages instead of simply reporting their absence. Packages are named with the software name, the version number, and the **.deb** extension. Check **www.debian.org/doc** for more information. File name format is as follows:

> the package name

> version number

> distribution label and build number. Packages created specifically for Ubuntu will have the ubuntu label here. Attached to it will be the build number, the number of times the package was built for Ubuntu.

> architecture   The type of system the package runs on, like i386 for Intel 32 bit x86 systems, or amd64 for both Intel and AMD 64 bit systems, x86_64.

> package format. This is always deb

For example, the package name for 3dchess is 3dchess, with a version and build number 0.0.1-13, and an architecture amd64 for a 64 bit system.

```
3dchess_0.0.1-13_amd64.deb
```

The following package has an Ubuntu label, a package specifically created for Ubuntu. The version number is 1.2 and build number is 4, with the Ubuntu label ubuntu2. The architecture is i386 for a 32 bit system.

```
spider_1.2-4ubuntu2_i386.deb
```

Managing software with apt-get

APT is designed to work with repositories, and will handle any dependencies for you. It uses **dpkg** to install and remove individual packages, but can also determine what dependent packages need to be installed, as well as query and download packages from repositories. There are several popular front ends for APT that let you manage your software easily, like synaptic, gnome-apt (Add/Remove Applications), aptitude, and deselect. Synaptic and gnome-apt rely on a desktop interface like GNOME. If you are using the command line interface, you can use **apt-get** to manage packages. Using the **apt-get** command on the command line you can install, update, and remove packages. Check the **apt-get** man page for a detailed listing of **apt-get** commands (see Table 4-2).

```
apt-get command package
```

Command	Description
update	Download and resynchronize the package listing of available and updated packages for APT supported repositories. APT repositories updated are those specified in **/etc/apt/sources.list**
upgrade	Update packages, install new versions of installed packages if available.
dist-upgrade	Update (upgrade) all your installed packages to a new release
install	Install a specific package, using its package name, not full package file name.
remove	Remove a software package from your system.
source	Download and extract a source code package
check	Check for broken dependencies
clean	Removes the downloaded packages held in the repository cache on your system. Used to free up disk space.

Table 4-2: apt-get commands

The **apt-get** tool takes two arguments: the command to perform and the name of the package. Other APT package tools follow the same format. The command is a term such as **install** for installing packages or **remove** to uninstall a package. Use the **install**, **remove**, or **update** commands respectively. You only need to specify the software name, not the package's full file name. APT will determine that. To install the MPlayer package you would use:

```
sudo apt-get install mplayer
```

To make sure that apt-get has current repository information, use the **apt-get update** command.

```
sudo apt-get update
```

To remove packages, you use the **remove** option.

```
sudo apt-get remove mplayer
```

You can use the **-s** option to check the remove or install first, especially to check if there are any dependency problems. For remove operations you can use **-s** to find out first what dependent packages will also be removed.

```
sudo apt-get remove -s mplayer
```

The **apt-get** command can be very helpful if your X Windows System server ever fails (your display driver). For example, if you installed a restricted vendor display driver, and then your desktop fails to start, you can start up the recover mode, drop to the root shell, and use apt-get to remove the restricted display driver. The following would remove the ATI (AMD) restricted display driver.

```
sudo apt-get remove fglrx*
```

Your former X open source display drivers would be automatically restored.

A complete log of all install, remove, and update operations are kept in the **/var/log/dpkg.log** file. You can consult this file to find out exactly what files were installed or removed.

Configuration for APT is held in the **/etc/apt** directory. Here the **sources.list** file lists the distribution repositories from where packages are installed. Source lists for additional third party repositories (like that for Wine) are kept in the /**etc/sources.list.d** directory. GPG database files hold validation keys for those repositories. Specific options for apt-get are kept in either a **/etc/apt.conf** file or in various files located in the **/etc/apt.conf.d** directory.

Updating packages (Upgrading) with apt-get

The apt-get tool also lets you easily update your entire system at once. The terms update and upgrade are used differently from other software tools. The update command just updates your package listing, checking for packages that may need to install newer version, but not installing those versions. Technically it updates the package list that APT uses to determine what packages need updated. The term upgrade is used to denote the actual update of a software package; a new version is downloaded and installed. What is referred to at updating by apt-get, other package managers refer to a obtaining the list of software packages to be updated. In apt-get, upgrading is what other package managers refer to as performing updates.

TIP: The terms **update** and **upgrade** can be confusing when used with apt-get. The **update** operation updates the Apt package list only, whereas **upgrade** downloads and installs all the packages for a new release.

Upgrading is a simple matter of using the `upgrade` command. With no package specified, apt-get with the `upgrade` command will upgrade your entire system, downloading from an FTP site or copying from a CD-ROM and installing packages as needed. Add the **-u** option to list packages as they are upgraded. First make sure your repository information (package list) is up to date with the **update** command.

```
sudo apt-get update
sudo apt-get -u upgrade
```

Command Line Search and Information: dpkg-query and apt-cache tools

The **dpkg-query** command lets you list detailed information about your packages. They operate on the command line (terminal window). **dpkg-query** with the **-l** option will list all your packages.

```
dpkg-query -l
```

The dpkg command can operate as a front end for dpkg-query, detecting its options to perform the appropriate task. The previous command could also be run as:

```
dpkg -l
```

To list a particular package requires and exact match on the package name, unless you use pattern matching operators. The following lists the **wine** package (Windows Compatibility Layer).

```
dpkg-query -l wine
```

A pattern matching operator, like *, placed after a patter will display any packages beginning with that pattern. The pattern with operators needs to be quoted to prevent an attempt by the shell to use the pattern to match on filenames on your current directory. The following example finds all packages beginning with the pattern "wine". This would include packages line **wine-doc** and **wine-utils**.

```
dpkg-query -l 'wine*'
```

You can further refine the results by using **grep** to perform an additional search. The following operation first outputs all packages beginning with **wine**, and from those results, the **grep** operations lists only those with the pattern *utils* in their name, like **wine-utils**.

```
dpkg -l 'wine*' | grep 'utils'
```

Use the **-L** option to just list the files that a package has installed.

```
dpkg-query  -L  wine
```

To see the status information about a package, including its dependencies and configuration files, use the **-s** option. Fields will include Status, Section, Architecture, Version, Depends (dependent packages), Suggests, Conflicts (conflicting packages), and Conffiles (configuration files).

```
dpkg-query -s  wine
```

The status information will also provide suggested dependencies. These are packages not installed, but like to be used. For the wine package, the **msttcorefonts** Windows fonts package is suggested.

```
dpkg-query  -s  wine | grep Suggests
```

Use the **-S** option to find what package a particular file belongs to.

```
dpkg-query  -S  filename
```

You can also obtain information with the **apt-cache** tool. Use the search command with **apt-cache** to perform a search.

```
apt-cache search wine
```

To find dependencies for a particular package, use the **depends** command.

```
apt-cache depends wine
```

To just display the package description use the **show** command.

```
apt-cache show wine
```

Note: If you have installed aptitude, you can use the **aptitude** command with the **search** and **show** options to find and display information about packages.

Managing non-repository packages with dpkg

You can use **dpkg** to install a software package you have already downloaded directly, not with an APT enabled software tool like **apt-get** or **Synaptic**. In this case you are not installing from a repository. Instead, you have manually downloaded the package file from a Web or FTP site to a folder on your system. Such a situation would be rare, reserved for software not available on the Ubuntu or any APT enabled repository. Keep in mind that most software is already on your Ubuntu or an APT enabled repository. Check there first before performing a direct download and install with **dpkg**. The **dpkg** configuration files are located in the **/etc/dpkg** directory. Configuration is held in the **dpkg.cfg** file. See the **dpkg** man page for a detailed listing of **dpkg** options.

One situation where you would use dpkg is for packages you have built yourself, like those created when converting a package in another format to a Debian package. This is the case when converting a RPM package (Red Hat Package Manager) to a Debian package format.

For **dpkg**, you use the **-i** option to install a package and **-r** to remove it.

```
sudo dpkg -i package.deb
```

The major failing for **dpkg** is that it provides no dependency support. It will inform you of needed dependencies, but you will have to install them separately. **dpkg** installs only the specified package. It is ideal for packages that have no dependencies.

You use the **-I** option to obtain package information directly from the DEB package file.

```
sudo dpkg -I package.deb
```

To remove a package you use the **-r** option with the package software name. You do not need version or extension information like **.386** or **.deb**. With **dpkg**, when removing a package with dependencies, you first have to remove all its dependencies manually. You will not be able to uninstall the package until you do. Configuration files are not removed.

```
sudo dpkg -r packagename
```

If you install a package that requires dependencies, and then fail to also install these dependencies, then your install database will be marked as having broken packages. In this case APT will not allow new packages to be installed until the broken packages are fixed. You can enter the **apt-get** command with the **-f** and install options. This will fix all broken packages at once.

```
sudo apt-get -f install
```

Using packages with other software formats

It is possible to convert software packages in other software formats into a deb packages that can then be installed on Ubuntu. To do this you use the **alien** tool. **alien** can convert several different kinds of formats such as RPM and even TGZ. You use the **--to-deb** option to convert to a Debian package format that Ubuntu can then install. The **--scripts** option attempts to also convert any pre or post install configuration scripts.

```
alien --scripts --to-deb  system-config-lvm-1.1.4-3.1.fc10.noarch.rpm
```

You can download and install **alien** from the Ubuntu repository using Synaptic.

Once you have generated the **.deb** package, you can use **dpkg** or Gdebi to install it.

The package used in this example is the Fedora LVM (Logical Volume Manager) GNOME configuration tool, available from the following site.

```
http://download.fedora.redhat.com/pub/fedora/linux/releases
```

5. Office Applications and Editors

Running Microsoft Office on Linux: CrossOver

OpenOffice

KOffice

GNOME Office

Document Viewers (PostScript, PDF, and DVI)

PDA Access

Editors

Database Management Systems

A variety of office suites are now available for Linux (see Table 5-1). These include professional-level word processors, presentation managers, drawing tools, and spreadsheets. The freely available versions are described in this chapter. Sun has initiated development of an Open Source Office suite using StarOffice code. The applications, known as OpenOffice, provide Office applications integrated with GNOME. OpenOffice is currently the primary office application supported by Ubuntu. KOffice is an entirely free office suite designed for use with KDE. The GNOME Office suite integrates GNOME applications into a productivity suite that is freely available. CodeWeavers CrossOver Office provides reliable support for running MS Office Windows applications directly on Linux, integrating with them with KDE and GNOME.

Web Site	Description
www.openoffice.org	OpenOffice open source office suite based on StarOffice
www.koffice.org	KOffice Suite, for KDE
www.gnome.org/gnome-office	GNOME Office, for GNOME
www.sun.com/staroffice	StarOffice Suite
www.codeweavers.com	CrossOver Office (MS Office support)
www.scribus.net	Scribus desktop publishing tool.

Table 5-1: Linux Office Suites

You can also purchase commercial office suites such as StarOffice from Sun. For desktop publishing, especially PDF generation, you can use Scribus, a cross-platform tool available from the Ubuntu repository. A variety of database management systems are also available for Linux. These include high-powered, commercial-level database management systems, such as Oracle, IBM's DB2, and Sybase. Most of the database management systems available for Linux are designed to support large relational databases. Ubuntu includes both MySQL and PostgreSQL databases in its distribution. For small personal databases, you can use the desktop database management systems being developed for KDE and GNOME. In addition, some software is available for databases accessed with the Xbase database programming language. These are smaller databases using formats originally developed for dBase on the PC. Various database management systems available to run under Linux are listed in Table 5-8 later in this chapter.

Linux also provides several text editors that range from simple text editors for simple notes to editors with more complex features such as spell-checkers, buffers, or pattern matching. All generate character text files and can be used to edit any Linux text files. Text editors are often used in system administration tasks to change or add entries in Linux configuration files found in the **/etc** directory or a user's initialization or application dot files located in a user's home directory. You can use any text editor to work on source code files for any of the programming languages or shell program scripts.

Running Microsoft Office on Linux: CrossOver

One of the primary concerns for new Linux users is what kind of access they will have to their Microsoft Office files, particularly Word files. The Linux operating system and many applications for it are designed to provide seamless access to MS Office files. The major Linux Office suites, including KOffice, OpenOffice, and StarOffice, all read and manage any Microsoft

Office files. In addition, these office suites are fast approaching the same level of features and support for office tasks as found in Microsoft Office.

Wine allows you to run many Windows applications directly, using a supporting virtual windows API. See the Wine website for a list of supported applications, **www.winehq.com**. Well written applications may run directly from Wine, like the newsbin newsreader. Often you will have to have a working Windows system from which to copy system DLLs needed by particular applications. You can also import your Windows fonts by directly copying them to the Wine font directory. Each user can install their own version of Wine with its own simulated C: partition on which Windows applications are installed. The simulated drive is installed as **drive_c** in your **.wine** directory. The **.wine** directory is a hidden directory. It is not normally displayed with the **ls** command or the GNOME file manager. You can also use any of your Linux directories for your Windows application data files instead of your simulated C: drive. These are referenced by Windows applications as the **z:** drive.

In a terminal window, using the **wine** command with an install program will automatically install that Windows application on the simulated C: drive. The following example installs Microsoft Office. Though there may be difficulties with latest Microsoft Office versions, earlier versions like 2003 should work fine. When you insert the Microsoft Office CD, it will be mounted to the /media directory using as its folder the disk label. Check the /media folder (Filesystem) to see what the actual name is. You want to run the setup.exe program for Office with wine. Depending on the version of Office you have, there may be further subfolders for the actual Office setup.exe program. The following example assumes that the label for Office is OFFICE and that the setup.exe program for Office is on the top level directory of that CD.

```
$ wine /media/OFFICE/setup.exe
```

The install program will start up and you will be prompted to enter your product key. Be sure to use uppercase. In the Wine menu in the Applications menu, you will also find entries for Microsoft Word (Applications | Wine | Programs | Microsoft Office). The application will start up normally. If you right-click on the menu entry, like the one for Microsoft Word, you can select the Add Launcher to Desktop entry to add an icon for the application on your desktop. The application is referenced by Wine on the user's simulated C drive, like the following for Word.

```
wine  "C:\Program Files\Microsoft Office\OFFICE11\WINWORD.EXE"
```

The Windows My Documents folder is set up by Wine to be the user's home directory. There you will find any files saved to My Documents.

Wine is constantly being updated to accommodate the latest versions of Windows applications. However, for some applications you may need to copy DLL files from a working Windows system to the Wine Windows folder, **.wine/drive_c/windows**, usually to the **system** or **system32** directories. Though effective, Wine support will not be as stable as Crossover.

CrossOver Office is a commercial product that lets you install and run most Microsoft Office applications. CrossOver Office was developed by CodeWeavers, which also supports Windows web browser plug-ins as well as several popular Windows applications like Adobe Photoshop. CrossOver features both standard and professional versions, providing reliable application support. You can find out more about CrossOver Office at **www.codeweavers.com**.

CrossOver can be installed either for private multi-user mode or managed multi-user mode. In private multi-user mode, each user installs Windows software, such as full versions of

Office. In managed multi-user mode, the Windows software is installed once and all users share it. When you install new software, you first open the CrossOver startup tool, and then on the Add/Remove panel you will see a list of supported software. This will include Office applications as well as some Adobe applications, including earlier versions of Photoshop. An Install Software panel will then let you select whether to install from a CD-ROM or an **.exe** file. For Office on a CD-ROM, select CD-ROM, place the Windows CD-ROM in your CD-ROM drive, and then click Next. The Windows Office installer will start up in a Linux window and will proceed as if you were on a Windows system. When the install requires a restart of the system, CrossOver will simulate it for you. Once the software is installed, you will see a Windows Applications menu on the main menu, from which you can start your installed Windows software. The applications will run within a Linux window, just as if they were running in Windows.

With VMware, you can run Windows under Linux, allowing you to run Windows applications, including Microsoft Office, on your Linux system. For more information, check the VMware Web site at **www.vmware.com**.

Note: Though Linux allows users to directly mount and access any of the old DOS or FAT32 partitions used for Windows 95, 98, and Me, it can mount NTFS partitions (Windows Vista, XP, 2000, and NT) with the NTFS, **ntfs-3g** and the original NTFS project drivers. The **ntfs-3g** drivers support writing NTFS partitions. The **ntfs-3g** drivers are installed on Ubuntu by default.

OpenOffice

OpenOffice (OO) is a fully integrated suite of office applications developed as an open source project and freely distributed to all. It is included as the primary office suite for Ubuntu, accessible from the Office menu. It includes word processing, spreadsheet, presentation, and drawing applications (see Table 5-2). Versions of OpenOffice exist for Linux, Windows, and Mac OS. You can obtain information such as online manuals and FAQs as well as current versions from the OpenOffice.org Web site at **www.openoffice.org**.

Note: Development for OpenOffice is being carried out as an open source project called OpenOffice.org. The core code is based on the original StarOffice. The code developed in the OpenOffice.org project will then be incorporated into future releases of StarOffice.

OpenOffice is an integrated suite of applications. You can open the writer, spreadsheet, or presentation application directly. Also, in most OpenOffice applications, you can select New from the File menu and select a different application if you wish. The Writer word processor supports standard word processing features, such as cut and paste, spell-checker, and text formatting, as well as paragraph styles (see Figure 5-1). Context menus let you format text easily. Wizards (Letter, Web page, Fax, and Agenda) let you generate different kinds of documents quickly. You can embed objects within documents, such as using Draw to create figures that you can then drag and drop to the Writer document. You can find out more about each component at their respective produce pages listed at, `www.openoffice.org/product`.

Figure 5-1: OpenOffice.org Writer word processor

Calc is a professional-level spreadsheet. With Math, you can create formulas that you can then embed in a text document. With the presentation manager (Impress), you can create images for presentations, such as circles, rectangles, and connecting elements like arrows, as well as vector-based illustrations. Impress supports advanced features such as morphing objects, grouping objects, and defining gradients. Draw is a sophisticated drawing tool that includes 3-D modeling tools. You can create simple or complex images, including animation text aligned on curves. OpenOffice also includes a printer setup tool with which you can select printers, fonts, paper sizes, and page formats.

Application	Description
Calc	OpenOffice spreadsheet
Draw	OpenOffice drawing application
Writer	OpenOffice word processor
Math	OpenOffice mathematical formula composer
Impress	OpenOffice presentation manager
Base	Database front end for accessing and managing a variety of different databases.

Table 5-2: OpenOffice.org Applications

Note: StarOffice is a fully integrated and Microsoft Office–compatible suite of office applications developed and supported by Sun Microsystems, **www.sun.com/staroffice**. Sun provides StarOffice as a commercial product, though educational use is free.

OpenOffice features an underlying component model that can be programmed to develop customized applications. Check the OpenOffice API project for more details (**api.openoffice.org**). The OpenOffice Software Development Kit (SDK) provides support for using OpenOffice components in applications written in C++ or Java. The Unified Network Objects (UNO) model is the component model for OpenOffice, providing interaction between programming languages, other object models, and network connections.

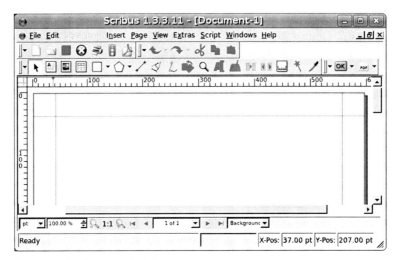

Figure 5-2: Scribus desktop publisher

Also for use on GNOME is Scribus, the desktop publishing tool (see Figure 5-2). (**www.scribus.net**)

KOffice

KOffice is an integrated office suite for the KDE (K Desktop Environment) consisting of several office applications, including a word processor, a spreadsheet, and graphic applications. You can download it using Synaptic Package Manager. All applications are written for the KOM component model, which allows components from any one application to be used in another. This means you can embed a spreadsheet from KSpread or diagrams from Karbon14 in a KWord document. You can obtain more information about KOffice from the KOffice Web site at **www.koffice.org**.

Tip: KOffice applications have import and export filters that allow them to import or export files from popular applications like Abiword, OpenOffice.org applications, MS Word, and even Palm documents. The reliability of these filters varies, and you should check the KOffice Filters Web page for a listing of the different filters and their stability.

KOffice Applications

Currently, KOffice includes KSpread, KPresenter, KWord, Karbon14, KFormula, KChart, Kugar, Krita, and Kivio (see Table 5-3). The contact application, Kontact, has been spun off as a separate project. Kontact is an integrated contact application including Kmail, Korganizer, Kaddressbook, and Knotes. KSpread is a spreadsheet, KPresenter is a presentation application, Karbon14 is a vector graphics program, KWord is a Publisher-like word processor, KFormula is a formula editor, and KChart generates charts and diagrams. Kugar is a report generator, Krita is a bitmap image editor, and Kivio creates flow charts. Kexi provides database integration with KOffice applications, currently supporting PostgreSQL and MySQL.

Application	Description
KSpread	Spreadsheet
KPresenter	Presentation program
Kontour	Vector drawing program
Karbon14	Vector graphics program
KWord	Word processor (desktop publisher)
KFormula	Mathematical formula editor
KChart	Tool for drawing charts and diagrams
Kugar	Report generator
Krita	Paint and image manipulation program
Kivio	Flow chart generator and editor (similar to Vivio)
Kexi	Database integration
KPlato	Project management and planning
Kontact (separate project)	Contact application including mail, address book, and organizer

Table 5-3: KOffice Applications

KSpread is the spreadsheet application, which incorporates the basic operations found in most spreadsheets, with formulas similar to those used in Excel. You can also embed charts, pictures, or formulas using KChart, Krita, Karbon14, or KFormula.

With KChart, you can create different kinds of charts, such as bar graphs, pie charts, and line graphs, as well as create diagrams. To generate a chart, you can use data in KSpread to enter your data. With KPresenter, you can create presentations consisting of text and graphics modeled using different fonts, orientations, and attributes such as colors. You can add such elements as speech bubbles, arrows, and clip art, as well as embed any KOffice component. Karbon14 is a vector-based graphics program, much like Adobe Illustrator and OpenOffice Draw. It supports the standard graphic operations such as rotating, scaling, and aligning objects.

KWord can best be described as a desktop publisher, with many of the features found in publishing applications like Microsoft Publisher and FrameMaker. Although it is also a fully functional word processor, KWord is not page-based like Word or WordPerfect. Instead, text is set up in frames that are placed on the page like objects. Frames, like objects in a drawing program, can be moved, resized, and even reoriented. You can organize frames into a frame set, having text flow from one to the other.

GNOME Office

The GNOME Office project supports three office applications: AbiWord, Gnumeric, and GNOME-DB. Former members of GNOME Office still provide certain Office tasks, like Novell's Evolution e-mail and contact client. Many former members are still GNOME projects, with information listed for them at **www.gnome.org/projects**. The GNOME Office applications, as well as other GNOME-based Office applications, are part of Ubuntu and can be downloaded with Add/Remove Applications. You can find out more from the GNOME Office site at **www.gnome.org/gnome-office**. A current listing for common GNOME Office applications, including those not part of the GNOME Office suite is shown in Table 5-4. All implement the CORBA model for embedding components, ensuring drag-and-drop capability throughout the GNOME interface.

AbiWord is a word processor, Gnumeric is a spreadsheet, and GNOME-DB provides database connectivity. Gnumeric is a GNOME spreadsheet, a professional-level program meant to replace commercial spreadsheets. Like GNOME, Gnumeric is freely available under the GNU Public License. Gnumeric is included with the GNOME release, and you will find it installed with GNOME on any distribution that supports GNOME. You can download current versions from **www.gnome.org/projects/gnumeric**. Gnumeric supports standard GUI spreadsheet features, including auto filling and cell formatting, and it provides an extensive number of formats. It supports drag-and-drop operations, enabling you to select and then move or copy cells to another location. Gnumeric also supports plug-ins, making it possible to extend and customize its capabilities easily.

AbiWord is an open source word processor that aims to be a complete cross-platform solution, running on Mac, Unix, and Windows, as well as Linux. It is part of a set of desktop productivity applications being developed by the AbiSource project (**www.abisource.com**).

Application	Description
GNOME **Office**	**Description**
AbiWord	Cross-platform word processor
Gnumeric	Spreadsheet
GNOME-DB	Database connectivity
Other GNOME Office Apps	**Description**
Evolution	Integrated e-mail, calendar, and personal organizer (Novell)
Dia	Diagram and flow chart editor (GNOME project)
GnuCash	Personal finance manager (GNOME project)
Balsa	E-mail client (GNOME project)
GnuCash	Personal finance manager (GNOME project)
Planner	Project manager (GNOME project)
OpenOffice	OpenOffice office suite

Table 5-4: GNOME Office and Other Office Applications for GNOME

The GNOME-DB project provides a GNOME Data Access (GDA) library supporting several kinds of databases, such as PostgreSQL, MySQL, Microsoft Access, and unixODBC. It provides an API to which databases can plug in. These back-end connections are based on CORBA. Through this API, GNOME applications can then access a database. You can find out more about GNOME-DB at **www.gnome-db.org**.

Dia is a drawing program designed to create diagrams (GNOME project). You can select different kinds of diagrams to create, such as database, circuit object, flow chart, and network diagrams. You can easily create elements along with lines and arcs with different types of endpoints such as arrows or diamonds. Data can be saved in XML format, making it easily transportable to other applications.

GnuCash (**www.gnucash.org**) is a personal finance application for managing accounts, stocks, and expenses (GNOME project). It includes support for home banking with the OpenHBCI interface. OpenHBCI is the open source home banking computer interface (**http://openhbci.sourceforge.net**).

Document Viewers (PostScript, PDF, and DVI)

Though located under Graphics submenu in the Applications menu, PostScript, PDF, and DVI viewers are more commonly used with Office applications (see Table 5-5). Evince and Okular can display both PostScript (**.ps**) and PDF (**.pdf**) files. Evince is the default document viewer for GNOME. It is automatically stared whenever you double-click a PDF file on the GNOME desktop. Its menu entry is Applications | Graphics | Document Viewer, but this is not turned on by default (use System | Preferences | Main Menu to have the menu entry appear). Okular is the default document viewer for KDE4, with its menu entry also as Applications | Graphics | Document Viewer.

Okular, Evince, and Xpdf are PDF viewers. They include many of the standard Adobe reader features such as zoom, two-page display, and full-screen mode. Alternatively, you can download Acrobat reader for Linux from **medibuntu.org** or Adobe to display PDF files. All these viewers also have the ability to print documents. To generate PDF documents you can use Scribus desktop publisher (**www.scribus.net**), and to edit PDF documents you can use **pdfedit**.

Viewer	Description
Evince	Document Viewer for PostScript, DVI, and PDF files
Okular	KDE4 tool for displaying PDF, DVI, and postscript files (replaces KPDF, Kghostview, and Kdvi)
xpdf	X Window System tool for displaying PDF files only
tkdvi	Tool for displaying TeX DVI files
Acrobat Reader for Linux	Adobe PDF and PostScript display application (**medibuntu.org** repository, **acroread** package)
Scribus	Desktop publisher for generating PDF documents
pdfedit	Edit PDF documents

Table 5-5: PostScript, PDF, and DVI viewers

Linux also features a professional-level typesetting tool, called TeX, commonly used to compose complex mathematical formulas. TeX generates a DVI document that can then be displayed by DVI viewers, of which there are several for Linux. DVI files generated by the TeX document application can be viewed by Evince, Okular, and tkdvi.

PDA Access

For many PDAs you can use the pilot tools to access your handheld, transferring information between it and your system. You can use the J-Pilot, KPilot, and GnomePilot applications to access your PDA from your desktop.

To use your PDA on GNOME, you can use the gnome-pilot applet from your GNOME panel to configure your connection. When you first start up gnome-pilot you are prompted to specify the deice settings. Serial is the default, but most palm devices now use USB. In the gnome-pilot applet's Preferences windows (right-click on applet), the Conduits panel lets you enable several hot sync operations to perform automatically, including e-mail, memos, and installing files. Click the Help button for a detailed manual.

J-Pilot provides a GUI interface that lets you perform basic tasks such as synchronizing address book and writing memos. J-Pilot is accessible from the Office menu and is part of Ubuntu.

KPilot works on the KDE4 desktop, and is installed as the **kpilot** package. On the KUbuntu desktop it is accessible from Applications | Utilities | PalmPilot Tool. It will first open the Kpilot configuration window to let you set up your device, HotSync, contact, calendar, and Conduit preferences.

The **pilot-link** package holds the tools you use access your PDA. Check **www.pilot-link.org** for detailed documentation and useful links. The tool name usually begins with "pilot"; for instance, **pilot-addresses** read addresses from an address book. Other tools whose names begin with "read" allow you to convert Palm data for access by other applications; **read-expenses**, for instance, outputs expense data as standard text. One of the more useful tools is **pilot-xfer**, used to back up your Palm.

Tip: The device name used for your PDA is **/dev/pilot**, which is managed by **udev**. Should you need to manually specify a port for your handheld, you would have to modify udev rules, not change the **/dev/pilot** file directly.

Editors

Traditionally, most Linux distributions, including Ubuntu, install the cursor-based editors Vim and Emacs. *Vim* is an enhanced version of the Vi text editor used on the Unix system. These editors use simple, cursor-based operations to give you a full-screen format. You can start these editors from the shell command line without any kind of X Window System support. In this mode, their cursor-based operations do not have the ease of use normally found in window-based editors. There are no menus, scroll bars, or mouse-click features. However, the K Desktop and GNOME do support powerful GUI text editors with all these features. These editors operate much more like those found on Macintosh and Windows systems. They have full mouse support, scroll bars, and menus. You may find them much easier to use than the Vi and Emacs editors. These editors operate from their respective desktops, requiring you first have either KDE or GNOME installed, though the editors can run on either desktop. Vi and Emacs have powerful editing features that have been refined over the years. Emacs, in particular, is extensible to a full-development environment for programming new applications. Newer versions of Emacs, such as GNU Emacs and XEmacs, provide X Window System support with mouse, menu, and window operations. They can run on any window manager or desktop. In addition, the gvim version of the Vim editor also provides basic window operations. You can access it on both GNOME and KDE desktops. Table 5-6 lists several GUI-based editors for Linux.

Note: Ubuntu Linux includes a fully functional word processor, Writer (OpenOffice). AbiWord is now part of Ubuntu, along with Kword, which is part of KOffice. You can find out more on AbiWord at **www.abiword.com**.

The K Desktop	Description
Kate	Text and program editor
Knotes	Sticky notes
KWord	Desktop publisher, part of KOffice
GNOME	
Gedit	Text editor
AbiWord	Word processor
X Window System	
GNU Emacs	Emacs editor with X Window System support
XEmacs	X Window System version of Emacs editor
gvim	Vim version with X Window System support
OpenWriter	OpenOffice word processor that can edit text files

Table 5-6: Desktop Editors

GNOME Text Editor: Gedit

The Gedit editor is a basic text editor for the GNOME desktop. It provides full mouse support, implementing standard GUI operations, such as cut and paste to move text, and click and drag to select text. It supports standard text editing operations such as Find and Replace. You can use Gedit to create and modify your text files, including configuration files. Gedit also provides more advanced features such as print preview and configurable levels of undo/redo operations, and it can read data from pipes. It features a plug-in menu that provides added functionality, and it includes plug-ins for spell-checking, encryption, e-mail, and text-based Web page display.

KDE Editor: Kate

The KDE editor Kate provide full mouse support, implementing standard GUI operations, such as cut and paste to move text, and click and drag to select text. The editors are accessible from the Applications | Utilities menu on the KDE desktop.. Kate is an advanced editor, with such features as spell-checking, font selection, and highlighting. Most commands can be selected using menus. A toolbar of icons for common operations is displayed across the top of the Kate window. A sidebar displays panels for a file selector and a file list. With the file selector, you can navigate through the file system selecting files to work on. Kate also supports multiple views of a document, letting you display segments in their own windows, vertically or horizontally. You can also open several documents at the same time, moving between them with the file list. Kate is designed to be a program editor for editing software programming/development-related source code files. Although Kate does not have all the features of Emacs or Vi, it can handle most major tasks. Kate can format the syntax for different programming languages, such as C, Perl, Java, and XML. In addition, Kate has the capability to access and edit files on an FTP or Web site.

The Emacs Editor

Emacs can best be described as a working environment featuring an editor, a mailer, a newsreader, and a Lisp interpreter. The editor is tailored for program development, enabling you to format source code according to the programming language you use. Many versions of Emacs are currently available for use on Unix and Linux systems. The versions usually included with Linux distributions are either GNU Emacs or XEmacs. The current version for GNU Emacs is X Window System–capable, enabling GUI features such as menus, scroll bars, and mouse-based editing operations. Check the update FTP sites for your distribution for new versions as they come out, and also check the GNU Web site at **www.gnu.org** and the Emacs Web site at **www.emacs.org**. You can find out more information about XEmacs at its Web site, **www.xemacs.org**.

Emacs derives much of its power and flexibility from its capability to manipulate buffers. Emacs can be described as a buffer-oriented editor. Whenever you edit a file in any editor, the file is copied into a work buffer, and editing operations are made on the work buffer. Emacs can manage many work buffers at once, enabling you to edit several files at the same time. You can edit buffers that hold deleted or copied text. You can even create buffers of your own; fill them with text, and later save them to a file. Emacs extends the concept of buffers to cover any task. When you compose mail, you open a mail buffer; when you read news, you open a news buffer. Switching from one task to another is simply a matter of switching to another buffer.

The Emacs editor operates much like a standard word processor. The keys on your keyboard represent input characters. Commands are implemented with special keys, such as control (CTRL) keys and alternate (ALT) keys. There is no special input mode, as in Vi. You type in your text, and if you need to execute an editing command, such as moving the cursor or saving text, you use a CTRL key. Such an organization makes the Emacs editor easy to use. However, Emacs is anything but simple—it is a sophisticated and flexible editor with several hundred commands. Emacs also has special features, such as multiple windows. You can display two windows for text at the same time. You can also open and work on more than one file at a time, displaying each on the screen in its own window. You invoke the Emacs editor with the command `emacs`. You can enter the name of the file you want to edit, and if the file does not exist, it is created. In the next example, the user prepares to edit the file **mydata** with Emacs:

```
$ emacs mydata
```

The GNU Emacs editor now supports an X Window System graphical user interface. To enable X support, start Emacs within an X Window System environment, such as a KDE, GNOME, or XFce desktop. The basic GUI editing operations are supported: selection of text with click-and-drag mouse operations; cut, copy, and paste; and a scroll bar for moving through text. The Mode line and Echo areas are displayed at the bottom of the window, where you can enter keyboard commands. The scroll bar is located on the left side. To move the scroll bar down, click it with the left mouse button. To move the scroll bar up, click it with the right mouse button.

Note: XEmacs is the complete Emacs editor with a graphical user interface and Internet applications, including a Web browser, a mail utility, and a newsreader.

The Vi Editor: Vim and Gvim

The Vim editor included with most Linux distributions is an enhanced version of the Vi editor. It includes all the commands and features of the Vi editor. Vi, which stands for *visual,* remains one of the most widely used editors in Linux. Keyboard-based editors like Vim and Emacs use a keyboard for two different operations: to specify editing commands and to receive character input. Used for editing commands, certain keys perform deletions, some execute changes, and others perform cursor movement. Used for character input, keys represent characters that can be entered into the file being edited. Usually, these two different functions are divided among different keys on the keyboard. Alphabetic keys are reserved for character input, while function keys and control keys specify editing commands, such as deleting text or moving the cursor. Such editors can rely on the existence of an extended keyboard that includes function and control keys. Editors in Unix, however, were designed to assume a minimal keyboard with alphanumeric characters and some control characters, as well as the ESC and ENTER keys. Instead of dividing the command and input functions among different keys, the Vi editor has three separate modes of operation for the keyboard: command and input modes, and a line editing mode. In *command* mode, all the keys on the keyboard become editing commands; in the *input* mode, the keys on the keyboard become input characters. Some of the editing commands, such as **a** or **i**, enter the input mode. On typing **i**, you leave the command mode and enter the input mode. Each key now represents a character to be input to the text. Pressing ESC automatically returns you to the command mode, and the keys once again become editor commands. As you edit text, you are constantly moving from the command mode to the input mode and back again. With Vim, you can use the CTRL-O command to jump quickly to the command mode and enter a command, and then automatically return to the input mode. Table 5-7 lists a very basic set of Vi commands to get you started.

Although the Vi command mode handles most editing operations, it cannot perform some, such as file saving and global substitutions. For such operations, you need to execute line editing commands. You enter the line editing mode using the Vi colon command. The colon is a special command that enables you to perform a one-line editing operation. When you type the colon, a line opens up at the bottom of the screen with the cursor placed at the beginning of the line. You are now in the line editing mode. In this mode, you enter an editing command on a line, press ENTER, and the command is executed. Entry into this mode is usually only temporary. Upon pressing ENTER, you are automatically returned to the Vi command mode, and the cursor returns to its previous position on the screen.

Although you can create, save, close, and quit files with the Vi editor, the commands for each are not all that similar. Saving and quitting a file involves the use of special line editing commands, whereas closing a file is a Vi editing command. Creation of a file is usually specified on the same shell command line that invokes the Vi editor. To edit a file, type **vi** or **vim** and the name of a file on the shell command line. If a file by that name does not exist, the system creates it. In effect, giving the name of a file that does not yet exist instructs the Vi editor to create that file. The following command invokes the Vi editor, working on the file **booklist**. If **booklist** does not yet exist, the Vi editor creates it.

```
$ vim booklist
```

Command	Description
h	Moves the cursor left one character.
l	Moves the cursor right one character.
k	Moves the cursor up one line.
j	Moves the cursor down one line.
CTRL-F	Moves forward by a screen of text; the next screen of text is displayed.
CTRL-B	Moves backward by a screen of text; the previous screen of text is displayed.
Input	*(All input commands place the user in input; the user leaves input with ESC.)*
a	Enters input after the cursor.
i	Enters input before the cursor.
o	Enters input below the line the cursor is on; inserts a new empty line below the one the cursor is currently on.
Text Selection (Vim)	
v	Visual mode; move the cursor to expand selected text by character. Once selected, press key to execute action: **c** change, **d** delete, **y** copy, **:** line editing command, **J** join lines, **U** uppercase, **u** lowercase.
V	Visual mode; move cursor to expand selected text by line.
Delete	
x	Deletes the character the cursor is on.
dd	Deletes the line the cursor is on.
Change	*(Except for the replace command, r, all change commands place the user into input after deleting text.)*
cw	Deletes the word the cursor is on and places the user into the input mode.
r	Replaces the character the cursor is on. After pressing **r**, the user enters the replacement character. The change is made without entering input; the user remains in the Vi command mode.
R	First places into input mode, and then overwrites character by character. Appears as an overwrite mode on the screen but actually is in input mode.
Move	Moves text by first deleting it, moving the cursor to desired place of insertion, and then pressing the **p** command. (When text is deleted, it is automatically held in a special buffer.)
p	Inserts deleted or copied text after the character or line the cursor is on.
P	Inserts deleted or copied text before the character or line the cursor is on.
dw p	Deletes a word, and then moves it to the place you indicate with the cursor (press **p** to insert the word *after* the word the cursor is on).
yy or Y p	Copies the line the cursor is on.

Search	The two search commands open up a line at the bottom of the screen and enable the user to enter a pattern to be searched for; press ENTER after typing in the pattern.
/*pattern*	Searches forward in the text for a pattern.
?*pattern*	Searches backward in the text for a pattern.
n	Repeats the previous search, whether it was forward or backward.
Line Editing Commands	**Effect**
w	Saves file.
q	Quits editor; q! quits without saving.

Table 5-7: Editor Commands

After executing the `vim` command, you enter Vi's command mode. Each key becomes a Vi editing command, and the screen becomes a window onto the text file. Text is displayed screen by screen. The first screen of text is displayed, and the cursor is positioned in the upper-left corner. With a newly created file, there is no text to display. This fact is indicated by a column of tildes at the left side of the screen. The tildes represent the part of a screen that is not part of the file.

When you first enter the Vi editor, you are in the command mode. To enter text, you need to enter the input mode. In the command mode, `a` is the editor command for appending text. Pressing this key places you in the input mode. Now the keyboard operates like a typewriter and you can input text to the file. If you press ENTER, you merely start a new line of text. With Vim, you can use the arrow keys to move from one part of the entered text to another and work on different parts of the text. After entering text, you can leave the input mode and return to the command mode by pressing ESC. Once finished with the editing session, you exit Vi by typing two capital Zs, `zz`. Hold down the SHIFT key and press z twice. This sequence first saves the file and then exits the Vi editor, returning you to the Linux shell. To save a file while editing, you use the line editing command `w`, which writes a file to the disk; `w` is equivalent to the Save command found in other word processors. You first type a colon to access the line editing mode, and then type `w` and press ENTER.

You can use the `:q` command to quit an editing session. Unlike the `zz` command, the `:q` command does not perform any save operation before it quits. In this respect, it has one major constraint. If any modifications have been made to your file since the last save operation, the `:q` command will fail and you will not leave the editor. However, you can override this restriction by placing a ! qualifier after the `:q` command. The command `:q!` will quit the Vi editor without saving any modifications made to the file in that session since the last save (the combination `:wq` is the same as `zz`).

To obtain online help, enter the `:help` command. This is a line editing command. Type a colon, enter the word `help` on the line that opens at the bottom of the screen, and then press ENTER. You can add the name of a specific command after the word `help`. The F1 key also brings up online help.

As an alternative to using Vim in a command line interface, you can use gvim, which provides X Window System–based menus for basic file, editing, and window operations. Gvim is installed as the **vim-gui-common** package, which includes several links to Gvim such as **evim**, **gview**, and **gex** (open Ex editor line). To use Gvim, you can enter the `gvim` command at an terminal prompt.

The standard Vi interface is displayed, but with several menu buttons displayed across the top along with a toolbar with button for common commands like searches and file saves. All the standard Vi commands work just as described previously. However, you can use your mouse to select items on these menus. You can open and close a file, or open several files using split windows or different windows. The editing menu enables you to cut, copy, and paste text as well as undo or redo operations. In the editing mode, you can select text with your mouse with a click-and-drag operation, or use the Editing menu to cut or copy and then paste the selected text. Text entry, however, is still performed using the `a`, `i`, or `o` command to enter the input mode. Searches and replacements are supported through a dialog window. There are also buttons on the toolbar for finding next and previous instances. Gview also features programming support, with color coding for programming syntax, for both shell scripts and C++ programs. There is even a Make button for running Make files.

You can also split the view into different windows to display parts of the same file or different files. Use the **:split** command to open a window, and **:hide** to close the current one. Use Ctrl-w with the up and down arrow keys to move between them. On Gvim, you use entries in the Windows menu to manage windows. Configuration preferences can be placed in the user's **.vimrc** file.

Database Management Systems

Database software can be generally organized into three categories: SQL, Xbase, and desktop databases. *SQL-based databases* are professional-level relational databases whose files are managed by a central database server program. Applications that use the database do not access the files directly. Instead, they send requests to the database server, which then performs the actual access. *SQL* is the query language used on these industrial-strength databases. Ubuntu includes both MySQL and PostgreSQL databases. Both are open source projects freely available for your use. Table 5-8 lists database management systems currently available for Linux.

Note: The *Xbase language* is an enhanced version of the dBase programming language used to access database files whose formats were originally developed for dBase on the PC. Xbase is used mainly for smaller personal databases, with database files often located on a user's own system.

SQL Databases (RDBMS)

SQL databases are relational database management systems (RDBMSs) designed for extensive database management tasks. Many of the major SQL databases now have Linux versions, including Oracle, Informix, Sybase, and IBM (but not, of course, Microsoft). These are commercial and professional database management systems of the highest order. Linux has proved itself capable of supporting complex and demanding database management tasks. In addition, many free SQL databases are available for Linux that offer much the same functionality. Most commercial databases also provide free personal versions, as do Oracle, Adabas D, and MySQL.

System	Site
OpenOffice.org	OpenOffice.org database: **www.openoffice.org**
PostgreSQL	The PostgreSQL database: **www.postgresql.org**
MySQL	MySQL database: **www.mysql.com**
Oracle	Oracle database: **www.oracle.com**
Sybase	Sybase database: **www.sybase.com**
DB2	IBM database: **ibm.com/software/data/db2**
Informix	Informix database: **ibm.com/software/data/informix**
MaxDB	SAP database: **www.sdn.sap.com/irj/sdn/maxdb**
GNU SQL	The GNU SQL database: **www.ispras.ru/~kml/gss**

Table 5-8: Database Management Systems for Linux

OpenOffice.org Base

OpenOffice provides a basic data base application, OpenOffice.org Base that can access many database files. You can set up and operate a simple database, as well as access and manage files from other database applications. When you start up OpenOffice. org Base, you will be prompted to either start a new database or connect to an existing one. File types supported include ODBC 3.0 (Open Database Connectivity), JDBC (Java), ADO, MySQL, dBase, CSV, PostgreSQL, and MDB (Microsoft Access) database files (install the **unixodbc** and **java-libmysql** packages). You can also create your own simple databases. Check the OpenOffice.org – Base page and Project page (**http://dba.openoffice.org**) for detailed information on drivers and supported databases.

PostgreSQL

PostgreSQL is based on the POSTURES database management system, though it uses SQL as its query language. POSTGRESQL is a next-generation research prototype developed at the University of California, Berkeley. Linux versions of PostgreSQL are included in most distributions, including the Red Hat, Fedora, Debian, and Ubuntu distributions. You can find more information on it from the PostgreSQL Web site at **www.postgresql.org**. PostgreSQL is an open source project, developed under the GPL license.

MySQL

MySQL, included with Ubuntu, is a true multi-user, multithreaded SQL database server, supported by MySQL AB. MySQL is an open source product available free under the GPL license. You can obtain current information on it from its Web site, **www.mysql.com**. The site includes detailed documentation, including manuals and FAQs.

6. Graphics and Multimedia

Graphics Applications

Multimedia

Sound Drivers and Interfaces

Music Applications

CD Burners

Video Applications

Ubuntu includes a wide range of both graphic and multimedia applications and tool, including simple image viewers like GwenView, sophisticated image manipulation programs like GIMP, music and CD players like Rhythmbox, and TV viewers like Totem. Several popular Linux multimedia sites are listed in Table 6-1. There is strong support for graphics and multimedia tasks from image management, video and DVD, to sound and music editing (see Tables 6.2, 6-5 and 6-6). Thousands of multimedia and graphic projects, as well as standard projects, are under development at sites like **www.gnomefiles.org**, **www.sourceforge.net**, **www.kde-apps.org**. Most are available on Ubuntu's multiverse and universe repositories. For information on graphics hardware and drivers, check **www.phoronix.com**. The Ubuntu Studio project has collected popular multimedia development software into several collections for audio, video, and graphics. The Mythbuntu project provides an Ubuntu version of MythTV for Home Theater PCs (HTPC).

Projects and Sites	Description
SourceForge	This site holds many development projects for Linux: **www.sourceforge.net**
Medibuntu.org	Ubuntu third party repository for multimedia and non-free codecs and applications: **medibuntu.org**
Sound & MIDI Software for Linux	Lists a wide range of multimedia and sound software. **linux-sound.org**
Advanced Linux Sound Architecture (ALSA)	The Advanced Linux Sound Architecture (ALSA) project for current sound drivers: **www.alsa-project.org**
Open Sound System	Open Sound System, drives for older devices: **www.opensound.com**
PulseAudio	PulseAudio sound interface, now the default for Ubuntu. **www.pulseaudio.org**
Phoronix	Site for the latest news and reviews of hardware compatibility, including graphics cards. **www.phoronix.com**
Ubuntu Studio	Ubuntu Studio multimedia development applications and desktop, audio, video, and graphics collection installed from ubuntustudio meta packages, Meta Packages (universe) **www.ubuntustudio.org**
Mythbuntu	MythTV implementation of HTPC multimedia software, **www.mythbuntu.org.**

Table 6-1: Linux and Ubuntu Multimedia Sites

Support for many popular multimedia operations, specifically MP3, DVD, and DivX, are not included with many distributions because of licensing and other restrictions. To play MP3, DVD, or DivX files, you will have to download and install support packages manually. For Ubuntu, precompiled packages for many popular media applications and libraries, such as MPlayer and XviD as well as MP3 and DVD video support, are available at Ubuntu multiverse and universe repositories.

Medibuntu.org

For applications and codecs with licensing issues, like Skype VoIP, AAC support, Real Player, Adobe reader, Google Earth, and the DVD Video commercial decoder (**libdvdcss**), you need to access the Medibuntu.org repository, **medibuntu.org**. Table 6-2 lists the applications and codec available on the Medibuntu repository.

See the following Web page for details on adding the Medibuntu repository to your repository listing. It is also accessible from the **medibuntu.org** site by clicking the Repository Howto button.

```
https://help.ubuntu.com/community/Medibuntu
```

You will have to both install respository configuration for the Medibuntu.org repository, and install the Medibuntu respository software authentication key.

Once you have set up repository access, you can use the Synaptic Package Manager to download and install any of the Medibuntu packages. If you want to use Add/Remove to install Medibuntu applications, you can use the Synaptic Package Manager to first install the **app-install-data-medibuntu** package. You will then see Medibuntu applications (though not all the packages) listed in Add/Remove Applications.

Medibuntu repository support

To add repository support, you have to create a **medibuntu.list** file in your **/etc/apt/sources.list.d** directory which will contain the apt source references for the Medibuntu repository. The contents of the medibuntu.list repository file for Ubuntu jaunty are available at **http://www.medibuntu.org/sources.list.d/jaunty.list**. Creating the file in the **/etc/apt/sources.list.d** directory requires administrative access, so you would have to use the **sudo** command. The entire operation can be performed by the following command run in a terminal window (you can just copy it form the Medibuntu help page).

```
sudo wget http://www.medibuntu.org/sources.list.d/jaunty.list --output-
document=/etc/apt/sources.list.d/medibuntu.list
```

Alternatively you could access the **jaunty list** on your browser and download it as a text file named **jaunty.list**.

```
http://www.medibuntu.org/sources.list.d/jaunty.list
```

Then copy the file to **the /etc/apt/sources.list.d** directory as **medibuntu.list**, using the **sudo** and **cp** commands.

```
sudo cp jaunty.list /etc/apt/sources.list.d/medibuntu.list
```

Medibuntu signature key

You then have to install the Medibuntu signature key, before you can download and install any packages. The Medibuntu key is held in the medibuntu-keyring packages which you need to install.

Package	Description
aacgain	AAC normalizer for MP4 video and MP3 media files
aacplusenc	AAC encoder
acroread	Adobe Acrobat reader
acroread-plugins	Support for Adobe reader features like fill-able forms.
acroread-dictionary-en	Adobe Acrobat reader dictionary, English. There are different packages for several languages
acroread-doc-en	Adobe Acrobat reader documentation, English. There are different packages for several languages.
alsa-firmware	Proprietary firmware support for several soundcards.
amrnb	AMR speech codec (Adaptive Multi-Rate)
amrwb	AMR speech wideband codec (H323)
app-install-data-medibuntu	Adds Medibuntu application entries to Add/Remove Applications (gnome-install), Applications | Add Remove. Allows you to use Add/Remove to install or remove Medibuntu applications.
gizmo	VoIP application
google-earth	Google Earth
libdvdcss2	Commercial DVD Video support
medibuntu-keyring	Medibuntu repository digital signature key
mozilla-acroread	Adobe Acrobat Reader plugin for Firefox and Konqueror
mplayer	Mplayer media player, with faac and amr support enabled.
memcoder	Mplayer movie encoder
non-free	Meta package for installing a wide range of non-free codecs at once. Install amr, w32codecs, and the restricted-extras packages for Ubuntu desktop and KUbuntu.
realplayer	RealPlayer 10 for Linux (based on Helix player)
rmconverter	Convert Real Player media
skype	Skype VoIP application
w32codecs, w64codecs	Windows media codecs, use **non-free** meta package to install, or download and install directly with Gdebi.

Table 6-2: Medibuntu.org codecs and applications

To install the key is to use the following command line in a terminal window, also available on the Medibuntu Ubuntu help page listed previously. You can copy it from your browser and paste it to the terminal window. Use the terminal window Edit menu Paste to copy.

```
sudo apt-get update && sudo apt-get install medibuntu-keyring && sudo apt-get
update
```

You will be prompted to install these packages without verification. Press **y** and then ENTER to continue.

You could also just download the **medibuntu-keyring** package directly from the **medibuntu.org** Web site and open it eth the GDebi package installer

```
http://packages.medibuntu.org/jaunty/medibuntu-keyring.html
```

You could also download it first and then use either Gdebi or **dpkg** to install it.

```
medibuntu-keyring_2008.04.20_all.deb
```

Alternatively, an easy way to install the **medibuntu-keyring** package is to start up the Synaptic Package Manager. Click the Reload button to read the Medibuntu repository listing. Then search for:

```
medibuntu-keyring
```

Select the package for install and click Apply. You will be warned that it is not authenticated, but install anyway. The key will be installed. Click Reload again. You can now download and install any Medibuntu package. Medibuntu packages will appear in the Synaptic Package Manager, which you can use to install Medibuntu packages.

Graphics Applications

GNOME, KDE, and the X Window System support an impressive number of graphics applications, including image viewers, window grabbers, image editors, and paint tools. On the KDE and GNOME desktops, these tools can be found under either a Graphics submenu or the Utilities menu.

The F-Spot Photo Manager provides a simple and powerful way to manage, display, and import your photos and images (**www.f-spot.org**). Photos can be organized by different categories such as events, people, and places. You can perform standard display operations like rotation or full-screen viewing, along with slide shows. Image editing support is provided. Selected photos can be directly burned to a CD (uses Nautilus burning capabilities).

Features include a simple and easy-to-use interface. A timeline feature lets you see photos as they were taken. You can also display photos in full-screen mode or as slide shows. F-Spot includes a photo editor that provides basic adjustments and changes like rotation, red eye correction, and standard color settings including temperature and saturation (see Figure 6-1). You can tag photos placing them in groups, making them easier to access. With a tag you can label a collection of photos. Then use the tag to instantly access them. The tag itself can be a user-selected icon, including one that the user can create with the included Tag icon editor. F-Spot provides several ways to upload photos to a Web site using a Flickr account (**www.flickr.com**). Gallery-supported sites (**http://gallery.menalto.com**). Photos can also be saved to a folder for later uploading a website, either as plain files or as static HTML files.

Cheese is a Web cam picture taking and video recording tool (**www.gnome.org/projects/cheese**). With Cheese you can snap pictures from your Web cam and apply simple effects (see Figure 6-2).

Tools	Description
F-Spot	GNOME digital camera application and image library manager (**wsw.f-spot.org**)
Cheese	GNOME Web cam application for taking pictures and videos
ubuntustudio-graphics	Ubuntu Studio meta package (Meta Packages (universe)), includes a collection of graphics applications.
KDE	
Gwenview	Image browser and viewer (default for KDE)
ShowFoto	Simple image viewer, works with digiKam (**www.digikam.org**)
KSnapshot	Screen grabber
KolourPaint	Paint program
Krita	Image editor (**www.koffice.org/krita**)
GNOME	
gThumb	Image browser, viewer, cataloger (**http://gthumb.sourceforge.net**)
Eye of Gnome	GNOME Image Viewer
GIMP	GNU Image Manipulation Program (**www.gimp.org**)
Inkscape	GNOME Vector graphics application (**www.inkscape.org**)
gpaint	GNOME paint program
OpenOffice Draw	OpenOffice Draw program
X Window System	
Xpaint	Paint program
Xfig	Drawing program
ImageMagick	Image format conversion and editing tool

Table 6-3: Graphics Tools for Linux

Photo Tools: F-Spot and Cheese

Click the Photo button to manage photos and the Video button to record video. Icons of photos and video will appear on the bottom panel, letting you select ones for effects or removal. The effects panel will show effects that can be turned on or off for the current image. To save a photo, right click on its icon on the lower panel and select Save to from the pop-up menu. You can also export the selected photo or video to F-Spot, as well as email it as an attachment. You can also use the pop-up menu on particular icons to remove a photo. The Edit menu has a "Move all to trash" option for removing all items.

Tip: The Windows version of Photoshop is now supported by Wine. You can install Photoshop CS on Ubuntu using Wine and then access it through the Wine Windows support tool. Once started, Photoshop will operate like any Linux desktop application.

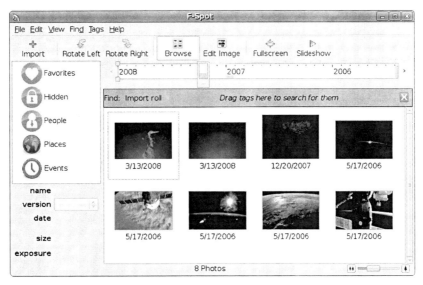

Figure 6-1: F-spot Photo Management

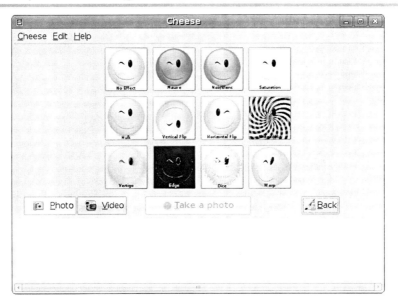

Figure 6-2: Cheese Web cam photo/video manager

KDE Graphics Tools

The KDE desktop features the same variety of tools found on the GNOME desktop. Many are available from the Ubuntu main repository. Most do not require a full installation of the KDE desktop. The KSnapshot program is a simple screen grabber for KDE, which currently supports only a few image formats. Gwenview is an easy-to-use, comfortable image browser and viewer supporting slide shows and numerous image formats. It is the default viewer for KDE and KDE4. KolourPaint is a simple paint program with brushes, shapes, and color effects; it supports numerous image formats. Krita is the KOffice professional image paint and editing application, with a wide range of features such as creating web images and modifying photographs (formerly known as Krayon and KImageShop).

GNOME Graphics Tools

GNOME features several powerful and easy-to-use graphic tools. Most are installed with Ubuntu or available on its repository. Also, many of the KDE tools work just as effectively in GNOME and are accessible from the GNOME desktop.

The gThumb application is a thumbnail image viewer that lets you browse images using thumbnails, display them, and organize them into catalogs or easy reference. The Eye of Gnome is the GNOME image viewer accessible from Applications | Graphics | Image Viewer. The menu item is not displayed by default, use System | Preferences | Main Menu to have it appear.

GIMP is the GNU Image Manipulation Program, a sophisticated image application much like Adobe Photoshop. You can use GIMP for such tasks as photo retouching, image composition, and image authoring. It supports features such as layers, channels, blends, and gradients. GIMP makes particular use of the GTK+ widget set. You can find out more about GIMP and download the newest versions from its Web site at **www.gimp.org**. GIMP is freely distributed under the GNU Public License.

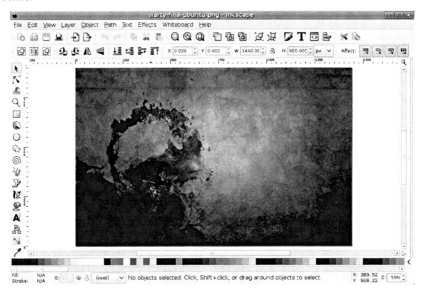

Figure 6-3: Inkscape

Inkscape is a Gnome based vector graphics application for SVG (scalable vector graphics) images (see Figure 6-3). It features capabilities similar to professional level vector graphics applications like Adobe Illustrator. The SVG format allows easy generation of images for Web use as well as complex art. Though its native format is SVG, it can also export to PNG format. It features layers and easy objects creation, including stars and spirals. A color bar lets you quickly change color fills.

The gPhoto project provides software for accessing digital cameras (**www.gphoto.org**). Several front-end interfaces are provided for a core library, called libgphoto2, consisting of drivers and tools that can access numerous digital cameras.

X Window System Graphic Programs

X Window System–based applications run directly on the underlying X Window System, which supports the more complex desktops like GNOME and KDE. These applications tend to be simpler, lacking the desktop functionality found in GNOME or KDE applications. Most are available on the Ubuntu Universe repository. Xpaint is a paint program much like MacPaint that allows you to load graphics or photographs and then create shapes, add text and colors, and use brush tools with various sizes and colors. Xfig is a drawing program. ImageMagick lets you convert images from one format to another; you can, for instance, change a TIFF image to a JPEG image. Table 6-3 lists some popular graphics tools for Linux.

Multimedia

Many applications are available for both video and sound, including sound editors, MP3 players, and video players (see Tables 6-5 and 6-6). Linux sound applications include mixers, digital audio tools, CD audio writers, MP3 players, and network audio support. There are literally thousands of projects currently under development.

Information about applications designed specifically for the GNOME or KDE user interface can be found at their respective software sites (**www.gnomefiles.org** and **www.kde-apps.org**). Precompiled binary DEB packages for most applications are at the Ubuntu repository.

To install support for most of the commonly used codecs, you can install the Ubuntu restricted extras package, **ubuntu-restricted-extras**. Use either Add/Remove or Synaptic to install, search on "restricted" on All packages, or locate the Meta Packages (multiverse) section. This package is a meta package that will download a collection of other packages that provide support for DVD, MP3, MPEG4, DivX, and AC3, as well as Flash (non-free) and Java runtime support. It will install all the Gstreamer bad, ugly, and ffmpeg packages, as well as Adobe flash and JRE packages. The Microsoft font collection (**msttcorefonts**) is also included, as well as RAR archive extraction (**unrar**). You are warned that licensing for these codecs may be restricted in some countries.

```
ubuntu-restricted-extras
```

For the KUbuntu desktop you would install the KDE version.

```
kubuntu-restricted-extras
```

For certified valid multimedia licensed codecs for Linux check **www.fluendo.com**. You can purchase supported and fully licensed codes for all the standard multimedia formats including DVD video, MP3, MPEG4, and AC3.

Ubuntu codec wizard

Ubuntu provides a codec wizard that will automatically detect whenever you need to install a new multimedia codec (see Figure 6-4). If you try to run a media file for which you do not have the proper codec, the codec wizard will pop-up and list the codecs you need to download an install. Often there are several choices. For MP3 you can use the lame codec or the licensed Fluendo codec, or both (see Figure 6-5). Alternatively, you could download and install these codecs manually. Most are available on the universe and multi-verse repositories, though you would need to know what packages to look for. For the Fluendo codecs, search on fluendo in the Synaptic Package Manager.

The codec wizard will select and install these packages for you, simplifying the process of installing the various multimedia codecs available for Linux.

A listing of popular multimedia codecs available is shown in Table 6-4. Of particular interest may be the liba52, faad2, and lame codecs for sound decoding, as well as the xvidcore, x264, libdvdcss, and libdvbpsi for video decoding. For GStreamer supported applications like the Totem movie player, you will need a special set of packages called gstreamer-bad and gstreamer-ugly. Most are installed by the **ubuntu-restricted-extras** package. The **ffmpeg**, **libmad**, and **libsmpeg** packages are supported directly in the main Ubuntu repository.

Figure 6-4: Ubuntu codec wizard prompt

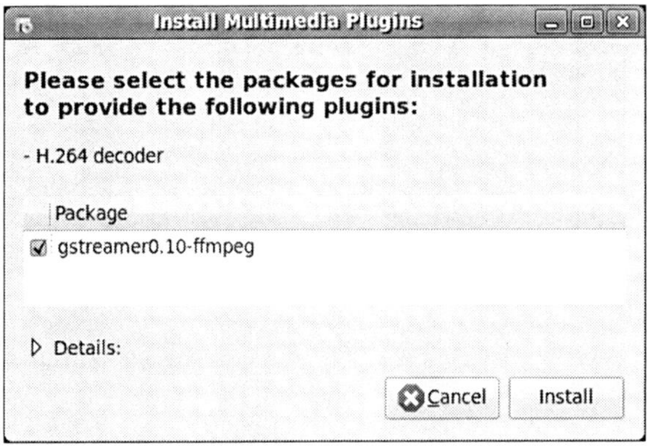

Figure 6-5: Ubuntu codec wizard selection

Some codecs, like libdvdcss, are available only from the Medibuntu.org repository. If you configure APT to use the Medibuntu repository, you can use the Synaptic Package Manager to download and install them. Medibuntu also provides a meta package called **non-free-codecs** that will select and install most of the codec for you, including DVD Video (**libdvdcss**), MP3, Flash, and Win32/64 codecs.

```
non-free-codecs
```

There are also several third party multimedia applications you may want. Three of the major applications with their recommended sites for Ubuntu are shown here. The Xine core media libraries are installed and supported by Ubuntu. The Xine user interface is part of the Universe repository.

Xine	Xine multimedia player	Ubuntu Main/Universe
MPlayer	MPlayer multimedia player	Multiverse
VideoLAN (vlc)	VideoLAN network/media	Multiverse

GStreamer

Many of the GNOME-based applications make use of GStreamer. GStreamer is a streaming media framework based on graphs and filters. Using a plug-in structure, GStreamer applications can accommodate a wide variety of media types. You can download modules and plug-ins from **http://gstreamer.freedesktop.org**. GNOME includes several GStreamer applications:

- The Totem video player uses GStreamer to play DVDs, VCDs, and MPEG media.

- Rhythmbox provides integrated music management; it is similar to the Apple iTunes music player.

- Sound Juicer is an audio CD ripper.

- A CD player, a sound recorder, and a volume control are all provided as part of the GStreamer GNOME Media package.

Note: GStreamer can be configured to use different input and output sound and video drivers and servers, using the GStreamer properties tool, the Multimedia System Selector. To open this tool you choose System | Preferences | Multimedia Selector (this menu item is hidden by default, use System | Preferences | Main Menu to display. You can also enter `gstreamer-properties` in a terminal window.

GStreamer Plug-ins: the Good, the Bad, and the Ugly

Many GNOME multimedia applications like Totem use GStreamer to provide multimedia support. To use such features as DVD Video and MP3, you have to install GStreamer extra plug-ins. You can find out more information about GStreamer and its supporting packages at **http://gstreamer.freedesktop.org**.

Package	Description
liba52	HDTV audio (ATSC A/52, AC3)
faad	MPEG2/ 4 AAC audio decoding, high quality (faad2)
faac	MPEG2/ 4 AAC sound encoding and decoding
ffmpeg	Play, record, convert, stream audio and video. Includes digital streaming server, conversion tool, and media player. libavcodec holds ffmpeg originally developed video and audio codec code (Ubuntu main repository).
gstreamer-ffmpeg	ffmpeg plug-in for GStreamer
gstreamer-bad	not fully reliable codecs and tools for GStreamer, some with possible licensing issues.
gstreamer-ugly	reliable video and audio codecs for GStreamer that may have licensing issues
gstreamer-fluendo-mp3	Fully licensed MP3 codec from Fluendo for GStreamer
gstreamer-fluendo-mpegdemux	Fully licensed MPEG2 TS video streams demuxing from Fluendo for GStreamer
audacious-plugins-extra	MP3, AAC, and WMA for Audacious
lame	MP3 playback capability, not an official MP3 decoder
libdts	DTS coherent acoustics playback
libdvbpsi	MPEG TS stream (DVB and PSI) decoding and encoding capability, VideoLAN project.
libdvdread	DVD playback (use **install-css.sh** to install libdvdcss for commercial DVD decoding)
libdvdnav	DVD video menu navigation
libdvdcss	DVD commercial decryption, available from **medibuntu.org** repository.
vdr-plugin-dvd	DVD playback and recording for VDR video recorder
libfame	Fast Assembly MPEG video encoding
libmad	MPEG1 audio decoding (Ubuntu main repository)
libmpeg	MPEG video audio decoding (MPEG1/2 audio and video, AC3, IFO, and VOB)
libquicktime	Quicktime playback
mt-daap	Itunes support
mpeg2dec	MPEG2 and MPEG1 playback
twolame	MPEG audio layer 2, MP2 encoding
x264	H264/AVC decoding and encoding (high definition media)
libxvidcore	OpenDivx codec (DivX and Xvid playback)

`libsmpeg`	Smpeg MPEG 1 video and audio decoder
`swfdec`	FLASH animation decoding
`totem-xine`	Totem movie player using Xine libraries
`libxine1-all-plugins`	Added video/ audio playback for Xine media player

Table 6-4: Multimedia third-party codecs

The supporting packages can be confusing. For version 1.0 and above, GStreamer establishes four different support packages called the base, the good, the bad, and the ugly. The base package is a set of useful and reliable plug-ins. These are in the Ubuntu main repository. The good package is a set of supported and tested plug-ins that meets all licensing requirements. This is also part of the Ubuntu main repository. The bad is a set of unsupported plug-ins whose performance is not guaranteed and may crash, but still meet licensing requirements. The ugly package contains plug-ins that work fine, but may not meet licensing requirements, like DVD support.

- **The base**   Reliable commonly used plug-ins

- **The good**   Reliable additional and useful plug-ins

- **The ugly**   Reliable but not fully licensed plug-ins (DVD/MP3 support)

- **The bad**   Possibly unreliable but useful plug-ins (possible crashes)

As an alternative to the ugly package, you can use Fluendo packages for MP3 and MPEG2 support, **gstreamer-fluendo-mp3** and **gstreamer-fluendo-mpegmux**. Another plug-in for GStreamer that you may want include is **ffmpeg** which provides H264 HDTV support. The codec wizard will automatically detect the codec you will need to use for your GStreamer application.

GStreamer MP3 Compatibility: iPod

For your iPod and other MP3 devices to work with GNOME applications like Rhythmbox, you will need to install MP3 support for GStreamer. MP3 support is not installed by Ubuntu because of licensing issues. You can, however, install the GStreamer **gstreamer-fluendo-mp3** (licensed MP3) or **gstreamer-plugins-ugly** support packages as noted previously.

To play songs from your iPod, Ubuntu provides the **libgpod3** library for GNOME and **ipodslave** for KDE. These allow player applications like Rythmbox and Amarok to use your iPod. To sync, import, or extract from your iPod, you can use iPod management software such as GUI for iPod, both **gtkpod** (Universe) and **gtkpod-aac** with aac and MP4 support (Multiverse). Several tools are currently available for iPod access; they include ipod, hipo, ipod-convenience (for IPod touch and iPhone).

Ubuntu Studio

Ubuntu Studio features Linux software for multimedia production, including sound, music, video, and graphics applications. You can install Ubuntu Studio as its own installation or as an added desktop on your Ubuntu desktop install. You can even choose different applicaton subsets to install.

You can download the Ubuntu Studio install DVD from **www.ubuntustudio.org**. This is an Alternate DVD that installs using the test install utility. Use the arrow keys and tabs to move the cursor, the spacebar to choose, and ENTER key to select. The install procedure is the same for the desktop, but adds a Software selection screen where you choose what collection of Ubuntu Studio software you want (see Figure 6-6). Use the arrow keys and spacebar to select entries. Select them all for the entire collection. When finished, use the Tab key to move to the Continue item and press ENTER.

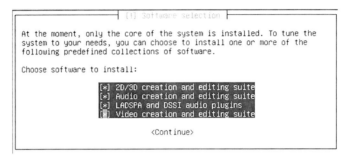

Figure 6-6: Ubuntu Studio text install Software selection

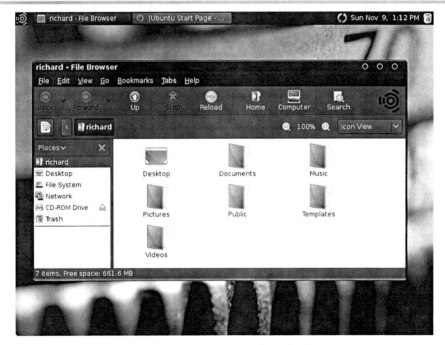

Figure 6-7: Ubuntu Studio desktop with Ubuntu Studio theme

Figure 6-8: Ubuntu studio menu

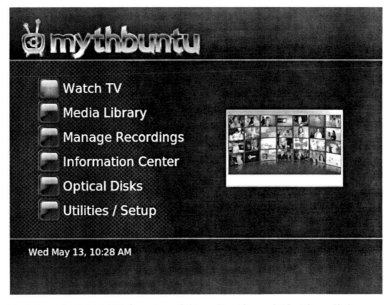

Figure 6-9: Mythbuntu MythTV front end (Applications | Multimedia)

Figure 6-10: Mythbuntu Control Centre

To just add Ubuntu Studio to your current desktop install, use Synaptic and find the Meta Package (universe) section. There you will find the **ubuntustudio-desktop** Meta package which will install all Ubuntu Studio packages. You can also choose to install collection subsets like **ubuntustudio-audio** or **ubuntustudio-video**. Ubuntu studio uses its own Ubuntu Studio desktop theme with a single panel at the top and one menu (see Figures 6-7 and 6-8).

Mythbuntu

Mythbuntu is the Ubuntu version of MythTV, a linux implementation of a multimedia center for Home Theater Personal Computers (HTPC). You can download Mythbuntu from **www.mythbuntu.org**, or install on an Ubuntu desktop with **mythbuntu-desktop** Meta package. In Synaptic you will find the Meta package in the Meta Packages (multiverse) section.

Installation adds several steps, one for selecting a graphics card driver, another or your remote, and another for configuring your Video and TV settings.

Mythbuntu uses the XFCE desktop which runs much more economically than either GNOME or KDE. Once installed, you can run the MythTV front end (Applications | Multimedia) to display the Mythbuntu interface for easily selecting media tasks like watching TV or viewing a recording (see Figure 6-9).

To configure Mythbuntu, use the Mythbuntu Control Centre, Applications | System menu (see Figure 6-10). Be sure to enable Medibuntu proprietary codec support to allow your system to play all kinds of media. To return to the Mythbuntu interface select Applications | Multimedia | MythTV front-end.

Sound Drivers and Interfaces

Sound devices on Linux are supported by hardware sound drivers. With the current Ubuntu kernel, hardware support is implemented by the Advanced Linux Sound Architecture (ALSA) system. ALSA replaces the free version of the Open Sound System used in previous releases, as well as the original built-in sound drivers. You can find more about ALSA at **www.alsa-project.org**. See Table 6-5 for a listing of sound device and interface tools.

Your sound cards are automatically detected for you when you start up your system. Your sound cards should all be detected for you. Your sound devices are automatically detected by ALSA, which is invoked by udev when your system starts up. Removable devices, like USB sound devices, will also be detected.

Sound tool	Description
GNOME Volume Control	GNOME sound connection configuration and volume tool
KMix	KDE sound connection configuration and volume tool
alsamixer	ALSA sound connection configuration and volume tool
amixer	ALSA command for sound connection configuration
Sound Preferences	GNOME Sound Preferences, used to select sound interface like ALSA or PulseAudio (System | Preferences | Hardware | Sound)
PulseAudio	PulseAudio sound interface, selected in Sound Preferences, **www.pulseaudio.org**
PulseAudio Volume Control	PulseAudio Volume Control (Applications | Sound and Video menu), controls stream input, output, and playback, **pavucontrol** package.
PulseAudio Volume Meter	Volume Meter (Applications | Sound and Video menu), displays active sound levels
PulseAudio Manager	Manager for information and managing PulseAudio, **pman** package (Applications | Sound and Video menu)
PulseAudio Device Chooser	Device selection (Applications | Sound and Video menu)
PulseAudio Preferences	Options for network access and virtual output. (System | Preferences menu)

Table 6-5: Sound device and interface tools

You select preferences for your sounds using the GNOME sound preferences. On GNOME choose System | Preferences | Sound. This opens the Sound Preferences window, which has two panels: Devices and Sounds (see Figure 6-11). On the Devices panel you can select the sound interface to use for Sound Events, Music and Movies, and Audio Conferencing, as well as for Default Mixer Tracks. Normally the ALSA interface is selected. You can use PulseAudio instead.

Figure 6-11: Sound Preferences

The Sounds panel lets you select a sound theme, enabling system sounds for particular tasks like check boxes or logouts. The Sound effects lets you use visual sounds like flashes on the desktop for your system sounds. Sound themes can be selected from the pop-up menu under the Sound Themes label (you can also select them from Volume Control). The Alerts and Sound Effects pane then lists the sound and effects supported by the theme. You can click on the Default entry for a sound to open a pop-up menu with entries for Disable, Default, and Custom. Disable to turn off that particular alert or effect. Custom will open a window with sound files where you can select your own sound to use. Sound themes are implemented according to the Freedesktop.org Sound Theme and Naming Specification.

GNOME Volume Control

Various output and input connections are then activated and configured during automatic configuration. The standard connections are activated, but others, like SPDIF digital connections, may not. You can mute and un-mute, as well as control the volume of different connection with either GNOME Volume Control or KDE KMix. KMix will provide a complete display of every connection on your system, whereas GNOME Volume Control will show only those selected for display. KMix will show SPDIF connections, but GNOME Volume Control may not.

GNOME volume control is displayed as an applet on the panel, the speaker icon. You can use it to quickly change your system's sound volume using a sliding bar (see Figure 6-12).

Figure 6-12: Volume Control dialog and panel icon

To perform more detailed configuration, you use the Volume Control tool. You can access the GNOME Volume Control tool either from the sound applet your top panel (click the volume control button, or right-click and select Open Volume Control), or from System | Preferences | Volume Control menu entry (not displayed by default, use System | Preferences | Main Menu to have the menu entry displayed) (see Figure 6-13).

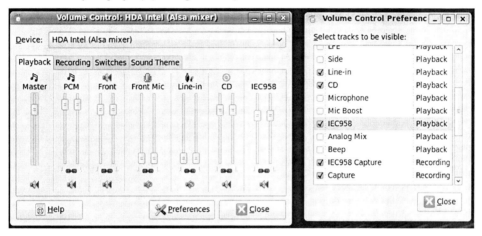

Figure 6-13: Volume Control, with SPDIF selection

Depending upon the kinds of devices displayed, there may be as many as four tabs: Playback, Recording, Switches, and Options, depending on the sound playback and recording sources selected. If recording devices (capture) are selected, then the recording tab is displayed showing those devices. The Switches tab usually has just an entry for headphones. If capture devices are displayed, the Options tab would show a pop-up menu for streams like PCM. In Figure 6-12, the digital playback sources are selected. This will display a Recording tab for digital capture and an Options panel for selecting a digital playback source.

On the Playback tab you can set the sound levels for different connections, both right or left, locking them together, or muting the connection altogether. Only a few commonly used connections are displayed. To display others, you need to configure the Volume Control properties.

To set the default sound device, select the device from the drop down menu labeled Device at the top of the Volume Control window. These are the same devices listed in the Sound Preferences Device pop-up menu. You can easily switch between defaults using just the Volume Control.

Configuring digital output for SPDIF (digital) connectors can be confusing. The digital output may be muted by default. You will have to first configure GNOME Volume Control

Preferences to display the SPDIF digital connection. To display the Preferences window, either right-click on the sound applet and select Preferences, or Click the Preferences button on the Volume Control window. The Preferences window will list all possible connections (tracks) on your system, with checks for those that will be displayed (see Figure 6-12). From the list of tracks find the device name of the optical output and click its checkbox. This will make it show up on the Volume control window.

The name of the SPDIF output is not always obvious. You may need to run **aplay -L** in a terminal window to see what the name of the digital output device is on your system. It will be the entry with Digital in it. On an Intel chip system this could be something like IEC958 for Intel HDA sound devices found on many computer motherboards.

Volume Control also features a tab for sound theme (see Figure 6-14). You can select the sound theme you want or choose to have no sound for alerts. The Ubuntu sound theme is selected by default.

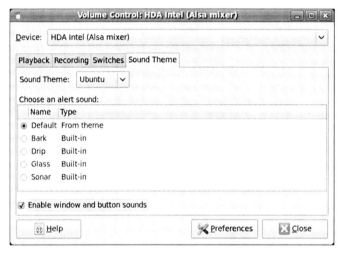

Figure 6-14: Volume Control Sound Theme tab

As an alternative to either GNOME Volume Control or KMix, you can also use the command-line ALSA control tool, **alsamixer**. This will display all connections and allow you to use keyboard command to select (arrow keys), mute (m key), or set sound levels (Page Up and Down). Use Escape to exit. The **amixer** command lets you perform the same tasks for different sound connections from the command line. To actually play and record from the command-line, you can use the **play** and **rec** commands.

PulseAudio and sound interfaces

In addition to hardware drivers, sound system also use sound interfaces to direct encoded sound streams from an application to the hardware drivers and devices. There are a many sound interfaces available, but Ubuntu now uses the PulseAudio server, as do many other distributions. PulseAudio aims to combine and consolidate all sound interfaces into a simple, flexible, and powerful server. The ALSA hardware drivers are still used, but the application interface are handled by PulseAudio.

Figure 6-15: PulseAudio selected in Sound Preferences, System | Preferences | Sound

PulseAudio provides packages for interfacing with Gstreamer, MPlayer, ALSA, and xmms, and Xine, replacing those sound interfaces with PulseAudio. The KDE aRts interface is not supported as aRts also performs its own synthesizing.

PulseAudio is cross-platform sound server, allowing you to modify the sound level for different audio streams separately. See **www.pulseaudio.org** for documentation and help. PulseAudio offers complete control over all your sound streams, letting you combine sound devices and direct the stream anywhere on your network. PulseAudio is not confined to a single system. It is network capable, letting you direct sound from one PC to another. Installed with Pulse Audio are the Pulse Audio tools. These are command line tools for managing Pulse Audio and playing sound files. The **paplay** and **pacat** will play a sound files, **pactl** will let you control the sound server and **pacmd** lets you reconfigure it.

Pulse audio is installed as the default set up for Ubuntu, the Auto selection. Each user can choose to use Pulse Audio or not. Activation is performed from GNOME or KDE desktop preferences (see Figure 6-15). On GNOME choose System | Preferences | Sound. Then on the Devices Panel, you can select Pulse Audio from the various pop-up menus.

For full easy configuration be sure to install all the Pulse Audio GUI tools (Universe repository). Most begin with the prefix **pa** in the package name. To select all of them for installation, search for and install either **paman** or **padevchooser**.

padevchooser

The **padevchooser** tool is a gnome applet that can be used to start up all the other pulseaudio tools. Except for PulseAudio Preferences and PulseAudio Device Chooser, menu entries are not set up for these tools. You would use the PulseAudio Device Chooser applet (**padevchooser**) to run them. Should you not want to run the applet, you can open a terminal window and enter their commands, starting them directly. They will then run as GUI GNOME applications. For example, you can open a terminal window and enter the command **paman** to run the PulseAudio Manager. The PulseAudio tools and their command names are shown here.

```
PulseAudio Volume Control, pavucontrol
PulseAudio Volume Meter, pavumeter
PulseAudio Manager, paman
PulseAudio Device Chooser, padevchooser
PulseAudio Preferences, papref
```

The PulseAudio tools and the Device Chooser are shown in Figure 6-16.

Figure 6-16: PulseAudio tools with PulseAudio Device Chooser applet

To run the PulseAudio Device Chooser applet select its entry in the Applications | Sound & Video menu. The PulseAudio Device Chooser applet will appear in the top panel to the right. The applet's Preferences dialog has an option for starting the Pulse Audio Device Chooser automatically. To select a PulseAudio tool, left-click on the PulseAudio Device Chooser icon and select the tool from the pop-up menu (see Figure 6-17). There are entries for Manager (PulseAudio Manager), Volume Control, Volume Meter (Playback and Recording), and Configure Local Sound

Server (PulseAudio Preferences, **papref**). You can also use the Device Chooser to select the default server, sink (output device), and source (input device) should there be more than one. Passing the mouse over an entry will display detailed information about the interface, device, or server. PulseAudio could be running on different hosts and configured by different users on a given host. You can choose which one to use.

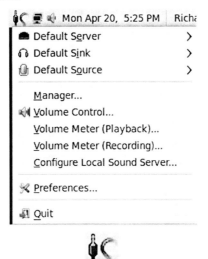

Figure 6-17: PulseAudio Device Chooser menu and applet icon, Applications | Sound & Video | PulseAudio Device Chooser

Once PulseAudio is activated, you can use the PulseAudio Volume Control tool to set the sound levels for different playback applications and sound devices (select Volume Control on the PulseAudio Device Chooser applet, or enter **pavucontrol** in a terminal window). The PulseAudio Volume Control applications will show three panels: Playback, Output Devices, and Input Devices (see Figure 6-18). The Playback panel shows all the applications currently use PulseAudio. You can adjust the volume for each application separately.

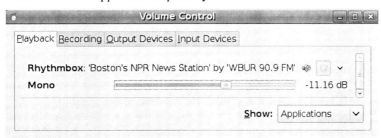

Figure 6-18: PulseAudio Volume Control, Playback

You can also use the Output devices panel to set the volume control at the source (see Figure 6-19). Input devices are for capture or microphone input, and can also be adjusted.

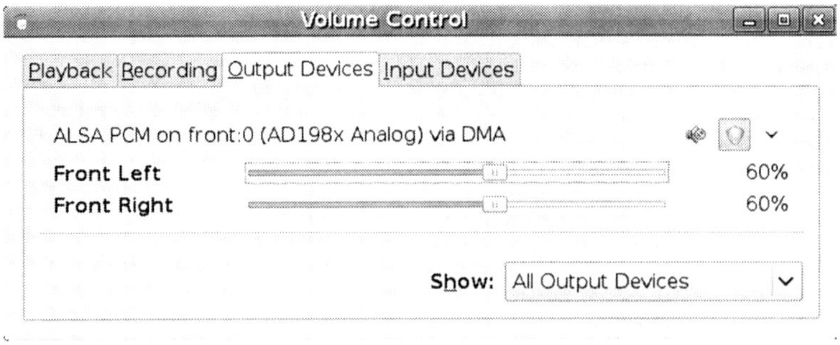

Figure 6-19: PulseAudio Volume Control, Devices

You can also use the PulseAudio Volume control to direct different applications (streams) to different outputs (devices). For example you could have two sound sources running, one for video and another for music. The video could be directed through one device to headphones and the music through another device to the speakers, or even to another PC. To redirect an application to a different device, right-click on it in the Playback panel. A pop-up menu will list the available devices and let you select the one you want to use.

The PulseAudio Volume Meter will show the actual volume of your devices Volume Meter, see Figure 6-20 (select Volume Meter, Playback or Recording, on the PulseAudio Device Chooser applet menu, or enter **pavumeter** in a terminal window).

Figure 6-20: PulseAudio Volume Meter

The PulseAudio Manager will show information about your PulseAudio configuration (select Manager on the PulseAudio Device Chooser applet menu; enter **paman** in a terminal window). Devices panel shows the currently active sinks (outputs or directed receivers) and sources (see Figure 6-21). The Clients panel will show all the applications currently using PulseAudio for sound.

To configure network access, you use the PulseAudio Configuration tool (System | Preferences | PulseAudio Preferences, or select Configure Local Sound Server on the PulseAudio Device Chooser applet menu). Here you can permit network access (see Figure 6-22). You can also enable multicast and simultaneous output. Simultaneous output creates a virtual output device to the same hardware device. This lets you channel two sources onto the same output. With PulseAudio Volume Control you could then channel playback streams to the same output device, but using a virtual device as the output for one. This lets you change the output volume for each stream independently. You could have music and voice directed to the same hardware device, using a virtual device for music and the standard device for voice. You can then reduce the music stream, or raise the voice stream.

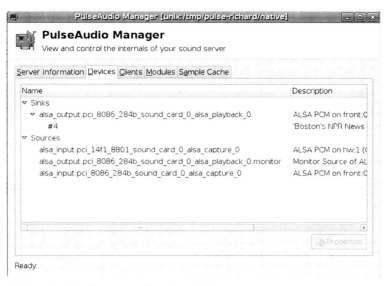

Figure 6-21: PulseAudio Manager Devices tab

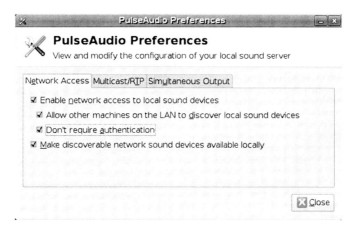

Figure 6-22: PulseAudio Preferences, System | Preferences | PulseAudio Preferences

Music Applications

Many music applications are currently available for GNOME, including sound editors, MP3 players, and audio players (see Table 6-6). You can use the Rhythmbox and Sound Juicer to play music from different sources, and the GNOME Sound Recorder to record sound sources. A variety of applications are also available for KDE, including the media players Amarok, a mixer (KMix), and a CD player (Kscd).

Application	Description
Xine	Multimedia player for video, DVD, and audio
Rhythmbox	Music management (GStreamer), default CD player with iPod support.
Sound Juicer	GNOME CD audio ripper (GStreamer)
Amarok	KDE4 multimedia audio player
Audacious	Multimedia player
Grip	CD audio ripper
Kscd	Music CD player
JuK	KDE4 Music player (jukebox) for managing music collections
GNOME CD Player	CD player
GNOME Sound Recorder	Sound recorder
XMMS	CD player
RealPlayer	RealMedia and RealAudio streaming media (**www.real.com**), download from **medibuntu.org**, the **realplayer** package.
HelixPlayer	Open source version of Real Player
ubuntustudio-audio	Ubuntu Studio meta package (Meta Packages (universe)), includes a collection of audio applications.

Table 6-6: Music Players and Rippers Applications

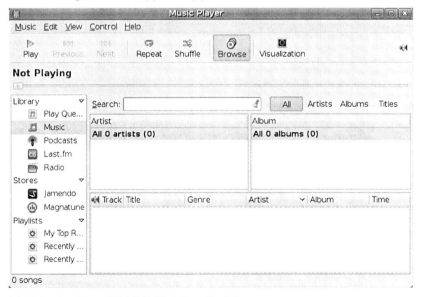

Figure 6-23: Rhythmbox GNOME Multimedia Player

GNOME includes sound applications like the XMMS2 multimedia player, GNOME CD Player, Sound Juicer (Audio CD Extractor), and Rhythmbox in the Sound And Video menu (see Figure 6-23). Rhythmbox is the default sound multimedia player, supporting music files, radio streams, and podcasts. KDE applications include Amarok and Juk (see Figure 6-24). Amarok is the primary multimedia player for KDE4. JuK (Music Jukebox) is the KDE4 music player for managing music collections. Linux systems also support HelixPlayer, the open source project used for RealPlayer.

Due to licensing and patent issues, Ubuntu does not install MP3 support by default. MP3 playback capability has been removed from multimedia players like Rhythmbox and Audacious. The Ubuntu codec wizard will prompt you to install MP3 support when you first try to play an MP3 file, usually the Gstreamer package. Another option is the free Fluendo MP3 codec. Just install the gsreamer-fluendo-mp3 package (Universe repository). As an alternative to MP3, you can use Ogg Vorbis compression for music files (**www.vorbis.com**).

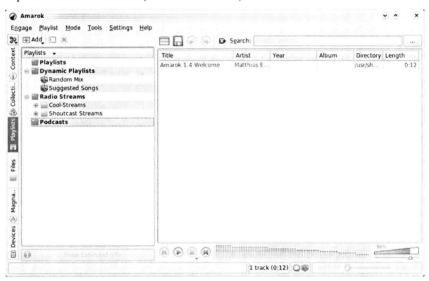

Figure 6-24: Amarok KDE Multimedia Player

CD/DVD Burners

Several CD/DVD ripper and writer programs that can be used for CD music and MP3 writing (burners and rippers). These include Sound Juicer, Brasero (see Chapter 3), K3b, and Grip (See Table 6-7).

GNOME also features two CD audio rippers installed with Ubuntu, Grip and Sound Juicer. For burning DVD/CD data discs, you can use Brasero and the Nautilus CD/DVD burner. The Nautilus CD/DVD burner is integrated into the Nautilus file manager, the default file manager for the GNOME desktop. For KDE you can use K3b

Qdvdauthor, dvdauthor, Brasero, and K3b can all be used to create DVD Video discs. All use mkisofs, cdrecord, and cdda2wav DVD/CD writing programs, which are installed as part of your distribution. DVD Video and CD music rippers may require addition codecs installed, which the codec wizard will prompt you for.

Application	Description
Brasero	Full service CD/DVD burner, for music, video, and data discs.
Sound Juicer	GNOME music player and CD burner and ripper
Serpentine	GNOME music CD burner and ripper.
ogmrip	DVD transcoding with DivX support
K3b	KDE CD writing interface
dvdauthor	Tools for creating DVDs
Qdvdauthor	KDE front end for dvdauthor (**www.kde-apps.org**)
Grip	GNOME Cd player, ripper, and encoder

Table 6-7: CD/DVD Burners

Video Applications

Several projects provide TV, video, DivX, DVD, and DTV support for Ubuntu (see Table 6-8).

Video and DVD Players

Most current DVD and media players are provided on the Ubuntu repositories

➢ The VideoLAN project (**www.videolan.org**) offers network streaming support for most media formats, including MPEG-4 and MPEG-2. It includes a multimedia player, VLC, which can work on any kind of system (**vlc** package, Universe repository).

➢ MPlayer is one of the most popular and capable multimedia/DVD players in use. It is a cross-platform open source alternative to RealPlayer and Windows Media Player, and it includes support for DivX (**www.mplayerhq.hu**). MPlayer uses an extensive set of supporting libraries and applications like **lirc**, **lame**, **lzo**, and **aalib**, which are also on the site. If you have trouble displaying video, be sure to check the preferences for different video devices and select one that works best (**mplayer** package, Multiverse repository).

➢ Xine is a multipurpose video player for Linux/Unix systems that can play video, DVD, and audio discs. Many applications like Totem, KMPLayer, and Kaffiene use Xine support to playback DVD Video. See **http://xinehq.de** for more information. (**xine** support packages, Ubuntu main repository).

➢ Dragon Player is a KDE4 multimedia player, installed with KDE4 desktop (see Figure 6-26)

➢ Totem is the GNOME movie player that uses GStreamer (see Figure 6-27). To expand Totem capabilities, you need to install added GStreamer plug-ins, like the DVB plugin for DVB broadcasts. The codec wizard will prompt you to install any needed media codecs and plugins. (**totem** package, Ubuntu main repository, installed with GNOME desktop).

➢ KMPlayer is a KDE movie player (older movie player)

➢ Kaffiene is a KDE multimedia player based on Xine (**kaffiene** package, Ubuntu main repository).

➢ Additional codec support is supplied by ffmpeg and x264. The x264 codec is an open source version of the high definition H.264 codec developed by Videolan (**x264** and **ffmpeg** packages, Multiverse repository, installed by codec wizard when first required).

Projects and Players	Sites
LinuxTV.org	Links to video, TV, and DVD sites: **www.linuxtv.org**
Xine	Xine video player: **www.xinehq.de**
Totem	Totem video and DVD player for GNOME based on Xine and using GStreamer, includes plugins for DVB, YouTube, nd MythTV: **www.xinehq.de**
Dragon Player	Dragon Player video and DVD player for KDE4
VLC Media Player (vlc)	Network multimedia streaming, includes x264 high definition support. **www.videolan.org**
MPlayer	MPlayer DVD/multimedia player (fully capable version at **medibuntu.org**) **www.mplayerhq.hu**
MythTV (Mythbuntu)	Home media center with DVD, DVR, and TV capabilities **www.mythtv.org** (use the Mythbuntu version, included on the Ubuntu Universe repository, **www.mythbuntu.org**)
kdetv	KDE TV viewer
tvtime	TV viewer, **http://tvtime.sourceforge.net**
DivX for Linux	**http://labs.divx.com/DivXLinuxCodec** (requires direct download)
XviD	Open Source DivX, **www.xvid.org**
ubuntustudio-video	Ubuntu Studio meta package (Meta Packages (universe)), includes a collection of video applications.
klear	KDE DVB TV and HDTV viewer
Kaffiene	KDE media player, including DVB, DVD, CD, and network streams.
KMPlayer	Basic KDE movie player

Table 6-8: Video and DVD Projects and Applications

Totem Plugins

The Totem movie player uses plugins to add capabilities like Internet video streaming. YouTube support is already installed as part of the desktop, along with the BBC content viewer. Select the menu item Edit | Plugins to open the Configure Plugins window (see Figure 6-25). Select the plugins you want. The YouTube and BBC plugins will already be selected.

For added support, install the totem-plugins-extra package.

```
totem-plugins extra
```

This provides the Coherence DLNA/UPnP client and the Gromit annotation tool. The Coherence plugin enables access to Universal Plug-n-Play (UPnP) media servers.

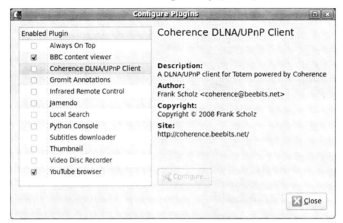

Figure 6-25: Totem Movie Player plugins

Figure 6-27: Totem Movie player

DVD Video support

None of the DVD Video applications will initially play commercial DVD Video discs. That requires CSS decryption of commercial DVDs which is provided by the **libdvdcss** package. This package is not available on the primary Ubuntu repositories. It is only available on the third-party **medibuntu.org** repository. The packages on medibuntu.org are fully compatible with an Ubuntu system, but the packages, due to licensing restrictions, are not considered part of the official Ubuntu software collection.

The **libdvdcss** library works around CSS decryption by treating the DVD as a block device, allowing you to use any of the DVD players to run commercial DVDs. It is also provides region-free access. See the following page for complete details

```
https://help.ubuntu.com/community/RestrictedFormats/PlayingDVDs
```

Figure 6-26: KDE4 Dragon Player

The three packages you need are:

```
gstreamer-plugins-ugly
libdvdread4
libdvdcss2
```

Both gstreamer-ugly and libdvdread4 are available on the Ubuntu repositories and can be installed with Synaptic Package Manager. The libdvdcss library is not available on the Ubuntu repository due to licensing restrictions, but is available from the **medibuntu.org** repository.

The easiest way to install the **libdvdcss** package is to configure medibuntu.org repository access, as described previously in this chapter, and in chapter 4. Once configured, just use the Synaptic Package Manager to search for the **libdvdcss** package, select it and install it.

Should you not want to configure medibuntu.org repository access, you can directly download the package with your Web browser using Gdebi. You have to be sure to select the correct architecture version. You can then use Gdebi to install it (see Figures 4-1 and 4-2, page 136).

```
http://packages.medibuntu.org/jaunty/libdvdcss2.html
```

Alternatively, you can use the **install-css.sh** script provided by the **libdvdread4** package. This script will download the **libdvdcss** decryption library from the **medibuntu.org** repository. Enter the following in a terminal window. You will have to provide your administrative password.

```
sudo /usr/share/doc/libdvdread4/install-css.sh
```

Originally, some of these players do not support DVD menus. With the **libdvdnav** library, these players now feature full DVD menu support. The **libdvdread4** library provides basic DVD interface support, such as reading IFO files.

TV Players

The site **www.linuxtv.org** provides detailed links to DVD, digital video broadcasting (DVB), and multicasting. The site also provides downloads of many Linux video applications.

TV player **tvtime** works with many common video capture cards, relying on drivers developed for TV tuner chips on those cards like the Conexant chips. It can only display a TV image. It has no recording or file playback capabilities. Check **http://tvtime.sourceforge.net** for more information.

Note: To play DivX media on Ubuntu you use the DivX for Linux codec at
   http://labs.divx.com/DivXLinuxCodec.

Dragon Player, Kaffiene, and Kdetv (Universe repository) are KDE multimedia players that will also play TV.

MythTV, popular video recording and playback application on Linux systems. (Mythbuntu release, multiverse repository). See **www.mythbuntu.org** for more information.

DVB and HDTV support

For DVB and HDTV reception you can use most DVB cards as well as many HDTV cars like the PCHDTV video card (**www.pdhdtv.com**). For example, the latest PCHDTV card uses the **cx88-dvb** drivers included with most recent Linux kernels. The DVB kernel driver is loaded automatically. You can use the **lsmod** command to see if your DVB module is loaded.

Tip: Many graphics cards do not provide support for HDTV (H264) hard ware acceleration in Linux, though software acceleration with the x264 codec is adequate.

Be sure appropriate decoders are installed like mpeg2, FFmpeg, and A52 (ac3) (**liba52**, **libxine-ffmpeg**, **gstreamer-ffmpeg**, and **libdvbps**). If the needed codec is not installed, you will be prompted to install it. The codec package will be located and installed for you.

For DVB broadcasts, many DVB capable players and tools like Kaffeine and Klear, as well as vdr will tune and record DVB broadcasts in t, s, and c formats. Some applications, like me-tv and Kaffeine, can scan DVB channels directly. Others, like Klear, require that you first generate a **channels.conf** file. You can do this with the **w_scan** command (**w-scan** package). Then copy the generated **channels.conf** file to the appropriate applications directory. Channel scans can be output in vdr, Kaffeine, and Xine formats for use with those applications as well as others like Mplayer and MythTV. The **w_scan** command can also generate **channel.conf** entries for ATSC channels (HDTV), though not all applications can tune ATSC channels (Kaffeine can tune HDTV as well as scan for HDTV channels). You can also use the **dvbscan** tool (**dvb-apps** package) for scanning your channels and the **azap** tool for accessing the signal directly. This tool makes use of channel frequencies kept in the **/usr/share/dvb/atsc** directory. There are files for ATSC broadcast as well as cable.

The DVB applications can also be used to record DVB broadcasts to TS (transport stream) files. The transport stream (**.ts** or **.tp**) file can then be viewed with a DVB capable viewer, such as Xine or Videolan VLC media player. You can use Kaffeine, MythTV, kvdr, and vdr (video disk recorder) to view and record. Check the MythTV site for details (**www.mythtv.org**).

The Kaffeine KDE media player can scan for both DVB and ATSC channels. You will need to have a DVD or ATSC tuner installed on your system. On the Settings menu, select Channels. This opens a Channel dialog (see Figure 6-28). Your tuner device will be selected on the Search on menu. Click on the Start scan button to begin scanning. Detected channels will be listed on the Found scrollbox. Select the ones you want and click Add Selected to place them in the Channels scrollbox. Close when finished. On the Kaffeine player, be sure to add the channel you want to watch on the Channel list. Kaffeine also provides Gstreamer support with the kaffeine-gstreamer package.

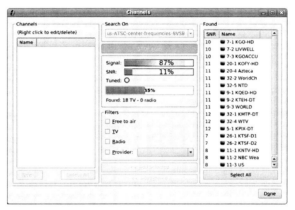

Figure 6-28: Kaffeine ATSC channel scan

The transport stream (**.ts** or **.tp**) files generated by HDTV cards like PCHDTV can be viewed with an HDTV capable viewer, such as Totem, Xine, Kaffeine, or Videolan VLC media player. You can use Kaffeine to both tune and record, but most applications cannot yet tune an HDTV signal for recording. One solution for recording HDTV is to use the **dvb-atsc-tools** provided by the PCHDTV Web site. The PCHDTV card and related cards using the connextant c88 chips (like most FusionTV); the c88x DVB kernel module will automatically be detected and loaded. You can then use the PCHDTV atsc tools to access and record programs. From the PCHDTV site, download the **atsc-dvb-tools** package (**http://www.pchdtv.com/downloads/dvb-atsc-tools-1.0.7.tgz**). These are source code programs you will have to compile. Uzip the archive file to a directory. You can use either the **tar** command or Archive Manager.

```
tar xvjf dvb-atsc-tools-1.0.7.tgz
```

In a terminal window change to that directory issue the **make** and **make install** commands. Be sure you have already downloaded and installed the kernel development packages.

```
make
make install
```

You can then use the **getatsc** and **dtvsignal** commands, among others to check and record HDTV receptions. The following records a channel to a file.

```
getatsc -dvb 0 12 > my.ts
```

This is an open ended process that will continue until you kill the process. To stop the recording you could do the following which uses the **ps** command to obtain the process id (pid) for the **getatsc** process. These getatsc and kill operations can be set up with cron tasks (KCRON) to implement automatic recording like a DVR or VCR.

```
kill `ps -C getatsc -o pid=`
```

You could then use any application like the VLC media player, Kaffeine, or an HDTV capable Mplayer to play back the file.

The **dtvscan** tool can also generate channels.conf files for Xine and Mplayer.

DivX and Xvid on Linux

MPEG-4 compressed files for provide DVD-quality video with relatively small file sizes. They have become popular for distributing high quality video files over the Internet. When you first try to play an MPEG-4, the codec wizard will prompt you to install the needed codec packages to play it. Many multimedia applications like VLC already support Mpeg4 files.

DivX is a commercial video version of MPEG-4 compress video files, free for personal use. You can download the Linux version of DivX for free from **http://labs.divx.com/DivXLinuxCodec**. You have to manually install the package.

An alternative, you can use the open source version of DivX known as Xvid (**libxvidcore** package, Multiverse repository). Most DivX files can be run using XviD. XviD is an entirely independent open source project, but it's compatible with DivX files. You can also download the XviD source code from **http://xvid.org**.

To convert DVD Video files to an MPEG-4/DivX format you can use **transcode** (Multiverse repository) or **ffmpeg** (Universe repository). Many DVD burners can these to convert DVD video files to DivX/Xvid files.

7. Mail and News

Your Linux system supports a wide range of both electronic mail and news clients. Mail clients enable you to send and receive messages with other users on your system or accessible from your network. News clients let you read articles and messages posted in a newsgroups, which are open to access by all users. This chapter reviews mail and news clients installed with Ubuntu Linux.

Mail Clients

You can send and receive e-mail messages in a variety of ways, depending on the type of mail client you use. Although all electronic mail utilities perform the same basic tasks of receiving and sending messages, they tend to have different interfaces. Some mail clients operate on a desktop, such as KDE or GNOME. Others run on any X Window System managers. Several popular mail clients were designed to use a screen-based interface and can be started only from the command line. Other traditional mail clients were developed for just the command line interface, which requires you to type your commands on a single command line. Most mail clients described here are included in standard Linux distributions and come in a standard RPM package for easy installation. For Web-based Internet mail services, such as Hotmail, GMail, and Yahoo, you use a Web browser instead of a mail client to access mail accounts provided by those services. Table 7-1 lists several popular Linux mail clients. Mail is transported to and from destinations using mail transport agents like Sendmail, Exim, and Postfix. To send mail over the Internet, they use the Simple Mail Transport Protocol (SMTP). Ubuntu automatically install and locally configure it for you. On starting up your system, having configured your network connections, you can send and receive messages over the Internet.

Mail Client	Description
Kontact (KMail, KAddressbook, KOrganizer)	Includes the K Desktop mail client, KMail; integrated mail, address book, and scheduler
Evolution	E-mail client, **http://projects.gnome.org/evolution/**
Thunderbird	Mozilla group stand-alone mail client and newsreader
Sylpheed	Gtk mail and news client
Claws-mail	Extended version of sylpheed Email client
GNUEmacs and XEmacs	Emacs mail clients
Mutt	Screen-based mail client
Mail	Original Unix-based command line mail client
Squirrel Mail	Web-based mail client

Table 7-1: Linux Mail Clients

You can sign your e-mail message with the same standard signature information, such as your name, Internet address or addresses, or farewell phrase. Having your signature information automatically added to your messages is helpful. To do so, you need to create a signature file in your home directory and enter your signature information in it. A *signature file* is a standard text file you can edit using any text editor. Mail clients such as KMail enable you to specify a file to function as your signature file. Others, such as Mail, expect the signature file to be named **.signature**.

MIME

MIME (the term stands for *Multipurpose Internet Mail Extensions*) is used to enable mail clients to send and receive multimedia files and files using different character sets such as those for different languages. Multimedia files can be images, sound clips, or even video. Mail clients that support MIME can send binary files automatically as attachments to messages. MIME-capable mail clients maintain a file called **mailcap** that maps different types of MIME messages to applications on your system that can view or display them. For example, an image file will be mapped to an application that can display images. Your mail clients can then run that program to display the image message. A sound file will be mapped to an application that can play sound files on your speakers. Most mail clients have MIME capabilities built in and use their own version of the **mailcap** file. Others use a program called metamail that adds MIME support. MIME is not only used in mail clients. Both the KDE and GNOME file managers use MIME to map a file to a particular application so that you can launch the application directly from the file.

The mime.types File

Applications are associated with binary files by means of the **mailcap** and **mime.types** files. The **mime.types** file defines different MIME types, associating a MIME type with a certain application. The **mailcap** file then associates each MIME type with a specified application. Your system maintains its own MIME types file, usually **/etc/mime.types**.

Entries in the MIME types file associate a MIME type and possible subtype of an application with a set of possible file extensions used for files that run on a given kind of application. The MIME type is usually further qualified by a subtype, separated from the major type by a slash. For example, a MIME type image can have several subtypes such as jpeg, gif, or tiff. A sample MIME type entry defining a MIME type for JPEG files are shown here. The MIME type is image/jpeg, and the list of possible file extensions is "jpeg jpg jpe":

```
image/jpeg jpeg jpg jpe
```

The applications specified will depend on those available on your particular system. The application is specified as part of the application type. In many cases, X Window System–based programs are specified. Comments are indicated with a **#**. The following entries associate **odt** files with the OpenOffice.org writer, **kwd** and **kwt** files with KOffice KWord, and **qtl** files with the Quicktime player.

```
application//vnd.oasis.opendcument.text   odt
application/x-kword                       kwd kwt
application/x-quicktimeplayer             qtl
```

Note: On KDE, use the KDE Control Center's File Association entry under KDE Components. This will list MIME types and their associated filename extensions. Select an entry to edit it and change the applications associated with it. KDE saves its MIME type information in a separate file called **mimelnk** in the KDE configuration directory.

MIME Standard Associations

Though you can create your own MIME types, a standard set already is in use. The types text, image, audio, video, application, multipart, and message, along with their subtypes, have already been defined for your system. You will find that commonly used file extensions such as **.tif** and **.jpg** for TIFF and JPEG image files are already associated with a MIME type and an application. Though you can easily change the associated application, it is best to keep the MIME types already installed. The current official MIME types are listed at the IANA Web site (**www.iana.org**) under the name Media Types, provided as part of their Assignment Services. You can access the media types file directly on their site.

OpenPGP/MIME and S/MIME Authentication and Encryption Protocols

S/MIME and OpenPGP/MIME are authentication protocols for signing and encrypting mail messages. S/MIME was originally developed by the RSA Data Security. OpenPGP is an open standard based on the PGP/MIME protocol developed by the PGP (Pretty Good Privacy) group. Clients like KMail and Evolution can use OpenPGP/MIME to authenticate messages. Check the Internet Mail Consortium for more information, **www.imc.org**.

Evolution

Evolution is the primary mail client for the GNOME desktop. It is installed by default along with OpenOffice. Though designed for GNOME, it will work equally well on KDE. Evolution is an integrated mail client, calendar, and address book. The Evolution mailer is a powerful tool with support for numerous protocols (SMTP, POP, and IMAP), multiple mail accounts, and encryption. With Evolution, you can create multiple mail accounts on different servers, including those that use different protocols such as POP or IMAP. You can also decrypt PGP- or GPG-encrypted messages. Messages are indexed for easy searching. Junk mail filtering is also provided. Evolution also provides collaboration server support like Microsoft Exchange (2000/2003) and GroupWise (Novell). Evolution can function as an Exchange or GroupWise client. As an added feature, you can now display Web calendars within evolution. See the Evolution Web site for a complete description of its features.

```
http://projects.gnome.org/evolution/
```

The Evolution mailer provides a simple GUI interface, with a toolbar for commonly used commands and a sidebar for shortcuts. A menu of Evolution commands allows access to other operations. The main panel is divided into two panes, one for listing the mail headers and the other for displaying the currently selected message. You can click any header title to sort your headers by that category. Evolution also supports the use of virtual folders. These are folders created by the user to hold mail that meets specified criteria. Incoming mail can be automatically distributed to their particular virtual folder.

To configure Evolution, select Preferences from the Edit menu. On the Evolution Preferences window, a sidebar holds icons for main accounts, auto-completion, mail preferences, composition preference, calendar and task and certificates. The main accounts entry displays a list of current accounts. An Add button lets you add new ones, and the Edit button allows you to change current accounts. When editing an account, you have Account Editor Displays panels for Identity, Receiving email (your incoming mail server), sending email (outgoing mail server), and security (encryption and digital signatures). The Mail Preferences entry is where you configure how Evolution displays and manages messages. In the Compose Preferences entry lets you set up composition features like signatures, formatting, and spell-checking. The Automatic Contact panel in Mail Preferences is where you can specify that addresses of mail you reply to should be automatically added to the Evolution address book. To see and manage the contacts in your address book, click on the Contacts button on the left lower sidebar.

With evolution you can also create search folders to organize access to your messages. A search folder is not an actual folder. It simply collects links to messages based on certain search criteria. Using search folders, you can quickly display messages on a given topic, subject, or from a specific user. In effect, it performs an automatic search on messages as they arrive. To set up a search folder, select Search Folders in the Edit menu and click Add to open the Add Rule window. Here you can add criteria for searches and the folders to search. You can also right-click a message header that meets criteria you want searched and select Create Rule from Message, and then one of the Search Rule entries.

To extend Evolution's capabilities, numerous plugins are available. Most are installed and enabled for you automatically, including the SpamAssasin plugin for handling junk mail. To manage your plugins, select the Plugin entry in the Edit menu. This opens the Plugin Manager, with plugins listed in a left side scroll window and configuration panels located for a selected plugin on the right side.

Evolution also supports filters. You can use filters to automatically direct some messages to certain folders, instead of having all incoming messages placed in the inbox folder. To create a filter, you can select the Message Filters entry in the Edit menu and click Add to open the Add Rule message. You can also right-click on the header of a message whose head meets your criteria, like a subject or sender, and select Create Rule from Message and select a Filter entry for sender, subject, or recipient. On the Add Rule window you can add other criteria and also specify the action to take, like moving the message to a certain folder. You can also add other actions like assigning a score, changing the color, copying the message, or just deleting it.

Note: Other GNOME mail clients include sylpheed and Claws-mail (both are on the Ubuntu Universe repository). Sylpheed is a mail and news client with an interface similar to Windows mail clients. Claws-mail is an extended version of Sylpheed with many additional features (**www.claws-mail.org**).

Thunderbird

Thunderbird is a full-featured stand-alone e-mail client provided by the Mozilla project (**www.mozilla.org**). It is designed to be easy to use, highly customized, and heavily secure. It features advanced intelligent spam filtering, as well as security features like encryption, digital signatures, and S/MIME. To protect against viruses, e-mail attachments can be examined without being run. Thunderbird supports both Internet Message Access Protocol (IMAP) and the Post Office Protocol (POP), as well as functioning as a newsreader. It also features a built-in RSS reader. Thunderbird also supports the use of the Lightweight Directory Access Protocol (LDAP) address books. Thunderbird is an extensible application, allowing customized modules to be added to enhance its capabilities. You can download extensions such as dictionary search and contact sidebars from its Web site. GPG encryption can be supported with the enigmail extension (Ubuntu main repository).

The interface uses a standard three-pane format, with a side pane for listing mail accounts and their boxes. The top pane lists main entries, and the bottom pane shows text. Command can be run using the toolbar, menus, or keyboard shortcuts. You can even change the appearance using different themes. Thunderbird also supports HTML mail, displaying Web components like URLs in mail messages.

The message list pane will show several fields by which you can sort your messages. Some use just symbols like the Threads, Attachments, and Read icons. Clicking Threads will gather the messages into respective threads with replies grouped together. The last icon in the message list fields is a pop-up menu letting you choose which fields to display. Thunderbird provides a variety of customizable display filters, such as People I Know, which displays only messages from those in your address book, and Attachments, which displays messages with attached files. You can even create your own display filters. Search and sorting capabilities also include filters that can match selected patterns in any field, including subject, date, or the message body.

When you first start up Thunderbird, you will be prompted to create an e-mail account. You can add more e-mail accounts or modify your current ones by selecting Account Settings from the Edit menu. Then click Add Account to open a dialog with four options, one of which is an e-mail account. Upon selecting the Email option, you are prompted to enter your e-mail address and name. In the next panel you specify either the POP or IMAP protocol and enter the name of the incoming e-mail server, such as **smtp.myemailserver.com**. You then specify an incoming user name, the user name given you by your e-mail service. Then you enter an account name label to identify the account on Thunderbird. A final verification screen lets you confirm your entries. In the Account Settings window you will see an entry for your news server, with panels for Server Settings, Copies & Folders, Composition & Addressing, Offline & Disk Space, Return Receipt, and Security. The Server Settings panel has entries for your server name, port, user name, and connection and task configurations such as automatically downloading new messages. The Security panel opens the Certificate Manager, where you can select security certificates to use to digitally sign or encrypt messages.

Thunderbird provides an address book where you can enter complete contact information, including e-mail addresses, street addresses, phone numbers, and notes. Select Address Book from the Tools menu to open the Address Book window. There are three panes, one for the address books available, one listing the address entries with field entries like name, e-mail, and organization, and one for displaying address information. You can sort the entries by these fields. Clicking an entry will display the address information, including e-mail address, street addresses, and phone. Only fields with values are displayed. To create a new entry in an address book, click New Card to open a window with panels for Contact and Address information. To create mailing lists from the address book entries, you click the New List button, specify the name of the list, and enter the e-mail addresses.

Once you have your address book set up, you can use its addresses when creating mail messages easily. On the Compose window, click the Contacts button to open a Contacts pane. Your address book entries will be listed using the contact's name. Just click the name to add it to the address box of your e-mail message. Alternatively, you can open the address book and drag and drop addresses to an address box on your message window.

A user's e-mail messages, addresses, and configuration information are kept in files located in the **.thunderbird** directory within the user's home directory. Backing up this information is as simple as making a copy of that directory. Messages for the different mail boxes are kept in a **Mail** subdirectory. If you are migrating to a new system, you can just copy the directory from the older system. To back up the mail for any given mail account, just copy the **Mail** subdirectory for that account. Though the default address books, **abook.mab** and **history.mab**, can be interchangeably copied, non-default address books need to be exported to an LDIF format and then imported to the new Thunderbird application. It is advisable to regularly export your address books to LDAP Data Interchange Format (LDIF) files as backups.

GNOME Mail Clients: Evolution, Sylpheed, and Others

Several GNOME-based mail clients are now available (see Table 7-2). These include Evolution, and Sylpheed (Evolution is included with Ubuntu). Check **www.gnomefiles.org** for more mail clients as they come out. Many are based on the GNOME mail client libraries (camel), which provides support for standard mail operations. As noted previously, Evolution is an integrated mail client, calendar, and contact manager from Novell. Sylpheed is a mail and news client with an interface similar to Windows mail clients. Claws-mail is an extended version of Sylpheed with many additional features (**www.claws-mail.org**).

Application	Description
Evolution	Integrated mail client, calendar, and contact manager
Sylpheed	Mail and news client similar to Windows clients
gnubiff	E-mail checker and notification tool
Mail Notification	E-mail checker and notification that works with numerous mail clients, including MH, Sylpheed, Gmail, Evolution, and Mail
Claws-mail	Extended version of sylpheed

Table 7-2: GNOME Mail Clients

The K Desktop Mail Client

The: KMail K Desktop mail client, KMail, provides a full-featured GUI interface for composing, sending, and receiving mail messages. KMail is now part of the KDE Personal Information Management suite, KDE-PIM, which also includes an address book (KAddressBook), an organizer and scheduler (KOrganizer), and a note writer (KNotes). All these components are also directly integrated on the desktop into Kontact. To start up KMail, you start the Kontact application. The KMail window displays three panes for folders, headers, and messages. The upper-left pane displays your mail folders. You have an inbox folder for received mail, an outbox folder for mail you have composed but have not sent yet, and a sent-mail folder for messages you have previously sent. You can create your own mail folders and save selected messages in them, if you wish. The top-right pane displays mail headers for the currently selected mail folder. To display a message, click its header. The message is then displayed in the large pane below the header list. You can also send and receive attachments, including binary files. Pictures and movies that are received are displayed using the appropriate K Desktop utility. If you right-click the message, a pop-up menu displays options for actions you may want to perform on it. You can move or copy it to another folder, or simply delete it. You can also compose a reply or forward the message. KMail, along with Kontact, KOrganizer, and KaddressBook, is accessible from the KDE Desktop, Office, and Internet menus.

To set up KMail for use with your mail accounts, you must enter account information. Select the Configure entry in the Settings menu. Several panels are available on the Settings window, which you can display by clicking their icons in the left column. For accounts, you select the Network panel. You may have more than one mail account on mail servers maintained by your ISP or LAN. A configure window is displayed where you can enter login, password, and host information. For secure access, KMail now supports the Secure Sockets Layer (SSL), provided OpenSSL is installed. Messages can now be encrypted and decoded by users. It also supports IMAP in addition to POP and SMTP protocols.

SquirrelMail

You Web Mail Client use the SquirrelMail Web mail tool to access mail on a Linux system using your Web browser. It will display a login screen for mail users. It features an inbox list and message reader, support for editing and sending new messages, and a plug-in structure for adding new features. You can find out more about SquirrelMail at **www.squirrelmail.org**. The Apache configuration file is **/etc/httpd/conf.d/squirrelmail.conf**, and SquirrelMail is installed in **/usr/share/squirrelmail**. Be sure that the IMAP mail server is also installed.

To configure SquirrelMail, you use the **config.pl** script in the **/usr/share/squirrelmail/config** directory. This displays a simple text-based menu where you can configure settings like the server to use, folder defaults, general options, and organizational preferences.

```
./config.pl
```

To access SquirrelMail, use the Web server address with the **/squirrelmail** extension, as in **localhost/squirrelmail** for users on the local system, or **www.mytrek.com/squirrelmail** for remote users.

Command Line Mail Clients

Several mail clients use a simple command line interface. They can be run without any other kind of support, such as the X Window System, desktops, or cursor support. They are simple and easy to use but include an extensive set of features and options. Two of the more widely used mail clients of this type are Mail and Mutt. Mail is the mailx mail client that was developed for the Unix system. It is considered a kind of default mail client that can be found on all Unix and Linux systems. Mutt is a cursor-based client that can be run from the command line.

Mutt

Mutt has an easy-to-use screen-based interface. Mutt has an extensive set of features, such as MIME support. You can find more information about Mutt from the Mutt Web site, **www.mutt.org**. Here you can download recent versions of Mutt and access online manuals and help resources. On most distributions, the Mutt manual is located in the **/usr/doc** directory under Mutt. The Mutt newsgroup is **comp.mail.mutt**, where you can post queries and discuss recent Mutt developments.

Mail

What is known now as the Mail utility was originally created for BSD Unix and called, simply, mail. Later versions of Unix System V adopted the BSD mail utility and renamed it mailx.

Now, it is simply referred to as Mail. Mail functions as a de facto default mail client on Unix and Linux systems. All systems have the mail client called Mail, whereas they may not have other mail clients.

To send a message with Mail, type `mail` along with the address of the person to whom you are sending the message. Press ENTER and you are prompted for a subject. Enter the subject of the message and press ENTER again. At this point, you are placed in input mode. Anything typed in is taken as the contents of the message. Pressing ENTER adds a new line to the text. When you finish typing your message, press CTRL-D on a line of its own to end the message. You will then be prompted to enter a user to whom to send a carbon copy of the message (Cc). If you do not want to send a carbon copy, just press ENTER. You will then see *EOT (end-of-transmission)* displayed after you press CTRL-D

You can send a message to several users at the same time by listing those users' addresses as arguments on the command line following the `mail` command. In the next example, the user sends the same message to both **chris** and **aleina**.

```
$ mail chris aleina
```

To receive mail, you enter only the `mail` command and press ENTER. This invokes a Mail shell with its own prompt and mail commands. A list of message headers is displayed. Header information is arranged into fields beginning with the status of the message and the message number. The status of a message is indicated by a single uppercase letter, usually **N** for *new* or **U** for *unread.* A message number, used for easy reference to your messages, follows the status field. The next field is the address of the sender, followed by the date and time the message was received, and then the number of lines and characters in the message. The last field contains the subject the sender gave for the message. After the headers, the Mail shell displays its prompt, an ampersand (**&**). At the Mail prompt, you enter commands that operate on the messages. An example of a Mail header and prompt follows:

```
$ mail
Mail version 8.1 6/6/93. Type ? for help.
"/var/spool/mail/larisa": 3 messages 2 unread
 1 chris@turtle.mytrek. Thu Jun 7 14:17 22/554 "trip"
>U 2 aleina@turtle.mytrek Thu Jun 7 14:18 22/525 "party"
 U 3 dylan@turtle.mytrek. Thu Jun 7 14:18 22/528 "newsletter"
& q
```

Mail references messages either through a message list or through the current message marker (**>**). The greater-than sign (**>**) is placed before a message considered the current message. The current message is referenced by default when no message number is included with a Mail command. You can also reference messages using a message list consisting of several message numbers. Given the messages in the preceding example, you can reference all three messages with **1-3**.

You use the **R** and **r** commands to reply to a message you have received. The **R** command entered with a message number generates a header for sending a message and then places you into the input mode to type in the message. The **q** command quits Mail. When you quit, messages you have already read are placed in a file called **mbox** in your home directory. Instead of saving messages in the **mbox** file, you can use the **s** command to save a message explicitly to a file of your choice. Mail has its own initialization file, called **.mailrc**, which is executed each time Mail is invoked, for either sending or receiving messages. Within it, you can define Mail options and create Mail aliases. You can set options that add different features to mail, such as changing the prompt or saving copies of messages you send. To define an alias, you enter the keyword `alias`, followed by the alias you have chosen and then the list of addresses it represents. In the next example, the alias `myclass` is defined in the **.mailrc** file.

```
alias myclass chris dylan aleina justin larisa
```

In the next example, the contents of the file **homework** are sent to all the users whose addresses are aliased by `myclass`.

```
$ mail myclass < homework
```

Notifications of Received Mail

As your mail messages are received, they are automatically placed in your mailbox file, but you are not automatically notified when you receive a message. You can use a mail client to retrieve any new messages, or you can use a mail monitor tool to tell you if you have any mail waiting. Several mail notification tools are also available, such as **gnubiff** and Mail Notification. Mail Notification will support Gmail, as well as Evolution (for Evolution, install the separate plug-in package). When you first log in after Mail Notification has been installed, the Mail Notification configuration window is displayed. Here you can add new mail accounts to check, such as Gmail accounts, as well as set other features like summary pop-ups. When you receive mail, a mail icon will appear in the notification applet of your panel. Move your cursor over it to check for any new mail. Clicking it will display the Mail Notification configuration window, though you can configure this to go directly to your e-mail application. **gnubiff** will notify you of any POP3 or IMAP mail arrivals.

The KDE Desktop has a mail monitor utility called Korn that works in much the same way. Korn shows an empty inbox tray when there is no mail and a tray with slanted letters in it when mail arrives. If old mail is still in your mailbox, letters are displayed in a neat square. You can set these icons as any image you want. You can also specify the mail client to use and the polling interval for checking for new mail. If you have several mail accounts, you can set up a Korn profile for each one. Different icons can appear for each account, telling you when mail arrives in one of them.

For command line interfaces, you can use the biff utility. The biff utility notifies you immediately when a message is received. This is helpful when you are expecting a message and want to know as soon as it arrives. Then biff automatically displays the header and beginning lines of messages as they are received. To turn on biff, you enter `biff y` on the command line. To turn it off, you enter `biff n`. To find out if biff is turned on, enter `biff` alone.

You can temporarily block biff by using the `mesg n` command to prevent any message displays on your screen. The `mesg n` command not only stops any Write and Talk messages, it also stops biff and Notify messages. Later, you can unblock biff with a `mesg y` command. A `mesg n` command comes in handy if you don't want to be disturbed while working on some project.

Accessing Mail on Remote POP Mail Servers

Most new mail clients are equipped to access mail accounts on remote servers. For such mail clients, you can specify a separate mail account with its own mailbox. For example, if you are using an ISP, most likely you will use that ISP's mail server to receive mail. You will have set up a mail account with a username and password for accessing your mail. Your e-mail address is usually your username and the ISP's domain name. For example, a username of **justin** for an ISP domain named **mynet.com** would have the address **justin@mynet.com**. The username would be **justin**. The address of the actual mail server could be something like **mail.mynet.com**. The user **justin** would log in to the **mail.mynet.com** server using the username **justin** and password to access mail sent to the address **justin@mynet.com**. Mail clients, such as Evolution, KMail, Sylpheed, and Thunderbird, enable you to set up a mailbox for such an account and access your ISP's mail server to check for and download received mail. You must specify what protocol a mail server uses. This is usually either the Post Office Protocol (POP) or the IMAP protocol (IMAP). This procedure is used for any remote mail server. Using a mail server address, you can access your account with your username and password.

Tip: Many mail clients, such as mutt and Thunderbird, support IMAP and POP directly.

Should you have several remote e-mail accounts, instead of creating separate mailboxes for each in a mail client, you can arrange to have mail from those accounts sent directly to the inbox maintained by your Linux system for your Linux account. All your mail, whether from other users on your Linux system or from remote mail accounts, will appear in your local inbox. Such a feature is helpful if you are using a mail client, such as Mail, that does not have the capability to access mail on your ISP's mail server. You can implement such a feature with Fetchmail. Fetchmail checks for mail on remote mail servers and downloads it to your local inbox, where it appears as newly received mail (you will have to be connected to the Internet or the remote mail server's network).

To use Fetchmail, you have to know a remote mail server's Internet address and mail protocol. Most remote mail servers use the POP3 protocol, but others may use the IMAP or POP2 protocols. Enter `fetchmail` on the command line with the mail server address and any needed options. The mail protocol is indicated with the **-p** option and the mail server type, usually POP3. If your e-mail username is different from your Linux login name, you use the **-u** option and the e-mail name. Once you execute the `fetchmail` command, you are prompted for a password. The syntax for the `fetchmail` command for a POP3 mail server follows:

```
fetchmail -p POP3 -u username mail-server
```

Connect to your ISP and then enter the `fetchmail` command with the options and the POP server name on the command line. You will see messages telling you if mail is there and, if so, how many messages are being downloaded. You can then use a mail client to read the messages from your inbox. You can run Fetchmail in daemon mode to have it automatically check for mail. You have to include an option specifying the interval in seconds for checking mail.

```
fetchmail -d 1200
```

You can specify options such as the server type, username, and password in a **.fetchmailrc** file in your home directory. You can also have entries for other mail servers and accounts you may have. Once it is configured, you can enter `fetchmail` with no arguments; it will read entries from your **.fetchmailrc** file. You can also make entries directly in the **.fetchmailrc** file. An entry in the **.fetchmailrc** file for a particular mail account consists of several fields and their values: poll, protocol, username, and password. *Poll* is used to specify the mail server name, and *protocol,* the type of protocol used. Notice you can also specify your password, instead of having to enter it each time Fetchmail accesses the mail server.

Mailing Lists

As an alternative to newsgroups, you can subscribe to mailing lists. Users on mailing lists automatically receive messages and articles sent to the lists. Mailing lists work much like a mail alias, broadcasting messages to all users on the list. Mailing lists were designed to serve small, specialized groups of people. Instead of posting articles for anyone to see, only those who subscribe receive them. Numerous mailing lists, as well as other subjects, are available for Linux. For example, at the **www.gnome.org** site, you can subscribe to any of several mailing lists on GNOME topics, such as **gnome-themes-list@gnome.org**, which deals with GNOME desktop themes. You can do the same at **lists.kde.org** for KDE topics. At **www.liszt.com**, you can search for mailing lists on various topics. By convention, to subscribe to a list, you send a request to the mailing list address with a –**request** term added to its username. For example, to subscribe to **gnome-themes-list@gnome.org**, you send a request to **gnome-themes-list-request@gnome.org**. At **www.linux.org**, on the Documentation page you can access a listing of mailing lists and submit subscriptions. Lists exist for such topics as the Linux kernel, administration, security, and different distributions. For example, **linux-admin** covers administration topics, and **linux-apps** discuses software applications; **http://vger.kernel.org** provides mailing list services for Linux kernel developers.

Note: You can use the Mailman and Majordomo programs to automatically manage your mailing lists. Mailman is the GNU mailing list manager, included with Ubuntu (**www.list.org**). You can find out more about Majordomo at **www.greatcircle.com/majordomo** and about Mailman at **www.sourceforge.net**.

Usenet News

Usenet is an open mail system on which users post messages that include news, discussions, and opinions. It operates like a mailbox that any user on your Linux system can read or send messages to. Users' messages are incorporated into Usenet files, which are distributed to any system signed up to receive them. Each system that receives Usenet files is referred to as a *site.* Certain sites perform organizational and distribution operations for Usenet, receiving messages from other sites and organizing them into Usenet files, which are then broadcast to many other sites. Such sites are called *backbone sites,* and they operate like publishers, receiving articles and organizing them into different groups.

To access Usenet news, you need access to a news server. A news server receives the daily Usenet newsfeeds and makes them accessible to other systems. Your network may have a system that operates as a news server. If you are using an Internet service provider (ISP), a news server is probably maintained by your ISP for your use. To read Usenet articles, you use a *newsreader*—a client program that connects to a news server and accesses the articles. On the Internet and in TCP/IP networks, news servers communicate with newsreaders using the Network News Transfer Protocol (NNTP) and are often referred to as NNTP news servers. Or you could also create your own news server on your Linux system to run a local Usenet news service or to download and maintain the full set of Usenet articles. Several Linux programs, called *news transport agents,* can be used to create such a server.

Usenet files were originally designed to function like journals. Messages contained in the files are referred to as *articles*. A user could write an article, post it in Usenet, and have it immediately distributed to other systems around the world. Someone could then read the article on Usenet, instead of waiting for a journal publication. Usenet files themselves were organized as journal publications. Because journals are designed to address specific groups, Usenet files were organized according to groups called *newsgroups*. When a user posts an article, it is assigned to a specific newsgroup. If another user wants to read that article, he or she looks at the articles in that newsgroup. You can think of each newsgroup as a constantly updated magazine. For example, to read articles on the Linux operating system, you would access the Usenet newsgroup on Linux. Usenet files are also used as bulletin boards on which people carry on debates. Again, such files are classified into newsgroups, though their articles read more like conversations than journal articles. You can also create articles of your own, which you can then add to a newsgroup for others to read. Adding an article to a newsgroup is called *posting* the article.

Linux has newsgroups on various topics. Some are for discussion, and others are sources of information about recent developments. On some, you can ask for help for specific problems. A selection of some of the popular Linux newsgroups is provided here:

Newsgroup	Topic
comp.os.linux.announce	Announcements of Linux developments
comp.os.linux.admin	System administration questions
comp.os.linux.misc	Special questions and issues
comp.os.linux.setup	Installation problems
comp.os.linux.help	Questions and answers for particular problems
linux.help	Obtain help for Linux problems

Newsreaders

You read Usenet articles with a newsreader, such as KNode, Pan, Mozilla, trn, or tin, which enables you to first select a specific newsgroup and then read the articles in it. A newsreader operates like a user interface, enabling you to browse through and select available articles for reading, saving, or printing. Most newsreaders employ a sophisticated retrieval feature called *threads* that pulls together articles on the same discussion or topic. Newsreaders are designed to operate using certain kinds of interfaces. For example, KNode is a KDE newsreader that has a KDE interface and is designed for the KDE desktop. Pan has a GNOME interface and is designed to operate on the GNOME desktop. Pine is a cursor-based newsreader, meaning that it provides a full-screen interface that you can work with using a simple screen-based cursor that you can move with arrow keys. It does not support a mouse or any other GUI feature. The **tin** program uses a simple command line interface with limited cursor support. Most commands you type in and press ENTER to execute. Several popular newsreaders are listed in Table 7-3.

Most newsreaders can read Usenet news provided on remote news servers that use the NNTP. Many such remote news servers are available through the Internet. Desktop newsreaders, such as KNode and Pan, have you specify the Internet address for the remote news server in their own configuration settings. Several shell-based newsreaders, however, such as trn and tin, obtain the news server's Internet address from the **NNTPSERVER** shell variable. Before you can connect to a remote news server with such newsreaders, you first have to assign the Internet address of the news server to the **NNTPSERVER** shell variable, and then export that variable. You can place the assignment and export of **NNTPSERVER** in a login initialization file, such as **.bash_profile**, so that it is performed automatically whenever you log in. Administrators could place this entry in the **/etc/profile** file for a news server available to all users on the system.

```
$ NNTPSERVER=news.domain.com
$ export NNTPSERVER
```

Newsreader	Description
Pan	GNOME Desktop newsreader
KNode	KDE Desktop newsreader
Thunderbird	Mail client with newsreader capabilities (X based)
Sylpheed	GNOME Windows-like newsreader
Slrn	Newsreader (cursor based)
Emacs	Emacs editor, mail client, and newsreader (cursor based)
trn	Newsreader (command line interface)
NewsBin	Newsreader (Windows version works under Wine)

Table 7-3: Linux Newsreaders

Newsbin under Wine

There is as yet not good binary based newsreader, one that can convert text messages to binary equivalents, like those found in **alt.binaries** newsgroups. One solution is to use the Windows version of the popular NewsBin newsreader running under Wine (Windows compatibility layer for Linux). You need to install Wine first. The current version of Newsbin runs stable and fast with Wine (you may need to use the video hardware drives for your graphics card).

You can download and install Wine using the Synaptic Package Manager. Then download and install Newsbin. The current version of Newsbin works on Wine and Ubuntu with no modifications needed. Newsbin will be accessible directly from an icon on your desktop as you would any application. It is advisable to disable the Message of the Day (MOTD) feature on the Options Advanced panel. You can save files directly on any Linux file system, as well as newsgroup downloads. The Autorar feature works effectively for binary files. Your entire Linux files system along with any mounted files systems is accessible as the **z:** drive. To test Par2 files for binaries you will need to also download and install QuickPar, another windows program the works effectively on Wine (**www.quickpar.org.uk**). QuickPar will be accessible from Newsbin.

slrn

The **slrn** newsreader is screen-based. Commands are displayed across the top of the screen and can be executed using the listed keys. Different types of screens exist for the newsgroup list, article list, and article content, each with its own set of commands. An initial screen lists your subscribed newsgroups with commands for posting, listing, and subscribing to your newsgroups. When you start slrn for the first time, you may have to create a **.jnewsrc** file in your home directory. Use the following command: `slrn -f .jnewsrc -create`. Also, you will have to set the `NNTPSERVER` variable and make sure it is exported.

The slrn newsreader features a new utility called **slrnpull** that you can use to automatically download articles in specified newsgroups. This allows you to view your selected newsgroups offline. The slrnpull utility was designed as a simple single-user version of Leafnode; it will access a news server and download its designated newsgroups, making them available through slrn whenever the user chooses to examine them. Newsgroup articles are downloaded to the `SLRNPULL_ROOT` directory. On Ubuntu, this is **/var/spool/srlnpull**. The selected newsgroups to be downloaded are entered in the **slrnpull.conf** configuration file placed in the `SLRNPULL_ROOT` directory. In this file, you can specify how many articles to download for each group and when they should expire. To use **slrn** with **slrnpull**, you will have to further configure the **.slrnrc** file to reference the **slrnpull** directories where newsgroup files are kept.

News Transport Agents

Usenet news is provided over the Internet as a daily newsfeed of articles and postings for thousands of newsgroups. This newsfeed is sent to sites that can then provide access to the news for other systems through newsreaders. These sites operate as news servers; the newsreaders used to access them are their clients. The news server software, called *news transport agents,* is what provides newsreaders with news, enabling you to read newsgroups and post articles. For Linux, three of the popular news transport agents are INN, Leafnode, and Cnews. Both Cnews and Leafnode are small and simple, and useful for small networks. INN is more powerful and complex, designed with large systems in mind (see **www.isc.org** for more details).

Daily newsfeeds on Usenet are often large and consume much of a news server's resources in both time and memory. For this reason, you may not want to set up your own Linux system to receive such newsfeeds. If you are operating in a network of Linux systems, you can designate one of them as the news server and install the news transport agent on it to receive and manage the Usenet newsfeeds. Users on other systems on your network can then access that news server with their own newsreaders.

If your network already has a news server, you needn't install a news transport agent at all. You only have to use your newsreaders to remotely access that server (see `NNTPSERVER` in the preceding section). In the case of an ISP, such providers often operate their own news servers, which you can also remotely access using your own newsreaders, such as KNode and Pan. Remember, though, that newsreaders must take the time to download the articles for selected newsgroups, as well as updated information on all the newsgroups.

You can also use news transport agents to run local versions of news for only the users on your system or your local network. To do this, install INN, Leafnode, slrnpull, or Cnews and configure them just to manage local newsgroups. Users on your system could then post articles and read local news.

8. Internet Applications

Web Clients

Web Browsers

The Mozilla Framework

Java for Linux

FTP Clients

Network File Transfer: FTP

Voice and Messenger Clients: VoIP, ICQ, IRC, and IM

Instant Messenger: Pidgin

VoIP: Ekiga and Skype

Ubuntu provides powerful Web and FTP clients for accessing the Internet. Many are installed automatically and are ready to use when you first start up your Linux system. Linux also includes full Java development support, letting you run and construct Java applets. This chapter will cover some of the more popular Web, Java, and FTP clients available on Linux. Web and FTP clients connect to sites that run servers, using Web pages and FTP files to provide services to users. There are also network tools for obtaining network information or setting up messaging connections, like Pidgin for Instant Messages (IM) and Ekiga for Voice over Internet Protocol (VoIP) connections.

Web Clients

The World Wide Web (WWW or the Web) is a hypertext database of different types of information, distributed across many different sites on the Internet. A *hypertext database* consists of items linked to other items, which, in turn, may be linked to yet other items, and so on. Upon retrieving an item, you can use that item to retrieve any related items. For example, you could retrieve an article on the Amazon rain forest and then use it to retrieve a map or a picture of the rain forest. In this respect, a hypertext database is like a web of interconnected data you can trace from one data item to another. Information is displayed in pages known as *Web pages.* On a Web page, certain keywords or graphics are highlighted that form links to other Web pages or to items, such as pictures, articles, or files.

On your Linux system, you can choose from several Web browsers, including Firefox, Konqueror, Epiphany, and Lynx. Firefox, Konqueror, and Epiphany are X Window System–based browsers that provide full picture, sound, and video display capabilities. Most distributions also include the Lynx browser, a line-mode browser that displays only lines of text. The K Desktop incorporates Web browser capabilities into its file manager, letting a directory window operate as a Web browser. GNOME-based browsers, such as Express and Mnemonic, are also designed to be easily enhanced.

Web browsers and FTP clients are commonly used to conduct secure transactions such as logging in to remote sites, ordering items, or transferring files. Such operations are currently secured by encryption methods provided by the Secure Sockets Layer (SSL). If you use a browser for secure transactions, it should be SSL enabled. Most browsers such as Mozilla and ELinks include SSL support. For FTP operations, you can use the SSH version of ftp, **sftp**, or the Kerberos 5 version. Linux distributions include SSL as part of a standard installation.

URL Addresses

An Internet resource is accessed using a Universal Resource Locator (URL). A URL is composed of three elements: the transfer protocol, the hostname, and the pathname. The transfer protocol and the hostname are separated by a colon and two slashes, **://**. The *pathname* always begins with a single slash:

`transfer-protocol://host-name/path-name`

The *transfer protocol* is usually HTTP (Hypertext Transfer Protocol), indicating a Web page. Other possible values for transfer protocols are **ftp**, and **file**. As their names suggest, **ftp** initiates FTP sessions, whereas **file** displays a local file on your own system, such as a text or HTML file. Table 8-1 lists the various transfer protocols.

Protocol	Description
`http`	Uses Hypertext Transfer Protocol for Web site access.
`ftp`	Uses File Transfer Protocol for FTP connections.
`fish`	Uses File Transfer Protocol using SSH secure connections
`telnet`	Makes a Telnet connection.
`news`	Reads Usenet news; uses Network News Transfer Protocol (NNTP).

Table 8-1: Web Protocols

The *hostname* is the computer on which a particular Web site is located. You can think of this as the address of the Web site. By convention, most hostnames begin with **www**. In the next example, the URL locates a Web page called **guides.html** on the **www.tldp.org** Web site:

```
http://tldp.org/guides.html
```

File Type	Description
`.html`	Web page document formatted using HTML, the Hypertext Markup Language
Graphics Files	
`.gif`	Graphics, using GIF compression
`.jpeg`	Graphics, using JPEG compression
`.png`	Graphics, using PNG compression (Portable Network Graphics)
Sound Files	
`.au`	Sun (Unix) sound file
`.wav`	Microsoft Windows sound file
`.aiff`	Macintosh sound file
Video Files	
`.QT`	QuickTime video file, multiplatform
`.mpeg`	Video file
`.avi`	Microsoft Windows video file

Table 8-2: Web File Types

If you do not want to access a particular Web page, you can leave the file reference out, and then you automatically access the Web site's home page. To access a Web site directly, use its hostname. If no home page is specified for a Web site, the file **index.html** in the top directory is often used as the home page. In the next example, the user brings up the GNOME home page:

```
http://www.gnome.org/
```

The pathname specifies the directory where the resource can be found on the host system, as well as the name of the resource's file. For example, **/pub/Linux/newdat.html** references an HTML document called **newdat** located in the **/pub/Linux** directory.

The resource file's extension indicates the type of action to be taken on it. A picture has a **.gif** or **.jpeg** extension and is converted for display. A sound file has an **.au** or **.wav** extension and is played. The following URL references a **.gif** file. Instead of displaying a Web page, your browser invokes a graphics viewer to display the picture. Table 8-2 provides a list of the more common file extensions.

```
http://www.train.com/engine/engine1.gif
```

Enabling Flash plugin

Ubuntu includes two free and open source versions of Flash: **swfdec** and **gnash**. It is preferable that you try these before trying to use the version provided directly by Adobe. The **swfdec** version is newer.

Adobe only provides a 32 bit version of Flash for Linux. To use the Adobe version of Flash on a 64 bit system you have to first install the 32bit **nspluginwrapper** packages for both **x86_64** and **i386** platforms, as well as the **pulseaudio-libs** package for the **i386** platform. Be sure to create a /usr/lib/mozilla/plugins directory. Then install the Adobe plugin. You can then run the **mozilla-plugin-config -i -g -v** to register the plugin.

Web Browsers

Most Web browsers are designed to access several different kinds of information. Web browsers can access a Web page on a remote Web site or a file on your own system. Some browsers can also access a remote news server or an FTP site. The type of information for a site is specified by the keyword **http** for Web sites, **nntp** for news servers, **ftp** for FTP sites, or **file** for files on your own system. As noted previously, several popular browsers are available for Linux. Three distinctive ones are described here: Mozilla, Konqueror, and Lynx. Mozilla is an X Window System–based Web browser capable of displaying graphics, video, and sound, as well as operating as a newsreader and mailer. Konqueror is the K Desktop file manager. KDE has integrated full Web-browsing capability into the Konqueror file manager, letting you seamlessly access the Web and your file system with the same application. Lynx and ELinks are command line–based browsers with no graphics capabilities, but in every other respect they are fully functional Web browsers.

To search for files on FTP sites, you can use search engines provided by Web sites, such as Yahoo! or Google. These usually search for both Web pages and FTP files. To find a particular Web page you want on the Internet, you can use any of these search engines or perform searches from any number of Web portals. Web searches have become a standard service of most Web sites. Searches carried out on documents within a Web site may use local search indexes set up and maintained by indexing programs like ht:/Dig. Sites using ht:/Dig use a standard Web page search interface. Hypertext databases are designed to access any kind of data, whether it is text, graphics, sound, or even video. Whether you can actually access such data depends to a large extent on the type of browser you use.

Note: Ubuntu now includes a free open source Flash plugin from swfdec

The Mozilla Framework

The Mozilla project is an open source project based on the original Netscape browser code that provides a development framework for Web-based applications, primarily the Web browser and e-mail client. Originally, the aim of the Mozilla project was to provide an end-user Web browser called Mozilla. Its purpose has since changed to providing a development framework that anyone can use to create Web applications, though the project also provides its own. Table 8-3 lists some Mozilla resources.

Currently the framework is used for Mozilla products like the Firefox Web browser and the Thunderbird mail client, as well for non-Mozilla products like the Netscape, Epiphany, and Galleon Web browsers. In addition, the framework is easily extensible, supporting numerous add-ons in the form of plug-ins and extensions. The Mozilla project site is **www.mozilla.org**, and the site commonly used for plug-in and extension development is **www.mozdev.org**.

Web Site	Description
`www.mozilla.org`	The Mozilla project
`www.mozdev.org`	Mozilla plug-ins and extensions
`www.oreillynet.com/mozilla`	Mozilla documentation and news
`www.mozillazine.org`	Mozilla news and articles
`www.mozillanews.org`	Mozilla news and articles
`www.bugzilla.org`	Mozilla bug reporting and tracking system

Table 8-3: Mozilla Resources

The first-generation product of the Mozilla project was the Mozilla Web browser, which is still available. Like the original Netscape, it included a mail client and newsreader, all in one integrated interface. The second generation products have split this integrated package into separate stand-alone applications, the Firefox Web browser and the Thunderbird e-mail/newsreader client. Also under development is the Camino Web browser for Mac OS X and the Sunbird calendar application.

In 1998, Netscape made its source code freely available under the Netscape Public License (NPL). Mozilla is developed on an open source model much like Linux, KDE, and GNOME. Developers can submit modifications and additions over the Internet to the Mozilla Web site. Mozilla releases are referred to as Milestones. Mozilla products are currently released under both the NPL license for modifications of Mozilla code and the MPL license (Mozilla Public License) for new additions.

The Firefox Web Browser

Firefox is the next generation of browsers based on the Netscape core source code known as Mozilla (see Figure 8-1). In current releases, Ubuntu uses Firefox as its primary browser. Firefox is a streamlined browser featuring fast web access. Firefox is based on the Netscape core source code known as mozilla. Firefox is an X Window System application you can operate from any desktop, including GNOME, KDE, and XFce. Firefox is installed by default with both a menu entry in the Main menu's Internet menu and an icon on the different desktop panels. When opened, Firefox displays an area at the top of the screen for entering a URI address and a Navigation toolbar with series of buttons for various web page operations. Menus on the top menu bar provide access to such Firefox features as Tools, View, History, and Bookmarks. A status bar at the bottom shows the state of the current page.

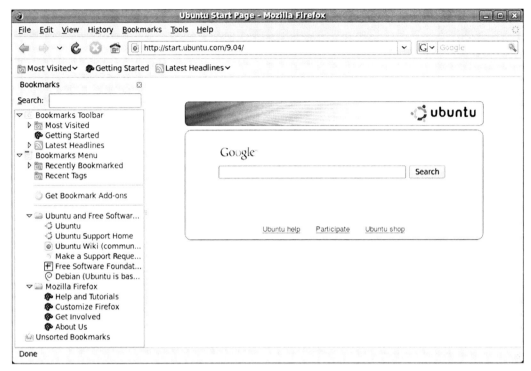

Figure 8-1: Firefox Web Browser

To the right of the URI box is a search box where you can use different search engines for searching the Web, selected sites, or particular items. A pop-up menu lets you select a search engine. Currently included are Google, Yahoo, Amazon, and eBay, along with Dictionary.com for looking up word definitions. Firefox also features button links and tabbed pages. You can drag the URI from the URI box to the button link bar to create a button with which to quickly access the site. Use this for frequently accessed sites.

For easy browsing, Firefox features tabbed panels for displaying web pages. To open an empty tabbed panel, press CTRL-T or select New Tab from the File menu. To display a page in that panel, drag it's URL from the URL box or from the bookmark list to the panel. You can have several panels open at once, moving from one page to the next by clicking their tabs. You can elect to open all your link buttons as tabbed panels by right-clicking the link bar and selecting Open In Tabs.

Tip: Right-clicking on the Web page background displays a pop-up menu with options for most basic operations like page navigation, saving and sending pages,

To search a current page for certain text, enter CTRL-F key. This opens a search toolbar at the bottom of Firefox where you can enter a search term. You have search options to highlight found entries or to match character case. Next and Previous buttons let you move to the next found pattern.

When you download a file using Firefox, the download is managed by the Download Manager. You can download several files at once. Downloads can be displayed in the Download

Manager toolbar. You can cancel a download at any time, or just pause a download, resuming it later. Right-clicking a download entry will display the site it was downloaded from as well as the directory you saved it in. To remove an entry, click Remove from toolbar.

Firefox Bookmarks and History

Firefox refers to the URIs of web pages you want to keep as *bookmarks,* marking pages you want to access directly. The Bookmarks menu enables you add your favorite web pages. You can also press CTRL-T to add a bookmark. You can then view a list of your bookmarks and select one to view. You can also edit your list, adding new ones or removing old ones. When adding a bookmark an Add Bookmark window opens with a pop-up menu for folders and tags. The Folder menu is set to Bookmarks folder by default. You can also select the Bookmarks Toolbar or unfilled bookmarks.

History is a list of previous URIs you have accessed. The URI box also features a pop-up menu listing your previous history sites. Bookmarks and History can be viewed as sidebars, selectable from the View menu.

Firefox also features Bookmark toolbar. Use this for frequently accessed sites. The Bookmark toolbar is displayed just above the Web page. You can drag the URI from the URI box to the Bookmark toolbar to create a button with which to quickly access the site. Buttons can also be folders, containing button links for several pages. Clicking on a folder button will display the button links in a pop-up menu. You can also right-click on the Bookmark toolbar to display a pop-up menu with entries for adding a bookmark and creating a new folder. Entries include an "Open all in Tabs", letting you open a whole group of commonly used Web pages at once.

To manage your bookmarks, click on the Show all bookmarks entry in the Bookmarks menu. This opens the Library window with bookmark folders displayed in a sidebar. Bookmarks in a folder are shown in the upper right panel, and properties for a selected bookmark in that list are displayed in the lower right panel. The Organize menu has an option to create a new folder. The View menu lets you sort your bookmarks. The Import and Backup menu has options to save backups of your bookmark, as well as export your bookmark for use on other systems using Firefox. You can also import exported Firefox bookmarks from other systems.

Bookmarks also maintains a Smart Bookmarks folder that keeps a list of Most Visited, Recently Bookmarked, and Recent Tags. This lets you easily find sites you visit most often, or ones you consider important.

Firefox supports live bookmarks. A live bookmark connects to a site that provides a live RSS feed. This is a page that is constantly being updated, like a news site. Live bookmarks are indicated by a live bookmark icon to the right of its URI. Click on this icon or select Subscribe to this Page from the Bookmark menu, to subscribe to the site. A pop-up menu is displayed in the main window with the prompt "Subscribe to this feed using". Live Bookmarks is selected by default, but you can also choose MY Yahoo, Bloglines, or Google. You can also choose to Always use Live bookmarks for feeds. You can then click Subscribe Now to set up the live bookmark. This opens a dialog where you can choose to place the live bookmark, either in the Bookmark menu, or on the Bookmark toolbar. In the Bookmark toolbar, the live bookmark becomes a pop-up menu listing the active pages, with an entry at the end for the main site.

When you click on the live bookmark either in the Bookmark toolbar or the live bookmark icon in its URI entry, a list of active pages is displayed. An "Open all in Tabs" entry at the bottom of the listing lets you open all the active pages at once. News pages on a site are often RSS feeds that you can set up as a live bookmark. At the Ubuntu site (**www.ubuntu.com**) many of the News links can be subscribed to as live bookmarks, like the Canonical Blog, the Fridge, and Planet Ubuntu. When you select a subscribed site on the bookmark menu, a submenu of active pages is displayed that you can choose from. On Ubuntu, the BBC site is a live bookmark available from the Latest Headlines Bookmark Toolbar button.

Firefox Configuration

The Preferences menu (Edit | Preferences) in Firefox enables you to set several different options. There are preference panels for Main, Tabs, Content, Applications, Privacy, Security, and Advanced (see Figure 8-2). On the Main panel you can set you home page, download options, and access add-on management. Tabs control tab opening and closing behavior. Content sets you set the font and fond size, as well as color and language to use. You can also block pop-ups and enable java. Applications associate content with applications to run it, like video or mp3. Privacy controls history, cookies, and private data. Security is where you can remember passwords and set warning messages. The Advanced panel has several panels: General, Network, Update, and Encryption. The General panel provides features like spell checking, and keyboard navigation. The Network panel has a Setting button for the Connection feature which is where you set up your network connections such as the direct connection to the internet or proxy settings. Here you can also set up offline storage size. The encryption panel is where you can manage certificates, setting up validation methods, viewing, and revocation.

Figure 8-2: Firefox Preferences

If you are on a network that connects to the Internet through a firewall, you must use the Proxies screen to enter the address of your network's firewall gateway computer. A *firewall* is a computer that operates as a controlled gateway to the Internet for your network. Several types of firewalls exist. The most restrictive kinds of firewalls use programs called *proxies,* which receive Internet requests from users and then make those requests on their behalf. There is no direct connection to the Internet.

Firefox also support profiles. You can set up different Firefox configurations, each with preferences and bookmarks. This is useful for computers like laptops that may connect to different networks or used for different purposes. You can select and create Profiles by starting up the profile manager. Enter the **firefox** command in a terminal window with the -P option.

```
firefox -P
```

A default profile is already set up. You can create a new profile which runs the profile wizard to prompt you for the profile name and directory to use. Select a profile to use and click Start Firefox. The last profile you used will be used up the next time you start Firefox. You have the option to prompt for the profile to use at start up, otherwise run the **firefox -P** command again to change your profile.

Add-on Management button, on the Preferences Main panel, opens a window with panels for Extensions, Themes, and Plugins. From the Add-ons window you can select the get Add-ons panel to link to the Add-ons sties and to load Ubuntu Extensions. The Get Ubuntu Extensions links opens an Install/Remove Extension window listing available extension packages designed to work well with Ubuntu. Check the ones you want and click Apply Changes. The Plugins panel lists all your current plugins, letting you enable or disable them (see Figure 8-3).

Figure 8-3: Firefox Add-ons Management

The K Desktop Web Browser: Konqueror

If you are using the K Desktop, you can use the Konqueror Web browser. It can display Web pages, including graphics and links. The K Desktop's file manager supports standard Web page operation, such as moving forward and backward through accessed pages. Clicking a link accesses and displays the Web page referenced. In this respect, the Web becomes seamlessly integrated into the K Desktop (see Chapter 10).

GNOME Web Browsers: Epiphany

Several GNOME-based Web browsers are also available. Epiphany, Galeon, and Kazehakase support standard Web operations. Epiphany is a GNOME Web browser designed to be fast with a simple interface (see Figure 8-4). The Bookmarks menu will hold entries for Ubuntu and Free Content sites like the Ubuntu Forum and Wikipedia. You can find out more about Epiphany at **http://epiphany.mozdev.org**. Epiphany is included with Ubuntu. Epiphany works well as a simple browser with a clean interface. It is also integrated with the desktop, featuring a download applet that will continue even after closing Epiphany.

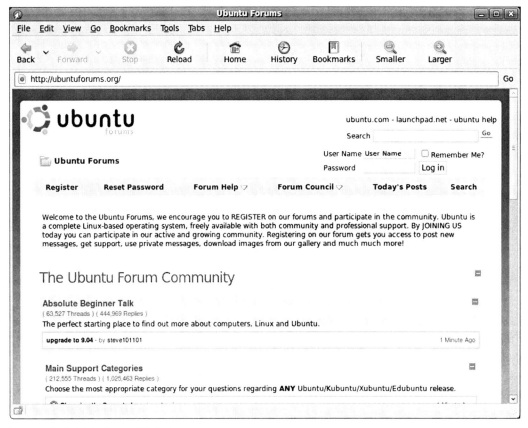

Figure 8-4: Epiphany Web browser

Epiphany also supports tabbed panels for multiple Web site access. Galeon is a fast, light browser also based on the Mozilla browser engine (Gecko). Kazehakase emphasizes a customizable interface with download boxes and RSS bookmarks.

For GNOME, you can also download numerous support tools, such as the RSSOwl to display news feeds and the GNOME Download Manager (Gwget) for controlling Web-based downloads.

Lynx and ELinks: Line-Mode Browsers

Lynx is a line-mode browser you can use without the X Window System. A Web page is displayed as text only. A text page can contain links to other Internet resources but does not display any graphics, video, or sound. Except for the display limitations, Lynx is a fully functional Web browser. You can also use Lynx to download files or access local pages. All information on the Web is still accessible to you. Because it does not require much of the overhead that graphics-based browsers need, Lynx can operate much faster, quickly displaying Web page text. To start the Lynx browser, you enter **lynx** on the command line and press ENTER.

Another useful text-based browser shipped with most distributions is ELinks. ELinks is a powerful screen-based browser that includes features such as frame, form, and table support. It also supports SSL secure encryption. To start ELinks, enter the **elinks** command in a terminal window.

Java for Linux

To develop Java applications, use Java tools, and run many Java products, you must install the Java 2 Software Development Kit (SDK) and the Java 2 Runtime Environment (JRE) on your system. The SDK is a superset of the JRE, adding development tools like compilers and debuggers. Together with other technologies like the Java API, they make up the Java 2 Platform, Standard Edition (J2SE).

Sun has open sourced Java as the OpenJDK. Sun supports and distributes Linux versions of this product. The JRE subset can be installed as OpenJRE. They are directly supported by Ubuntu as packages on the main repository. You can install them with the Synaptic Package Manager. On Ubuntu, use **openjdk-6-jre** to install the Java runtime environment, and **openjdk-6-jdk** to install both the JRE and Java the development tools. Java packages and applications are listed in Table 8-4.

The compatible set of GNU packages (Java-like) are provided that allows you to run Java applets using GNU free Java support. This collection provides a GNU licensed and open source environment, consisting of three packages: GNU Java compiler (**gcj**), the Eclipse Java compiler (**ecj**), and a set of wrappers and links (**java-gcj-compat**). They are available as part of the Ubuntu main repository. Use the **gcj-web-plugin** for supporting JAVA in Web browsers.

You can also download and install the Sun version of the JRE, now included in the Ubuntu multiverse repository. Use the Synaptic Package Manager and search on "sun-java5", like the **sun-java6-jdk** and **sun-java5-jdk** packages. These are Debian versions packaged for installation on Ubuntu (Mulitverse development repository). Alternatively, you could download and install the JRE and SDK directly from Sun (**www.java.com**). The SDK and JRE are available in the form of self-extracting compressed archives, **.bin**.

Application	Description
Java Development Kit, OpenJDK	An open source Java development environment with a compiler, interpreters, debugger, and more (include the JRE), **http://openjdk.java.net**. Included on the Ubuntu main repository **openjdk-6-jdk**
Java Runtime Environment, OpenJRE	An open source Java runtime environment, including the Java virtual machine, included on the Ubuntu main repository, **openjdk-6-jre**. **www.java.com**
Java Platform Standard Edition (JSE)	Complete Java collection, including JRE, JDK, and API, **http://java.sun.com/javase**.
Java-like environment	The Java-like Free and Open Environment, consisting of the GNU Java runtime (libgcj), the Eclipse Java compiler (ecj), and supporting wrappers and links (**java-gcj-compat**). Included on Ubuntu main repository.
Java System Web Server	A Web server implemented with Java. Available at Java Web site at **http://java.sun.com**. (commercial).
GNU Java Compiler	GNU Public Licensed Java Compiler (GCJ) to compile Java programs, **http://gcc.gnu.org/java**. Included on Ubuntu main repository, **gcj**.
Jakarta Project	Apache Software Foundation project for open source Java applications, **http://jakarta.apache.org**.
CACAO	A just-in-time (jit) compiler only implementation of the Java Virtual Machine (JVM), included on the Ubuntu main repository, **cacao-oj6-jdk**, .**www.cacaojvm.org**.
Classpath	GNU license Java open source libraries, Universe repository, **www.gnu.org/software/classpath**

Table 8-4: Java Packages and Java Web Applications

Also available is CACAO, the open source GNU licensed Java Virtual Machine that uses the compiler only, instead of the interpreter, **cacao-oj6-jre** and **cacao-oj6-jdk** (**www.cacaojvm.org**). CACAO is supported directly on the Ubuntu main respository.

For those that want an entire open source and GNU licensed version of the Java libraries, you can install the classpath Java libraries, also available on the Universe repository, **www.gnu.org/software/classpath**.

Note: Numerous additional Java-based products and tools are currently adaptable for Linux. Many of the products such as the Java web server run directly as provided by Sun. You can download several directly from the Sun Java website at **http://java.sun.com**.

Sun now provides an open source development environment called Iced Tea designed for developing completely open source Java applications (OpenJDK). OpenJDK provides a Java development platform for entirely open source Java applications. Detailed descriptions of features can be found in the SDK documentation, **http://java.sun.com/docs**.

BitTorrent Clients (transmission)

GNOME and KDE provide several very effective BitTorrent clients. With BitTorrent you can download very large files quickly in a shared distributed download operation where several users participate in downloading different parts of a file, sending their parts of the download to other participants, known as peers. Instead of everyone trying to access a few central servers, all peers participating in the BitTorrent operation become sources for the file being downloaded. Certain peers function as seeders, those who have already downloaded the file, but continue to send parts to those who need them.

Ubuntu will install and use the GNOME BitTorrent client, Transmission (Applications | Internet | Transmission BitTorrent Client). For KUbuntu you can use the Ktorrent BitTorrent client. To perform a BitTorrent download you need the BitTorrent file for the file you want to download. The BitTorrent file for the Ubuntu Alternate CD iso image is **ubuntu-9.04-alternate-amd64.iso.torrent**. When you download the file from the **http://releases.ubuntu.com** site, you will be prompted to either open it directly with Transmission or save it to a file.

Transmission can handle several torrents at once. On the toolbar are buttons for starting, pausing, and remove a download. The Add button can be used to load a BitTorrent file (**.torrent**), setting up a download. When you first open a torrent file, the Torrent Options window opens where you can specify the destination folder and the priority. The option to start the download automatically will be selected by default. Figure 8-5 shows Transmission with two BitTorrent operations set up, one of which is active. A progress bar shows how much of the file has been downloaded.

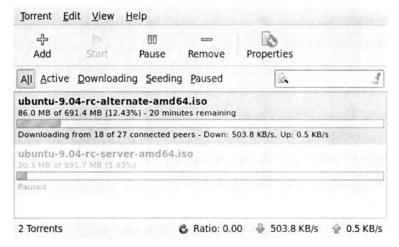

Figure 8-5: Transmission BitTorrent client

You could set up Transmission to manage several BitTorrents, of which only a few many be active, others paused, and still others that have finished but continue to functions as seeders. There are display buttons for All, Active, Downloading, Seeding, and Paused torrents.

To see more information about a torrent, select it and then click the Details button. This opens a Details window with tabs for Activity, Peers, Tracker, Information, Files, and Options. Activity shows statistics like the progress, times, and errors. Peers show all the peers participating in the download. Tracker displays the location of the tracker, the server that manages the torrent operation. Files shows the progress of the file download (a torrent could download more than one file). Information shows description, origin, and locations of the download folder and torrent file. The Options tab lets you set bandwidth and connection parameters, limiting the download or upload, and the number of peers.

FTP Clients

With FTP clients, you can connect to a corresponding FTP site and download files from it. FTP clients are commonly used to download software from public FTP sites that operate as software repositories. Most Linux software applications can be downloaded to your Linux system from such sites. These sites feature anonymous logins that let any user access their files. Basic FTP client capabilities are incorporated into the Konqueror (KDE) and Nautilus (GNOME) file managers. You can use a file manager window to access an FTP site and drag files to local directories to download them. Effective FTP clients are also now incorporated into most Web browsers, making Web browsers a primary downloading tool. Firefox in particular has strong FTP download capabilities.

Though file managers and Web browsers provide effective access to public (anonymous login) sites, to access private sites, you may need a stand-alone FTP client like curl, wget, gFTP or **ftp**. These clients let you enter user names and passwords with which you can access a private FTP site. The stand-alone clients are also useful for large downloads from public FTP sites, especially those with little or no Web display support. Popular Linux FTP clients are listed in Table 8-5.

FTP Clients	Description
Firefox	Mozilla Web and FTP browser
Konqueror	K Desktop file manager
Nautilus	GNOME file manager
gFTP	GNOME FTP client, **gftp-gtk**
ftp	Command line FTP client
lftp	Command line FTP client capable of multiple connections
NcFTP	Screen-based FTP client
curl	Internet transfer client (FTP and HTTP)

Table 8-5: Linux FTP Clients

Network File Transfer: FTP

With File Transfer Protocol (FTP) clients you can transfer extremely large files directly from one site to another. FTP can handle both text and binary files. This is one of the TCP/IP protocols, and it operates on systems connected to networks that use the TCP/IP protocols, such as the Internet. FTP performs a remote login to another account on another system connected to you on a network. Once logged in to that other system, you can transfer files to and from it. To log in, you need to know the login name and password for the account on the remote system. For example, if you have accounts at two different sites on the Internet, you can use FTP to transfer files from one to the other. Many sites on the Internet allow public access using FTP, however. Such sites serve as depositories for large files anyone can access and download. These sites are often referred to as *FTP sites,* and in many cases, their Internet addresses begin with the word *ftp,* such as **ftp.gnome.org**. These public sites allow anonymous FTP login from any user. For the login name, you use the word "anonymous," and for the password, you use your email address. You can then transfer files from that site to your own system.

You can perform FTP operations using any one of a number of FTP client programs. For Linux systems, you can choose from several FTP clients. Many now operate using GUI interfaces such as GNOME. Some, such as Firefox, have limited capabilities, whereas others, such as NcFTP, include an extensive set of enhancements. The original FTP client is just as effective, though not as easy to use. It operates using a simple command line interface and requires no GUI or cursor support, as do other clients.

The Internet has a great many sites open to public access that contain files anyone can obtain using file transfer programs. Unless you already know where a file is located, however, finding it can be difficult. To search for files on FTP sites, you can use search engines provided by websites, such as Yahoo! or Google. For Linux software, you can check sites such as **www.freshmeat.net, www.sourceforge.net**, **www.kde-apps.org**, and **www.gnome.org**. These sites usually search for both web pages and FTP files.

Web Browser–Based FTP: Firefox

You access an FTP site and download files from it with any Web browser. A Web browser is effective for checking out an FTP site to see what files are listed there. When you access an FTP site with a Web browser, the entire list of files in a directory is listed as a Web page. You can move to a subdirectory by clicking its entry. With Firefox, you can easily browse through an FTP site to download files. To download a file with Firefox, click the download link. This will start the transfer operation, opening a box for selecting your local directory and the name for the file. The default name is the same as on the remote system. You can manage your downloads with the download manager, which will let you cancel a download operation in progress or remove other downloads requested. The manager will show the time remaining, the speed, and the amount transferred for the current download. Browsers are useful for locating individual files, though not for downloading a large set of files, as is usually required for a system update.

The KDE File Managers: Konqueror and Dolphin

On the KDE Desktop, the desktop file managers (Konqueror and Dolphin) have built-in FTP capability. The FTP operation has been seamlessly integrated into standard desktop file operations. Downloading files from an FTP site is as simple as copying files by dragging them from one directory window to another, but one of the directories happens to be located on a remote FTP site. On KDE, you can use a file manager window to access a remote FTP site. Files in the remote directory are listed just as your local files are. To download files from an FTP site, you open a window to access that site, entering the URL for the FTP site in the window's location box. Use the **ftp://** protocol for FTP access. You can also use the **fish://** protocol for FTP access using SSH secure connections. Once connected, open the directory you want, and then open another window for the local directory to which you want the remote files copied. In the window showing the FTP files, select the ones you want to download. Then simply click and drag those files to the window for the local directory. A pop-up menu appears with choices for Copy, Link, or Move. Select Copy.

The selected files are then downloaded. Another window then opens, showing the download progress and displaying the name of each file in turn, along with a bar indicating the percentage downloaded so far.

GNOME Desktop FTP: Nautilus

The easiest way to download files is to use the built-in FTP capabilities of the GNOME file manager, Nautilus. On GNOME, the desktop file manager—Nautilus—has a built-in FTP capability much like the KDE file manager. The FTP operation has been seamlessly integrated into standard desktop file operations. Downloading files from an FTP site is as simple as dragging files from one directory window to another, where one of the directories happens to be located on a remote FTP site. Use the GNOME file manager to access a remote FTP site, listing files in the remote directory, just as local files are. Just enter the FTP URL following the prefix **ftp://** and press ENTER. The top directory of the remote FTP site will be displayed. Simply use the file manager to progress through the remote FTP site's directory tree until you find the file you want. Then open another window for the local directory to which you want the remote files copied. In the window showing the FTP files, select those you want to download. Then CTRL-click and drag those files to the window for the local directory. CTRL-clicking performs a copy operation, not a move. As files are downloaded, a dialog window appears showing the progress.

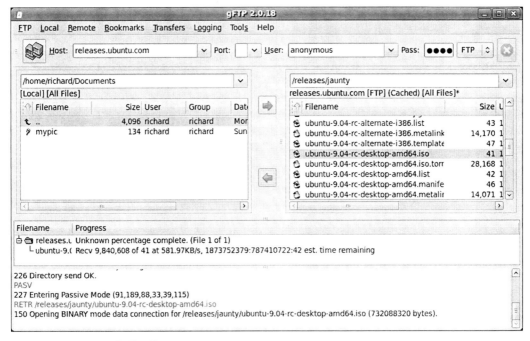

Figure 8-6: gFTP FTP client

gFTP

The gFTP program is a simpler GNOME FTP client designed to let you make standard FTP file transfers (see Figure 8-6). The package name for gFTP is **gftp-gtk**, located in the Ubuntu main repository. The gFTP window consists of several panes. The top-left pane lists files in your local directory, and the top-right pane lists your remote directory. Subdirectories have folder icons preceding their names. The parent directory can be referenced by the double period entry (..) with an up arrow at the top of each list. Double-click a directory entry to access it. The pathnames for all directories are displayed in boxes above each pane. You can enter a new pathname for a different directory to change to it, if you want.

Two buttons between the panes are used for transferring files. The left arrow button, <-, downloads selected files in the remote directory, and the right arrow button, ->, uploads files from the local directory. To download a file, click it in the right-side pane and then click the left arrow button, <-. When the file is downloaded, its name appears in the left pane, your local directory. Menus across the top of the window can be used to manage your transfers. A connection manager enables you to enter login information about a specific site. You can specify whether to perform an anonymous login or to provide a username and password. Click Connect to connect to that site. A drop-down menu for sites enables you to choose the site you want. Interrupted downloads can be restarted easily.

wget

The wget tool lets you easily access Web and FTP sites for particular directories and files. Directories can be recursively downloaded, letting you copy an entire Web site. **wget** takes as its option the URL for the file or directory you want. Helpful options include **-q** for quiet, **-r** for recursive (directories), **-b** to download in the background, and **-c** to continue downloading an interrupted file. One of the drawbacks is that your URL reference can be very complex. You have to know the URL already. You cannot interactively locate an item as you would with an FTP client. The following would download the Ubuntu Install DVD in the background.

```
wget -b  ftp://cdimages.ubuntu.com/dvd/currnet/jaunty-dvd-amd64.iso
```

TIP: With the Gnome Wget tool you can run wget downloads using a GUI interface.

curl

The **curl** Internet client operates much like wget, but with much more flexibility. With curl you can specify multiple URLs on its command line. You can also use braces to specify multiple matching URLs, like different Web sites with the same domain name. You can list the different Web site host names within braces, followed by their domain name (or visa versa). You can also use brackets to specify a range of multiple items. This can be very useful for downloading archived files that have the same root name with varying extensions, like different issues of the same magazine. curl can download using any protocol, and will try to intelligently guess the protocol to use if none is given. Check the curl man page for more information.

ftp

The name ftp designates the original FTP client used on Unix and Linux systems. The ftp client uses a command line interface, and it has an extensive set of commands and options you can use to manage your FTP transfers. Alternatively you can use **sftp** for more secure access. The **sftp** client has the same commands as **ftp**, but provided SSH (Secure SHell) encryption. Also, if you installed the Kerberos clients, a Kerberized version of ftp is setup which provides for secure authentication from Kereberos servers. It has the same name as the **ftp** client (an **ftp** link to Kerberos ftp) and also the same commands.

You start the ftp client by entering the command **ftp** at a shell prompt. If you have a specific site you want to connect to, you can include the name of that site on the command line after the ftp keyword. Otherwise, you need to connect to the remote system with the ftp command **open**. You are then prompted for the name of the remote system with the prompt "(to)". When you enter the remote system name, ftp connects you to the system and then prompts you for a login name. The prompt for the login name consists of the word "Name" and, in parentheses, the system name and your local login name. Sometimes the login name on the remote system is the same as the login name on your own system. If the names are the same, press ENTER at the prompt. If they are different, enter the remote system's login name. After entering the login name, you are prompted for the password. In the next example, the user connects to the remote system **garnet** and logs in to the **robert** account:

```
$ ftp
ftp> open
(to) garnet
Connected to garnet.berkeley.edu.
220 garnet.berkeley.edu FTP server ready.
Name (garnet.berkeley.edu:root): robert
password required
Password:
user robert logged in
ftp>
```

Once logged in, you can execute Linux commands on either the remote system or your local system. You execute a command on your local system in ftp by preceding the command with an exclamation point. Any Linux commands without an exclamation point are executed on the remote system. One exception exists to this rule. Whereas you can change directories on the remote system with the **cd** command, to change directories on your local system, you need to use a special ftp command called **lcd** (local **cd**). In the next example, the first command lists files in the remote system, while the second command lists files in the local system:

```
ftp> ls
ftp> !ls
```

The ftp program provides a basic set of commands for managing files and directories on your remote site, provided you have the permission to do so (see Table 8-6). You can use **mkdir** to create a remote directory, and **rmdir** to remove one. Use the **delete** command to erase a remote file. With the **rename** command, you can change the names of files. You close your connection to a system with the **close** command. You can then open another connection if you want. To end the ftp session, use the **quit** or **bye** command.

```
ftp> close
ftp> bye
Good-bye
$
```

Command	Effect
`ftp`	Invokes the ftp program.
open *site-address*	Opens a connection to another system.
`close`	Closes connection to a system.
`quit` or **bye**	Ends ftp session.
`ls`	Lists the contents of a directory.
`dir`	Lists the contents of a directory in long form.
get *filename*	Sends file from remote system to local system.
put *filename*	Sends file from local system to remote system.
mget *regular-expression*	Enables you to download several files at once from a remote system. You can use special characters to specify the files.
mput *regular-expression*	Enables you to send several files at once to a remote system. You can use special characters to specify the files.
`runique`	Toggles storing of files with unique filenames. If a file already exists with the same filename on the local system, a new filename is generated.
reget *filename*	Resumes transfer of an interrupted file from where you left off.
`binary`	Transfers files in binary mode.
`ascii`	Transfers files in ASCII mode.
cd *directory*	Changes directories on the remote system.
lcd *directory*	Changes directories on the local system.
`help` or ?	Lists ftp commands.
mkdir *directory*	Creates a directory on the remote system.
`rmdir`	Deletes a remote directory.
delete *filename*	Deletes a file on the remote system.
mdelete *file-list*	Deletes several remote files at once.
`rename`	Renames a file on a remote system.
`hash`	Displays progressive hash signs during download.
`status`	Displays current status of ftp.

Table 8-6: The ftp Client Commands

To transfer files to and from the remote system, use the `get` and `put` commands. The `get` command receives files from the remote system to your local system, and the `put` command sends files from your local system to the remote system. In a sense, your local system gets files *from* the remote and puts files *to* the remote. In the next example, the file **weather** is sent from the local system to the remote system using the `put` command:

```
ftp> put weather
PORT command successful.
ASCII data connection
ASCII Transfer complete.
ftp>
```

If a download is ever interrupted, you can resume the download with **reget**. This is helpful for an extremely large file. The download resumes from where it left off, so the whole file needn't be downloaded again. Also, be sure to download binary files in binary mode. For most FTP sites, the binary mode is the default, but some sites might have ASCII (text) as the default. The command **ascii** sets the character mode, and the command **binary** sets the binary mode. Most software packages available at Internet sites are archived and compressed files, which are binary files. In the next example, the transfer mode is set to binary, and the archived software package **mydata.tar.gz** is sent from the remote system to your local system using the **get** command:

```
ftp> binary
ftp> get mydata.tar.gz
PORT command successful.
Binary data connection
Binary Transfer complete.
ftp>
```

You may often want to send several files, specifying their names with wildcard characters. The **put** and **get** commands, however, operate only on a single file and do not work with special characters. To transfer several files at a time, you have to use two other commands, **mput** and **mget**. When you use **mput** or **mget**, you are prompted for a file list. You can then either enter the list of files or a file-list specification using special characters. For example, *.c specifies all the files with a **.c** extension, and * specifies all files in the current directory. In the case of **mget**, files are sent one by one from the remote system to your local system. Each time, you are prompted with the name of the file being sent. You can type **y** to send the file or **n** to cancel the transmission. You are then prompted for the next file. The **mput** command works in the same way, but it sends files from your local system to the remote system. In the next example, all files with a **.c** extension are sent to your local system using **mget**:

```
ftp> mget
(remote-files) *.c
mget calc.c? y
PORT command successful
ASCII data connection
ASCII transfer complete
mget main.c? y
PORT command successful
ASCII data connection
ASCII transfer complete
ftp>
```

Answering the prompt for each file can be a tedious prospect if you plan to download a large number of files, such as those for a system update. In this case, you can turn off the prompt with the **prompt** command, which toggles the interactive mode on and off. The **mget** operation then downloads all files it matches, one after the other.

```
ftp> prompt
Interactive mode off.
ftp> mget
(remote-files) *.c
 PORT command successful
ASCII data connection
ASCII transfer complete
PORT command successful
ASCII data connection
ASCII transfer complete
ftp>
```

lftp

The **lftp** program is an enhanced FTP client with advanced features such as the capabilities to download mirror sites and to run several FTP operations in the background at the same time. It uses a command set similar to that for the ftp client. You use `get` and `mget` commands to download files, with the `-o` option to specify local locations for them. Use `lcd` and `cd` to change local and remote directories.

Note: To access a public FTP site, you have to perform an anonymous login. Instead of a login name, you enter the keyword **anonymous** (or **ftp**). Then, for the password, you enter your email address. Once the ftp prompt is displayed, you are ready to transfer files. You may need to change to the appropriate directory first or set the transfer mode to binary.

To manage background commands, you use many of the same commands as for the shell. The `&` placed at the end of a command puts it into the background. Use CTRL-Z to put a job already running into the background. Commands can be grouped with parentheses and placed together into the background. Use the `jobs` command to list your background jobs and the `wait` or `fg` command to move jobs from the background to the foreground. When you exit lftp, the program will continue to run any background jobs. In effect, lftp becomes a background job itself.

When you connect to a site, you can queue commands with the `queue` command, setting up a list of FTP operations to perform. With this feature, you could queue several download operations to a site. The queue can be reordered and entries deleted if you wish. You can also connect to several sites and set up a queue for each one. The `mirror` command lets you maintain a local version of a mirror site. You can download an entire site or just update newer files, as well as removing files no longer present on the mirror.

You can tailor lftp with options set in the **.lftprc** file. System-wide settings are placed in the **/etc/lftp.conf** file. Here, you can set features like the prompt to use and your anonymous password. The **.lftp** directory holds support files for command history, logs, bookmarks, and startup commands. The lftp program also supports the **.netrc** file, checking it for login information.

Tip: The NcFTP program runs as a command line operation similar to ftp with many of the same commands (Ubuntu Universe repository). To start up NcFTP, you enter the `ncftp` command on the command line. It also provides **ncftpput** and **ncftpget** for use in shell scripts.

Voice and Messenger Clients: VoIP, ICQ, and IM

You may, at times, want to communicate directly with other users on your network. You can do so with VoIP, ICQ, and IM (Instant Messenger clients, provided the other user is also logged in to a connected at the same time (see Table 8-7). With Voice over the Internet Protocol applications, you can speak over Internet connections, talking as if on a telephone.

ICQ (I Seek You) is an Internet tool that notifies you when other users are online and enables you to communicate with them. ICQ works much like an instant messenger. With an Internet Relay Chat utility (IRC), you can connect to a remote server where other users are also connected and talk with them. Instant messenger (IM) clients operate much the same way, allowing users on the same IM system to communicate anywhere across the Internet. Ubuntu uses Pidgin as its standard interface for IM messaging.

Clients	Description
Ekiga	VoIP application
Pidgin	Messenger interface for all instant messenger protocols including MSN, AIM, Yahoo, MySpaceIM, ICQ, XMPP, and IRC. Pidgin was formerly GAIM.
X-Chat	Internet Relay Chat (IRC) client, also has a GNOME version, **gnome-xchat**.
Konversation	KDE IRC client
Jabber	Jabber client (XMPP)
psi	Jabber client using QT (KDE), XMPP
Finch	Command line cursor-based IRC, ICQ, and AIM client
naim	Command line cursor-based IRC, ICQ, and AIM client
empathy	GNOME 2.24 new instant messenger client, Pidgin remains the preferred default for Ubuntu 9.04.

Table 8-7: Talk and Messenger Clients

Instant Messenger: Pidgin

Instant messenger (IM) clients allow users on the same IM system to communicate anywhere across the Internet. Currently some of the major IM systems are AIM (AOL), Microsoft Network (MSN), Yahoo, ICQ, and Jabber. Some use an XML protocol called XMPP, Extensible Messaging and Presence Protocol (**www.xmpp.org**).

When you run an IM application like Pidgen or Empathy, the user switcher applet will display IM options: Online, Away, Busy, and Offline (see Figure 8-7). A symbol next to the user will show the current status. You can use the user switcher to quickly change your IM status.

Pidgin Instant Messenger will not start up unless you have at least one account configured. The first time you start Pidgin, the Add Account window is displayed with Basic and Advanced panels for setting up an account. Later you can edit the account by selecting it in the Accounts window (Accounts | Manage menu item) and clicking the Modify button.

Available	◯
Away	▲
Busy	◔
Invisible	⬠
Offline	▢
Lock screen	

Figure 8-7: User Switcher with IM options

Ubuntu will install Pidgin as its standard interface for Instant Messaging (Pidgin was formerly GAIM). Pidgin is a multi-protocol IM client that works with most IM protocols including AIM, MSN, Jabber, Google Talk, ICQ, IRC, Yahoo, MySpaceIM, and more. Pidgin is accessible from Applications | Internet | Instant Messenger.

Note: Empathy is the new GNOME 2.24 instant messenger client. Pidgin remains the preferred default or Ubuntu 9.04, due to its reliability and user interface. Empathy can be installed from the Universe repository.

To create a new account, select Manage from the Accounts menu. This opens an Add Account window with a Basic and Advanced panels. On Basic panel the protocol and account settings. On the Advanced panel you specify the server and network connection settings. On the Basic panel, you choose the protocol to use from a pop-up menu that shows items like AIM, Bonjour, MySpaceIM, Yahoo, and IRC. The configuration entries for both Basic and Advanced will changes depending on the protocol. For AIM, there are entries for Screen name, password, and alias. You can also select a buddy icon. On the Advanced panel the AIM server will already be entered.

To configure your setup, select Preferences from the Tools menu. The Conversations panel lets you set the font, images, and smiley icons for your messages. The Network panel lets to configure your network connection, and the Logging panel lets you turn logging of your messages on or off. The Sounds panel allows you to choose sounds for different events. You can find out more about Pidgin at **http://pidgin.im**. Pidgin is a GNOME front end that used the libpurple library for is actual IM tasks (formerly libgaim). The libpurple library is used by many different IM applications such as Finch.

Ekiga

Ekiga is GNOME's VoIP application providing Internet IP Telephone and video conferencing support (see Figure 8-8). It was formerly called GnomeMeeting, and its web site is still at **www.gnomemeeting.org**. Ekiga supports both the H.323 and SIP (Session Initiation Protocol) protocols. It is compatible with Microsoft's NetMeeting. H.323 is a comprehensive protocol that includes the digital broadcasting protocols like DVB and H.261 for video streaming, as well as the supporting protocols like the H.450 series for managing calls.

To use Ekiga you will need a SIP address. You can obtain a free one from **www.ekiga.net**. You will first have to subscribe to the service. When you first start Ekiga, you will be prompted to configure your connection. Here you can provide information like contact information, your connection method, sound driver, and video device. Use the address book to connect to another Ekiga user. A white pages directory lets you search for people who are also using Ekiga.

Figure 8-8: Ekiga VoIP

Skype

An Ubuntu compliant version of Skype is available on the Medibuntu repository. It is recommended that you use this version. If you have already configured access to the Medibuntu.org repository, you just use the Synaptic Package Manager to search for Skype. The Skype package will be listed. Select it for installation and click Apply. Additional supporting packages will be selected and installed for you.

Even if you have not configured access to the Medibuntu repository, you can still download and install Skype directly from the Medibuntu.org Web site using your browser and Gdebi.

```
http://packages.medibuntu.org/jaunty/index.html
```

Alternatively you could try to install the Ubuntu i386 version that Skype provides on its Web site, though this is not recommended. You can download the DEB package from the Skype site and then use the **dpkg** command to install it. This is an i386 version that is meant to run only on the 32bit version of Ubuntu, not the 64bit, x86_64, version.

```
sudo dpkg -i skype-debian_2.0.0.72-1_i386.deb
```

It may be possible to make it run on the x86_64 bit version, but may be unstable. Use the **--force-architecture** option to force the install.

```
sudo dpkg -i --force-architecture skype-debian_2.0.0.72-1_i386.deb
```

Once installed, you can access Skype from the Applications | Internet menu. The interface is similar to the Windows version (see Figure 8-9). A Skype panel icon will appear on the panel, once you start Skype. You can use it to easily access Skype throughout your session.

Figure 8-9: Skype VoIP and panel icon

ubuntu

Part 3: Interfaces

GNOME

KDE

The Shell

9. GNOME

The Network Object Model Environment, also known as *GNOME,* is a powerful and easy-to-use environment consisting primarily of a panel, a desktop, and a set of GUI tools with which program interfaces can be constructed. GNOME is designed to provide a flexible platform for the development of powerful applications. Currently, GNOME is supported by several distributions and is the primary interface for Ubuntu. GNOME is free and released under the GNU Public License.

The core components of the GNOME desktop consist of a panel for starting programs and desktop functionality. Other components normally found in a desktop, such as a file manager, Web browser, and window manager, are provided by GNOME-compliant applications. GNOME provides libraries of GNOME GUI tools that developers can use to create GNOME applications. Programs that use buttons, menus, and windows that adhere to a GNOME standard can be said to be GNOME-compliant. The official file manager for the GNOME desktop is Nautilus. The GNOME desktop does not have its own window manager as KDE does. Instead, it uses any GNOME-compliant window manager. The Metacity window manager is the one bundled with the GNOME distribution.

You can find out more about GNOME at its Web site, **www.gnome.org**. The Web site provides online documentation, such as the GNOME User's Guide and FAQs, and also maintains extensive mailing lists for GNOME projects to which you can subscribe. The **www.gnomefiles.org** site provides a detailed software listing of current GNOME applications and projects. For detailed documentation check the GNOME documentation site at **http://library.gnome.org**. Documentation is organized by Users, Administrators, and Developers. The Desktop Users Guide provides a complete tutorial on desktop use. For administrators, the GNOME Desktop System Administration Guide details how administrators can manage user desktops. The Desktop Administrators' Guide to GNOME Lockdown and Pre-configuration shows how administrators can control access to tasks like printing or saving files. Table 9-1 offers a listing of useful GNOME sites.

Web Sites	Descriptions
www.gnome.org	Official GNOME Web site
http://library.gnome.org	GNOME documentation Web site for Users, Administrators, and Developers
http://art.gnome.org	Desktop themes and background art
http://www.gnomefiles.org	GNOME Software applications, applets, and tools.
www.gnome.org/gnome-office	GNOME Office applications.
http://developer.gnome.org	Gnome developers site, see library.gnome.org for developer documentation.

Table 9-1: GNOME Resources

If you want to develop GNOME programs, check the Developers section at the GNOME documentation site as well as **http://developer.gnome.org**, which provides tutorials, programming guides, and development tools. Here you can links to extensive support tools such as tutorials and integrated development environments (IDEs). The GNOME documentation site includes detailed online documentation for the GTK+ library, GNOME widgets, and the GNOME desktop, as well as the complete API reference manual online. The Overview of the GNOME Platform provides a comprehensive description of all GNOME components. For offline developer help, install and use the DevHelp utility (part of the GNOME Developer's Tools release). Table 9-1 offers a listing of useful GNOME sites.

GTK+ is the widget set used for GNOME applications. The GTK+ widget set is entirely free under the Lesser General Public License (LGPL). The LGPL enables developers to use the widget set with proprietary software, as well as free software (the GPL would restrict it to just free software). The drag-and-drop functionality supports drag-and-drop operations with other widget sets that support these protocols, such as Qt.

GNOME 2 Features

Check **www.gnome.org** for a detailed description of GNOME features and enhancements, with screen shots and references. GNOME releases new revisions on a frequent schedule. Several versions since the 2.0 release have added many new capabilities. GNOME now has efficiencies in load time and memory use, making for a faster response time. For laptops, power management has been improved along with battery monitoring. For developers, there is a new version of the GTK+ toolkit, better documentation, and improved development tools. GVFS (GNOME Virtual File System) provides direct file manager support for virtual file systems, letting you access Samba shares and FTP sites directly.

Ubuntu 9.04 uses GNOME 2.26, with many features included from GNOME 2.22 (Ubuntu 8.04) and GNOME 2.24 (Ubuntu 8.10). Key changes with GNOME 2.24, GNOME 2.22, and GNOME 2.26 are described in detail at:

```
http://library.gnome.org/misc/release-notes/2.26/
http://library.gnome.org/misc/release-notes/2.24/
http://library.gnome.org/misc/release-notes/2.22/
```

GNOME Desktop Features

- File Roller can work on archives on networked systems. You can also copy and paste or drag and drop files between archives.

- For right-to-left languages, window, menu, and workspace components are now mirrored, also positioned right-to-left.

- GNOME documentation site is **http://library.gnome.org**, which organizes documentation into Users, Administrators, and Developers sections.

- Home directories now have data specific folders set up including Pictures, Documents, Videos, and Music. Gnome applications may use these as defaults.

- With the GNOME Volume Manager, a computer window is now included listing your file system devices, including CD-ROMs as well as network file system devices.

- GNOME automatically mounts removable devices at the **/media** directory.

- GNOME now supports sound themes, providing a whole range of customized themes with a simple selection.

- The GNOME video player, Totem, supports Web access, DVB, and DVD. It also provides YouTube and MythTV support.

- The International Clock Applet is now used for the time applet on the top GNOME panel. It lets you see the time at any location on the planet, as well as the weather.

GNOME File Manager Features

Nautilus is the official file manager for the GNOME desktop. You can find out more about Nautilus from the Nautilus user's manual that is part of the GNOME User's Guide at **www.gnome.org**. The Nautilus file manager, as part of GNOME, also has several new features added.

- Nautilus supports tabs for displaying several folders in the same file manager window.

- Removable media and mounted shares can be ejected and unmounted on the Places sidebar by clicking an Eject button.

- Nautilus File Manager includes disk usage chart when displaying properties for file systems. Images are displayed with their appropriate orientation using EXIF camera information.

- Nautilus is now more integrated into other applications such as File Roller for archives, the image viewer for pictures, and the GNOME media player for audio and video. You can now preview sound and video files within a Nautilus window.

- Nautilus uses GVFS (GNOME Virtual File System) for remote file systems, which replaces GnomeVFS. GVFS uses the GO object-based abstraction layer for I/0, GIO. With GVFS nautilus can support FUSE user based file system access. Applications no longer have to be written for GNOME virtual file system access. Any application can access a GVFS mounted file system.

- With GVFS, Nautilus now manages automounts for remote file systems. Access is stateful, requiring a user password only once, before granting continual access.

- Context-sensitive menus let you perform appropriate actions, such as extracting archive files. An Open With option lets you choose from a selection of appropriate applications. Multiple applications can now be registered for use with a file.

- The file manager can display network shares on local networks, using DNS-based service discovery. The file manager also supports access to password-protected FTP sites.

- The file manager can display audio tracks on music CDs with the **cdda://** protocol, and access connected digital cameras with the **gphoto2://** protocol.

The GNOME Interface

The GNOME interface consists of the panel and a desktop, as shown in Figure 9-1. The panel appears as a long bar across the bottom of the screen. It holds menus, programs, and applets. (An *applet* is a small program designed to be run within the panel.) On the top panel is a menu labeled Applications. The menu operates like the Start menu lists entries for applications you can run on your desktop. You can display panels horizontally or vertically, and have them automatically hide to show you a full screen. The Applications menu is reserved for applications.

Other tasks like opening a home directory window or logging out are located in the Places menu. The System menu holds the Preferences menu for configuring your GNOME interface, as well as the Administration menu for accessing the Ubuntu administrative tools.

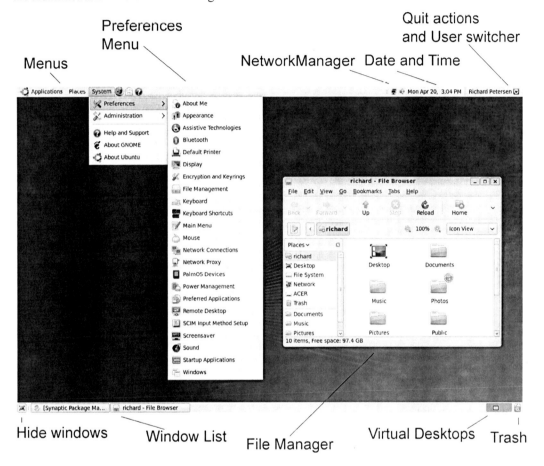

Figure 9-1: GNOME with Preferences menu

Note: The current Ubuntu GNOME interface uses two panels, one on top for menus and notification tasks like your clock, and one on the bottom for interactive features for workspaces and docking applications. Three main menus are now used instead of one: an Applications menu, a Places menu, and the System. The System menu is used to log out of your session (Quit).

The remainder of the screen is the desktop. Here, you can place directories, files, or programs. You can create them on the desktop directly or drag them from a file manager window. A click-and-drag operation will move a file from one window to another or to the desktop. A click and drag with the CTRL key held down will copy a file. A click-and-drag operation with the middle mouse button (two buttons at once on a two-button mouse) enables you to create links on the desktop to installed programs. Initially, the desktop holds only an icon for your home directory. Clicking it opens a file manager window to that directory. A right-click anywhere on the desktop displays a desktop menu with which you can open new windows and create new folders.

Tip: You can display your GNOME desktop using different themes that change the appearance of desktop objects such as windows, buttons, and scroll bars. GNOME functionality is not affected in any way. You can choose from a variety of themes. Many are posted on the Internet at **http://art.gnome.org**. Technically referred to as *GTK themes,* these allow the GTK widget set to change its look and feel. To select a theme, select Theme panel in the Appearance tool in the System | Preferences menu. The default GNOME theme is Nadoka

GNOME Components

From a user's point of view, you can think of the GNOME interface as having four components: the desktop, the panel, the main menus, and the file manager. You have two panels displayed, one used for menus, application icons, and running applets at the top of the screen, and one at the bottom of the screen used primarily for managing your windows and desktop spaces. In its standard default configuration for Ubuntu, the GNOME desktop will display nothing. If have any removable media, like CD/DVD discs, or attached partitions, icons for those will be displayed.

You home directory as wells as any partitions, removable media, and remote file systems, can be accessed from entries on the Places menu on the top panel. If you want icons for them displayed on your desktop, right-click on the item in the Places. A pop-up menu is displayed with an option "Add to Desktop". Select it. To add the Computer icon to the desktop, you would right-click on Computer from the Places menu and select "Add this launcher to the desktop". A Computer icon will appear on the desktop. You can do the same for Network which will show just your remote directories and devices. The home directory icon cannot be added to the desktop.

To start a program, you can select its entry in the Applications menu. You can also click its application icon in the panel (if there is one) or drag a data file to its icon. To add an icon for an application to the desktop, right-click on it entry in the Applications menu and select "Add this launcher to the desktop."

Quitting GNOME

To quit GNOME, you select the Quit entry in the System menu. This displays a dialog with two rows of buttons. The top row has Logout, Lock Screen, and Switch User buttons, and bottom row has Suspend, Hibernate, Restart, and Shut Down button. The Logout button quits GNOME, returning you to the login window. The Shut Down button shuts down the system. The Restart button shuts down and reboots your system. A cancel button lets you return to the desktop.

GNOME Help

The GNOME Help browser (Yelp) provides a browser-like interface for displaying the GNOME user's manual, Man pages, and info documents. You can select it from the System menu. It features a toolbar that enables you to move through the list of previously viewed documents. You can even bookmark specific items. A browser interface enables you to use links to connect to different documents. On the main page, expandable links for several Gnome desktop topics are displayed on left side, with entries for the Gnome User Manual, Administration Guide, and Ubuntu release notes on the right side. At the bottom of the left side listing are links for the Man and Info pages. You can use these links to display Man and Info pages easily. Use the Search box to quickly locate help documents. Special URL-like protocols are supported for the different types of documents: **ghelp**, for GNOME help; **man**, for man pages; and **info**, for the info documents, like **man:fstab** to display the Man page for the **fstab** file.

The GNOME Help Browser provides a detailed manual on every aspect of your GNOME interface. The left hand links display GNOME categories for different application categories like, like the System tools and Gnome Applets. The Gnome Applets entry will provide detailed descriptions of all available GNOME applets. Applications categories like Internet, Programming, System Tools, and Sound and Video will provide help documents for applications developed as part of the GNOME project, like the Evolution mail client, the Totem movie player, the Disk Usage Analyzer, and the GNOME System Monitor. Click on the Desktop entry at the top of the left hand list, to display links for Gnome User and Administration manuals

The GNOME Desktop

The GNOME desktop provides you with all the capabilities of GUI-based operating systems (see Figure 9-1). You can drag files, applications, and directories to the desktop, and then back to GNOME-compliant applications. If the desktop stops functioning, you can restart it by starting the GNOME file manager (Nautilus). The desktop is actually a back-end process in the GNOME file manager. But you needn't have the file manager open to use the desktop.

Note: As an alternative to using the desktop, you can drag any program, file, or directory to the panel and use the panel instead.

Drag and Drop Files to the Desktop

Any icon for an item that you drag from a file manager window to the desktop also appears on the desktop. However, the default drag-and-drop operation is a **move** operation. If you select a file in your file manager window and drag it to the desktop, you are actually moving the file from its current directory to the GNOME desktop directory, which is located in your home directory and holds all items on the desktop. For GNOME, the desktop directory is **DESKTOP**. In the case of dragging directory folders to the desktop, the entire directory and its subdirectories will be moved to the GNOME desktop directory. To remove an icon from the desktop, you move it to the trash.

You can also copy a file to your desktop by pressing the CTRL key and then clicking and dragging it from a file manager window to your desktop. You will see the small arrow in the upper-right corner of the copied icon change to a + symbol, indicating that you are creating a copy, instead of moving the original.

You can also create a link on the desktop to any file. This is useful if you want to keep a single version in a specified directory and just be able to access it from the desktop. You could also use links for customized programs that you may not want on the menu or panel. There are two ways to create a link. While hold down the CTRL AND SHIFT KEYS, CTRL-SHIFT, drag the file to where you want the like created. A copy of the icon then appears with a small arrow in the right corner indicating it is a link. You can click this link to start the program, open the file, or open the directory, depending on what kind of file you linked to. Alternatively, first click and drag the file out of the window, and after moving the file but before lifting up the mouse button, press the ALT key. This will display a pop-up menu with selections for Cut, Copy, and Link. Select the Link option to create a link.

GNOME's drag-and-drop file operation works on virtual desktops provided by the GNOME Workspace Switcher. The GNOME Workspace Switcher on the bottom panel creates icons for each virtual desktop in the panel, along with task buttons for any applications open on them.

Applications on the Desktop

In most cases, you only want to create on the desktop another way to access a file without moving it from its original directory. You can do this either by using a GNOME application launcher button or by creating a link to the original program. Application launcher buttons are the GNOME components used in menus and panels to display and access applications. The Open Office buttons on the top panel are application launcher buttons. To place an icon for the application on your desktop, you can simply drag the application button from the panel or from a menu. For example, to place an icon for the Firefox Web browser on your desktop, just drag the Web browser icon on the top panel to anywhere on your desktop space.

For applications that are not on the panel or in the menu, you can either create an application launcher button for it or create a direct link, as described in the preceding section. To create an application launcher, first right-click the desktop background to display the desktop menu. Then select the Create Launcher entry.

GNOME Desktop Menu

You can also right-click anywhere on the empty desktop to display the GNOME desktop menu. This will list entries for common tasks, such as creating an application launcher, creating a new folder, or organizing the icon display. Keep in mind that the New Folder entry creates a new directory on your desktop, specifically in your GNOME desktop directory (**DESKTOP**), not your home directory. The entries for this menu are listed in Table 9-2.

Menu Item	Description
Create Launcher	Creates a new desktop icon for an application.
Create Folder	Creates a new directory on your desktop, within your DESKTOP directory.
Create Document	Creates files using installed templates
Clean Up by Name	Arranges your desktop icons.
Keep Aligned	Aligns your desktop icons.
Cut, Copy, Paste	Cuts, copies, or pastes files, letting you move or copy files between folders.
Change Desktop Background	Opens a Background Preferences dialog to let you select a new background for your desktop.

Table 9-2: The GNOME Desktop Menu

Window Manager

GNOME works with any window manager. However, desktop functionality, such as drag-and-drop capabilities and the GNOME Workspace Switcher (discussed later), works only with window managers that are GNOME-compliant. The current release of GNOME uses the Metacity window manager. It is completely GNOME-compliant and is designed to integrate with the GNOME desktop without any duplication of functionality.

Metacity employs much the same window operations as used on other window managers. You can resize a window by clicking any of its sides or corners and dragging. You can move the window with a click-and-drag operation on its title bar. You can also right-click and drag any border to move the window, as well as ALT-click anywhere on the window. The upper-right corner shows the Maximize, Minimize, and Close buttons. Minimize creates a button for the window in the panel that you can click to restore it. You can right-click the title bar of a window to display a window menu with entries for window operations. These include workspace entries to move the window to another workspace (virtual desktop) or to all workspaces, which displays the window no matter to what workspace you move.

Compiz-Fusion

For 3D support you can use compositing window manager support provided by Compiz-fusion. Windows are displayed using window decorators, allowing windows to wobble, bend, and move in unusual ways. Desktops can also be accessed using 3D tools like the Desktop Wall or the Desktop Cube. They employ features similar to current Mac and Vista desktops. A compositing window manager support relies on a graphics card OpenGL 3D acceleration support. Be sure your graphics card is supported. Compiz-fusion is a merger of Compiz and Beryl compositing window managers. See **http://wiki.compiz-fusion.org** for more information. Several keyboard shortcuts are supported for popular effects (see Table 9-3)

Keys	Description
ALT-TAB	Switchers: Application, Shift, and Ring
CTRL-TAB-ARROW (LEFT, RIGHT, UP, DOWN)	Viewport switcher, moving to different workspaces
MOUSE SCROLL BUTTON, UP OR DOWN	Viewport switcher, moving to different workspaces
CTRL-ALT-(LEFT-MOUSE-CLICK AND DRAG)	Desktop Wall or Desktop Cube

Table 9-3: Compiz-Fusion Keyboard Shortcuts

Compiz-fusion is now integrated into your Ubuntu GNOME desktop. To enable Compiz-fusion effect, you use the Appearance preferences tool, and select the Visual Effects panel (System | Appearance, Visual Effects). On this panel select the Normal or Extra entries. Selecting either will change window managers, from Metacity (GNOME default) to Compiz-fusion. The Normal option returns to Metacity. Change to Normal if the Compiz-fusion window manager becomes unstable.

Not all Compiz-Fusion features are enabled. Some will conflict, requiring other to be turned off. To enable specific Compiz-fusion effects, you should first install a Compiz configuration manager. There are two available: the Simple CompizConfig Settings Manager (**simple-ccsm**) and the CompizConfig Settings Manager (**compizconfig-settings-manager**). Install either with the Synaptic Package Manager. Then access them from the System | Preferences menu as CompizConfig Settings Manager or as the Simple CompizConfig Settings Manager

The Simple CompizConfig Settings Manager display a window with tabs for different types of features: Animations, Effects, Desktop, Accessibility, and Edges (see Figure 9-2). Certain features in one tab will depend on settings in another. On the Desktop tab you would select the Desktop Cube (see Figure 9-3), which would then enable Cube effects on the Effects tab. By default the Desktop Wall is selected which disables Cube effects entries. You can also configure profiles, selecting different sets of features at once.

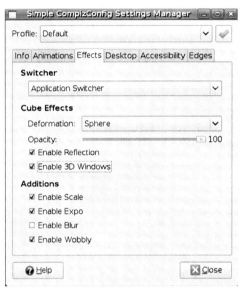

Figure 9-2: Simple CompizConfig Settings Manager, Effects

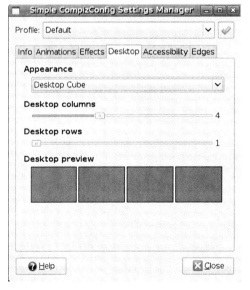

Figure 9-3: Simple CompizConfig Settings Manager, Desktop

Tip: When you install the Simple CompizConfig Settings Manager, a Custom option will be added to the Visual Effects tab in the Appearance preferences tool (System | Preferences | Appearance). Here you can click a Preferences button to open the SCCSM directly.

The CompizConfig Settings Manager provides a more detailed interface with all effects directly selectable with a separate configuration pane for each effect (see Figure 9-4). Select the effect you want. Conflicting features will be turned off automatically. Double click an effect entry to open a configuration pane with options for configuring the effect. The CompizConfig Settings Manager (CCSM) offers much more details configuration options than the Simple Compiz Config Settings Manager (SCCSM), but conflicts can be more complicated to resolve. The Simple CompizConfig Settings Manager will handle conflicts transparently for you. Should you have difficulty with settings configured with the CCSM, you can use SCCSM to instead.

An important difference between the two is that the CCSM will use the original default keys for certain effects, whereas the SCCSM will use the same key for several effects. For the Switchers, the SCCSM will always use the At-Tab keys, whereas the CCSM will use the super-Tab keys for the Shift and Ring switchers. The super key is the Windows Start key on found on most keyboards. Using different keys would allow you to have both switchers enabled at the same time.

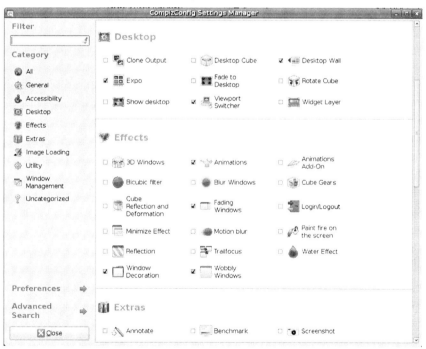

Figure 9-4: CompizConfig Settings Manager

Switchers

Compiz provides several switchers for browsing quickly through open windows, selecting the one you want. Alt-Tab views open windows in current workspace. To list windows in all your workspaces, press Ctrl-Alt-Tab. Should you have numerous windows open across several workspaces, this becomes a way to quickly browse through them, stopping at and selecting the one you want. On the Simple CompizConfig Settings Manager you can choose the switcher you want from the Switcher drop down menu on the Effects panel. The options are: Application Switcher, Static Application Switcher, Shift Switcher (Cover), Shift Switcher (Flip), and Ring Switcher

Application switcher will display a central dialog showing images of your open windows. If you have many windows open, the Application Switcher is a very fast way to locate and select a window (see Figure 9-5). Press the Alt-Tab key to display the Application Switcher. Your current active window will be centrally displayed and highlighted. Continually pressing Alt-Tab will move you through the sequence of window images, making the next window the central and thereby selected one. The Shift-Alt-Tab keys will move you backward to the previous window.

A variation on the Application switcher, the static application switcher, displays all windows side by side, but moves the highlighted selection across them, instead of moving the window images.

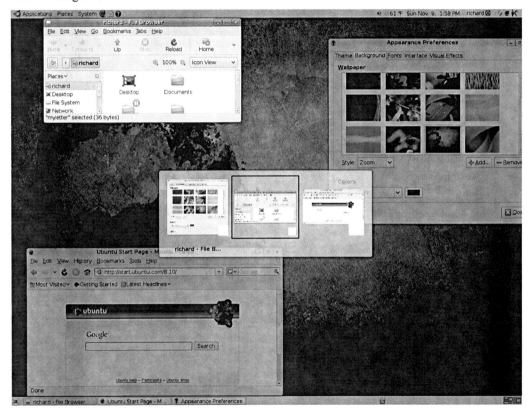

Figure 9-5: Applications switcher (Alt-Tab)

The Shift Switcher performs the same task as the Application Switcher, but will display the non-central windows stacked to the sides (see Figure 9-6). If you configured with the SCCSM (Simple), press the Alt key with the Tab key. If you configured with the CCSM, you use the original Compiz default keys for Shift Switcher, the super key with the Tab key. The super key is the Windows start key on Windows keyboards.

The cover shift switcher displays non-selected windows on either side, whereas the flip shift switcher displays them as a stack to the left.

The Ring Switcher displays the windows in a ring, moving the ring of windows around to a central selected position.

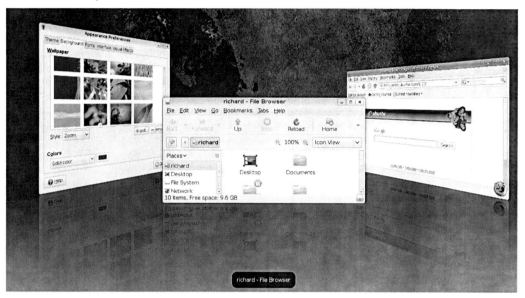

Figure 9-6: Cover Shift Switcher (Alt-Tab or Super-Tab, Super is Windows Start key)

Window previews

The Window Previews feature displays thumbnails of open windows as you pass the mouse over their taskbar labels on the panel (see Figure 9-7). It is turned off by default.

Figure 9-7: Windows previews, thumbnails of open windows as mouse passes over on lower panel

Viewport Switcher

The Viewport switcher lets you use the mouse scroll button or the Ctrl-Alt-Arrow keys to switch quickly between workspaces. Click on the desktop, deselecting any active windows, and then use the scroll button to move directly between workspaces. Scrolling up moves to the right, and scrolling down moves to the left. You can also use Ctrl-alt-arrow, right left up or down to move between workspaces. The Viewport switcher is designed to work with either the Desktop Wall or the Desktop Cube.

Desktop Wall

By default, compiz-fusion will enable the Desktop Wall for easy switching between workspaces. You can use Ctrl-Alt-arrow, right or left to quickly move from one workspace to another. Desktop Wall is incompatible with the Desktop Cube. Should you choose to use the Desktop Cube instead, then the Desktop Wall will be disabled. Desktop Wall is the more stable of the two, requiring only normal graphics card support.

As you move from one workspace to another, the Desktop Wall will display a small dialog containing boxes with simple arrow images for each desktop. This is the Show Viewport Switcher Preview option which is enabled by default. You can configure the Desktop Wall using the CompizConfig Settings Manager to display an image of the desktop instead of just the arrow image (see Figure 9-8). Enable the Show Live Viewport Previews option. For no desktop wall dialog deselect both. Desktop Wall will then just change desktops directly, without displaying a dialog,

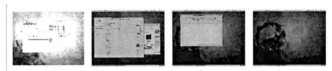

Figure 9-8: Desktop Wall with Viewport switcher and Live previews enabled (Ctrl-Alt-arrow, arrow can be left, right, up, or down)

Desktop Cube with 3D and Deformation

The Desktop Cube displays your desktop workspaces on a cube. When in use, the cube is displayed on the entire screen, replacing your desktop display. The Desktop Cube is not active by default. It conflicts with Desktop Wall. You will have to use a configuration tool to turn it on, turning off Desktop Wall at the same time. To display the Desktop Cube, press Ctrl-Alt with a mouse left-click and drag. As long as you hold the mouse button down, the cube is displayed. Move the mouse to move around the cube to different workspaces (see Figure 9-9).

You need to have more than two workspaces set up to see the cube (right-click on workspace switcher applet on bottom right panel and then add desktop columns).

The Viewport Switcher will work with Desktop Cube, letting you use the scroll button as well as Ctrl-Alt-arrow keys to move quickly between workspaces.

If you have 3d windows also selected (Effects section), then the open windows will be displayed above their respective workspaces (see Figure 9-9).

With the Cube Reflection and Deformation feature the cube is displayed as a circular sphere or cylinder. You can even set the top and bottom images or colors (see Figure 9-10).

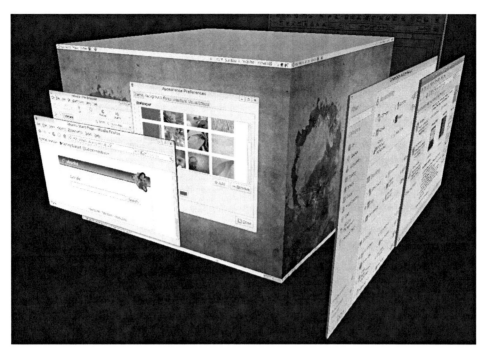

Figure 9-9: Cube with 3D Windows (Ctrl-Alt with mouse left-click and drag)

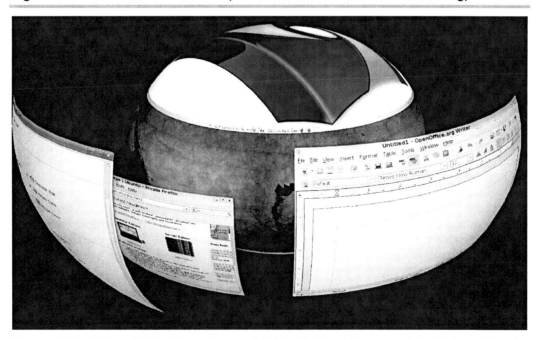

Figure 9-10: Cube with Deformation and 3D (Ctrl-Alt with mouse left-click and drag)

GNOME Preferences

You can configure different parts of your GNOME interface using tools listed in the Preferences menu in the System menu. Ubuntu provides several tools for configuring your GNOME desktop. These are listed in the System | Preferences menu. The GNOME preferences are listed in Table 9-4. The Help button on each preference window will display detailed descriptions and examples. Some of the more important tools are discussed here. Appearance, Fonts, and Sessions are discussed in following sections.

The keyboard shortcuts configuration (Keyboard Shortcuts) lets you map keys to certain tasks, like mapping multimedia keys on a keyboard to media tasks like play and pause. Just select the task and then press the key. There are tasks for the desktop, multimedia, and window management. With window management you can also map keys to perform workspace switching. Keys that are already assigned will be shown.

The Windows configuration (Windows) is where you can enable features like window roll up, window movement key, and mouse window selection.

The Mouse and Keyboard preferences are the primary tools for configuring your mouse and keyboard (Mouse). The Mouse preferences let you choose a mouse image, configure its motion, and hand orientation. The Keyboard preferences window shows several panels for selecting your keyboard model (layout), configuring keys (Layout Options), repeat delay (Keyboard), and even enforcing breaks from power typing as a health precaution.

To select a sound driver to use for different tasks, as well ad specify the sounds to use for desktop events, you use the Sound Preferences tool (Sound). On the Devices panel you can select the sound driver to use, if more than one, for the Sound Events, Music and Videos, and conferencing. Defaults will already be chosen. On the Sounds tab you can enable software sound mixing letting you choose the sound you want for different desktop events. On the Sounds tab you can enable alerts and sound effects. GNOME now uses sound themes for specify an entire set of sounds for different effects and alerts.

Appearance

Several appearance related configuration tasks have been combined into the Appearance tool. These include Themes, Background, Fonts, Interfaces, and Visual Effects. To change your theme or background image, or configure your fonts, use the Appearance tool (System | Preferences | Appearance). The Appearance window shows five panels: Theme, Background, Fonts, Interface, and Visual Effects (see Figure 9-11). The Background panel was discussed in Chapter 3. The Theme and Fonts panels are covered in the following sections. The Interface panel lets you modify the appearance of toolbar and menu items, whether to display icons and where to display text. A preview sections shows how menus and toolbar items will appears depending on your choices. The Visual Effects panel lets you choose the level of desktop effects ranging from just a simple display to full for 3-D effects for windows (wobble, shrink, and explode).

Desktop Themes

You use the Themes panel on the Appearance Preferences tool to select or customize a theme. Themes control your desktop appearance. The Themes panel will list icons for currently installed themes (see Figure 9-11). The icons will show key aspects or each theme like window, folder, and button images, in effect previewing the theme for you.

Preferences	Description
Assistive Technologies	Enables features like accessible login and keyboard screen.
About Me	Personal information like image, addresses, and password.
Appearance	Desktop Appearance configuration: Themes, Fonts, Backgrounds, and interface.
Bluetooth	Bluetooth notification icon display options
Default Printer	Choose a default printer if more than one.
Encryption and Keyrings	Seahorse encryption management configuration.
Keyboard	Configure your keyboard: selecting options, models, and typing breaks, as well as accessibility features like repeating, slow, and sticking, and mouse keys.
Keyboard Shortcuts	Configure keys for special tasks, like multimedia operations.
Main Menu	Add or remove categories and menu items for the Applications and System menus.
Mouse	Mouse configuration: select hand orientation, mouse image, and motion.
Network Configuration	Manage all network connections using Network Manager
Network Proxy	Specify proxy configuration if needed: manual or automatic
Power Management	Power management options for battery use and sleep options.
Preferred Applications	Set default Web browser, Mail application, and Terminal window.
Remote Desktop	Allow remote users to view or control your desktop. Can control access with password.
Removable Drives and Media	Set removable drives and media preferences.
SCIM Input Method	Specify custom input methods for keyboard
Screen Resolution	Change your screen resolution, refresh rate, and screen orientation.
Screensaver	Select and manage your screen saver
Seahorse Preferences	Encryption key management
Search and Indexing	Set search and indexing preferences for Desktop searches.
Sessions	Manage your session with start up programs and save options.
Sound	Select the sound driver for events, video and music, and conferencing. Also select sounds to use for desktop events.
Windows	Enable certain window capabilities like roll up on title bar, movement key, window selection.

Table 9-4: The GNOME Preferences

The Ubuntu theme is initially selected. You can move through the icons to select a different theme if you wish. If you have downloaded additional themes from sites like

http://art.gnome.org, you can click the install button to locate and install them. Once installed, the additional themes will also be displayed in the Theme panel. If you download and install a theme or icon set from the Ubuntu repository, it will be automatically installed for you. Three new themes have been added: Dust, Dust Sand, and New Wave.

Note: GNOME also supports sound themes, selectable from the Sounds tab on the System | Preferences | Sound window. See Chapter 6.

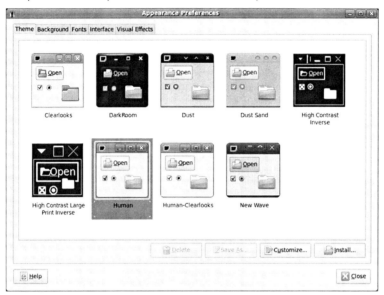

Figure 9-11: Selecting GNOME themes

The true power of Themes is shown in the ability it let users customize any given theme. Themes are organized into three components: controls, window border, and icons. Controls covers the appearance of window and dialog controls like buttons and slider bars. Window border specifies how title bars, borders, window buttons are displayed. Icons specify how all icons used on the desktop are displayed, whether on the file manager, desktop, or the panel. You can actually mix and match components from any installed theme to make your own theme. You can even download and install separate components like specific icon sets, which you can then use in a customized theme.

Clicking the Customize button will open a Themes Details window with panels the different theme components. The ones used for the current theme will be already selected. The controls panel will list. An additional color panel lets you set the background and text colors for windows, input boxes, and selected items. In the control, window border, and icon panels you will see listings of the different themes. You can then mix and match different components from those themes, creating your own customized theme. Upon selecting a component, you desktop will automatically change showing you how it looks. If you have added a component, like a new icon set, it will also be listed.

One you have created a new customized theme, a Custom Theme icon will appear in the theme list. To save the customized theme, click the Save As button. This opens a dialog where you can enter a theme name, any notes, and specify whether you want to also keep the theme background. The save theme then appears in the theme listing.

Themes and icons installed directly by a user are placed in the **.themes** and **.icons** directories in the user's home directory. Should you want these themes made available for all users, you can move them from the **.themes** and **.icons** directories to the **/usr/share/icons** and **/usr/share/themes** directories. Be sure to login as the root user. You then need to change ownership of the moved themes and icons to the root user.

```
chown -R root:root  /usr/share/themes/newtheme
```

Fonts

Ubuntu uses the fontconfig method for managing fonts (**http://fontconfig.org**). You can easily change font sizes, add new fonts, and configure features like anti-aliasing. Both Gnome and KDE provide tools for selecting, resizing, and adding fonts.

Resizing Desktop Fonts

With very large monitors and their high resolutions becoming more common, one feature users find helpful is the ability to increase the desktop font sizes. On a large widescreen monitor, resolutions less than the native one tend not to scale well. A monitor always looks best in its native resolution. However, with a large native resolution like 1900 × 1200, text sizes become so small they are hard to read. You can overcome this issue by increasing the font size. The default size is 10; increasing it to 12 makes text in all desktop features like windows and menus much more readable.

To increase the font size, open the Font Panel on the Appearance tool by clicking System | Preferences | Appearance and selecting the Fonts panel. The Font panel is shown in Figure 9-12. You can even change the font itself as well as choose bold or italic. You can further refine your fonts display by clicking the Details button to open a window where you can set features like the dots-per-inch, hinting, and smoothing. To examine a font in more detail, click the Go To Fonts Folder button and click the font.

Adding Fonts

To add fonts you open the font viewer. You can do this directly by entering the fonts:/ URL in any file manager window. Select Open Location from the File menu to open the URL box. Once the font viewer is open, you can add a font by simply dragging it to the font viewer window. When you restart, your font will be available for use on your desktop. KDE will have Personal and System folders for fonts, initially showing icons for each. For user fonts, open the Personal fonts window. Fonts that are Zip archived, should first be opened with the Archive manager and the can be dragged from the archive manager to the font viewer. To remove a font, right-click it in the font viewer select Move to Trash or Delete.

User fonts will be installed to a user's **.fonts** directory. For fonts to be available to all users, they have to be installed in the **/usr/share/fonts** directory, making them system fonts. Numerous font packages are available on the Ubuntu repositories. Many true type font packages begin with **ttf-** prefix. When you install the font packages, the fonts are automatically installed on your system and ready for use. Microsoft true type fonts are available from the **msttcorefonts** package (Multiverse repository).

You can also manually install fonts yourself by dragging fonts to the font directory. On KDE, you do this by opening the System folder, instead of the Personal folder when you start up the fonts viewer. You can do this from any user login. They drag any fonts packages to this **fonts:/System** window. On Gnome, you have manually copy fonts to the **/user/share/fonts** directory (use **sudo** command). If your system has installed both Gnome and KDE, you can install system fonts using KDE (konqueror file manager) and they will be available on Gnome. For dual boot systems, where Windows is installed as one of the operating systems, you can copy fonts directly from the Windows font directory on the Windows partition (will be mounted automatically in **/media**) to the **fonts:/System** or **fonts:/** window (**/usr/share/fonts** or **.fonts**).

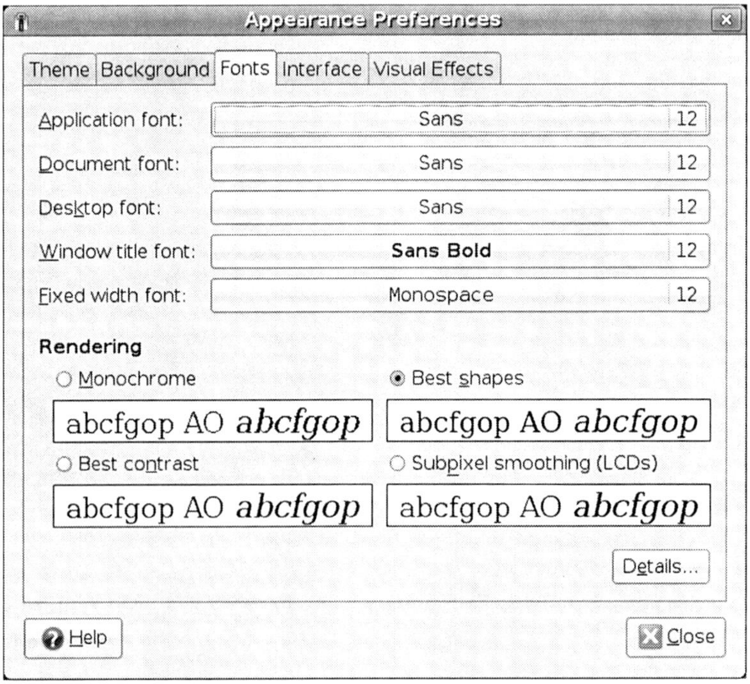

Figure 9-12: Fonts

Configuring Fonts

To better refine your font display, you can use the font rendering tool. Open the Fonts panel on the Appearance tool (System | Preferences | Appearance, Fonts panel). In the Font Rendering section are basic font rendering features like Monochrome, Best contrast, Best shapes, and Subpixel smoothing. Choose the one that works best. For LCDS choose subpixel smoothing. For detailed configuration, click on the Details button. Here you can set smoothing, hinting (anti-aliasing), and subpixel color order features. The sub-pixel color order is hardware dependent.

On Gnome, clicking on a font entry in the Fonts Preferences tool will open a Pick a font dialog that will list all available fonts. You can also generate a listing with the **fc-list** command. The list will be unsorted, so you should pipe it first to the sort command. You can use **fc-list** with any font name or name pattern to search for fonts, with options to search by language, family, or styles. See the **/etc/share/fontconfig** documentation for more details.

```
fc-list | sort
```

Startup Applications Preferences

You can configure your desktop to restore your previously opened windows and applications, as well as specify startup programs. When you log out, you may want the windows you have open and the applications you have running to be automatically started when you log back in. In effect, you are saving you current session, and having it restored it when you log back in. For example, if you are in the middle of working on a spread sheet, you can save your work, but not close the file. Then logout. When you log back in, your spreadsheet will be opened automatically to where you left off.

Restoring a session is not turned on by default. You use the Startup Applications Preferences dialog's Options tab (System | Preferences| Startup Applications Preferences) to turn on (see Figure 9-13). You can set the option "Automatically remember running applications when logging out".

You can also use the Startup Applications Preferences dialog to select programs that you may want started up automatically. Some are already selected like the Software updater and the NetworkManager. On the Startup Programs tab you can select programs you want started, as well as un-select the ones you don't want.

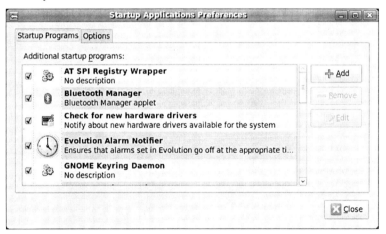

Figure 9-13: Startup Applications Preferences

The GNOME File Manager

Nautilus is the GNOME file manager, supporting the standard features for copying, removing, and deleting items as well as setting permissions and displaying items. It also provides enhancements such as zooming capabilities, user levels, and theme support. You can enlarge or reduce the size of your file icons, select from novice, intermediate, or expert levels of use, and customize the look and feel of Nautilus with different themes. Nautilus also lets you set up customized views of file listings, enabling you to display images for directory icons and run component applications within the file manager window. Nautilus implements a spatial approach to file browsing. A new window is opened for each new folder.

For GNOME 2.22, Nautilus is based on the GVFS which allows any application to access a virtually mounted file system. File system mounted with FUSE, the user base file systems access, will be displayed and accessed by Nautilus.

Home Folder Subdirectories

Ubuntu uses the Common User Directory Structure (xdg-user-dirs at **freedesktop.org**) to set up subdirectories such as **Music** and **Video** in the user home directory. Folders will include Documents, Music, Pictures, and Videos. These localized user directories are used as defaults by many desktop applications. Users can change their directory names or place them within each other using the GNOME file browser. For example, Music can be moved into **Documents**, **Documents/Music**. Local configuration is held in the **.config/user-dirs.dirs** file. System-wide defaults are set up in the **/etc/xdg/user-dirs.defaults** file.

Nautilus Windows

Nautilus was designed as a desktop shell in which different components can be employed to add functionality. An image viewer can display images. The GNOME media player can run sound and video files. The GNOME File Roller tool can archive files, as well as extract them from archives. Archives can also be managed directly by the Nautilus file manager. With the implementation of GStreamer, multimedia tools such as the GNOME audio recorder are now more easily integrated into Nautilus.

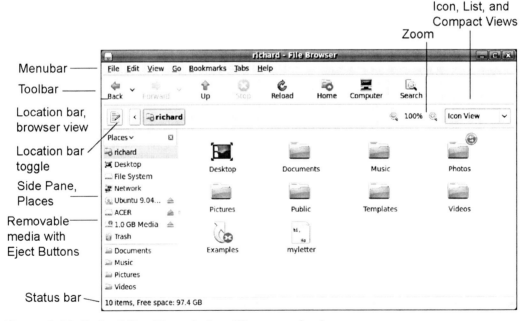

Figure 9-14: Default Nautilus window (Browser view)

When you click the folder for your home directory on your desktop, a file manager window opens showing your home directory. There are two methods for displaying folder: browser and spatial. Ubuntu uses the browser method by default. The browser view displays several components, including a browser toolbar, location bar, and side pane commonly found on most traditional file managers (see Figure 9-14). The rest of the window is divided into two panes. The left pane is a side pane used to display information about the current working directory. The right pane is the main panel that displays the list of files and subdirectories in the current working directory. A status bar at the bottom of the window displays information about a selected file or directory. You can turn any of these elements on or off by selecting their entries in the View menu.

When you open a new directory from a Browser Folder window, the same window is used to display it, and you can use the forward and back arrows to move through previously opened directories. In the location window, you can enter the pathname for a directory to move directly to it. Next to the Location bar (box or button) is an element for zooming in and out of the view of the files. Click the + button to zoom in and the – button to zoom out. Next to the zoom element is a drop-down menu for selecting the different views for your files, such as icons, small icons, or details.

Though the browser mode is the default for Ubuntu, it is possible to also enable the spatial view. The spatial view provides a streamlined display with no toolbars or side pane. Much of its functionality has been moved to menus and pop-up windows, leaving more space to display files and folders. If you want to use the spatial method for viewing folders, you need to changes the file manager behavior preferences. Open any folder and select Preferences from the Edit menu. This opens the File Manager Preferences window. Then in the Behavior panel de-select the entry Always open in Browser window. The file manager will then open a new window for each subdirectory you open. A directory window will show only the menus for managing files and the icons (see Figure 9-15). An information bar at the bottom displays information about the directory or selected files. The menu entries provide the full range of tasks involved in managing your files. On the lower-left bar of the window is a pop-up menu to access parent directories. The name of the currently displayed directory is shown.

To use to the Browser view for a particular folder, while in using the spatial view, right-click on the folder's icon to display a pop-up menu, and then select Browser Folder. This will open that folder with the enhanced format. Also, you can select a folder and then select Browser view from the File menu.

Nautilus Side Pane: Tree, History, and Notes

The side pane has several different views, selectable from a pop-up menu, for displaying additional information about files and directories: Places, Information, Tree, History, and Notes. Places show your file system locations that you would normally access, starting with your home directory. File System places you at top of the file system, letting you move to any accessible part of it. Information displays detailed information about the current directory or selected file. For example, if you double-click an image file, the Information pane will display detailed data on the image, while the window pane displays the full image. The Tree view will display a tree-based hierarchical view of the directories and files on your system, highlighting the one you have currently selected. You can use this tree to move to other directories and files. The tree maps all the directories on your system, starting from the root directory. You can expand or shrink any directory by clicking the + or – symbol before its name. Select a directory by clicking the directory name. The contents of that directory are then displayed in the main panel. The History view shows previous files or directories you have accessed, handy for moving back and forth between directories or files.

The Notes view will display notes you have entered about an item or directory. The Notes view opens an editable text window within the side pane. Just select the Notes view and type in your notes. To add a note for a particular item, such as an image or sound file, just double-click the item to display or run it, and then select the Note view to type in your note. You can also right-click the item, to display the item's pop-up menu and select preferences, from which you can click a Notes panel. After you have added a note, you will see a note image added to the item's icon in the Nautilus window.

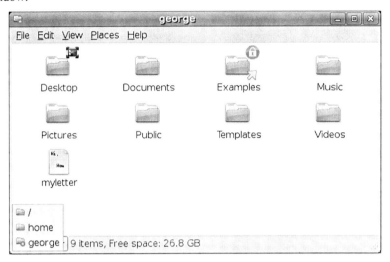

Figure 9-15: Nautilus file manager window (spatial view)

Tabs

The GNOME file manager now supports tabs. You can open up several folders in the same file manager window. To open a tabbed pane, select New Tab from the File menu or press **Ctrl-t**. You can then use the entries in the Tabs menu to move from one tab to another, or to rearrange tabs. You can also use the Ctrl-PageUp and Ctrl-PageDown keys to move from one tab to another. Use the Shift-Ctrl-PageUp and Shift-Ctrl-PageDown keys to rearrange the tabs.

Displaying Files and Folders

You can view a directory's contents as icons, a compact list, or as a detailed list. In the Browser view, you use the pop-up menu located on the right side of the Location bar. The List view provides the name, permissions, size, date, owner, and group. In the View as List view, buttons are displayed for each field across the top of the main panel. You can use these buttons to sort the lists according to that field. For example, to sort the files by date, click the Date button; to sort by size, click Size. In the Spatial view, you select the different options from the View menu.

In the Icon view, you can sort icons and preview their contents without opening them. To sort items in the Icon view, select the Arrange Items entry in the View menu (spatial or browser views) and then select a layout option. Certain types of file icons will display previews of their contents—for example, the icons for image files will display a small version of the image. A text file will display in its icon the first few words of its text. The Zoom In entry enlarges your view of the window, making icons bigger, and Zoom Out reduces your view, making them smaller. Normal

Size restores them to the standard size. You can also use the + and – buttons on the Location bar to change sizes.

In both the spatial and browser views, you can also change the size of individual icons. Select the icon and then choose the Stretch entry from the Edit menu. Handles will appear on the icon image. Click and drag the handles to change its size. To restore the icon, select Restore Icon's Original Size in the Edit menu.

To add an emblem to any file or directory icon, just select the Background & Emblems entry from the Edit menu to open the Background And Emblems window. Here you will see three icons to display panels for color and pattern backgrounds, as well as file and directory emblems. Click emblems to display the selection of emblems. To add an emblem to a file or directory icon, click and drag the emblem from the Emblem panel to the file or directory icon. The emblem will appear on that icon. If you want to add your own emblem, click the Add Emblem button to can search for an emblem image file by name, or browse your file system for the image you want to use (click the image icon).

Nautilus Menu

You can click anywhere on the main panel to display a pop-up menu with entries for managing and arranging your file manager icons (see Table 9-5). The menu is the same for both spatial and browser views. To create a new folder, select Create Folder. The Arrange Items entry displays a submenu with entries for sorting your icons by name, size, type, date, or even emblem. The Manually entry lets you move icons wherever you want on the main panel. You can also cut, copy, and paste files to more easily move or copy them between folders.

Menu Item	Description
Create Folder	Creates a new subdirectory in the directory.
Create Document	Creates a new document using installed templates.
Arrange Items	Displays a submenu to arrange files by name, size, type, date, or emblem.
Cut, Copy, Paste	Cuts, copies, or pastes files, letting you move or copy files between folders.
Zoom In	Provides a close-up view of icons, making them appear larger.
Zoom Out	Provides a distant view of icons, making them appear smaller.
Normal Size	Restores view of icons to standard size.
Properties	Opens the Properties panels for the directory
Clean Up by Name	Arranges icons by name.

Table 9-5: Nautilus File Manager Menu

Tip: To change the background used on the File Manager window, you now select "Background and Emblems" from the Edit menu, dragging the background you want to the file manager window. Choose from either colors or patterns.

Navigating Directories

The spatial and browser views use different tools for navigating directories. The spatial view relies more on direct window operations, whereas the browse view works more like a browser. Recall that to open a directory with the browser view, you need to right-click the directory icon and select Browse Folder.

Navigating in the Browser View

The browser view of the Nautilus file manager operates similarly to a Web browser, using the same window to display opened directories. It maintains a list of previously viewed directories, and you can move back and forth through that list using the toolbar buttons. The left arrow button moves you to the previously displayed directory, and the right arrow button moves you to the next displayed directory. The up arrow button moves you to the parent directory, and the Home button moves you to your home directory. To use a pathname to go directly to a given directory, you can type the pathname in the Location box and press ENTER. Use the toggle icon at the left of the location bar to toggle between box and button location views.

To open a subdirectory, you can double-click its icon or single-click the icon and select Open from the File menu. If you want to open a separate Nautilus browser view window for that directory, right-click the directory's icon and select Open In A New Window.

Navigating in the Spatial View

In the spatial view, Nautilus will open a new window for each directory selected. To open a directory, either double-click it or right-click and select the Open entry. The parent directory pop-up menu at the bottom left lets you open a window for any parent directories, in effect, moving to a previous directory. To jump to a specific directory, select the Open Location entry from the File menu. This will, of course, open a new window for that directory. The Open Parent entry on the File menu lets you quickly open a new window for your parent. You will quickly find that moving to different directories entails opening many new windows.

Managing Files

As a GNOME-compliant file manager, Nautilus supports GUI drag-and-drop operations for copying and moving files. To move a file or directory, click and drag from one directory to another as you would on Windows or Mac interfaces. The move operation is the default drag-and-drop operation in GNOME. To copy a file, click and drag normally while pressing the CTRL key.

Note: If you move a file to a directory on another partition (File System in Computer window), it will be copied instead of moved.

The File Manager pop-up menu for files and directories

You can also perform remove, rename, and link creation operations on a file by right-clicking its icon and selecting the action you want from the pop-up menu that appears (see Table 9-6). For example, to remove an item, right-click it and select the Move To Trash entry from the pop-up menu. This places it in the Trash directory, where you can later delete it by selecting Empty Trash from the Nautilus File menu. To create a link, right-click the file and select Make Link from the pop-up menu. This creates a new link file that begins with the term "link."

Renaming Files

To rename a file, you can either right-click the file's icon and select the Rename entry from the pop-up menu or click its icon and press the F2 key. The name of the icon will be highlighted in a black background, encased in a small text box. You can then click the name and delete the old name, typing a new one. You can also rename a file by entering a new name in its Properties dialog box. Use a right-click and select Properties from the pop-up menu to display the Properties dialog box. On the Basic tab, you can change the name of the file.

Menu Item	Description
Open	Opens the file with its associated application. Directories are opened in the file manager. Associated applications will be listed.
Open In A New Window	Opens a file or directory in a separate window. Alternate view only.
Open With Other Application	Selects an application with which to open this file. A submenu of possible applications is displayed.
Cut, Copy, Paste files	Entries to cut, copy, paste files.
Make Link	Creates a link to that file in the same directory.
Rename (F2)	Renames the file.
Move To Trash	Moves a file to the Trash directory, where you can later delete it.
Create Archive	Archives file using File Roller.
Send To	Email the file
Properties	Displays the Properties dialog.

Table 9-6: The Nautilus File and Directory Pop-Up Menu

File Grouping

File operations can be performed on a selected group of files and directories. You can select a group of items in several ways. You can click the first item and then hold down the SHIFT key while clicking the last item. You can also click and drag the mouse across items you want to select. To select separated items, hold the CTRL key down as you click the individual icons. If you want to select all the items in the directory, choose the Select All entry in the Edit menu. You can then click and drag a set of items at once. This enables you to copy, move, or even delete several files at once.

Applications and Files: MIME Types

You can start any application in the file manager by double-clicking either the application itself or a data file used for that application. If you want to open the file with a specific application, you can right-click the file and select the Open With entry. A submenu displays a list of possible applications. If your application is not listed, you can select Other Application to open a Select An Application dialog box where you can choose the application with which you want to open this file. You can also use a text viewer to display the bare contents of a file within the file manager window. Drag-and-drop operations are also supported for applications. You can drag a data file to its associated application icon (say, one on the desktop); the application then starts up using that data file.

To change or set the default application to use for a certain type of file, you open a file's Properties window and select the Open With tab. Here you can choose the default application to use for that kind of file. Once you select your application, it will appear in the Open With list for this file. If there is an application on the Open With panel you do not want listed in the Open With options, select it and click the Remove button.

If the application you want is not listed, click the Add button in the Open With panel to display a listing of applications. Choose the one you want. This displays an Add Application box and a Browse button. Commonly used applications are already listed. If you already know the full pathname of the application, you can enter it directly. If the application is not listed, you can click Browse to display a Select An Application box that will list applications you can choose. Initially, applications in the **/usr/bin** directory are listed, though you can browse to other directories.

For example, to associate BitTorrent files, with the original BitTorrent application, you would right-click any BitTorrent file (one with a **.torrent** extension), select the Properties entry, and then select the Open With panel. A list of installed applications will be displayed, such as Ktorrent, Azureus, and BitTorrent. Click BitTorrent to use the original BitTorrent application, and then close. BitTorrent is now the default for **.torrent** files.

Hint: The Preferred Applications tool will let you set default applications for Internet and System applications, namely the Web browser, mail client, and terminal window console. Available applications are listed in pop-up menus. You can even select from a list of installed applications for select a custom program. You access the Preferred Applications tool from the Personal submenu located in the System | Preferences menu.

Application Launcher

Certain files, such as shell scripts, are meant to be executed as applications. To run the file using an icon as you would other installed applications, you can create an application launcher for it. You can create application launchers using the Create Launcher tool. This tool is accessible either from the desktop menu as the Create Launcher entry, or from the panel menu's Add To box as the Custom Application Launcher entry. When accessed from the desktop, the new launcher is placed on the desktop, and from the panel, it will be placed directly on the panel.

The Create Launcher tool will prompt you for the application name, the command that invokes it, and its type. For the type you have the choice for application, file, or file within a terminal. For shell scripts, you would use an Application In Terminal option, running the script within a shell.

Use the file type for a data file for which an associated application will be automatically started, opening the file, for example, a Web page, which will then start a Web browser. Instead of a command, you will be prompted to enter the location of the file.

For Applications and Applications In Terminal, you will be prompted to select the command to use. To select the command to use (the actual application or script file), you can either enter its pathname, if you know it, or use the Browse button to open a file browser window to select it.

To select an icon for your launcher, click the Icon button, initially labeled No Icon. This opens the Icon Browser window, listing icons from which you can choose.

Preferred Applications for Web, Mail, Accessibility, and terminal windows

Certain types of files will have default applications already associated with them. For example, double-clicking a Web page file will open the file in the Firefox Web browser. If you prefer to set a different default application, you can use the Preferred Applications tool (see Figure 9-16). This tool will let you set default applications for Web pages, Mail readers, Accessibility tools, and the Terminal window. Available applications are listed in popup menus. In Figure 9-16 the default mail reader is Evolution. You can even select from a list of installed applications for select a custom program. You access the Preferred Applications tool from the Preferences menu (System | Preferences | Preferred Applications). The Preferred applications tool has panels for Internet, Multimedia, System, and Accessibility. On the Multimedia panel you can select default multimedia applications to run. The Accessibility panel has options for selecting a magnifier.

Figure 9-16: Preferred Applications tool

Default Applications for Media

Nautilus directly handles preferences for media operations. You set the preferences using the File Management Preferences window. It is accessible from either the Edit | Preferences menu item on any Nautilus file manager window, or from the System | Preferences | File Management. The System | Administration menu entry for File Management is not displayed by default. Use the System | Preferences | Main Menu tool to make it visible.

The Media tab of the File Management Preferences window lists entries for Cd Audio, DVD Video, Music Player, Photos, and Software. Pop-up menus let you select the application to use for the different media (see Figure 9-17). You also have options for Ask what to do, Do Nothing, and Open folder. The Open Folder options will just open a window displaying the files on the disc. A segment labeled "Other media" lets you set up an association for less used media like

Blu-Ray discs. Initially the "Ask what to do" option will be set for al entries. Possible options are listed for each drop down menu, like Rhythmbox Music Player for Cd Audio discs and Movie Player (Totem) for DVD Video. Photos can be opened with the F-Spot Photo-manager. Once you select an option, when you insert removable media, like a CD Audio discs, its associated application is automatically started.

If you just want to turn off the startup for a particular kind of media, you can select the Do Nothing entry from its application pop-up menu. If you want to be prompted for options, then set the "Ask what to do" entry in the Media panel pop-up menu. When you insert a disc, a dialog with a pop-up menu for possible actions is displayed. The default application is already selected. You can select another application or select the Do Nothing or Open Folder options.

You can turn the automatic start up off for all media by checking the box for "Never prompt or start programs on media insertion" at the bottom of the Media panel. You can also enable the option "browse media when inserted" to just open a folder showing its files.

Figure 9-17: File Management Preferences

File and Directory Properties

With the Properties dialog box, you can view detailed information on a file and set options and permissions (see Figure 9-18). A Properties box has five tabs: Basic, Emblems, Permissions, Open With, Sharing, and Notes. The *Basic* tab shows detailed information such as type, size, location, and date modified. The type is a MIME type, indicating the type of application associated with it. The file's icon is displayed at the top with a text box showing the file's name. You can edit the filename in this text box, changing that name. If you want to change the icon image used for the file or folder, just click the icon image on the Basic tab (next to the name). A Select Custom Icon dialog will open showing available icons you can use. You can select the one you want from that window. The **pixmaps** directory holds the set of current default images, though you can select your own images also. Click the image entry to see its icon displayed in the right pane. Double-clicking effects the icon image change.

The *Emblems* tab enables you to set the emblem you want displayed for this file, displaying all the emblems available. An emblem will appear in the upper-right corner of the icon, giving an indication of the file's contents or importance.

The *Permissions* tab for files shows the read, write, and execute permissions for owner, group, and other, as set for this file. You can change any of the permissions here, provided the file belongs to you. You configure access for owner, group, and others, using pop-up menus. You can set owner permissions as Read Only or Read And Write. For group and others, you can also set the None option, denying access. The group name expands to a pop-up menu listing different groups, allowing you to select one to change the file's group. If you want to execute this as an application (say a shell script) you check the Allow Executing File As Program entry. This has the effect of setting the execute permission.

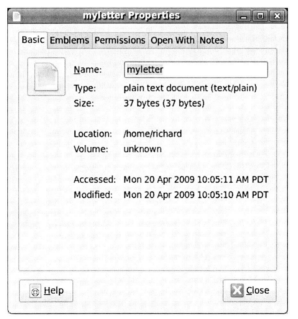

Figure 9-18: File properties on Nautilus

The *Permissions* tab for directories operates much the same way, but it includes two access entries, Folder Access and File Access. The Folder Access entry controls access to the folder with options for List Files Only, Access Files, and Create And Delete Files. These correspond to read, read and execute, and read/write/execute permissions given to directories. The File Access entry lets you set permissions for all those files in the directory. They are the same as for files; for the owner, Read or Read and Write; for the group and others, the entry adds a None option to deny access. To set the permissions for all the files in the directory accordingly (not just the folder), you click the Apply Permissions To Enclosed Files button.

The *Sharing* tab for directories allows you to share folders as network shares. If you have Samba or NFS, these will allow your folders and files to be shared with users on other systems. You have the option to specify whether the shared directory or file will be read only or allow write access. Access can be open to all users.

The Open With tab lists all the applications associated with this kind of file. You can select which one you want as the default. This can be particularly useful for media files, where you may prefer a specific player for a certain file, or a particular image viewer for pictures. The *Notes* tab will list any notes you want to make for the file or directory. It is an editable text window, so you can change or add to your notes, directly.

Certain kind of files will have added tabs, providing information about the item. For example, an audio file will have an *Audio* tab listing the type of audio file and any other information like the song title or compressions method used. An image file will have an *Image* tab listing the resolution and type of image. A video file will contain a *Video* tab showing the type of video file along with compression and resolution information.

Nautilus Preferences

You can set preferences for your Nautilus file manager in the Preferences dialog box, accessible by selecting the Preferences item in any Nautilus file manager window's Edit menu. You can also choose System | Preferences | File Management (menu item hidden by default, use System | Preferences | Main Menu to display). The Preferences dialog box shows a main window with a side pane with several configuration entries, including Views, Behavior, Display, List Columns, Preview, and Media. You use these dialog boxes to set the default display properties for your Nautilus file manager.

> The Views tab allows you to select how files are displayed by default, such as the list, icon, or compact view. The list view provides detailed information, whereas the compact view shows a simple listing.

> Behavior lets you choose how to select files, manage the trash, and handle scripts, as well as whether to use the Browse File alternate view as the default.

> Display lets you choose what added information you want displayed in an icon caption, like the size or date.

> List view lets you choose both the features to display in the detailed list and the order to display them in. In addition to the already-selected Name, Size, Date, and Type, you can add permissions, group, MIME type, and owner.

> The Preview tab lets you choose whether you want small preview content displayed in the icons, like beginning text for text files.

> Media tab lets you select default applications for certain media, like Music CDs or blank DVD discs (see previous section on Default Applications for Media).

Tip: To display a Delete option on the file menus, on the Behavior tab of the File
Management Preferences click the "Include a Delete Command that bypasses
Trash" entry in the Trash section.

Nautilus as a FTP Browser

Nautilus works as an operational FTP browser. You can use the Location box (toggle to
box view) or the Open Location entry on the File menu to access any FTP site. Just enter the URL
for the FTP site in the Location box and press ENTER (you do not need to specify **ftp://**). Folders on
the FTP site will be displayed, and you can drag files to a local directory to download them. The
first time you connect to a site, an Authentication dialog will open letting you select either
Anonymous access or access as a User. If you select User, you can then enter your username and
password for that site. You can then choose to remember the password for just this session or
permanently by storing it in a keyring.

Once you have accessed the site, you can navigate through the folders as you would with
any Nautilus folder, opening directories or returning to parent directories. To download a file, just
drag it from the ftp window to a local directory window. A small dialog will appear showing
download progress. To upload a file, just drag it from your local folder to the window for the open
ftp directory. Your file will be uploaded to that ftp site (should you have permission to do so). You
can also delete files on the site's directories.

Note: Nautilus is not a functional Web browser. It is preferable that you use the Web
browsers for access the Web.

The GNOME Panel

The *panel* is the main component of the GNOME interface (see Figures 9-19). Through it
you can start your applications, run applets, and access desktop areas. You can think of the
GNOME panel as a type of tool you can use on your desktop. You can have several GNOME
panels displayed on your desktop, each with applets and menus you have placed in them. In this
respect, GNOME is flexible, enabling you to configure your panels any way you want. In fact, the
default GNOME desktop that Ubuntu uses features two panels, a menu panel at the top for your
applications and actions, and a panel at the bottom used for minimized windows and the workspace
switcher. You can customize a panel to fit your own needs, holding applets and menus of your own
selection. You may add new panels, add applications to the panel, and add various applets.

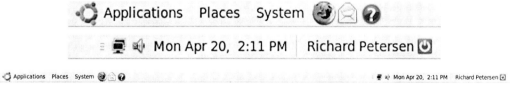

Figure 9-19: The GNOME panel, at the top of Ubuntu desktop

Panel configuration tasks such as adding applications, selecting applets, setting up menus,
and creating new panels are handled from the Panel pop-up menu. Just right-click anywhere on
your panel to display a menu with entries for Properties, New Panel, Add To Panel, and Delete This
Panel, along with Help and About entries. New Panel lets you create other panels; Add To Panel
lets you add items to the panel such as application launchers, applets for simple tasks like the

Workspace Switcher, and menus like the main applications menu. The Properties entry will display a dialog for configuring the features for that panel, like the position of the panel and its hiding capabilities.

To add a new panel, select the New Panel entry in the Panel pop-up menu. A new expanded panel is automatically created and displayed on the side of your screen. You can then use the panel's properties box to set different display and background features, as described in the following sections.

Panel Properties

To configure individual panels, you use the Panel Properties dialog box. To display this dialog box, you right-click the particular panel and select the Properties entry in the pop-up menu. For individual panels, you can set general configuration features and the background. The Panel Properties dialog box includes a tabbed pane, General and Background. With version 2.4, GNOME abandoned the different panel types in favor of just one kind of panel with different possible features that give it the same capabilities as the old panel types.

Displaying Panels

On the General pane of a panel's properties box, you determine how you want the panel displayed. Here you have options for orientation, size, and whether to expand, auto-hide, or display hide buttons. The Orientation entry lets you select which side of screen you want the panel placed on. You can then choose whether you want a panel expanded or not. An expanded panel will fill the edges of the screen, whereas a non-expanded panel is sized to the number of items in the panel and shows handles at each end. Expanded panels will remain fixed to the edge of screen, whereas unexpanded panels can be moved, provided the Show Hide Buttons feature is not selected.

Moving and Hiding Expanded Panels

Expanded panels can be positioned at any edge of your screen. You can move expanded panels from one edge of a screen to another by simply dragging the panel to another edge. If a panel is already there, the new one will stack on top of the current one. You cannot move unexpanded panels in this way. Bear in mind that if you place an expanded panel on the side edge, any menus will be displayed across at the top corner to allow proper pop-up display. The panel on the side edge will expand in size to accommodate its menus. If you have several menus or a menu with lengthy names, you could end up with a very large panel.

You can hide expanded panels either automatically or manually. These are features specified in the panel properties General box as Auto Hide and Show Hide Buttons. To automatically hide panels, select the Auto Hide feature. To redisplay the panel, move your mouse to the edge where the panel is located. You can enable or disable the Hide buttons in the panel's properties window.

If you want to be able to hide a panel manually, select the Show Hide Buttons. Two handles will be displayed at either end of the panel. You can further choose whether to have these handles display arrows or not. You can then hide the panel at any time by clicking either of the Hide buttons located on each end of the panel. The Hide buttons are thin buttons showing a small arrow. This is the direction in which the panel will hide.

Unexpanded Panels: Movable and Fixed

Whereas an expanded panel is always located at the edge of the screen, an unexpanded panel is movable. It can be located at the edge of a screen, working like a shrunken version of an Expanded panel, or you can move it to any place on your desktop, just as you would an icon.

An unexpanded panel will shrink to the number of its components, showing handles at either end. You can then move the panel by dragging its handles. To access the panel menu with its properties entry, right-click either of its handles.

To fix an unexpanded panel at its current position, select the Show Hide Buttons feature on its properties box. This will replace the handles with Hide buttons and make the panel fixed. Clicking a Hide button will hide the panel to the edge of the screen, just as with Expanded panels. If an expanded panel is already located on that edge, the button for a hidden unexpanded panel will be on top of it, just as with a hidden expanded panel. The Auto Hide feature will work for unexpanded panels placed at the edge of a screen.

If you want to fix an unexpanded panel to the edge of a screen, make sure it is placed at the edge you want, and then set its Show Hide Buttons feature.

Panel Background

With a panel's Background pane on its properties box, you can change the panel's background color or image. For a color background you click a color button to display a color selection window where you can choose a color from a color wheel or a list of color boxes, or else you can enter its number. Once your color is selected, you can use the Style slide bar to make it more transparent or opaque. To use an image instead of a color, select the image entry and use the Browse button to locate the image file you want. For an image, you can also drag and drop an image file from the file manager to the panel; that image then becomes the background image for the panel.

Panel Objects

A panel can contain several different types of objects. These include menus, launchers, applets, drawers, and special objects.

Menus   The Applications menu is an example of a panel menu. Launchers are buttons used to start an application or execute a command.

Launchers   The Web browser icon is an example of a launcher button. You can select any application entry in the Applications menu and create a launcher for it on the panel.

Applets   An applet is a small application designed to run within the panel. The Workspace Switcher showing the different desktops is an example of a GNOME applet.

Drawers   A drawer is an extension of the panel that can be open or closed. You can think of a drawer as a shrinkable part of the panel. You can add anything to it that you can to a regular panel, including applets, menus, and even other drawers.

Special objects   These are used for special tasks not supported by other panel objects. For example, the Logout and Lock buttons are special objects.

Moving, Removing, and Locking Objects

To move any object within the panel, right-click it and choose Move Entry. You can move it either to a different place on the same panel or to a different panel. For launchers, you can just drag the object directly where you want it to be. To remove an object from the panel, right-click it to display a pop-up menu for it, and then choose the Remove From Panel entry. To prevent an object from being moved or removed, you set its lock feature (right-click the object and select the Lock entry). To later allow it to be moved, you first have to unlock the object (right-click it and select Unlock).

Tip: On the panel Add To list, common objects like the clock and the CD player are intermixed with object types like menus and applications. When adding a kind of object, like an application, you will have to search through the list to find the entry for that type; in the case of applications, it is the application launcher entry.

Adding Objects

To add an object to a panel, select the object from the panel's Add To box (see Figure 9-20). To display the Add To box, right-click on the panel and select the Add To Panel entry. This Add To box displays a lengthy list of common objects as well as object types. For example, it will display the Main menu as well as an entry for creating custom menus. You can choose to add an application that is already in the GNOME Application menu or to create an application launcher for one that is not. Launchers can be added to a panel by just dragging them directly. Launchers include applications, windows, and files.

Figure 9-20: Panel Add To Box listing panel objects

Application Launchers

To Add an application that already has an application launcher to a panel is easy. You just have to drag the application launcher to the panel. This will automatically create a copy of the launcher for use on that panel. Launchers can be menu items or desktop icons. All the entries in your Application menu are application launchers. To add an application from the menu, just select it and drag it to the panel. You can also drag any desktop application icon to a panel to add a copy of it to that panel.

For any menu item, you can also go to its entry and right-click it. Then select the Add This Launcher To Panel entry. An application launcher for that application is then automatically added to the panel. Suppose you use Gedit frequently and want to add its icon to the panel, instead of having to go through the Application menu all the time. Right-click the Text Editor menu entry in the Accessories menu, and select the Add This Launcher To Panel option. The Gedit icon now appears in your panel.

You can also select the Add To Panel entry from the panel menu and then choose the Application Launcher entry. This will display a box with a listing of all the Application menu entries along with Preferences and Administration menus, expandable to their items. Just find the application you want added and select it. This may be an easier approach if you are working with many different panels.

Keep in mind that for any launcher that you previously created on the desktop, you can just drag it to the panel, to have copy of the launcher placed on the panel.

Folder and File Launchers

To add a folder to a panel, just drag it directly from the file manager window or from the desktop. To add a file, also drag it directly to the panel, but you will then have to create a launcher for it. The Create Launcher window will be displayed, and you can give the file launcher a name and select an icon for it.

Adding Drawers

You can also group applications under a Drawer icon. Clicking the Drawer icon displays a list of the different application icons you can then select. To add a drawer to your panel, right-click the panel and select the Add To Panel entry to display the Add To list. From that list select the Drawer entry. This will create a drawer on your panel. You can then drag any items from desktop, menus, or windows to the drawer icon on the panel to have them listed in the drawer.

If you want to add, as a drawer, a whole menu of applications on the main menu to your panel, right-click any item in that menu, and then select Entire Menu from the pop-up menu, and then select the Add This As Drawer To Panel entry. The entire menu appears as a drawer on your panel, holding icons instead of menu entries. For example, suppose you want to place the Internet Applications menu on your panel. Right-click any entry item, selecting Entire Menu, and select Add This As Drawer To Panel. A drawer appears on your panel labeled Internet, and clicking it displays a pop-up list of icons for all the Internet applications.

Adding Menus

A menu differs from a drawer in that a *drawer* holds application icons instead of menu entries. You can add menus to your panel, much as you add drawers. To add a submenu from the Applications menu to your panel, right-click any item and select Entire Menu, and then select the Add This As Menu To Panel entry. The menu title appears in the panel; you can click it to display the menu entries. You can also add a menu from the panel's Add To list, by selecting Custom menu.

Adding Folders

You can also add directory folders to a panel. Click and drag the Folder icon from the file manager window to your panel. Whenever you click this Folder button, a file manager window opens, displaying that directory. You already have a Folder button for your home directory. You can add directory folders to any drawer on your panel.

GNOME Applets

Applets are small programs that perform tasks within the panel. To add an applet, right-click the panel and select Add To Panel from the pop-up menu. This displays the Add To box listing common applets along with other types of objects, such as launchers. Select the one you want. For example, to add the clock to your panel, select Clock from the panel's Add To box. Once added, the applet will show up in the panel. If you want to remove an applet, right-click it and select the Remove From Panel entry.

GNOME features a number of helpful applets. Some applets monitor your system, such as the Battery Charge Monitor, which checks the battery in laptops, and System Monitor, which shows a graph indicating your current CPU and memory use. The Volume Control applet displays a small scroll bar for adjusting sound levels. The new Deskbar searches for files on your desktop.

Several helpful utility applets provide added functionality to your desktop. The Clock applet can display time in a 12- or 24-hour format. Right-click the Clock applet and select the Preferences entry to change its setup. The CPU Frequency Scaling Monitor displays CPU usage for CPUs like AMD and the new Intel processors that run at lower speeds when idle.

Workspace Switcher

The *Workspace Switcher* appears in the panel and shows a view of your virtual desktops (see Figure 9-21). Virtual desktops are defined in the window manager. On the current Ubuntu configuration, the Workspace Switcher is located on the right side of the lower panel. The Workspace Switcher lets you easily move from one desktop to another with the click of a mouse. It is a panel applet that works only in the panel. You can add the Workspace Switcher to any panel by selecting it from that panel's Add To box. If Compiz-fusion is enabled you can also use the scroll button on your mouse, or the Ctrl-Alt-arrow keys to move from one workspace to another.

The Workspace Switcher shows your entire virtual desktop as separate rectangles listed next to each other. Open windows show up as small colored rectangles in these squares. You can move any window from one virtual desktop to another by clicking and dragging its image in the Workspace Switcher. To configure the Workspace Switcher, right-click it and select Preferences to display the Preferences dialog box. Here, you can select the number of workspaces and name them. The default is two. If Compiz-Fusion is enables, then the Workspace Switcher Preferences shows a simple dialog with entries for column and rows number which can change to add workspaces.

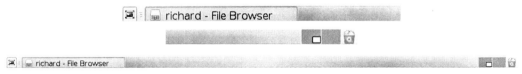

Figure 9-21: Panel with workspace switcher and window list, at the bottom of Ubuntu desktop

GNOME Window List

The *Window List* shows currently opened windows. The Window List arranges opened windows in a series of buttons, one for each window. A window can include applications such as a Web browser or a file manager window displaying a directory. You can move from one window to another by clicking its button. When you minimize a window, you can later restore it by clicking its entry in the Window List.

Right-clicking a window's Window List button opens a menu that lets you Minimize or Unminimize, Roll Up, Move, Resize, Maximize, or Close the window. The Minimize operation will reduce the window to its Window List entry. Right-clicking the entry will display the menu with an Unminimize option instead of a Minimize one, which you can then use to redisplay the window. The Roll Up entry will reduce the window to its title bar. The Close entry will close the window, ending its application.

If there is not enough space on the Window List applet to display a separate button for each window, then common windows will be grouped under a button that will expand like a menu, listing each window in that group. For example, all open terminal windows would be grouped under a single button, which when clicked would pop up a list of their buttons.

The Window List applet is represented by a small serrated bar at the beginning of the window button list. To configure the Window List, right-click on this bar and select the Properties entry. Here, you can set features such as the size in pixels, whether to group windows, whether to show all open windows or those from just the current workspace, or which workspace to restore windows to.

Sound, mouse, and keyboard configuration tools are found in the System | Preferences menu. For the sound configuration, the Sound applet lets you select sound files to play for events in different GNOME applications. For your keyboard, you can set the repeat sensitivity and click sound with the Keyboard applet. You can configure mouse buttons for your right or left hand, and adjust the mouse motion.

GNOME Directories and Files

Ubuntu installs GNOME binaries in the **/usr/bin** directory on your system. GNOME libraries are located in the **/usr/lib** directory. GNOME also has its own **include** directories with header files for use in compiling and developing GNOME applications, **/usr/include/libgnome-2.0/libgnome** and **/usr/include/libgnomeui** (see Table 9-7). The directories located in **/usr/share/gnome** contain files used to configure your GNOME environment.

GNOME User Directories

GNOME sets up several configuration files and directories in your home directory. The **.gnome2** and **.gconf** directories hold configuration files for different desktop components, such as **nautilus** for the file manager and **panel** for the panels. The **Desktop** directory holds all the items you placed on your desktop.

The GConf Configuration Editor

GConf Configuration Editor provides underlying configuration support. GConf corresponds to the Registry used on Windows system. It consists of a series of libraries used to implement a configuration database for a GNOME desktop. This standardized configuration database allows for consistent interactions between GNOME applications. This is not the preferred way to configure your GNOME desktop. You should always use the Preferences tools or the applications own configuration interface if possible.

System GNOME Directories	Contents
`/usr/bin`	GNOME programs
`/usr/lib`	GNOME libraries
`/usr/include/libgnome-2.0/libgnome`	Header files for use in compiling and developing GNOME applications
`/usr/include/libgnomeui`	Header files for use in compiling and developing GNOME user interface components
`/usr/share/gnome`	Files used by GNOME applications
`/usr/share/doc/gnome*`	Documentation for various GNOME packages, including libraries
`/etc/gconf`	GConf configuration files
User GNOME Directories	**Contents**
`.gnome, .gnome2`	Holds configuration files for the user's GNOME desktop and GNOME applications.
`DESKTOP`	Directory where files, directories, and links you place on the desktop will reside
`.gnome2_private`	The user's private GNOME directory
`.gtkrc`	GTK+ configuration file
`.gconf`	GConf configuration database
`.gconfd`	GConf **gconfd** daemon management files
`.gstreamer`	GNOME GStreamer multimedia configuration files
`.nautilus`	Configuration files for the Nautilus file manager

Table 9-7: GNOME Configuration Directories

GNOME applications that are built from a variety of other programs, as Nautilus is, can use GConf to configure all those programs according to a single standard, maintaining configurations in a single database. Currently the GConf database is implemented as XML files in the user's **.gconf** directory. Database interaction and access is carried out by the GConf daemon, **gconfd**.

You can use the GConf editor to configure different GNOME applications and desktop functions. To start the GConf editor, enter `gconf-editor` in a terminal window, or select Configuration Editor from the Applications | System Tools menu (this menu item is turned off by default, use System | Preferences | Main Menu to have it displayed).

Configuration elements are specified keys that are organized by application and program. You can edit the keys, changing their values. Figure 9-22 shows the GConf editor settings for the dialog display features used for the Epiphany Web browser.

The GConf editor has three panes:

Tree A tree pane for navigating keys, with expandable trees for each application, is located on the left. Application entries expand to subentries, grouping keys into different parts or functions for the application. For example, the Epiphany entry expands to dialog, general, Web, and directories entries.

Modification A modification pane to the top right will display the keys for a selected entry. The name field will include an icon indicating its type, and the Value field is an editable field showing the current value. You can directly change this value.

Documentation The documentation field at the bottom right displays information about the selected key, showing the key name, the application that owns it, and a short and detailed description.

Results The results pane, displayed at the bottom, only appears when you do a search for a key.

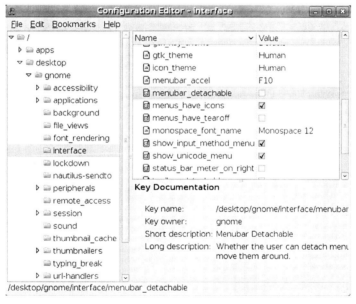

Figure 9-22: GConf editor

A key has a specific type such as numeric or string, and you will only be able to make changes using the appropriate type. Each key entry has an icon specifying its type, such as a check mark for the Boolean values, a number *1* for numeric values, and a letter a for string values. Some keys have pop-up menus with limited selections to choose from, represented by an icon with a row of lines. To change the value of a key, click its value field. You can then edit the value. For pop-up menus, you right-click the value field to display the menu.

There are many keys distributed over several applications and groups. To locate one, you can use the search function. Select Find from the Edit menu and enter a pattern. The results are displayed in a Results pane, which you can use to scroll through matching keys, selecting the one you want.

Changes can be made either by users or by administrators. Administrators can set default or mandatory values for keys. Mandatory values will prevent users from making changes. For user changes, you can open a Settings window by selecting Settings from the File menu. This opens an identical GConf Editor window. For administrative changes, you first log in as the root user. For default changes, you select the Default entry from the File menu, and for mandatory changes, select the Mandatory entry.

10. The K Desktop Environment: KUbuntu

KDE Install Options

The KDE 4 Desktop

Kickoff menu

Plasma

Dashboard

Zoom User Interface (ZUI)

KWin: Desktop Effects

KDE File Manager: Dolphin

Web and FTP Access: Konqueror

KDE Configuration: KDE System Settings

KDE Directories and Files

The *K Desktop Environment (KDE)* is a network-transparent desktop that includes the standard desktop features, such as a window manager and a file manager, as well as an extensive set of applications that cover most Linux tasks. KDE is an Internet-aware system that includes a full set of integrated network/Internet applications, including a mailer, a newsreader, and a Web browser. KDE aims to provide a level of desktop functionality and ease of use found in Macintosh and Windows systems, combined with the power and flexibility of the Unix operating system.

KUbuntu

The KUbuntu edition of Ubuntu installs KDE as the primary desktop from the KUbuntu install disc. KUbuntu officially supports KDE 4.1. It will install KDE 4.1. You can download this disc from the KUbuntu site at

```
http://www.kubuntu.org/
```

You can also download the discs directly from **http://releases.ubuntu.com**.

```
http://releases.ubuntu.com/kubuntu/jaunty/
```

You can obtain the DVD disc for KUbuntu from **http://cdimage.unbuntu.com**

```
http://cdimages.ubuntu.com/kubuntu/releases/jaunty/release/
```

You can also add KUbuntu as a desktop to an Ubuntu desktop (GNOME) installation. KDE includes numerous packages. Instead of trying to install each one, you should install KDE using its meta packages specified in the Synaptic Package Manager, Meta Packages. KDE will then become an option you can select from the Sessions menu. You will be prompted to keep the GDM (GNOME display manager) for logins, though you can change to KDM, the KDE Display Manager.

```
kubuntu-desktop
```

If you are installing KUbuntu from the KUbuntu CD, you will follow the same steps as those used for the Ubuntu CD/DVD: language, time zone, keyboard, partition, user and host name, and ready to install.

If you are using the KDM to login, a box will be displayed at the center of the screen where you can enter your user name and password. Users will be listed in a sidebar. Selecting the user will enter the user name in the user box. You can then enter your password.

A Session Type and Menu menus are displayed at the bottom right of the screen with the date. The Session Type lets you change the desktop interface, like GNOME should it be installed. The Menu has entries for Switch User, Restart X Server, Remote Login, Console Login, and Shutdown. The Shutdown entry will open a dialog with selections to either Restart or Turn off the system.

Upon entering your user name and password and pressing ENTER, your KDE session starts up. Several Plasmoids are displayed on the desktop including a Folder View set to the user's Desktop folder, and the Notetaker for entering notes.

Keep in mind that KUbuntu will use the KDE system administration tools if available, not the Ubuntu GNOME based counterparts. Instead of GNOME's **users-admin** you would use KUser to manage users and groups. For network connections you would use KNetworkManager, the KDE version of Network Manager. For Printing you still use system-config-printer-kde, the KDE version of system-config-printer that uses the older interface. On a system that uses only KUbuntu, for Software management and installation you use KDE KPackageKit manager, not Synaptic or Add/Remove. The system administration tools are accessible from the Applications | System menu.

The administration tools issue can be confusing. If you installed Ubuntu using the Ubuntu desktop CD, then GNOME is installed with al the Ubuntu GNOME administration tools. If you then later add the KUbuntu desktop, kubuntu-desktop, then you will be able to access both the GNOME administration tools and the KDE administration tools.

If, instead, you installed directly from a KUbuntu CD, then only KUbuntu is installed and you only have access to the KDE administration tools. Should you later decide to install the GNOME desktop (ubuntu-desktop) then the Ubuntu GNOME administration tools will become available. You can still manually install specific GNOME based administration tools using the KPackageKit software manager, in which case the needed supporting GNOME libraries will be also installed. You can then run these administration tools from your KDE desktop.

Also keep in mind that KUbuntu has a **kubuntu-restricted-extras** package for multimedia codecs.

The K Desktop

The KDE desktop is developed and distributed by the KDE Project, which is a large open group of hundreds of programmers around the world. KDE is entirely free and open software provided under a GNU Public License and is available free of charge along with its source code. KDE development is managed by a core group: the KDE Core Team. Anyone can apply, though membership is based on merit.

Numerous applications written specifically for KDE are easily accessible from the desktop. These include editors, photo and paint image applications, spreadsheets, and office applications. Such applications usually have the letter *K* as part of their name—for example, KWord or KMail. A variety of tools are provided with the KDE desktop. These include calculators, console windows, notepads, and even software package managers. On a system administration level, KDE provides several tools for configuring your system. With KUser, you can manage user accounts, adding new ones or removing old ones. Practically all your Linux tasks can be performed from the KDE desktop. KDE applications also feature a built-in Help application. Choosing the Contents entry in the Help menu starts the KDE Help viewer, which provides a Web page–like interface with links for navigating through the Help documents. KDE includes support for the office application suite KOffice, based on KDE's KParts technology. KOffice includes a presentation application, a spreadsheet, an illustrator, and a word processor, among other components. In addition, an integrated development environment (IDE), called KDevelop, is available to help programmers create KDE-based software.

Note: On KDE, menus will show more KDE applications than are shown on GNOME, including access to the KDE Control Center on the main menu.

KDE, initiated by Matthias Ettrich in October 1996, has an extensive list of sponsors, including SUSE, Red Hat, Ubuntu, Mandrake, O'Reilly, and others. KDE is designed to run on any Unix implementation, including Linux, Solaris, HP-UX, and FreeBSD. The official KDE Web site is **www.kde.org**, which provides news updates, download links, and documentation. KDE software packages can be downloaded from the KDE FTP site at **ftp.kde.org** and its mirror sites. Several

KDE mailing lists are available for users and developers, including announcements, administration, and other topics (see the KDE Web site to subscribe). A great many software applications are currently available for KDE at **www.kde-apps.org**. Development support and documentation can be obtained at **http://developer.kde.org**. Various KDE Web sites are listed in Table 10-1.

Web Site	Description
www.kde.org	KDE Web site
www.kubuntu.org	KUbuntu site
ftp.kde.org	KDE FTP site
www.kde-apps.org	KDE software repository
developer.kde.org	KDE developer site
www.trolltech.com	Site for Qt libraries
www.koffice.org	KOffice office suite
www.kde-look.org	KDE desktop themes, select KDE entry
http://lists.kde.org	KDE mailing lists

Table 10-1: KDE Web Sites

Currently, new versions of KDE are being released frequently, sometimes every few months. KDE releases are designed to enable users to upgrade their older versions easily. Your Ubuntu software updater will automatically update KDE from distribution repositories, as updates become available. Alternatively, you can download new KDE packages from your distribution's FTP site and install them manually.

Note: KDE uses as its library of GUI tools the Qt library, developed and supported by Trolltech (**www.trolltech.com**). Qt is considered one of the best GUI libraries available for Unix/Linux systems. Using Qt has the advantage of relying on a commercially developed and supported GUI library. Trolltech provides the Qt libraries as Open Source software that is freely distributable.

KDE 4

The KDE 4 release is a major reworking of the KDE desktop. KDE 4.1 is included with the Ubuntu 9.04 distribution. Check the KDE site for detailed information on KDE 4, including the visual guide.

```
www.kde.org/announcements/4.0/
```

For features added with KDE 4.2 (current KUbuntu edition), check:

```
www.kde.org/announcements/4.2/
```

Every aspect of KDE has been reworked with KDE4. There is a new files manager, desktop, theme, panel, and configuration interface. KDE Window manager supports advanced compositing effects. Oxygen artwork for user interface theme, icons, and windows.

Device interfaces are managed by Phonon for multimedia devices, and Solid for power, network, and bluetooth devices. Phonon multimedia framework provides can support different backends for media playback. Currently it uses the Xine backend. With Phonon you can direct media files to specific devices. Solid hardware integration framework integrates fixed and removable devices, as well as network and bluetooth connections. Solid also connects to your hardware's power management features. Threadweaver makes efficient use of multi-core processors.

New applications include the Okular document viewer for numerous document formats with various display features like zoom, page thumbnails, search, and bookmarks. It allows you to add notes to documents. Gwenview is the KDE image viewer with browsing, display, and slideshow features for your images. Terminal window supports tabbed panels, split views for large output, background transparency, and search dialog for commands. Large output can be scrolled.

Configuration and Administration Access with KDE

KDE uses a different set of menus and access points than GNOME for accessing system administration tools. There are also different ways to access KDE configuration tasks, as well as KDE system administration tools not available through GNOME.

Access GNOME and Ubuntu system administration tools from both the Applications | Settings and Applications | System entries. Here you will find Ubuntu desktop (GNOME) administration tools like Users and Groups, Printing, Login Window, and Synaptic Package Manager.

> **System Settings**   Accessible from Kickoff at Computer | System Settings and from Favorites | System Settings, this is the comprehensive KDE configuration tool, which lists all the KDE configuration tools for your managing your desktop, file manager, and system, as well as KDE's own administration tools that could be used instead of the GNOME ones.

> **Settings**   Accessible from Applications | Settings. On a mixed desktop with the Ubuntu desktop (GNOME) installed, this is smaller collection of Ubuntu desktop (GNOME) administrative tools (Ubuntu desktop) corresponding to those found in your Ubuntu desktop (GNOME) Administration menu. Many are also found on the KDE Applications | System menu.

> **System**. Accessible from Applications | System, this is collection of both Ubuntu and KUbuntu administration tools. On a mixed desktop with the Ubuntu desktop (GNOME) installed, this is a collection of system tools corresponding to those found in your GNOME System | Administration menu, including Add/Remove Applications and the Synaptic Package Manager. Many Ubuntu tools, including Printing, Login Window, and Services, are listed here. Other tools use the KUbuntu version only, like KRandR instead of Display. KUbuntu tools are also listed like KPackageKit and KUser.

Plasma: desktop, panel, and plasmoids (applets)

Plasma has containments and applets. Applets are referred to as plasmoids. These plasmoids are applets that operate within containments. On KDE4 there are two Plasma containments, the panel and the desktop. The desktop and the panel are now features of an underlying Plasma operation. They are not separate programs. Both can have plasmoids (applets).

302 Part 3: Interfaces

Each containment will have its own toolbox for configuration. The desktop has a toolbox at the top right corner, and panels will have toolbox on the right side. The panel toolbox features configuration tools for sizing and positioning the panel. See Table 10-2 for keyboard shortcuts.

Keys	Description
ALT-F1	Kickoff menu
ALT-F2	Krunner, command execution, entry can be any search string for a relevant operation, including bookmarks and contacts, not just applications.
UP/DOWN ARROWS	Move among entries in menus, including Kickoff and menus
LEFT/RIGHT ARROWS	Move to submenus menus, including Kickoff and Quick Access submenus menus
ENTER	Select a menu entry, including a Kickoff or QuickAccess
PAGE UP, PAGE DOWN	Scroll up fast
ALT-F4	Close current window
ALT-F3	Window menu for current window
CTRL-ALT-F6	Command Line Interface
CTRL-ALT-F8	Return to desktop from command line interface
CTRL-R	Remove a selected plasmoid
CTRL-S	Open a selected plasmoid configuration settings
CTRL-A	Open the Add Widgets window to add a plasmoid to the desktop
CTRL-L	Lock your widgets to prevent removal, adding new ones, or changing settings
ALT-TAB	Cover Switch or Box Switch for open windows
CTRL-F8	Desktop Grid
CTRL-F9	Present Windows Current Desktop
CTRL-F10	Present Windows All Desktops

Table 10-2: Desktop, Plasma, and KWin Keyboard Shortcuts

Ubuntu KDE 4.2 also supports the Zoom User Interface (ZUI) with its support for multiple plasma desktop containments (Activities). The Toolbox icon shows entries for Add widgets, Lock widgets, and Zoom out (ZUI interface), along with standard desktop operations like run command and configure desktop (background image and theme). . Use the Zoom In entry to access the ZUI interface: adding, removing, and selecting desktop containments.

The KDE Help Center

The KDE Help Center provides a browser-like interface for accessing and displaying both KDE Help files and Linux Man and info files (see Figure 10-1). You can start the Help Center by selecting its entry in Kickoff Applications menu. The Help window displays a sidebar that holds three tabbed panels, one listing contents, one providing a glossary, and one for search options (boolean operators, scope, and number of results). The main pane displays currently selected documents. A help tree on the contents tab in the sidebar lets you choose the kind of Help documents you want to access. Here you can choose KDE manuals, Man pages, or info documents, even application manuals. The Help Center includes a detailed user manual, a FAQ, and KDE Web site access.

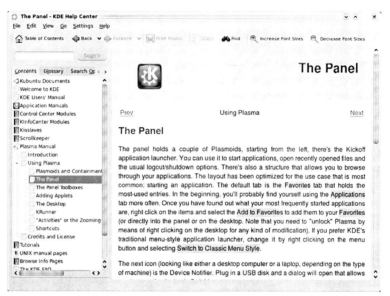

Figure 10-1: KDE Help Center

A navigation toolbar enables you to move through previously viewed documents. KDE Help documents use an HTML format with links you can click to access other documents. The Back and Forward commands move you through the list of previously viewed documents. The KDE Help system provides an effective search tool for searching for patterns in Help documents, including Man and info pages. Enter the search pattern in the Search box above the sidebar, or select the Find entry from the Edit menu or toolbar to display a page where you can enter a more detailed query.

The KDE 4 Desktop

One of KDE's aims is to provide users with a consistent integrated desktop, where all applications use GUI interfaces (see Figure 10-2). To this end, KDE provides its own window manager (KWM), file manager (Dolphin), program manager, and desktop and panel (Plasma). You can run any other X Window System–compliant application, such as Firefox, in KDE, as well as any GNOME application. In turn, you can also run any KDE application, including the Konqueror file manager in GNOME. The KDE 4 desktop features the Plasma desktop shell with new panel, menu, and widgets, and adds a dashboard function. Plasma replaces desktop and Kicker panel, managing both the desktop and panel.

The desktop supports drag-and-drop operations. For example, to print a document, drag it to the Printer icon. You can place any directories on the desktop by simply dragging them from a file manager window to the desktop. A small menu will appear with options to copy or link the folder. To just create an icon on the desktop for the same folder, select the link entry.

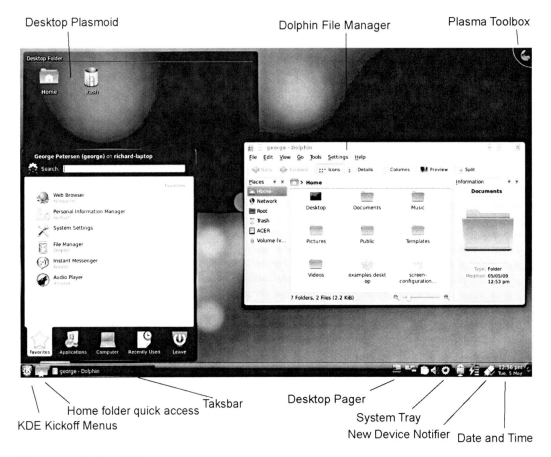

Figure 10-2: The KDE desktop

The desktop also supports copy-and-paste operations, holding text you copied from one application in a desktop clipboard that you can then use to paste to another application. You can even copy and paste from a Konsole window.

To configure your desktop, you use the Look & Feel tool in the System Settings window (Applications | Settings | System Settings). These include Appearance, Desktop, Notifications, and Window Behavior. Appearance holds the most configuration tasks, including Theme selection, Fonts, Styles, and Icons. Desktop is where you control Desktop Effects and the Screensaver. Windows Behavior controls window display features like shortcut keys, titlebar shading, and window movement. One key exception is the background. This is set by right-clicking on the desktop background to display the desktop menu and then selecting Configure Desktop. This entry only configures the background, called wallpaper in KDE. You can select other wallpaper from a drop-down menu, select your own image and even download directly from **www.kde-look.org**, by clicking the New Wallpaper button.

For your desktop, you can also select a variety of different themes. A *theme* changes the look and feel of your desktop, affecting the appearance of GUI elements, such as scroll bars, buttons, and icons. For example, you use the Plastik theme to make your K Desktop look like a

KDE 3.5 desktop. You can use the Theme Manager in the System Settings Appearance tool (System Settings | Look and Feel | Appearance | Themes) to select a theme and install new ones. Several will be installed for you. You can click the Get New Themes link to open the theme Web page at the **www.kde-look.org**. You can then download a new theme, and then click the Install New Theme button to locate the theme and install it.

Quitting KDE

To quit KDE, you first click the Leave button on the KDE Kickoff menu (see Figure 10-3). Here you will find options to logout, lock, switch user, shutdown, and restart. You can also right-click anywhere on the desktop and select the Logout entry from the pop-up menu. If you leave any KDE applications or windows open when you quit, they are automatically restored when you start up again. If you just want to lock your desktop, you can select the Lock entry on the Kickoff Leave menu, and your screen saver will appear. To access a locked desktop, click on the screen and a box appears prompting you for your login password. When you enter the password, your desktop reappears.

Figure 10-3: The Kickoff menu Leave

KDE Kickoff and Quick Access menus

KickOff application launcher (see Figure 10-4) organizes menu entries tabbed panels accessed by icons at the bottom of the menu window. There are panels for Favorites, Applications, Computer, Recently Used, and Leave. You can add and remove applications to the Favorites panel by right-clicking and selecting add or remove to favorites. The Applications panel shows application categories. The Computer button will open a window with all your fixed and removable storage. The Recently Used panel shows both documents and applications. KickOff also provides a Search box where you can search for a particular application, instead of working through menus.

To configure KDE, you use the KDE System Settings referenced by the System Settings item in the Favorites or Applications panel.

Use the Leave panel to logout or shut down (see Figure 10-3). There Session and System sections. The Session section has entries for Logout, Lock, and Switch User. The System section features system-wide operations, including Shutdown, Restart, and Suspend (either to RAM or Disk).

Figure 10-4: The Kickoff menu Favorites

Figure 10-5: The Kickoff menu Computer

The Computer menu has Applications and Places sections (see Figure 10-5). The Applications section has an entry for System Settings. The Places section is similar to the Places menu in GNOME, with entries for your home folder, network folder, root folder and the trash, as well as removable devices like USB drives and DVD/CD discs.

The Applications menu has most of the same entries as those found on GNOME. The entries have been standardized for both interfaces (see Figure 10-6). You can find entries for categories such as Internet, Graphics, and Office. These menus list both GNOME and KDE applications you can use. However, some of the KDE menus contain entries for a few more alternate KDE applications, like KMail on the Internet menu. Some entries will invoke the KDE version of a tool, like the Terminal entry in the System Tools menu, which will invoke the KDE terminal window, KConsole. There is no Preferences menu.

Figure 10-6: The Kickoff menu Applications

The QuickAcces menu is a plasmoid that will let you quickly access items like folder, files, bookmarks, or contacts. A QuickAccess plasmoid is set up on your panel for your home folder. It has been customized with the home folder icon. Clicking on it display a pop up dialog with entries for folders in your home folders as well as any files you may have there (see Figure 10-7). Click on a folder entry to open a file Manager window on your desktop for that folder. For a file, its associated application will be opened with that file. Clicking on the upper right sort button lets you change the sort sequence of your items.

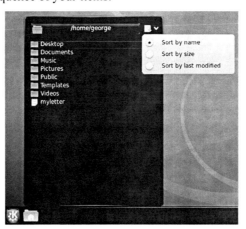

Figure 10-7: The Quick Access applet customized with home folder image

Figure 10-8: The Quick Access configuration

Use the Add Widgets tool on either the panel or desktop to create your own QuickAccess plasmoids. You can customize the QuickAcces plasmoid with its Setting dialog (see Figure 10-8). This has three tabs: General, Appearance, and Preview. On the General tab you can specify the folder you want displayed. The Appearance tab lets you change the icon used. The Preview tab enables previews of folders and files. On the Appearance tab, clicking on the Custom icon image opens an Icon source window where you can choose the icon you want to use.

Krunner

For fast access to applications, bookmarks, contacts, and other desktop items, you can use Krunner. The Krunner plasmoid operates as a search tool for applications and other items. To find an application, enter a search pattern and an icon for the application is displayed. Click on the icon to start the application. For applications where you know the name, part of the name, or just its basic topic, Krunner is a very fast way to access the applications. To start Krunner, press Alt-F2, right-click on the desktop to display the desktop menu and select Run command. Enter the pattern for the application you want to search for and press enter. The pattern "software" or "package" would both display the KPackageKit software manager icon. Entering the pattern "office" displays icons for all the OpenOffice.org applications (see Figure 10-9).

Figure 10-9: Krunner application search

Removable Devices: Device Notifier

Installed on the panel to the left, next to the date, is the Device Notifier plasmoid. When you insert a removable device like a CD/DVD-ROM disc or a USB drive, the New Device Notifier briefly displays a window showing all your removable devices, including the new one. You can click on the New Device Notifier any time to display this window. Figure 10-10 shows the New Device Notifier displayed on the panel and its applet icon.

Removable devices are not displayed as icons on your desktop. Instead, to open the devices, you use the New Device Notifier. Click on the Device Notifier icon in the panel to open its dialog. Then click on the device you want to open, like your DVD/CD disc or your USB drive. A file manager window will open showing your device contents. A USB drive will be automatically mounted when you click on its New Device Notifier entry to open up a file manager window for it.

Figure 10-10: Device Notifier and its panel plasmoid icon

You can use the Device Notifier to eject a removable device. When you select the device entry, an eject button will appear. Clicking on an entry for a DVD/CD-ROM disc will physically eject it, whereas for a USB drive, the drive will be unmounted and prepared for removal. You can then safely remove the USB drive.

Network Manager (network-manager-kde)

On KDE the Network Manager plasmoid provides panel access for NetworkManager. This is the same Network Manager application, but adapted to the KDE4 interface (network-manager-kde). Clicking on the plasmoid open a set of detachable dialogs listing your current available connections (see Figure 10-11). Wireless, Ethernet, and VPN connections will be displayed.

To configure display options, right-click on the Network Manager icon and select Network Management Settings. This opens a dialog where you can choose what kinds of connections you want displayed.

Figure 10-11: NetworkManager connections and plasmoid icon.

To configure your connections, right-click on the Network Manager icon and select Manage Connections. This opens the Network Manager Network Connections window (KDE4 interface) with the same tabs for wired, wireless, mobile broadband, VPN, and DSL.

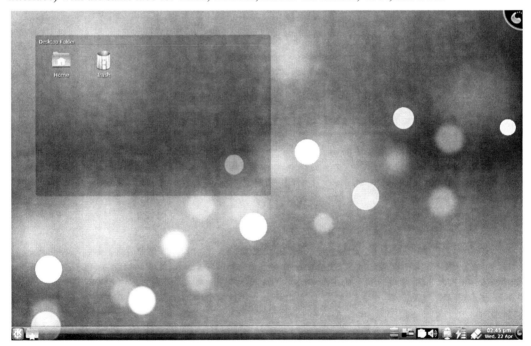

Figure 10-12: Initial KUbuntu screen with Desktop folder plasmoid

Desktop Plasmoids (applets)

The KDE 4 desktop features the Plasma desktop that treats applets differently. Plasma designates its applets as plasmoids. It is designed to deal with plasmoids on the same level as windows and icons. Just as a desktop can display windows, it can also display plasmoids. Plasmoids, or applets, are taking on more responsibility in desktop operations, running essential operations, every replacing to a limited extent the need for file manager windows. To this end, the dashboard tool can hide all other desktop items, showing just the plasmoids.

When you first login, your desktop will show one plasmoid, Desktop folder view (see Figure 10-12)

Managing desktop plasmoids

When you pass your mouse over a plasmoid, its sidebar is displayed with button for resizing, refreshing, settings, and closing the plasmoid (see Figure 10-13). Click and drag the resize button to change the plasmoid size. Clicking the settings button (wrench icon) opens that plasmoid's settings dialog (see Figure 10-14).

Figure 10-13: Clock Plasmoid with task sidebar

Figure 10-14: Clock Plasmoid Configuration

To add a widget (plasmoid) to the desktop, right-click anywhere on the desktop and select Add Widgets from the pop-up menu. This opens the Add Widgets window that lists widgets you can add (see Figure 10-15). A drop-down menu at the top of the window lets you see different widget categories like Date & Time, Online Services, and Graphics. You can also see recently used widgets as well as set up favorite widgets.

Figure 10-15: Adding a plasmoid: Add Widgets

Figure 10-16: Desktop window, Folder window, Calculator, Digital clock, and Notetaker plasmoids.

Figure 10-16 shows Desktop, digital clock, calculator, and folder view plasmoids. The Desktop plasmoid is just a folder view plasmoid set to the Desktop folder. When you add a Folder View plasmoid, it will default to your home directory.

The desktop toolbox menu entries with Zoom Out (ZUI) is shown here.

Dashboard

The dashboard is designed to display plasmoids (applets) only. It hides all windows and icons, showing all your desktop plasmoids. To start the dashboard, click the dashboard applet in the panel. When in use, the screen will display the Plasma Dashboard label at the top (see Figure 10-16). To return to the desktop, select Hide Dashboard from the top-right corner menu (Plasma desktop toolbox).

When the dashboard is in use, the screen will display the Plasma Dashboard label at the top (see Figure 10-17). To return to the desktop, select Hide Dashboard from the top-right corner menu (Plasma desktop toolbox).

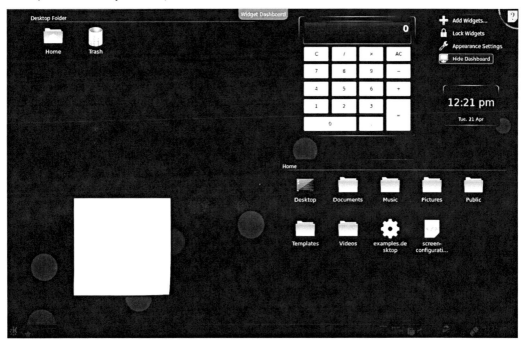

Figure 10-17: The Dashboard and Dashboard applet

Activities and ZUI (zoom)

KDE also supports multiple activities. Activities are different plasma desktop containments, each with it own set of plasmoids. An activity is not the same as virtual desktop. Virtual desktops affect windows, displaying a different set of windows on each desktop. An activity uses the current virtual desktop, but has its own set of plasmoids that are also displayed. You can use different activities, with different plasmoids on the same virtual desktop. Technically, each activity is a Plasma desktop containment that has its own collection of plasmids. You can switch to a different activity (desktop containment) and display a different collection of plasmoids on your desktop.

An activity is a way to set up as set of plasmoids for a certain task. You could have one activity for office work, another for news, and yet another for media. Each activity could have its own set of appropriate plasmoids, like clock, calculator, dictionary, and document folder for an office activity. A media activity might have a now playing plasmoid for audio, picture frame for photos, news ticker for latest news. You could have an activity for home, one for office, one for work, or one for entertainment, each with its own set of plasmoids.

Multiple activities are managed using the Zooming User Interface (ZUI). This interface is accessed through the Zoom Out entry on the desktop toolbox menu, shown here.

You zoom out to display your different activities, and zoom in to select an activity or move to a lower zoom level. There are two zoom out levels, the first showing a few activities (see Figure 10-18), and the second showing all of them. On the first level your mouse becomes a hand that can move to different activities (your screen shows only a few at a time). You can zoom out fully to display all your activities on a single screen (see Figure 10-19).

On the Zoom out levels, a toolbar appears at the bottom of each activity. There are buttons for Add Widgets, Add Activity, Zoom in (first looking glass), zoom out (second looking glass, and desktop settings like the background (wrench icon). From the first level, you can use the looking glasses on any activity to zoom out to top level. On the top level, only one looking glass icon is shown on each activity. Use any of them to zoom back to the first level.

Any additional activities will also have a delete icon on their toolbar (a red X). Your original desktop will not have one. You can remove any additional activities you set up by clicking their delete icon.

Tip: The Zoomed display will still show any open windows on your original desktop using the entire screen as if it where one desktop. To fully see your zoomed activities (not having them blocked by open windows), you should close or minimize your windows before zooming.

To add a new activity, click on the Add Activity button on the toolbar of any activity desktop (initially you will have only one). This creates a new activity, which will be displayed as a desktop.

To use an activity, from the first level, click on its zoom in icon (first looking glass) on its toolbar to zoom in on it. Your desktop will be restored to its original display, but now showing the desktop plasmoids for that activity.

To change from one activity to another, first select Zoom Out on the desktop toolbox to enter the Zoom Out mode. Find the activity you want (displayed as desktops with their different plasmoids). Then click on the activity's zoom in icon (first looking glass). The new activity with its own set of plasmoids is then displayed on your desktop.

You can add plasmoids to any activity by clicking on the activities Add Widget button. The Add widget dialog will open and you can select a widget to add.

While in the Zoom Out mode, showing your multiple activities, you can manage plasmoids on any of the activities. You can move plasmoids to different positions within an activity, remove a plasmoid, or even configure it. As you pass your mouse over a plasmoid, its sidebar will be displayed with items for moving, resizing, removing, and configuring the plasmoid. To move a plasmoid, click and drag anywhere on it, except on the sidebar items.

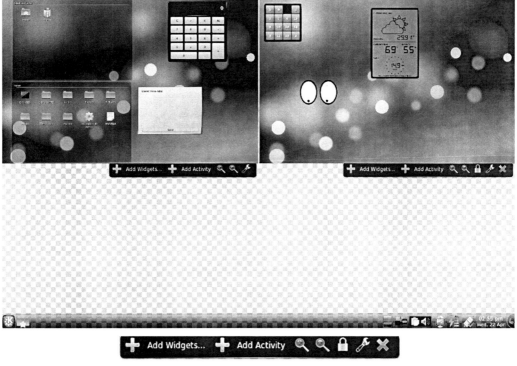

Figure 10-18: Zoom with added activities and activity toolbar

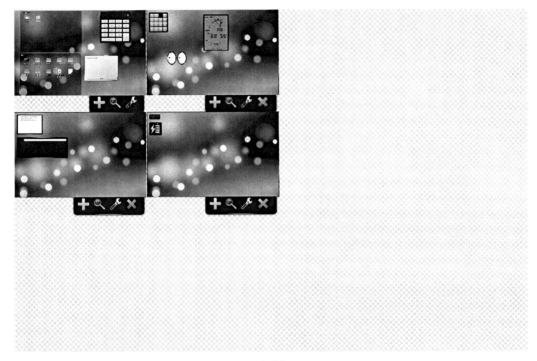

Figure 10-19: Full Zoom with multiple activities

KDE Windows

A KDE window has the same functionality you find in other window managers and desktops. You can resize the window by clicking and dragging any of its corners or sides. A click-and-drag operation on a side extends the window in that dimension, whereas a corner extends both height and width at the same time. The top of the window has a title bar showing the name of the window, the program name in the case of applications, and the current directory name for the file manager windows. The active window has the title bar highlighted. To move the window, click this title bar and drag it where you want. Right-clicking the window title bar displays a pop-up menu with entries for window operations, such as closing or resizing the window. Within the window, menus, icons, and toolbars for the particular application are displayed.

You can configure the appearance and operation of a window by selecting the Configure Window Behavior entry from the Window menu (right-click the title bar). Here you can set appearance (Window Decorations), button and key operations (Actions), the focus policy such as a mouse click on the window or just passing the mouse over it (Focus), how the window is displayed when moving it (Moving), and advanced features like moving a window directly to another virtual desktop, Active Desktop Borders. All these features can be configured also using the System Setting Look & Feel tools.

Opened windows are also shown as buttons on the KDE taskbar located on the panel. The taskbar shows the different programs you are running or windows you have open. This is essentially a docking mechanism that lets you change to a window or application just by clicking its button. When you minimize (iconify) a window, it is reduced to its taskbar button. You can then restore the window by clicking its taskbar button.

To the right of the title bar are three small buttons for minimizing, maximizing, or closing the window (down, up, and x symbols). You can switch to a window at any time by clicking its taskbar button. From the keyboard, you can use the ALT-TAB key combination to display a list of current open windows. Holding down the ALT key and sequentially pressing TAB moves you through the list.

Application and configuration windows may display a Help Notes button, shown next to the iconify button and displaying a question mark. Clicking this button changes your cursor to a question mark. You can then move the cursor to an item such as an icon on a toolbar, and then click it to display a small help note explaining what the item does. For example, moving the mouse to the Forward button in the file manager taskbar will show a note explaining that this button performs a browser forward operation.

Applications

You can start an application in KDE in several ways. If an entry for it is in the Kickoff Applications menu, you can select that entry to start the application. You can right-click on any application entry in the Applications menu to display a pop-up menu with "Add to Panel" and "Add to Desktop" entries. Select either to add a shortcut icon for the application to the desktop or the panel. You can then start an application by single clicking its desktop or panel icon.

An application icon on the desktop is implemented as desktop plasmoid. Passing the mouse over the application icon on the desktop displays a sidebar with the wrench icon for the icon settings. This opens a Setting window with tabs for general, permissions, application, and preview. On the general tab you can select an icon image and set the displayed name. The application tab references the actual application program file with possible options. Permissions set standard access permissions by the owner, group, or others.

You can also run an application by right-clicking on the desktop and selecting select Run Command (or press ALT-F2) which will display the Krunner tool consisting of a box to enter a single command. Previous commands can be accessed from a pop-up menu. You need only enter a pattern to search for the application. Results will be displayed in the Krunner window. Choose the one you want. A Show Options button will list options for running the program.

Virtual Desktops: Desktop Pager

KDE, like most Linux window managers, supports virtual desktops. In effect, this extends the desktop area on which you can work. You could have Mozilla running on one desktop and be using a text editor in another. KDE can support up to 16 virtual desktops, though the default is 4. Your virtual desktops can be displayed and accessed using the KDE Desktop Pager located on the panel. The KDE Desktop Pager represents your virtual desktops as miniature screens showing small squares for each desktop. It works much like the GNOME Workspace Switcher. On Ubuntu, by default, there are 2 squares, one on top of the other. To move from one desktop to another, click the square for the destination desktop. The selected desktop will be highlighted.

If you want to move a window to a different desktop, first open the window's menu by right-clicking the window's title bar. Then select the To Desktop entry, which lists the available desktops. Choose the one you want. Just passing your mouse over a desktop image on the panel will open a message displaying the desktop number.

You can also configure KDE so that if you move the mouse over the edge of a desktop screen, it automatically moves to the adjoining desktop. You need to imagine the desktops arranged in a four-square configuration, with two top desktops next to each other and two desktops below them. You enable this feature by enabling the Active Desktop Borders feature in the System Settings | Window Behavior | Window Behavior | Advanced pane.

Figure 10-20: Virtual desktop configuration and Pager plasmoid icon.

To change the number of virtual desktops, you right-click on the Desktop Pager on the panel, and the select the Configure Desktop entry in the pop-up menu. This opens the Multiple Desktops window which displays entries for your active desktops. By default, Ubuntu will set up two virtual desktops for you (see Figure 10-20). The text box labeled "Number of Desktops" controls the number of active desktops. Use the arrows or enter a number to change the number of active desktops. You can change any of the desktop names by clicking an active name and entering a new one. You can also access the Multiple Desktop window from System Settings | Desktop | Multiple Desktops. Choosing to display four desktops shows then stacked as shown here.

To change how the pager displays desktops on the panel, right-click and choose Pager Settings. Here you can configure the pager to display numbers or names for desktops. You can also decide on the number of rows to use. Choosing just one row would display the desktops side by side as shown here.

Tip: Use the CTRL-TAB keys to move to the next desktop, and CTRL-SHIFT-TAB to go the previous desktop. Use CTRL key in combination with a function key to switch to a specific desktop: for example, CTRL-F1 switches to the first desktop and CTRL-F3 to the third desktop.

KDE Panel

The KDE panel, located at the bottom of the screen, provides access to most KDE functions (see Figure 10-21). The panel is a specially configured Plasma containment, just as the desktop is a specially configured Plasma containment. The panel includes icons for menus, directory windows, specific programs, and virtual desktops. These are plasmoids that are configured for use on the panel. At the left end of the panel is a button for the Kickoff menu, a KDE *K* icon.

To add an application to the panel, right-click on its entry in the Kickoff menu to open a pop-up menu and select Add to Panel.

Figure 10-21: KDE panel

Figure 10-22: KDE Add Widgets for panel

To add a widget to the panel, right-click anywhere on the panel and select Add Widgets from the pop-up menu. This opens the Add Widgets window that lists widgets you can add (see

Figure 10-22). A drop-down menu at the top of the window lets you see different widget categories like Date & Time, Online Services, and Graphics. You can also see recently used widgets as well as set up favorite widgets. This is the same Add Widgets used for the desktop.

The Plasma panel supports several kinds of Windows and Tasks widgets including the taskbar, system tray, and pager. The system tray (highlighted in black) holds widgets for desktop operations like sound settings (kmix), update notifier (update-notifier-kde), and the clipboard (klipper) (see Figure 10-23). Next to the system tray are other commonly used widgets like the dashboard, pager, and device notifier. Figure 10-22 shows, from left to right, the pager, dashboard, the system tray (clipboard, sound settings, and update notifier), device notifier, power manager, NetworkManager, and time and date.

Figure 10-23: KDE panel plasmoids; including pager, system tray, device notifier

KDE Panel Configuration

To configure a panel, changing its position, size, and display features, you use the panel's toolbox. The panel toolbox is located at the right side of the panel. Click on it to open an additional panel configuration panel with buttons for adding widgets, moving the panel, changing its size and position, and with a More Settings menu for setting visibility and alignment features. Figure 10-24 shows the configuration panel as it will appear on your desktop. Figure 10-25 provides a more detailed description, including the More Settings menu entries.

Figure 10-24: KDE Panel Configuration

With the configuration panel activated, you can also move plasmoids around the panel. Clicking on a plasmoid will overlay a movement icon, letting you then move the plasmoid icon to a different location on the panel.

The lower part of the configuration panel is used for panel position settings. On the left side is a slider for positioning the panel on the edge of the screen. On the right side are two sliders for the minimum (bottom) and maximum (top) size of the panel.

The top part of the panel has button for changing the location and the size of the panel. The Screen Edge button lets you move the panel to another side of the screen (left, right, top, bottom). Just click and drag. The height button lets you change the panel size, larger or smaller.

The Add Widgets button will open the Add Widgets dialog letting you add new plasmoids to the panel.

The More Setting menu lets you set Visibility and Alignment features. You can choose and AutoHide setting that will hide the panel until you move the mouse to its location. The Windows can cover lets a window overlap the panel. For smaller panels, you can align to the right, left, or center of the screen edge.

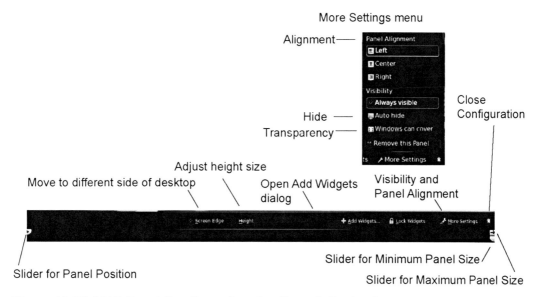

Figure 10-25: KDE Panel Configuration details and display features

The More Settings menu also has an entry to remove the panel. Use this entry to delete a panel you no longer want.

When you are finished with the configuration, click the red x icon the upper right side.

KWin - Desktop Effects

KWin desktop effects can be enabled on the System Settings Desktop tool (System Settings | Desktop | Desktop Effects). The All Effects tab will list available effects (see Figure 10-26). The more dramatic effects are found in the Windows Management section.

Several Windows effects will be selected by default, depending on whether your graphics card can support them. A check mark is placed next to active effects. IF there is wrench icon in the effects entry, it means the effect can be configured. Click on the icon to open its configuration dialog. For several effects, you use certain keys to start them. The more commonly used effects are Cover Switch, Desktop Grid, and Present Windows. The keys for these effects are listed in Table 10-3.

KEY	Operation
ALT-TAB	Cover Switch or Box Switch for open windows
CTRL-F8	Desktop Grid
CTRL-F9	Present Windows Current Desktop
CTRL-F10	Present Windows All Desktops

Table 10-3: KWin desktop effects keyboard shortcuts

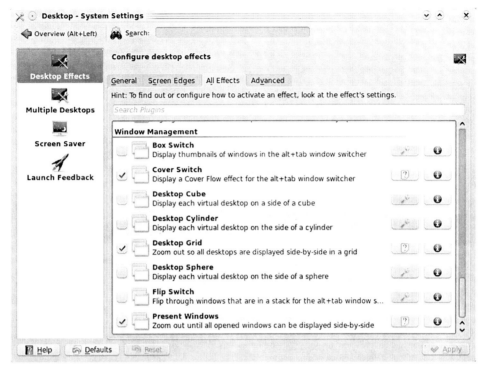

Figure 10-26: Desktop Effect selection and configuration

Most effects will occur automatically. The Taskbar Thumbnails effect will display a live thumbnail of window on the taskbar as your mouse passes over it, showing information on the widget in an expanded window (see Figure 10-27).

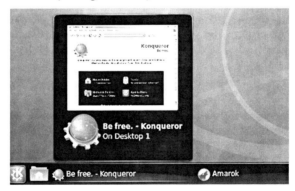

Figure 10-27: Taskbar Thumbnails effect, showing thumbnails of minimized applications

Figure 10-28: Present Windows (Windows effects) Ctrl-F9 for current desktop, Ctrl-f10 for all desktops

The Present Windows effect will display images of your open windows on your screen. The selected one will be highlighted (see Figure 10-28). You can use your mouse to select another. This provides an easy way to browse your open windows. Use Ctrl-F9 to display windows just on your current desktop, and use Ctrl-F10 to display all your open windows across all your desktops. Press the ESC key to return to the desktop.

The Box Switch and Cover Switch effects let you quickly browse through and select an open window (Figures 10-29 and 10-30). Open windows are arranges in a sequence, with the selected one centered. Continuing to press Alt-Tab moves you through the sequence. Box Switch displays windows in a boxed dialog, whereas Cover switch arranges unselected windows stacked to the sides.

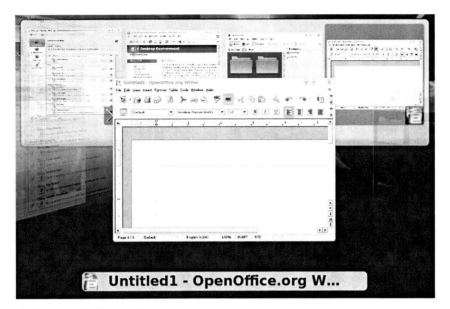

Figure 10-29: Box Switch - Alt-Tab

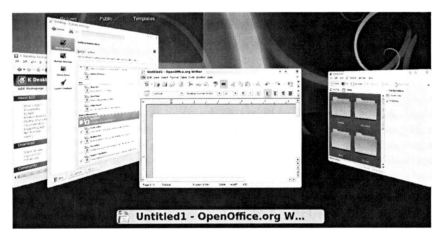

Figure 10-30: Cover Switch - Alt-Tab (Box Switch disabled)

Desktop Grid will show a grid of all your virtual desktops (Ctrl-F8), letting you see all your virtual desktops on the screen at once (see Figure 10-31). You can then move windows and open applications between desktops. Clicking on a desktop makes it the current one.

Figure 10-31: Desktop Grid - Ctrl-F8

KDE File Manager: Dolphin

Dolphin is KDE's dedicated file manager (Konqueror is used as a Web browser). A path for the current directory is displayed at the top of the file window and you can use it to move to different directories and their subdirectories (see Figure 10-32). With the split view you can open directories in the same window, letting you copy and move items between them. A side bar will display different panels. The Places panel will show icons for often used folders like Home, Network, and Trash, as well as removable devices. To add a folder to the Places panel, just drag it there. The files listed in a folder can be viewed in several different ways, such as icons, compact listing, detailed listing, and columns (View | View Mode menu). See Table 10-4 for keyboard shortcuts.

Tip: Configuration files, known as hidden files, are not usually displayed. To have the file manager display these files, select Show Hidden Files from the View menu (Ctrl-.). Dolphin also supports split views, letting you view different directories in the same window (Windows menu). You can split it vertically or horizontally.

You can open a file either by clicking it or by selecting it and then choosing the Open entry in the File menu. If you want to select the file or directory, you need to hold down the CTRL key while you click it. A single-click opens the file. If the file is a program, that program starts up. If it is a data file, such as a text file, the associated application is run using that data file. For example, if you single-click a text file, the Kate application starts displaying that file.

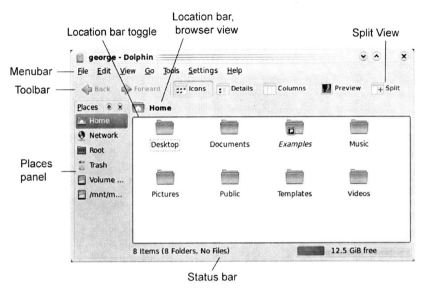

Figure 10-32: The KDE file manager (dolphin)

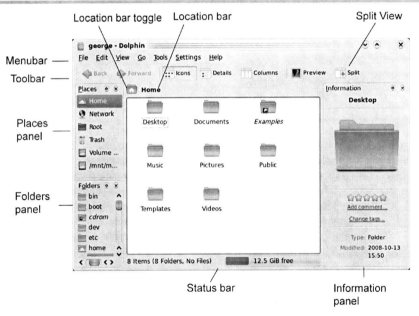

Figure 10-33: The KDE file manager (dolphin), multiple sidebars

If Dolphin cannot determine the application to use, it opens a dialog box prompting you to enter the application name. You can click the Browse button on this box to use a directory tree to locate the application program you want. To configure Dolphin, click Configure Dolphin from the Setting menu.

You can display additional panels by selecting them from the View | Panels menu (see Figure 10-33). The Information panel will display detailed information about a selected file or folder, and the Folders panel will display a directory tree for the file system. The panels are detachable from the file manager window (see Figure 10-34). Dolphin file manager also features integrated desktop search and meta-data extraction.

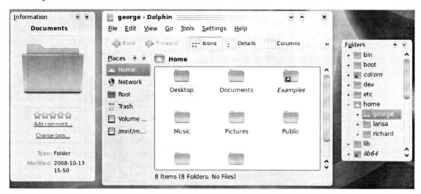

Figure 10-34: The KDE file manager with detached sidebars

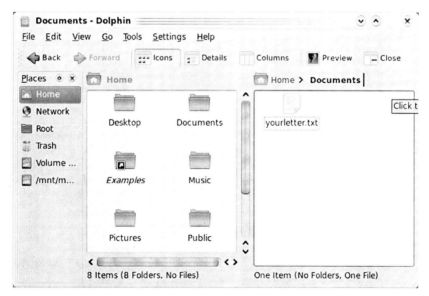

Figure 10-35: The KDE file manager with split views

Dolphin also supports split views, where you can open two different folders in the same window. Click the Split button in the toolbar. You can then drag folder and files from one folder to the other (see Figure 10-35).

Tip: Configuration files, known as hidden files, are not usually displayed. To have the file manager display these files, select Show Hidden Files from the View menu.

The file manager can also extract tar archives and install RPM packages. An *archive* is a file ending in **.tar.gz**, **.tar**, or **.tgz**. Clicking the archive lists the files in it. You can extract a particular file simply by dragging it out of the window. Clicking a text file in the archive displays it with Kate, while clicking an image file displays it with GwenView. Selecting an RPM package opens it with the package-manager utility, which you can then use to install the package.

Keys	Description
ALT-LEFT ARROW, ALT-RIGHT ARROW	Backward and Forward in History
ALT-UP ARROW	One directory up
ENTER	Open a file/directory
ESC	Open a pop-up menu for the current file
LEFT/RIGHT/UP/DOWN ARROWS	Move among the icons
SPACEBAR	Select/unselect file
PAGE UP, PAGE DOWN	Scroll up fast
CTRL-C	Copy selected file to clipboard
CTRL-V	Paste files from clipboard to current directory
CTRL-S	Select files by pattern
CTRL-L	Open new location
CTRL-F	Find files
CTRL-W	Close window

Table 10-4: KDE File Manager Keyboard Shortcuts

Search

To search for files, select the Find Files entry in the Tools menu. This opens the Kfind tool with several panes for searching files. There are three panes: Name/Location, Contents, and Properties. The Name/Location pane lets you perform a standard search on file and directory names. You can use wildcard matching symbols, such as *. The search results are displayed in a pane in the lower half of the Find window. You can click a file and have it open with its appropriate application. Text files are displayed by the Kate text editor. Images are displayed by GwenView. Applications are run. The search program also enables you to save your search results for later reference.

On the Properties pane you can search by date, size, owner, or group, and on the Contents pane you can search files for phrases or words, even including their meta info.

Navigating Directories

Within a file manager window, a single-click on a directory icon moves to that directory and displays its file and subdirectory icons. To move back up to the parent directory, you click the up arrow button located on the left end of the navigation toolbar. A single-click on a directory icon moves you down the directory tree, one directory at a time. By clicking the up arrow button, you move up the tree. The Navigation bar can display either the directory path for the current folder or an editable location box where you can enter in a pathname. For the directory path, you can click on any displayed directory name to moving you quickly to an upper level folder. Initially only the directories in the path name are displayed. To use the location box, select Show Full Location in the View | Navigation Bar menu (or press Ctrl-L). The navigation bar changes to an editable text box where you can type a path name.

Like a Web browser, the file manager remembers the previous directories it has displayed. You can use the back and forward arrow buttons to move through this list of prior directories. You can also use several keyboard shortcuts to perform such operations, like Atl-uparrow to move up a directory, and the arrow keys to move to different icons.

Copy, Move, Delete, Rename, and Link Operations

To perform an operation on a file or directory, you first have to select it. To select a file or directory, you click the file's icon or listing. To select more than one file, continue to hold the CTRL key down while you click the files you want. You can also use the keyboard arrow keys to move from one file icon to another and then use the ENTER key to select the file you want.

To copy and move files, you can use the standard drag-and-drop method with your mouse. To copy a file, you locate it by using the file manager. Open another file manager window to the directory to which you want the file copied. Then click and drag the File icon to that window. A pop-up menu appears with selections for Move, Copy, or Link. Choose Copy. To move a file to another directory, follow the same procedure, but select Move from the pop-up menu. To copy or move a directory, use the same procedure as for files. All the directory's files and subdirectories are also copied or moved.

To rename a file, Ctrl-click its icon and press F2, or right-click the icon and select Rename from the pop-up menu. The name below the icon will become boxed, editable text that you can then change.

You delete a file either by selecting it and deleting it or placing it in the Trash folder to delete later. To delete a file, select it and then choose the Delete entry in the File menu (also SHIFT-DEL key). To place a file in the Trash folder, click and drag it to the Trash icon on your desktop or select Move To Trash from the Edit menu (DEL key). You can later open the Trash folder and delete the files. To delete all the files in the Trash folder, right-click the Trash icon in Dolphin file manager sidebar, and select Remove Trash from the pop-up menu. To restore any files in the Trash bin, open the Trash window and drag them out of the Trash folder.

Each file or directory has properties associated with it that include permissions, the filename, and its directory. To display the Properties window for a given file, right-click the file's icon and select the Properties entry. On the General panel, you see the name of the file displayed. To change the file's name, replace the name there with a new one. Permissions are set on the Permissions panel. Here, you can set read, write, and execute permissions for user, group, or other access to the file. The Group entry enables you to change the group for a file. The Meta Info panel lists information specific to that kind of file, for example, the number of lines and characters in a text file. An image file will list features like resolution, bit depth, and color.

Tip: KDE automatically searches for and reads an existing **.directory** file located in a directory. A **.directory** file holds KDE configuration information used to determine how the directory is displayed. You can create such a file in a directory and place a setting in it to set display features, such as the icon to use to display the directory folder.

Web and FTP Access: Konqueror

The KDE Konqueror is a full-featured Web browser and an FTP client. It includes a box for entering either a pathname for a local file or a URL for a Web page on the Internet or your intranet. The initial default page is your Bookmarks page (see Figure 10-36). A navigation toolbar can be used to display previous Web pages. The Home button will always return you to your home page. When accessing a Web page, the page is displayed as on any Web browser. With the navigation toolbar, you can move back and forth through the list of previously displayed pages in that session.

The Konqueror also operates as an FTP client. When you access an FTP site, you navigate the remote directories as you would your own. The operations to download a file arc the same as copying a file on your local system. Just select the file's icon or entry in the file manager window and drag it to a window showing the local directory to which you want it downloaded. Then, select the Copy entry from the pop-up menu that appears.

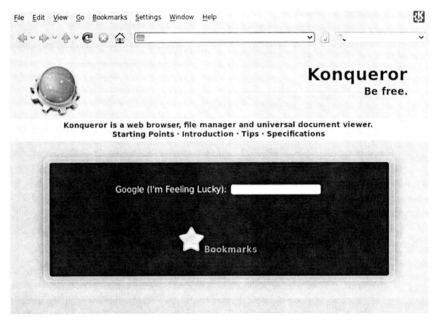

Figure 10-36: Konqueror

Tip: KDE features the KGet tool for Konqueror, which manages FTP downloads, letting you select, queue, suspend, and schedule downloads, while displaying status information on current downloads.

Figure 10-37: Konqueror as file manager with split views and sidebar

To configure Konqueror, select Configure Konqueror from a Konqueror window Settings menu. You can perform configuration tasks like specifying proxies, and Web page displays, fonts to use, cookie management, and encryption methods. The History category lets you specify the number of history items and their expiration date. With the Plugins category you can see a listing of current browser plug-ins as well as scan for new ones.

Konqueror also supports split views as well as a navigation sidebar. You can select vertical or horizontal split views from the Window menu. Also you can add split view icons to the toolbar by selecting Settings | Toolbar | Extra Toolbar (see Figure 10-34). With split views you can display two different Web sites at the same time in the same Konqueror window.

The Navigation panel can display bookmarks, folder links, and system tools. From the Setting menu select Show Navigation Panel (The Extra toolbar will also display a "Show Navigation Panel" icon that will display the Navigation Panel). The Navigation Panel displays bookmarks, history, home folder, root folder, network folder, and services. There are buttons for each on the left side of the Panel. In effect, Konqueror can be used as an alternative file manager to Dolphin.

Konqueror also supports tabbed displays. Instead of opening a folder or site in the same Konqueror window or a new one, you can open a new tab for it using the same Konqueror window. One tab can display the initial folder or site opened, and other tabs can be used for folders or sites opened later. You can then move from viewing one folder to another by simply clicking the latter folder's tab. This way you can view multiple folders or sites with just one Konqueror window. To open a folder as a tab, right-click its icon and select Open In New Tab. To later close the folder, right-click its tab label and select Close Tab. You can also detach a tab, opening it up in its own file manager window.

Konqueror can also operate as a file manager. To use Konqueror as a file manager, on the Konqueor window, choose Settings | Load View Profile | File Management. Konqueror will open to your home folder and the sidebar will list your file system directories (see Figure 10-37). You can also use split views on different folders, showing two or more open side by side. You can then move files directly between the displayed folders.

KDE Software Management: KPackageKit

KUbuntu uses the KDE version of PackageKit called KPackageKit to manage software (see Figure 10-38). This replaces the older Adept software manager. You can access PackageKit from Applications | Software Management. To list packages use the package categories listed in the drop down menu located to the right of the toolbar. You can also search for packages. Clicking on a package open an information box with a button bar with Description File List, Depends on, and Required by buttons. Description is selected initially displaying information about the packages like its name, PackageKit group, software development home page, and package size. The Depends on button will list dependent packages that the package needs. These will be installed along with the package, if not installed already. The Required by button shows what packages need this package, and can be useful if you plan to later remove the package.

Click the plush sign to the right of the package entry, to select the package for installation. Packages selected for download and installation will have a down arrow emblem on their package icon.

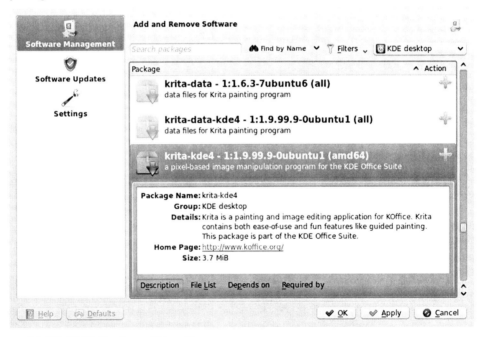

Figure 10-38: KDE PackageKit software manager.

Installed packages will have a disk emblem on their package icon. A minus sign will be displayed to the right of the package entry. To select the package for removal, click on this sign.

krita-kde4 - 1:1.9.99.9-0ubuntu1 (amd64)
a pixel-based image manipulation program for the KDE Office Suite

KDE Configuration: KDE System Settings

With the KDE configuration panels, you can configure your desktop and system, changing the way it is displayed and the features it supports. The configurations are accessed on the System Settings window (Scc Figure 10-39). On KUbuntu, you can access this window from the System Settings entry in the Kickoff Favorites panel. From a standard Ubuntu desktop installation, where KDE is one of several available desktops, including GNOME, access to the administrative tools is more complicated.

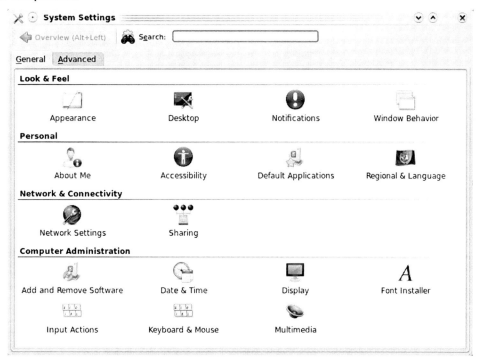

Figure 10-39: KDE System Settings General tab

From Applications, you would select Settings, and then from the Setting menu, you select System Settings. You should use the KDE System Settings tools to configure your KDE desktop. Keep in mind that most system configurations tasks are still performed by the GNOME-based Ubuntu administration tools. You can use the KDE versions if you wish.

The System Settings window shows two tabs, one General and the other Advanced. The General tab is divided into icons for Personal, Look & Feel, Computer Administration, and Network & Connectivity. The Advanced tab has icons for System administration and Advanced User Settings. Use the icons to display a window with sidebar icon list for configuration panes, with the panes selected shown on the right. The selected pane may also have tabs.

To change your theme, you would select the Appearance icon on the System Settings General tab located in the Look & Feel section. This opens an Appearances window with a sidebar listing icons for appearance features like fonts and styles (see Figure 10-40). To change the theme, select the Style icon. This displays the style pane on the right side of the window. There are three tabbed panels: Style, Effects, and Toolbar. On the Style panel you can select the widget style. For Icons you would use the Icon panel selected from the sidebar.

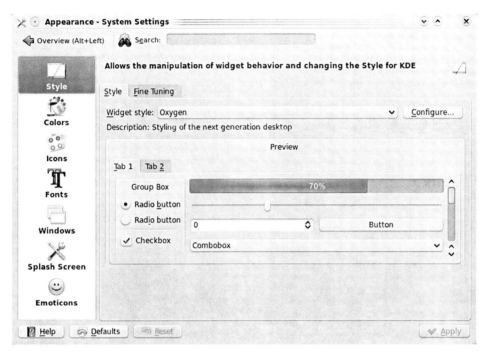

Figure 10-40: KDE System Settings: Appearance Style pane

The Network & Connectivity segment holds icons for configuring the KDE file manager's network tools, including Web browser features as well as Samba (Windows) access and Wireless connectivity. The Personal segment has icons for personal information (About Me), Accessibility features, designating default applications to use, and selecting the region and language. Computer Administration lets you set the settings for the Date and time, keyboard, mouse, and joystick configuration, font management, sound device configuration, and your display resolution.

The Advanced panel tools for Advanced Users Settings like the Solid hardware interface for Bluetooth and HAL power management (see Figure 10-41). File Associations lets you associate file types with applications (MIME types). The Sessions manager allows you to configure sessions. The System segment has entries for Login manager and Samba. The login manager applies only to the KDE login manager (KDM), not GDM. You would have to first choose to use the KDM instead of GDM. In the System segment, the GRUB editor allows you to change your GRUB boot selections easily, designating different kernel or operating systems as the default, as well as providing any needed parameters.

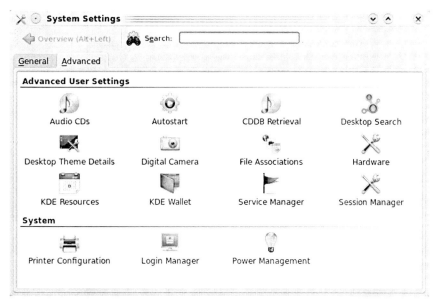

Figure 10-41: KDE System Settings Advanced tab

KDE Directories and Files

When KDE is installed on your system, its system-wide application, configuration, and support files may be installed in the same system directories as other GUIs and user applications. On Ubuntu, KDE is installed in the standard system directories with some variations, such as **/usr/bin** for KDE program files, **/usr/lib/kde4**, which holds KDE libraries, and **/usr/include/kde**, which contains KDE header files used in application development.

Your **.kde** directory holds files and directories used to maintain your KDE desktop. As with GNOME, the **Desktop** directory holds KDE desktop files whose icons are displayed on the desktop. Configuration files are located in the **.kde/share/config** directory. Here you can find the general configuration files for different KDE components: **kwinrc** holds configuration commands for the window manager, **kmailrc** for mail, while **kdeglobals** holds keyboard shortcuts along with other global definitions. You can place configuration directives directly in any of these files; **.kde/share/mimelnk** holds the desktop files for the menu entries added by the user. The **.kde/share/apps** directory contains files and directories for configuring KDE applications, including **koffice**, **kmail**, and even **konqueror**.

Each user has a **Desktop** directory that holds KDE link files for all icons and folders on the user's desktop (see Table 10-5). These include the Trash folders and the CD-ROM and home directory links.

System KDE Directories	Description
`/usr/bin`	KDE programs
`/usr/lib/kde4`	KDE libraries
`/usr/include/kde`	Header files for use in compiling and developing KDE applications
`/usr/share/config`	KDE desktop and application configuration files
`/usr/share/mimelnk`	Desktop files used to build the main menu
`/usr/share/apps`	Files used by KDE applications
`/usr/share/icons`	Icons used in KDE desktop and applications
`/usr/share/doc`	KDE Help system
User KDE Directories	Description
`.kde/AutoStart`	Applications automatically started up with KDE
`.kde/share/config`	User KDE desktop and application configuration files for user-specified features
`.kde/share/apps`	Directories and files used by KDE applications
`Desktop`	Desktop files for icons and folders displayed on the user's KDE desktop
`.kde/share/config/plasma-appletsrc`	Plasma applet configuration

Table 10-5: KDE Installation Directories

The directories located in **share** directory contain files used to configure system defaults for your KDE environment (the system **share** directory is located at **/usr/share**). The **share/apps** directory contains files and directories set up by KDE applications; **share/config** contains the configuration files for particular KDE applications. These are the system-wide defaults that can be overridden by users' own configurations in their own **.kde/share/config** directories. The **share/icons** directory holds the default icons used on your KDE desktop and by KDE applications. As noted previously, in the user's home directory, the **.kde** directory holds a user's own KDE configuration for the desktop and its applications.

11. Shells

The Command Line

History

Filename Expansion: *, ?, [ ]

Standard Input/Output and Redirection

Linux Files

The File Structure

Listing, Displaying, and Printing Files

Managing Directories: mkdir, rmdir, ls, cd, pwd

File and Directory Operations: find, cp, mv, rm, ln

The *shell* is a command interpreter that provides a line-oriented interactive and non-interactive interface between the user and the operating system. You enter commands on a command line; they are interpreted by the shell and then sent as instructions to the operating system (the command line interface is accessible from Gnome and KDE through a Terminal windows – Applications/Accessories menu). You can also place commands in a script file to be consecutively executed much like a program. This interpretive capability of the shell provides for many sophisticated features. For example, the shell has a set of file expansion characters that can generate filenames. The shell can redirect input and output, as well as run operations in the background, freeing you to perform other tasks.

Shell	Web Site
www.gnu.org/software/bash	BASH Web site with online manual, FAQ, and current releases
www.gnu.org/software/bash/manual/bash.html	BASH online manual
www.zsh.org	Z shell Web site with referrals to FAQs and current downloads.
www.tcsh.org	TCSH Web site with detailed support including manual, tips, FAQ, and recent releases
www.kornshell.com	Korn shell site with manual, FAQ, and references

Table 11-1: Linux Shells

Several different types of shells have been developed for Linux: the Bourne Again shell (BASH), the Korn shell, the TCSH shell, and the Z shell. All shells are available for your use, although the BASH shell is the default. You only need one type of shell to do your work. Ubuntu Linux includes all the major shells, although it installs and uses the BASH shell as the default. If you use the command line shell, you will be using the BASH shell unless you specify another. This chapter discusses the BASH shell, which shares many of the same features as other shells.

You can find out more about shells at their respective Web sites as listed in Table 11-1. Also, a detailed online manual is available for each installed shell. Use the `man` command and the shell's keyword to access them, **bash** for the BASH shell, **ksh** for the Korn shell, **zsh** for the Z shell, and **tsch** for the TSCH shell. For example, the command `man bash` will access the BASH shell online manual.

Note: You can find out more about the BASH shell at **www.gnu.org/software/bash**. A detailed online manual is available on your Linux system using the `man` command with the `bash` keyword.

The Command Line

The Linux command line interface consists of a single line into which you enter commands with any of their options and arguments. From GNOME or KDE, you can access the command line interface by opening a terminal window. Should you start Linux with the command line interface, you will be presented with a BASH shell command line when you log in.

By default, the BASH shell has a dollar sign ($) prompt, but Linux has several other types of shells, each with its own prompt (like **%** for the C shell). The root user will have a different prompt, the #. A shell *prompt,* such as the one shown here, marks the beginning of the command line:

```
$
```

You can enter a command along with options and arguments at the prompt. For example, with an -l option, the ls command will display a line of information about each file, listing such data as its size and the date and time it was last modified. In the next example, the user enters the ls command followed by a -l option. The dash before the -l option is required. Linux uses it to distinguish an option from an argument.

```
$ ls -l
```

If you wanted only the information displayed for a particular file, you could add that file's name as the argument, following the -l option:

```
$ ls -l mydata
-rw-r--r-- 1 chris weather 207 Feb 20 11:55 mydata
```

Tip: Some commands can be complex and take some time to execute. When you mistakenly execute the wrong command, you can interrupt and stop such commands with the interrupt key—CTRL-C.

You can enter a command on several lines by typing a backslash just before you press ENTER. The backslash "escapes" the ENTER key, effectively continuing the same command line to the next line. In the next example, the cp command is entered on three lines. The first two lines end in a backslash, effectively making all three lines one command line.

```
$ cp -i \
mydata \
/home/george/myproject/newdata
```

You can also enter several commands on the same line by separating them with a semicolon (;). In effect the semicolon operates as an execute operation. Commands will be executed in the sequence they are entered. The following command executes an ls command followed by a date command.

```
$ ls ; date
```

You can also conditionally run several commands on the same line with the && operator. A command is executed only if the previous one is true. This feature is useful for running several dependent scripts on the same line. In the next example, the ls command is run only if the date command is successfully executed.

```
$ date && ls
```

TIP: Command can also be run as arguments on a command line, using their results for other commands. To run a command within a command line, you encase the command in back quotes.

Command Line Editing

The BASH shell, which is your default shell, has special command line editing capabilities that you may find helpful as you learn Linux (see Table 11-2). You can easily modify commands you have entered before executing them, moving anywhere on the command line and inserting or deleting characters. This is particularly helpful for complex commands. You can use the CTRL-F or RIGHT ARROW key to move forward a character, or the CTRL-B or LEFT ARROW key to move back a character. CTRL-D or DEL deletes the character the cursor is on, and CTRL-H or BACKSPACE deletes the character before the cursor. To add text, you use the arrow keys to move the cursor to where you want to insert text and type the new characters.

Movement Commands	Operation
CTRL-F, RIGHT-ARROW	Move forward a character
CTRL-B, LEFT-ARROW	Move backward a character
CTRL-A or HOME	Move to beginning of line
CTRL-E or END	Move to end of line
ALT-F	Move forward a word
ALT-B	Move backward a word
CTRL-L	Clear screen and place line at top
Editing Commands	**Operation**
CTRL-D or DEL	Delete character cursor is on
CTRL-H or BACKSPACE	Delete character before the cursor
CTRL-K	Cut remainder of line from cursor position
CTRL-U	Cut from cursor position to beginning of line
CTRL-W	Cut previous word
CTRL-C	Cut entire line
ALT-D	Cut the remainder of a word
ALT-DEL	Cut from the cursor to the beginning of a word
CTRL-Y	Paste previous cut text
ALT-Y	Paste from set of previously cut text
CTRL-Y	Paste previous cut text
CTRL-V	Insert quoted text, used for inserting control or meta (Alt) keys as text, such as CTRL-B for backspace or CTRL-T for tabs
ALT-T	Transpose current and previous word
ALT-L	Lowercase current word
ALT-U	Uppercase current word
ALT-C	Capitalize current word
CTRL-SHIFT-_	Undo previous change

Table 11-2: Command Line Editing Operations

You can even cut words with the CTRL-W or ALT-D key and then use the CTRL-Y key to paste them back in at a different position, effectively moving the words. As a rule, the CTRL version of the command operates on characters, and the ALT version works on words, such as CTRL-T to transpose characters and ALT-T to transpose words. At any time, you can press ENTER to execute the command.

For example, if you make a spelling mistake when entering a command, rather than reentering the entire command, you can use the editing operations to correct the mistake. The actual associations of keys and their tasks, along with global settings, are specified in the **/etc/inputrc** file.

The editing capabilities of the BASH shell command line are provided by Readline. Readline supports numerous editing operations. You can even bind a key to a selected editing operation. Readline uses the **/etc/inputrc** file to configure key bindings. This file is read automatically by your **/etc/profile** shell configuration file when you log in. Users can customize their editing commands by creating an **.inputrc** file in their home directory (this is a dot file). It may be best to first copy the **/etc/inputrc** file as your **.inputrc** file and then edit it. **/etc/profile** will first check for a local **.inputrc** file before accessing the **/etc/inputrc** file. You can find out more about Readline in the BASH shell reference manual at **www.gnu.org/manual/bash**.

Command and Filename Completion

The BASH command line has a built-in feature that performs command line and file name completion. Automatic completions can be effected using the TAB key. If you enter an incomplete pattern as a command or filename argument, you can then press the TAB key to activate the command and filename completion feature, which completes the pattern. Directories will have a / attached to their name. If more than one command or file has the same prefix, the shell simply beeps and waits for you to press the TAB key again. It then displays a list of possible command completions and waits for you to add enough characters to select a unique command or filename. For situations where you know there are likely multiple possibilities, you can just press the ESC key instead of two TABs. In the next example, the user issues a `cat` command with an incomplete filename. When the user presses the TAB key, the system searches for a match and, when it finds one, fills in the filename. The user can then press ENTER to execute the command.

```
$ cat pre tab
$ cat preface
```

The automatic completions also work with the names of variables, users, and hosts. In this case, the partial text needs to be preceded by a special character, indicating the type of name. A listing of possible automatic completions follows:

- Filenames begin with any text or /.

- Shell variable text begins with a $ sign.

- User name text begins with a ~ sign.

- Host name text begins with a @.

- Commands, aliases, and text in files begin with normal text.

Variables begin with a **$** sign, so any text beginning with a dollar sign is treated as a variable to be completed. Variables are selected from previously defined variables, like system shell variables. User names begin with a tilde (~). Host names begin with a @ sign, with possible names taken from the **/etc/hosts** file. For example, to complete the variable HOME given just $HOM, simply press a tab key.

```
$ echo $HOM <tab>
$ echo $HOME
```

If you entered just an H, then you could enter two tabs to see all possible variables beginning with H. The command line is redisplayed, letting you complete the name.

```
$ echo $H <tab> <tab>
$HISTCMD $HISTFILE $HOME $HOSTTYPE HISTFILE  $HISTSIZE $HISTNAME
$ echo $H
```

You can also specifically select the kind of text to complete, using corresponding command keys. In this case, it does not matter what kind of sign a name begins with.

Command (CTRL-R for listing possible completions)	Description
TAB	Automatic completion
TAB TAB or ESC	List possible completions
ALT-/, CTRL-R-/	Filename completion, normal text for automatic
ALT-$, CTRL-R-$	Shell variable completion, $ for automatic
ALT-~, CTRL-R-~	User name completion, ~ for automatic
ALT-@, CTRL-R-@	Host name completion, @ for automatic
ALT-!, CTRL-R-!	Command name completion, normal text for automatic

Table 11-3: Command Line Text Completion Commands

For example, the ALT-~ will treat the current text as a user name. ALT-@ will treat it as a host name, and ALT-$, as a variable. ALT-! will treat it as a command. To display a list of possible completions, use the CTRL-X key with the appropriate completion key, as in CTRL-X-$ to list possible variable completions. See Table 11-3 for a complete listing.

History

The BASH shell keeps a list, called a *history list,* of your previously entered commands. You can display each command, in turn, on your command line by pressing the UP ARROW key. The DOWN ARROW key moves you down the list. You can modify and execute any of these previous commands when you display them on your command line.

Tip: The capability to redisplay a previous command is helpful when you've already executed a command you had entered incorrectly. In this case, you would be presented with an error message and a new, empty command line. By pressing the UP ARROW key, you can redisplay your previous command, make corrections to it, and then execute it again. This way, you would not have to enter the whole command again.

History Events

In the BASH shell, the *history utility* keeps a record of the most recent commands you have executed. The commands are numbered starting at 1, and a limit exists to the number of commands remembered—the default is 500. The history utility is a kind of short-term memory, keeping track of the most recent commands you have executed. To see the set of your most recent commands, type **history** on the command line and press ENTER. A list of your most recent commands is then displayed, preceded by a number.

```
$ history
1 cp mydata today
2 vi mydata
3 mv mydata reports
4 cd reports
5 ls
```

Each of these commands is technically referred to as an event. An *event* describes an action that has been taken—a command that has been executed. The events are numbered according to their sequence of execution. The most recent event has the highest number. Each of these events can be identified by its number or beginning characters in the command.

History Commands	Description
CTRL-N or DOWN ARROW	Moves down to the next event in the history list
CTRL-P or UP ARROW	Moves up to the previous event in the history list
ALT-<	Moves to the beginning of the history event list
ALT->	Moves to the end of the history event list
ALT-N	Forward Search, next matching item
ALT-P	Backward Search, previous matching item
CTRL-S	Forward Search History, forward incremental search
CTRL-R	Reverse Search History, reverse incremental search
fc *event-reference*	Edits an event with the standard editor and then executes it **Options** **-l** List recent history events; same as **history** command **-e** *editor event-reference* Invokes a specified editor to edit a specific event
History Event References	
! *event num*	References an event with an event number
!!	References the previous command
! *characters*	References an event with beginning characters
!? *pattern*?	References an event with a pattern in the event
!- *event num*	References an event with an offset from the first event
! *num–num*	References a range of events

Table 11-4: History Commands and History Event References

The history utility enables you to reference a former event, placing it on your command line and enabling you to execute it. The easiest way to do this is to use the UP ARROW and DOWN ARROW keys to place history events on your command line, one at a time. You needn't display the list first with `history`. Pressing the UP ARROW key once places the last history event on your command line. Pressing it again places the next history event on your command. Pressing the DOWN ARROW key places the previous event on the command line.

You can use certain control and meta keys to perform other history operations like searching the history list. A meta key is the ALT key, and the ESC key on keyboards that have no ALT key. The ALT key is used here. ALT-< will move you to the beginning of the history list; ALT-N will search it. CTRL-S and CTRL-R will perform incremental searches, display matching commands as you type in a search string. Table 11-4 lists the different commands for referencing the history list.

Tip: If more than one history event matches what you have entered, you will hear a beep, and you can then enter more characters to help uniquely identify the event.

You can also reference and execute history events using the ! history command. The ! is followed by a reference that identifies the command. The reference can be either the number of the event or a beginning set of characters in the event. In the next example, the third command in the history list is referenced first by number and then by the beginning characters:

```
$ !3
mv mydata reports
$ !mv my
mv mydata reports
```

You can also reference an event using an offset from the end of the list. A negative number will offset from the end of the list to that event, thereby referencing it. In the next example, the fourth command, `cd mydata`, is referenced using a negative offset, and then executed. Remember that you are offsetting from the end of the list—in this case, event 5—up toward the beginning of the list, event 1. An offset of 4 beginning from event 5 places you at event 2.

```
$ !-4
vi mydata
```

To reference the last event, you use a following !, as in `!!`. In the next example, the command `!!` executes the last command the user executed—in this case, `ls`:

```
$ !!
ls
mydata today reports
```

Filename Expansion: *, ?, [ ]

Filenames are the most common arguments used in a command. Often you may know only part of the filename, or you may want to reference several filenames that have the same extension or begin with the same characters. The shell provides a set of special characters that search out, match, and generate a list of filenames. These are the asterisk, the question mark, and brackets (`*`, `?`, `[]`). Given a partial filename, the shell uses these matching operators to search for files and expand to a list of filenames found. The shell replaces the partial filename argument with the expanded list of matched filenames. This list of filenames can then become the arguments for commands such as `ls`, which can operate on many files. Table 11-5 lists the shell's file expansion characters.

Common Shell Symbols	Execution
ENTER	Execute a command line.
;	Separate commands on the same command line.
`` `command` ``	Execute a command.
$ (*command*)	Execute a command.
[ ]	Match on a class of possible characters in filenames.
\	Quote the following character. Used to quote special characters.
|	Pipe the standard output of one command as input for another command.
&	Execute a command in the background.
!	History command.
File Expansion Symbols	**Execution**
*	Match on any set of characters in filenames.
?	Match on any single character in filenames.
[ ]	Match on a class of characters in filenames.
Redirection Symbols	**Execution**
>	Redirect the standard output to a file or device, creating the file if it does not exist and overwriting the file if it does exist.
>!	The exclamation point forces the overwriting of a file if it already exists.
<	Redirect the standard input from a file or device to a program.
>>	Redirect the standard output to a file or device, appending the output to the end of the file.
Standard Error Redirection Symbols	**Execution**
2>	Redirect the standard error to a file or device.
2>>	Redirect and append the standard error to a file or device.
2>&1	Redirect the standard error to the standard output.

Table 11-5: Shell Symbols

Matching Multiple Characters

The asterisk (*) references files beginning or ending with a specific set of characters. You place the asterisk before or after a set of characters that form a pattern to be searched for in filenames.

If the asterisk is placed before the pattern, filenames that end in that pattern are searched for. If the asterisk is placed after the pattern, filenames that begin with that pattern are searched for. Any matching filename is copied into a list of filenames generated by this operation.

In the next example, all filenames beginning with the pattern "doc" are searched for and a list generated. Then all filenames ending with the pattern "day" are searched for and a list is generated. The last example shows how the * can be used in any combination of characters.

```
$ ls
doc1 doc2 document docs mydoc monday tuesday
$ ls doc*
doc1 doc2 document docs
$ ls *day
monday tuesday
$ ls m*d*
monday
$
```

Filenames often include an extension specified with a period and followed by a string denoting the file type, such as **.c** for C files, **.cpp** for C++ files, or even **.jpg** for JPEG image files. The extension has no special status and is only part of the characters making up the filename. Using the asterisk makes it easy to select files with a given extension. In the next example, the asterisk is used to list only those files with a **.c** extension. The asterisk placed before the **.c** constitutes the argument for **ls**.

```
$ ls *.c
calc.c main.c
```

You can use * with the **rm** command to erase several files at once. The asterisk first selects a list of files with a given extension, or beginning or ending with a given set of characters, and then it presents this list of files to the **rm** command to be erased. In the next example, the **rm** command erases all files beginning with the pattern "doc":

```
$ rm doc*
```

Tip: Use the * file expansion character carefully and sparingly with the **rm** command. The combination can be dangerous. A misplaced * in an **rm** command without the -i option could easily erase all the files in your current directory. The -i option will first prompt the user to confirm whether the file should be deleted.

Matching Single Characters

The question mark (?) matches only a single incomplete character in filenames. Suppose you want to match the files **doc1** and **docA**, but not the file **document**. Whereas the asterisk will match filenames of any length, the question mark limits the match to just one extra character. The next example matches files that begin with the word "doc" followed by a single differing letter:

```
$ ls
doc1 docA document
$ ls doc?
doc1 docA
```

Matching a Range of Characters

Whereas the * and ? file expansion characters specify incomplete portions of a filename, the brackets ([]) enable you to specify a set of valid characters to search for. Any character placed within the brackets will be matched in the filename. Suppose you want to list files beginning with "doc", but only ending in *1* or *A*. You are not interested in filenames ending in *2* or *B*, or any other character. Here is how it's done:

```
$ ls
doc1 doc2 doc3 docA docB docD document
$ ls doc[1A]
doc1 docA
```

You can also specify a set of characters as a range, rather than listing them one by one. A dash placed between the upper and lower bounds of a set of characters selects all characters within that range. The range is usually determined by the character set in use. In an ASCII character set, the range "a-g" will select all lowercase alphabetic characters from *a* through *g,* inclusive. In the next example, files beginning with the pattern "doc" and ending in characters *1* through *3* are selected. Then, those ending in characters *B* through *E* are matched.

```
$ ls doc[1-3]
doc1 doc2 doc3
$ ls doc[B-E]
docB docD
```

You can combine the brackets with other file expansion characters to form flexible matching operators. Suppose you want to list only filenames ending in either a **.c** or **.o** extension, but no other extension. You can use a combination of the asterisk and brackets: * [co]. The asterisk matches all filenames, and the brackets match only filenames with extension **.c** or **.o**.

```
$ ls *.[co]
main.c  main.o  calc.c
```

Matching Shell Symbols

At times, a file expansion character is actually part of a filename. In these cases, you need to quote the character by preceding it with a backslash to reference the file. In the next example, the user needs to reference a file that ends with the ? character, **answers?**. The ? is, however, a file expansion character and would match any filename beginning with "answers" that has one or more characters. In this case, the user quotes the ? with a preceding backslash to reference the filename.

```
$ ls answers\?
answers?
```

Placing the filename in double quotes will also quote the character.

```
$ ls "answers?"
answers?
```

This is also true for filenames or directories that have white space characters like the space character. In this case you could either use the backslash to quote the space character in the file or directory name, or place the entire name in double quotes.

```
$ ls My\ Documents
My Documents
```

```
$ ls "My Documents"
My Documents
```

Generating Patterns

Though not a file expansion operation, {} is often useful for generating names that you can use to create or modify files and directories. The braces operation only generates a list of names. It does not match on existing filenames. Patterns are placed within the braces and separated with commas. Any pattern placed within the braces will be used to generate a version of the pattern, using either the preceding or following pattern, or both. Suppose you want to generate a list of names beginning with "doc", but only ending in the patterns "ument", "final", and "draft". Here is how it's done:

```
$ echo doc{ument,final,draft}
document docfinal docdraft
```

Since the names generated do not have to exist, you could use the {} operation in a command to create directories, as shown here:

```
$ mkdir {fall,winter,spring}report
$ ls
fallreport springreport winterreport
```

Standard Input/Output and Redirection

The data in input and output operations is organized like a file. Data input at the keyboard is placed in a data stream arranged as a continuous set of bytes. Data output from a command or program is also placed in a data stream and arranged as a continuous set of bytes. This input data stream is referred to in Linux as the *standard input,* while the output data stream is called the *standard output.* There is also a separate output data stream reserved solely for error messages, called the *standard error.*

Because the standard input and standard output have the same organization as that of a file, they can easily interact with files. Linux has a redirection capability that lets you easily move data in and out of files. You can redirect the standard output so that, instead of displaying the output on a screen, you can save it in a file. You can also redirect the standard input away from the keyboard to a file, so that input is read from a file instead of from your keyboard.

When a Linux command is executed that produces output, this output is placed in the standard output data stream. The default destination for the standard output data stream is a device—in this case, the screen. *Devices,* such as the keyboard and screen, are treated as files. They receive and send out streams of bytes with the same organization as that of a byte-stream file. The screen is a device that displays a continuous stream of bytes. By default, the standard output will send its data to the screen device, which will then display the data.

For example, the `ls` command generates a list of all filenames and outputs this list to the standard output. Next, this stream of bytes in the standard output is directed to the screen device. The list of filenames is then printed on the screen. The `cat` command also sends output to the standard output. The contents of a file are copied to the standard output, whose default destination is the screen. The contents of the file are then displayed on the screen.

Redirecting the Standard Output: > and >>

Suppose that instead of displaying a list of files on the screen, you would like to save this list in a file. In other words, you would like to direct the standard output to a file rather than the screen. To do this, you place the output redirection operator, the greater-than sign (>), followed by the name of a file on the command line after the Linux command. Table 11-6 lists the different ways you can use the redirection operators. In the next example, the output of the `ls` command is redirected from the screen device to a file:

```
$ ls -l *.c > programlist
```

Command	Execution
ENTER	Execute a command line.
;	Separate commands on the same command line.
command *opts args*	Enter backslash before carriage return to continue entering a command on the next line.
`` `command` ``	Execute a command.
Special Characters **for Filename Expansion**	**Execution**
*	Match on any set of characters.
?	Match on any single characters.
[]	Match on a class of possible characters.
\	Quote the following character. Used to quote special characters.
Redirection	**Execution**
command > filename	Redirect the standard output to a file or device, creating the file if it does not exist and overwriting the file if it does exist.
command < filename	Redirect the standard input from a file or device to a program.
command >> filename	Redirect the standard output to a file or device, appending the output to the end of the file.
command 2> filename	Redirect the standard error to a file or device
command 2>> filename	Redirect and append the standard error to a file or device
command 2>&1	Redirect the standard error to the standard output in the Bourne shell.
command >& filename	Redirect the standard error to a file or device in the C shell.
Pipes	**Execution**
*command	command*	Pipe the standard output of one command as input for another command.

Table 11-6: The Shell Operations

The redirection operation creates the new destination file. If the file already exists, it will be overwritten with the data in the standard output. You can set the `noclobber` feature to prevent overwriting an existing file with the redirection operation. In this case, the redirection operation on an existing file will fail. You can overcome the `noclobber` feature by placing an exclamation point after the redirection operator. You can place the `noclobber` command in a shell configuration file to make it an automatic default operation. The next example sets the `noclobber` feature for the BASH shell and then forces the overwriting of the **oldarticle** file if it already exists:

```
$ set -o noclobber
$ cat myarticle >! oldarticle
```

Although the redirection operator and the filename are placed after the command, the redirection operation is not executed after the command. In fact, it is executed before the command. The redirection operation creates the file and sets up the redirection before it receives any data from the standard output. If the file already exists, it will be destroyed and replaced by a file of the same name. In effect, the command generating the output is executed only after the redirected file has been created.

In the next example, the output of the `ls` command is redirected from the screen device to a file. First the `ls` command lists files, and in the next command, `ls` redirects its file list to the **listf** file. Then the `cat` command displays the list of files saved in **listf**. Notice the list of files in **listf** includes the **listf** filename. The list of filenames generated by the `ls` command includes the name of the file created by the redirection operation—in this case, **listf**. The **listf** file is first created by the redirection operation, and then the `ls` command lists it along with other files. This file list output by `ls` is then redirected to the **listf** file, instead of being printed on the screen.

```
$ ls
mydata intro preface
$ ls > listf
$ cat listf
mydata intro listf preface
```

Tip: Errors occur when you try to use the same filename for both an input file for the command and the redirected destination file. In this case, because the redirection operation is executed first, the input file, because it exists, is destroyed and replaced by a file of the same name. When the command is executed, it finds an input file that is empty.

You can also append the standard output to an existing file using the `>>` redirection operator. Instead of overwriting the file, the data in the standard output is added at the end of the file. In the next example, the **myarticle** and **oldarticle** files are appended to the **allarticles** file. The **allarticles** file will then contain the contents of both **myarticle** and **oldarticle**.

```
$ cat myarticle >> allarticles
$ cat oldarticle >> allarticles
```

The Standard Input

Many Linux commands can receive data from the standard input. The standard input itself receives data from a device or a file. The default device for the standard input is the keyboard. Characters typed on the keyboard are placed in the standard input, which is then directed to the Linux command. Just as with the standard output, you can also redirect the standard input, receiving input from a file rather than the keyboard. The operator for redirecting the standard input is the less-than sign (<). In the next example, the standard input is redirected to receive input from the **myarticle** file, rather than the keyboard device (use CTRL-D to end the typed input). The contents of **myarticle** are read into the standard input by the redirection operation. Then the `cat` command reads the standard input and displays the contents of **myarticle**.

```
$ cat < myarticle
hello Christopher
How are you today
$
```

You can combine the redirection operations for both standard input and standard output. In the next example, the `cat` command has no filename arguments. Without filename arguments, the `cat` command receives input from the standard input and sends output to the standard output. However, the standard input has been redirected to receive its data from a file, while the standard output has been redirected to place its data in a file.

```
$ cat < myarticle > newarticle
```

Pipes: |

You may find yourself in situations in which you need to send data from one command to another. In other words, you may want to send the standard output of a command to another command, not to a destination file. Suppose you want to send a list of your filenames to the printer to be printed. You need two commands to do this: the `ls` command to generate a list of filenames and the `lpr` command to send the list to the printer. In effect, you need to take the output of the `ls` command and use it as input for the `lpr` command. You can think of the data as flowing from one command to another. To form such a connection in Linux, you use what is called a *pipe*. The *pipe operator* (|, the vertical bar character) placed between two commands forms a connection between them. The standard output of one command becomes the standard input for the other. The pipe operation receives output from the command placed before the pipe and sends this data as input to the command placed after the pipe. As shown in the next example, you can connect the `ls` command and the `lpr` command with a pipe. The list of filenames output by the `ls` command is piped into the `lpr` command.

```
$ ls | lpr
```

You can combine the **pipe** operation with other shell features, such as file expansion characters, to perform specialized operations. The next example prints only files with a .c extension. The `ls` command is used with the asterisk and ".c" to generate a list of filenames with the .c extension. Then this list is piped to the `lpr` command.

```
$ ls *.c | lpr
```

In the preceding example, a list of filenames was used as input, but what is important to note is that pipes operate on the standard output of a command, whatever that might be. The contents of whole files or even several files can be piped from one command to another. In the next example, the `cat` command reads and outputs the contents of the **mydata** file, which are then piped to the `lpr` command:

```
$ cat mydata | lpr
```

Linux has many commands that generate modified output. For example, the `sort` command takes the contents of a file and generates a version with each line sorted in alphabetic order. The `sort` command works best with files that are lists of items. Commands such as `sort` that output a modified version of its input are referred to as *filters.* Filters are often used with pipes. In the next example, a sorted version of **mylist** is generated and piped into the `more` command for display on the screen. Note that the original file, **mylist**, has not been changed and is not itself sorted. Only the output of `sort` in the standard output is sorted.

```
$ sort mylist | more
```

The standard input piped into a command can be more carefully controlled with the standard input argument (`-`). When you use the dash as an argument for a command, it represents the standard input.

Linux Files

You can name a file using any letters, underscores, and numbers. You can also include periods and commas. Except in certain special cases, you should never begin a filename with a period. Other characters, such as slashes, question marks, or asterisks, are reserved for use as special characters by the system and should not be part of a filename. Filenames can be as long as 256 characters. Filenames can also include spaces, though to reference such filenames from the command line, be sure to encase them in quotes. On a desktop like GNOME or KDE you do not need quotes.

You can include an extension as part of a filename. A period is used to distinguish the filename proper from the extension. Extensions can be useful for categorizing your files. You are probably familiar with certain standard extensions that have been adopted by convention. For example, C source code files always have an extension of **.c**. Files that contain compiled object code have an **.o** extension. You can, of course, make up your own file extensions. The following examples are all valid Linux filenames. Keep in mind that to reference the last of these names on the command line, you would have to encase it in quotes as "New book review":

```
preface
chapter2
9700info
New_Revisions
calc.c
intro.bk1
New book review
```

Special initialization files are also used to hold shell configuration commands. These are the hidden, or dot, files, which begin with a period. Dot files used by commands and applications have predetermined names, such as the **.mozilla** directory used to hold your Mozilla data and configuration files. Recall that when you use `ls` to display your filenames, the dot files will not be displayed. To include the dot files, you need to use `ls` with the `-a` option.

The `ls -l` command displays detailed information about a file. First the permissions are displayed, followed by the number of links, the owner of the file, the name of the group the user belongs to, the file size in bytes, the date and time the file was last modified, and the name of the file. Permissions indicate who can access the file: the user, members of a group, or all other users. The group name indicates the group permitted to access the file object. The file type for **mydata** is that of an ordinary file. Only one link exists, indicating the file has no other names and no other links. The owner's name is **chris**, the same as the login name, and the group name is **weather**. Other users probably also belong to the **weather** group. The size of the file is 207 bytes, and it was last modified on February 20 at 11:55 A.M. The name of the file is **mydata**.

If you want to display this detailed information for all the files in a directory, simply use the `ls -l` command without an argument.

```
$ ls -l
-rw-r--r-- 1 chris weather 207 Feb 20 11:55 mydata
-rw-rw-r-- 1 chris weather 568 Feb 14 10:30 today
-rw-rw-r-- 1 chris weather 308 Feb 17 12:40 monday
```

All files in Linux have one physical format—a byte stream. A *byte stream* is just a sequence of bytes. This allows Linux to apply the file concept to every data component in the system. Directories are classified as files, as are devices. Treating everything as a file allows Linux to organize and exchange data more easily. The data in a file can be sent directly to a device such as a screen because a device interfaces with the system using the same byte-stream file format as regular files.

This same file format is used to implement other operating system components. The interface to a device, such as the screen or keyboard, is designated as a file. Other components, such as directories, are themselves byte-stream files, but they have a special internal organization. A directory file contains information about a directory, organized in a special directory format. Because these different components are treated as files, they can be said to constitute different *file types.* A character device is one file type. A directory is another file type. The number of these file types may vary according to your specific implementation of Linux. Five common types of files exist, however: ordinary files, directory files, first-in first-out pipes, character device files, and block device files. Although you may rarely reference a file's type, it can be useful when searching for directories or devices.

Although all ordinary files have a byte-stream format, they may be used in different ways. The most significant difference is between binary and text files. Compiled programs are examples of binary files. However, even text files can be classified according to their different uses. You can have files that contain C programming source code or shell commands, or even a file that is empty. The file could be an executable program or a directory file. The Linux `file` command helps you determine what a file is used for. It examines the first few lines of a file and tries to determine a classification for it. The `file` command looks for special keywords or special numbers in those first few lines, but it is not always accurate. In the next example, the `file` command examines the contents of two files and determines a classification for them:

```
$ file monday reports
monday: text
reports: directory
```

If you need to examine the entire file byte by byte, you can do so with the `od` (octal dump) command. The `od` command performs a dump of a file. By default, it prints every byte in its octal representation. However, you can also specify a character, decimal, or hexadecimal representation. The `od` command is helpful when you need to detect any special character in your file or if you want to display a binary file.

The File Structure

Linux organizes files into a hierarchically connected set of directories. Each directory may contain either files or other directories. In this respect, directories perform two important functions. A *directory* holds files, much like files held in a file drawer, and a directory connects to other directories, much as a branch in a tree is connected to other branches. Because of the similarities to a tree, such a structure is often referred to as a *tree structure.*

The Linux file structure branches into several directories beginning with a root directory, /. Within the root directory, several system directories contain files and programs that are features of the Linux system. The root directory also contains a directory called **/home** that contains the home directories of all the users in the system. Each user's home directory, in turn, contains the directories the user has made for their own use. Each of these can also contain directories. Such nested directories branch out from the user's home directory.

Note: The user's home directory can be any directory, though it is usually the directory that bears the user's login name. This directory is located in the directory named **/home** on your Linux system. For example, a user named **dylan** will have a home directory called **dylan** located in the system's **/home** directory. The user's home directory is a subdirectory of the directory called **/home** on your system.

Directory	Function
/	Begins the file system structure, called the *root.*
/home	Contains users' home directories.
/bin	Holds all the standard commands and utility programs.
/usr	Holds those files and commands used by the system; this directory breaks down into several subdirectories.
/usr/bin	Holds user-oriented commands and utility programs.
/usr/sbin	Holds system administration commands.
/usr/lib	Holds libraries for programming languages.
/usr/share/doc	Holds Linux documentation.
/usr/share/man	Holds the online Man files.
/var/spool	Holds spooled files, such as those generated for printing jobs and network transfers.
/sbin	Holds system administration commands for booting the system.
/var	Holds files that vary, such as mailbox files.
/dev	Holds file interfaces for devices such as the terminals and printers (dynamically generated by udev, do not edit).
/etc	Holds system configuration files and any other system files.

Table 11-7: Standard System Directories in Linux

Home Directories

When you log in to the system, you are placed within your home directory. The name given to this directory by the system is the same as your login name. Any files you create when you first log in are organized within your home directory. Within your home directory, however, you can create more directories. You can then change to these directories and store files in them. The same is true for other users on the system. Each user has a home directory, identified by the appropriate login name. Users, in turn, can create their own directories.

You can access a directory either through its name or by making it your working directory. Each directory is given a name when it is created. You can use this name in file operations to access files in that directory. You can also make the directory your working directory. If you do not use any directory names in a file operation, the working directory will be accessed. The working directory is the one from which you are currently working. When you log in, the working directory is your home directory, usually having the same name as your login name. You can change the working directory by using the **cd** command to designate another directory as the working directory.

Pathnames

The name you give to a directory or file when you create it is not its full name. The full name of a directory is its *pathname*. The hierarchically nested relationship among directories forms paths, and these paths can be used to identify and reference any directory or file uniquely or absolutely. Each directory in the file structure can be said to have its own unique path. The actual name by which the system identifies a directory always begins with the root directory and consists of all directories nested below that directory.

In Linux, you write a pathname by listing each directory in the path separated from the last by a forward slash. A slash preceding the first directory in the path represents the root. The pathname for the **robert** directory is **/home/robert**. The pathname for the **reports** directory is **/home/chris/reports**. Pathnames also apply to files. When you create a file within a directory, you give the file a name. The actual name by which the system identifies the file, however, is the filename combined with the path of directories from the root to the file's directory. As an example, the pathname for **monday** is **/home/chris/reports/monday** (the root directory is represented by the first slash). The path for the **monday** file consists of the root, **home**, **chris**, and **reports** directories and the filename **monday**.

Pathnames may be absolute or relative. An *absolute pathname* is the complete pathname of a file or directory beginning with the root directory. A *relative pathname* begins from your working directory; it is the path of a file relative to your working directory. The working directory is the one you are currently operating in. Using the previous example, if **chris** is your working directory, the relative pathname for the file **monday** is **reports/monday**. The absolute pathname for **monday** is **/home/chris/reports/monday**.

The absolute pathname from the root to your home directory can be especially complex and, at times, even subject to change by the system administrator. To make it easier to reference, you can use a special character, the tilde (~), which represents the absolute pathname of your home directory. In the next example, from the **thankyou** directory, the user references the **monday** file in the home directory by placing a tilde and slash before **monday**:

```
$ pwd
/home/chris/letters/thankyou
$ cat ~/monday
raining and warm
$
```

You must specify the rest of the path from your home directory. In the next example, the user references the **monday** file in the **reports** directory. The tilde represents the path to the user's home directory, **/home/chris**, and then the rest of the path to the **monday** file is specified.

```
$ cat ~/reports/monday
```

System Directories

The root directory that begins the Linux file structure contains several system directories. The system directories contain files and programs used to run and maintain the system. Many contain other subdirectories with programs for executing specific features of Linux. For example, the directory **/usr/bin** contains the various Linux commands that users execute, such as `lpl`. The directory **/bin** holds system level commands. Table 11-7 lists the basic system directories.

Listing, Displaying, and Printing Files: ls, cat, more, less, and lpr

One of the primary functions of an operating system is the management of files. You may need to perform certain basic output operations on your files, such as displaying them on your screen or printing them. The Linux system provides a set of commands that perform basic file-management operations, such as listing, displaying, and printing files, as well as copying, renaming, and erasing files. These commands are usually made up of abbreviated versions of words. For example, the `ls` command is a shortened form of "list" and lists the files in your directory. The `lpr` command is an abbreviated form of "line print" and will print a file. The `cat`, `less`, and `more` commands display the contents of a file on the screen. Table 11-8 lists these commands with their different options. When you log in to your Linux system, you may want a list of the files in your home directory. The `ls` command, which outputs a list of your file and directory names, is useful for this. The `ls` command has many possible options for displaying filenames according to specific features.

Displaying Files: cat, less, and more

You may also need to look at the contents of a file. The `cat` and `more` commands display the contents of a file on the screen. The name `cat` stands for *concatenate*.

```
$ cat mydata
computers
```

The `cat` command outputs the entire text of a file to the screen at once. This presents a problem when the file is large because its text quickly speeds past on the screen. The `more` and `less` commands are designed to overcome this limitation by displaying one screen of text at a time. You can then move forward or backward in the text at your leisure. You invoke the `more` or `less` command by entering the command name followed by the name of the file you want to view (`less` is a more powerful and configurable display utility).

```
$ less mydata
```

Command or Option	Execution
`ls`	This command lists file and directory names.
`cat` *filenames*	This filter can be used to display a file. It can take filenames for its arguments. It outputs the contents of those files directly to the standard output, which, by default, is directed to the screen.
`more` *filenames*	This utility displays a file screen by screen. Press the SPACEBAR to continue to the next screen and **q** to quit.
`less` *filenames*	This utility also displays a file screen by screen. Press the SPACEBAR to continue to the next screen and **q** to quit.
`lpr` *filenames*	Sends a file to the line printer to be printed; a list of files may be used as arguments. Use the **-P** option to specify a printer.
`lpq`	Lists the print queue for printing jobs.
`lprm`	Removes a printing job from the print queue.

Table 11-8: Listing, Displaying, and Printing Files

When `more` or `less` invoke a file, the first screen of text is displayed. To continue to the next screen, you press the F key or the SPACEBAR. To move back in the text, you press the B key. You can quit at any time by pressing the Q key.

Printing Files: lpr, lpq, and lprm

With the printer commands such as `lpr` and `lprm`, you can perform printing operations such as printing files or canceling print jobs (see Table 11-8). When you need to print files, use the `lpr` command to send files to the printer connected to your system. In the next example, the user prints the **mydata** file:

```
$ lpr mydata
```

If you want to print several files at once, you can specify more than one file on the command line after the `lpr` command. In the next example, the user prints out both the **mydata** and **preface** files:

```
$ lpr mydata preface
```

Printing jobs are placed in a queue and printed one at a time in the background. You can continue with other work as your files print. You can see the position of a particular printing job at any given time with the `lpq` command, which gives the owner of the printing job (the login name of the user who sent the job), the print job ID, the size in bytes, and the temporary file in which it is currently held.

If you need to cancel an unwanted printing job, you can do so with the `lprm` command, which takes as its argument either the ID number of the printing job or the owner's name. It then removes the print job from the print queue. For this task, `lpq` is helpful, for it provides you with the ID number and owner of the printing job you need to use with `lprm`.

Managing Directories: mkdir, rmdir, ls, cd, pwd

You can create and remove your own directories, as well as change your working directory, with the `mkdir`, `rmdir`, and `cd` commands. Each of these commands can take as its argument the pathname for a directory. The `pwd` command displays the absolute pathname of your working directory. In addition to these commands, the special characters represented by a single dot, a double dot, and a tilde can be used to reference the working directory, the parent of the working directory, and the home directory, respectively. Taken together, these commands enable you to manage your directories. You can create nested directories, move from one directory to another, and use pathnames to reference any of your directories. Those commands commonly used to manage directories are listed in Table 11-9.

Command	Execution
`mkdir` *directory*	Creates a directory.
`rmdir` *directory*	Erases a directory.
`ls -F`	Lists directory name with a preceding slash.
`ls -R`	Lists working directory as well as all subdirectories.
`cd` *directory name*	Changes to the specified directory, making it the working directory. **cd** without a directory name changes back to the home directory: **$ cd reports**
`pwd`	Displays the pathname of the working directory.
directory name / filename	A slash is used in pathnames to separate each directory name. In the case of pathnames for files, a slash separates the preceding directory names from the filename.
`..`	References the parent directory. You can use it as an argument or as part of a pathname: **$ cd ..** **$ mv ../larisa oldarticles**
`.`	References the working directory. You can use it as an argument or as part of a pathname: **$ ls .**
`~ / pathname`	The tilde is a special character that represents the pathname for the home directory. It is useful when you need to use an absolute pathname for a file or directory: **$ cp monday ~/today**

Table 11-9: Directory Commands

Creating and Deleting Directories

You create and remove directories with the `mkdir` and `rmdir` commands. In either case, you can also use pathnames for the directories. In the next example, the user creates the directory **reports**. Then the user creates the directory **articles** using a pathname:

```
$ mkdir reports
$ mkdir /home/chris/articles
```

You can remove a directory with the `rmdir` command followed by the directory name. In the next example, the user removes the directory **reports** with the `rmdir` command:

```
$ rmdir reports
```

To remove a directory and all its subdirectories, you use the `rm` command with the `-r` option. This is a very powerful command and could easily be used to erase all your files. You will be prompted for each file. To simply remove all files and subdirectories without prompts, add the `-f` option. The following example deletes the **reports** directory and all its subdirectories:

```
rm -rf reports
```

Displaying Directory Contents

You have seen how to use the `ls` command to list the files and directories within your working directory. To distinguish between file and directory names, however, you need to use the `ls` command with the `-F` option. A slash is then placed after each directory name in the list.

```
$ ls
weather reports articles
$ ls -F
weather reports/ articles/
```

The `ls` command also takes as an argument any directory name or directory pathname. This enables you to list the files in any directory without first having to change to that directory. In the next example, the `ls` command takes as its argument the name of a directory, **reports**. Then the `ls` command is executed again, only this time the absolute pathname of **reports** is used.

```
$ ls reports
monday tuesday
$ ls /home/chris/reports
monday tuesday
$
```

Moving Through Directories

The `cd` command takes as its argument the name of the directory to which you want to change. The name of the directory can be the name of a subdirectory in your working directory or the full pathname of any directory on the system. If you want to change back to your home directory, you only need to enter the `cd` command by itself, without a filename argument.

```
$ cd props
$ pwd
/home/dylan/props
```

Referencing the Parent Directory

A directory always has a parent (except, of course, for the root). For example, in the preceding listing, the parent for **travel** is the **articles** directory. When a directory is created, two entries are made: one represented with a dot (.), and the other with double dots (. .). The dot represents the pathnames of the directory, and the double dots represent the pathname of its parent directory. Double dots, used as an argument in a command, reference a parent directory. The single dot references the directory itself.

You can use the single dot to reference your working directory, instead of using its pathname. For example, to copy a file to the working directory retaining the same name, the dot can be used in place of the working directory's pathname. In this sense, the dot is another name for the working directory. In the next example, the user copies the **weather** file from the **chris** directory to the **reports** directory. The **reports** directory is the working directory and can be represented with the single dot.

```
$ cd reports
$ cp /home/chris/weather .
```

The .. symbol is often used to reference files in the parent directory. In the next example, the **cat** command displays the **weather** file in the parent directory. The pathname for the file is the .. symbol followed by a slash and the filename.

```
$ cat ../weather
raining and warm
```

Tip: You can use the cd command with the .. symbol to step back through successive parent directories of the directory tree from a lower directory.

File and Directory Operations: find, cp, mv, rm, ln

As you create more and more files, you may want to back them up, change their names, erase some of them, or even give them added names. Linux provides you with several file commands that enable you to search for files, copy files, rename files, or remove files (see Tables 11-5). If you have a large number of files, you can also search them to locate a specific one. The commands are shortened forms of full words, consisting of only two characters. The **cp** command stands for "copy" and copies a file, **mv** stands for "move" and renames or moves a file, **rm** stands for "remove" and erases a file, and **ln** stands for "link" and adds another name for a file, often used as a shortcut to the original. One exception to the two-character rule is the **find** command, which performs searches of your filenames to find a file. All these operations can be handled by the GUI desktops, like GNOME and KDE.

Searching Directories: find

Once you have a large number of files in many different directories, you may need to search them to locate a specific file, or files, of a certain type. The **find** command enables you to perform such a search from the command line. The **find** command takes as its arguments directory names followed by several possible options that specify the type of search and the criteria for the search; it then searches within the directories listed and their subdirectories for files that meet these criteria. The **find** command can search for a file by name, type, owner, and even the time of the last update.

```
$ find directory-list -option criteria
```

Tip: From the GNOME desktop you can use the "Search" tool in the Places menu to search for files. From the KDE Desktop you can use the find tool in the file manager. Select find from the file manager (Konqueror) tools menu.

The **-name** option has as its criteria a pattern and instructs **find** to search for the filename that matches that pattern. To search for a file by name, you use the **find** command with the directory name followed by the **-name** option and the name of the file.

$ **find** *directory-list* -name *filename*

Command or Option	Execution
find	Searches directories for files according to search criteria. This command has several options that specify the type of criteria and actions to be taken.
-name *pattern*	Searches for files with the *pattern* in the name.
-lname *pattern*	Searches for symbolic link files.
-group *name*	Searches for files belonging to the group *name*.
-gid *name*	Searches for files belonging to a group according to group ID.
-user *name*	Searches for files belonging to a user.
-uid *name*	Searches for files belonging to a user according to user ID.
-mtime *num*	Searches for files last modified *num* days ago.
-context *scontext*	Searches for files according to security context (SE Linux).
-print	Outputs the result of the search to the standard output. The result is usually a list of filenames, including their full pathnames.
-type *filetype*	Searches for files with the specified file type. File type can be **b** for block device, **c** for character device, **d** for directory, **f** for file, or **I** for symbolic link.
-perm *permission*	Searches for files with certain permissions set. Use octal or symbolic format for permissions.
-ls	Provides a detailed listing of each file, with owner, permission, size, and date information.
-exec *command*	Executes command when files found.

Table 11-10: The find Command

The **find** command also has options that merely perform actions, such as outputting the results of a search. If you want **find** to display the filenames it has found, you simply include the **-print** option on the command line along with any other options. The **-print** option is an action that instructs **find** to write to the standard output the names of all the files it locates (you can also use the **-ls** option instead to list files in the long format). In the next example, the user searches for all the files in the **reports** directory with the name **monday**. Once located, the file, with its relative pathname, is printed.

$ **find reports -name monday -print**
reports/monday

The **find** command prints out the filenames using the directory name specified in the directory list. If you specify an absolute pathname, the absolute path of the found directories will be output. If you specify a relative pathname, only the relative pathname is output. In the preceding example, the user specified a relative pathname, **reports**, in the directory list. Located filenames were output beginning with this relative pathname. In the next example, the user specifies an absolute pathname in the directory list. Located filenames are then output using this absolute pathname.

```
$ find /home/chris -name monday -print
/home/chris/reports/monday
```

Tip: Should you need to find the location of a specific program or configuration file, you could use `find` to search for the file from the root directory. Log in as the root user and use *l* as the directory. This command searched for the location of the `more` command and files on the entire file system: `find / -name more -print`.

Searching the Working Directory

If you want to search your working directory, you can use the dot in the directory pathname to represent your working directory. The double dots would represent the parent directory. The next example searches all files and subdirectories in the working directory, using the dot to represent the working directory. If you are located in your home directory, this is a convenient way to search through all your own directories. Notice the located filenames are output beginning with a dot.

```
$ find . -name weather -print
./weather
```

You can use shell wildcard characters as part of the pattern criteria for searching files. The special character must be quoted, however, to avoid evaluation by the shell. In the next example, all files with the **.c** extension in the **programs** directory are searched for and then displayed in the long format using the `-ls` action:

```
$ find programs -name '*.c' -ls
```

Locating Directories

You can also use the `find` command to locate other directories. In Linux, a directory is officially classified as a special type of file. Although all files have a byte-stream format, some files, such as directories, are used in special ways. In this sense, a file can be said to have a file type. The `find` command has an option called `-type` that searches for a file of a given type. The `-type` option takes a one-character modifier that represents the file type. The modifier that represents a directory is a **d**. In the next example, both the directory name and the directory file type are used to search for the directory called **travel**:

```
$ find /home/chris -name travel -type d -print
/home/chris/articles/travel
$
```

File types are not so much different types of files as they are the file format applied to other components of the operating system, such as devices. In this sense, a device is treated as a type of file, and you can use `find` to search for devices and directories, as well as ordinary files. Table 11-10 lists the different types available for the `find` command's `-type` option.

You can also use the find operation to search for files by ownership or security criteria, like those belonging to a specific user or those with a certain security context. The user option lets to locate all files belonging to a certain user. The following example lists all files that the user **chris** has created or owns on the entire system. To list those just in the users' home directories, you would use **/home** for the starting search directory. This would find all those in a user's home directory as well as any owned by that user in other user directories.

```
$ find / -user chris -print
```

Copying Files

To make a copy of a file, you simply give cp two filenames as its arguments (see Table 11-11). The first filename is the name of the file to be copied—the one that already exists. This is often referred to as the *source file*. The second filename is the name you want for the copy. This will be a new file containing a copy of all the data in the source file. This second argument is often referred to as the *destination file*. The syntax for the cp command follows:

Command	Execution
cp *filename filename*	Copies a file. **cp** takes two arguments: the original file and the name of the new copy. You can use pathnames for the files to copy across directories:
cp -r *dirname dirname*	Copies a subdirectory from one directory to another. The copied directory includes all its own subdirectories:
mv *filename filename*	Moves (renames) a file. The **mv** command takes two arguments: the first is the file to be moved. The second argument can be the new filename or the pathname of a directory. If it is the name of a directory, then the file is literally moved to that directory, changing the file's pathname:
mv *dirname dirname*	Moves directories. In this case, the first and last arguments are directories:
ln *filename filename*	Creates added names for files referred to as links. A link can be created in one directory that references a file in another directory:
rm *filenames*	Removes (erases) a file. Can take any number of filenames as its arguments. Literally removes links to a file. If a file has more than one link, you need to remove all of them to erase a file:

Table 11-11: File Operations

```
$ cp source-file destination-file
```

In the next example, the user copies a file called **proposal** to a new file called **oldprop**:

```
$ cp proposal oldprop
```

You could unintentionally destroy another file with the cp command. The cp command generates a copy by first creating a file and then copying data into it. If another file has the same name as the destination file, that file is destroyed and a new file with that name is created. By default Ubuntu configures your system to check for an existing copy by the same name (cp is aliased with the -i option). To copy a file from your working directory to another directory, you only need to use that directory name as the second argument in the `cp` command. In the next example, the **proposal** file is overwritten by the **newprop** file. The **proposal** file already exists.

```
$ cp newprop proposal
```

You can use any of the wildcard characters to generate a list of filenames to use with `cp` or `mv`. For example, suppose you need to copy all your C source code files to a given directory. Instead of listing each one individually on the command line, you could use an `*` character with the **.c** extension to match on and generate a list of C source code files (all files with a **.c** extension). In the next example, the user copies all source code files in the current directory to the **sourcebks** directory:

```
$ cp *.c sourcebks
```

If you want to copy all the files in a given directory to another directory, you could use `*` to match on and generate a list of all those files in a `cp` command. In the next example, the user copies all the files in the **props** directory to the **oldprop** directory. Notice the use of a **props** pathname preceding the `*` special characters. In this context, **props** is a pathname that will be appended before each file in the list that `*` generates.

```
$ cp props/* oldprop
```

You can, of course, use any of the other special characters, such as `.`, `?`, or `[]`. In the next example, the user copies both source code and object code files (**.c** and **.o**) to the **projbk** directory:

```
$ cp *.[oc] projbk
```

When you copy a file, you may want to give the copy a different name than the original. To do so, place the new filename after the directory name, separated by a slash.

```
$ cp filename directory-name/new-filename
```

Moving Files

You can use the `mv` command either to rename a file or to move a file from one directory to another. When using `mv` to rename a file, you simply use the new filename as the second argument. The first argument is the current name of the file you are renaming. If you want to rename a file when you move it, you can specify the new name of the file after the directory name. In the next example, the **proposal** file is renamed with the name **version1**:

```
$ mv proposal version1
```

As with `cp`, it is easy for `mv` to erase a file accidentally. When renaming a file, you might accidentally choose a filename already used by another file. In this case, that other file will be erased. The `mv` command also has an `-i` option that checks first to see if a file by that name already exists.

You can also use any of the special characters to generate a list of filenames to use with `mv`. In the next example, the user moves all source code files in the current directory to the **newproj** directory:

```
$ mv *.c newproj
```

If you want to move all the files in a given directory to another directory, you can use * to match on and generate a list of all those files. In the next example, the user moves all the files in the **reports** directory to the **repbks** directory:

```
$ mv reports/* repbks
```

Note: The easiest way to copy files to a CD-R/RW or DVD-R/RW disc is to use the built-in Nautilus burning capability. Just insert a blank disk, open it as a folder, and drag and drop files on to it. You will be prompted automatically to burn the files.

Copying and Moving Directories

You can also copy or move whole directories at once. Both **cp** and **mv** can take as their first argument a directory name, enabling you to copy or move subdirectories from one directory into another (see Table 11-11). The first argument is the name of the directory to be moved or copied, while the second argument is the name of the directory within which it is to be placed. The same pathname structure used for files applies to moving or copying directories.

You can just as easily copy subdirectories from one directory to another. To copy a directory, the **cp** command requires you to use the **-r** option. The **-r** option stands for "recursive." It directs the **cp** command to copy a directory, as well as any subdirectories it may contain. In other words, the entire directory subtree, from that directory on, will be copied. In the next example, the **travel** directory is copied to the **oldarticles** directory. Now two **travel** subdirectories exist, one in **articles** and one in **oldarticles**.

```
$ cp -r articles/travel oldarticles
$ ls -F articles
/travel
$ ls -F oldarticles
/travel
```

Erasing Files and Directories: the rm Command

As you use Linux, you will find the number of files you use increases rapidly. Generating files in Linux is easy. Applications such as editors, and commands such as **cp**, easily create files. Eventually, many of these files may become outdated and useless. You can then remove them with the **rm** command. The **rm** command can take any number of arguments, enabling you to list several filenames and erase them all at the same time. In the next example, the user erases the file **oldprop**:

```
$ rm oldprop
```

Be careful when using the **rm** command, because it is irrevocable. Once a file is removed, it cannot be restored (there is no undo). With the **-i** option, you are prompted separately for each file and asked whether to remove it. If you enter **y**, the file will be removed. If you enter anything else, the file is not removed. In the next example, the **rm** command is instructed to erase the files **proposal** and **oldprop**. The **rm** command then asks for confirmation for each file. The user decides to remove **oldprop**, but not **proposal**.

```
$ rm -i proposal oldprop
Remove proposal? n
Remove oldprop? y
$
```

Links: the ln Command

You can give a file more than one name using the `ln` command. You might want to reference a file using different filenames to access it from different directories. The added names are often referred to as *links*. Linux supports two different types of links, hard and symbolic. *Hard* links are literally another name for the same file, whereas *symbolic* links function like shortcuts referencing another file. Symbolic links are much more flexible and can work over many different file systems, whereas hard links are limited to your local file system. Furthermore, hard links introduce security concerns, as they allow direct access from a link that may have public access to an original file that you may want protected. Links are usually implemented as symbolic links.

Symbolic Links

To set up a symbolic link, you use the `ln` command with the `-s` option and two arguments: the name of the original file and the new, added filename. The `ls` operation lists both filenames, but only one physical file will exist.

```
$ ln -s original-file-name added-file-name
```

In the next example, the **today** file is given the additional name **weather**. It is just another name for the **today** file.

```
$ ls
today
$ ln -s today weather
$ ls
today weather
```

You can give the same file several names by using the `ln` command on the same file many times. In the next example, the file **today** is given both the names **weather** and **weekend**:

```
$ ln -s today weather
$ ln -s today weekend
$ ls
today weather weekend
```

If you list the full information about a symbolic link and its file, you will find the information displayed is different. In the next example, the user lists the full information for both **lunch** and **/home/george/veglist** using the `ls` command with the `-l` option. The first character in the line specifies the file type. Symbolic links have their own file type, represented by an l. The file type for **lunch** is l, indicating it is a symbolic link, not an ordinary file. The number after the term "group" is the size of the file. Notice the sizes differ. The size of the **lunch** file is only four bytes. This is because **lunch** is only a symbolic link—a file that holds the pathname of another file—and a pathname takes up only a few bytes. It is not a direct hard link to the **veglist** file.

```
$ ls -l lunch /home/george/veglist
lrw-rw-r-- 1 chris group 4 Feb 14 10:30 lunch
-rw-rw-r-- 1 george group 793 Feb 14 10:30 veglist
```

To erase a file, you need to remove only its original name (and any hard links to it). If any symbolic links are left over, they will be unable to access the file. In this case, a symbolic link would hold the pathname of a file that no longer exists.

Hard Links

You can give the same file several names by using the `ln` command on the same file many times. To set up a hard link, you use the `ln` command with no `-s` option and two arguments: the name of the original file and the new, added filename. The `ls` operation lists both filenames, but only one physical file will exist.

```
$ ln original-file-name added-file-name
```

In the next example, the **monday** file is given the additional name **storm**. It is just another name for the **monday** file.

```
$ ls
today
$ ln monday storm
$ ls
monday storm
```

To erase a file that has hard links, you need to remove all its hard links. The name of a file is actually considered a link to that file—hence the command `rm` that removes the link to the file. If you have several links to the file and remove only one of them, the others stay in place and you can reference the file through them. The same is true even if you remove the original link—the original name of the file.

Part 4: Administration

System Tools
System Administration
Network Connections
Printing

12. System Tools

GNOME System Monitor

Terminal Window

Login Window

Scheduling Tasks

Log Viewer

Disk Usage Analyzer

Virus Protection

Hardware Sensors

Computer Janitor

Useful system tools as well as user specific configuration tools can be found in the Applications | System Tools, System | Preferences, and System | Administration menus (see Table 12-1). The Administration menu holds tools like the System Monitor for checking on resource usage by processes and storage devices, whereas the Preferences menu holds user specific tools for customizing your desktop and device usage (see Chapter 3). In particular, mouse and keyboard configurations are handled by GNOME or KDE directly (System | Preferences). Software management is handled by the Synaptic Package Manager (System | Administration | Synaptic Package Manager). The System Tools menu holds third party or Universe packages like the ClamTK Virus Scanner and GNOME Schedule.

Ubuntu System Tools	Menu entry	Description
gnome-system-monitor	System Monitor	GNOME System Monitor
gnome-system-log	System Log	GNOME system log viewer
gnome-terminal	Terminal	GNOME Terminal Window
baobab	Disk Usage Analyzer	Disk usage analyzer
gdmsetup	Login Window	Configure Login Window
gnome-nettool	Network Tools	Network analysis
kcron	KCRON	KDE Cron schedule manager
gnome-schedule	Scheduled tasks	GNOME cron schedule manager
ClamTK	Virus Scanner	Clam Virus scanner
sensors-applet	Hardware Sensors Monitor	GNOME applet for temperature readings
	CPU Frequency Scaling	GNOME applet for CPU frequency, included with gnome-applets

Table 12-1: Ubuntu System Tools

GNOME System Monitor

Ubuntu provides the GNOME System Monitor for displaying system information and monitoring system processes, accessible from System | Administration | System Monitor. There are four panels; one for system information, one for processes, one for resources, and one for file systems (see Figure 12-1). The System panel shows the amount of memory, available disk space, and the type of CPU on your system. The Resources panel displays graphs for CPU, Memory and Swap memory, and Network usage.

Your File Systems panel lists your file systems, where they are mounted, and their type, as well as the amount of disk space used and how much is free. The Processes panel lists your processes, letting you sort or search for processes. You can use field buttons to sort by name, process ID, user, and memory. The View pop-up menu lets you select all processes, just your own, or active processes. You can easily stop any process by selecting it and then clicking the End Process button. Right-clicking an item displays actions you can take on the process such as stopping or hiding it. The Memory Maps display, selected from the View menu, shows information on virtual memory, inodes, and flags.

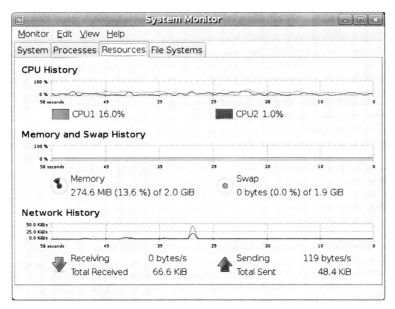

Figure 12-1: GNOME System Monitor: Resources

Managing Processes

Should you have to force a process or application to quit, you can use the Gnome System Monitor Processes tab to find, select, and stop the process. You should be sure of the process you want to stop. Ending a critical process could cripple your system. Application processes will bear the name of the application, and you can use those to force an application to quit. Ending processes manually is usually preformed for open ended operations that you are unable to stop normally. In Figure 12-2, the firefox application has been selected. Clicking the End Process button on the lower right will then force the Firefox Web browser to end.

The Edit menu provides several other options for managing a selected process. You can also right-click on a process entry to display a pop-up menu with the same options. There are corresponding keyboard keys for each option. The options are: stop, continue, end, kill, and change priority. The stop and continue operations work together. You can stop (pause) and process, and then later start it again with the continue option. The end process stops a process safely, whereas a kill option forces an immediate end to the process. The end process option is preferred, but if it does not work, you can use the kill process option. Change priority can give a process a lower or higher priority, letting run faster or slower.

You can also use the kill command in a terminal window to end a process. The **kill** command takes as its argument a process number. Be sure you obtain the correct one. Use the **ps** command to display a process id. Entering in the incorrect process number could also cripple your system. The **ps** command with the **-C** option searches for a particular application name. The **-o pid=** will display only the process id, instead of the process id, time, application name, and tty.

Once you have the process id, you can use the kill command with the process id as its argument to end the process.

```
$ ps -C firefox -o pic=
5555
$ kill 5555
```

One way to insure the correct number is to use the **ps** command to return the process number directly as an argument to a **kill** command. In the following example, an open ended process was started to record a program from channel 12 from a digital video broadcast device, using the **getatsc** command.

```
getatsc -dvb 0 12 > my.ts
```

The process is then ended by first executing the **ps** command to obtain the process id for the **getatsc** process (backquotes), and then using that process id in the **kill** command to end the process. The **-o pid=** option displays only the process id.

```
kill `ps -C getatsc -o pid=`
```

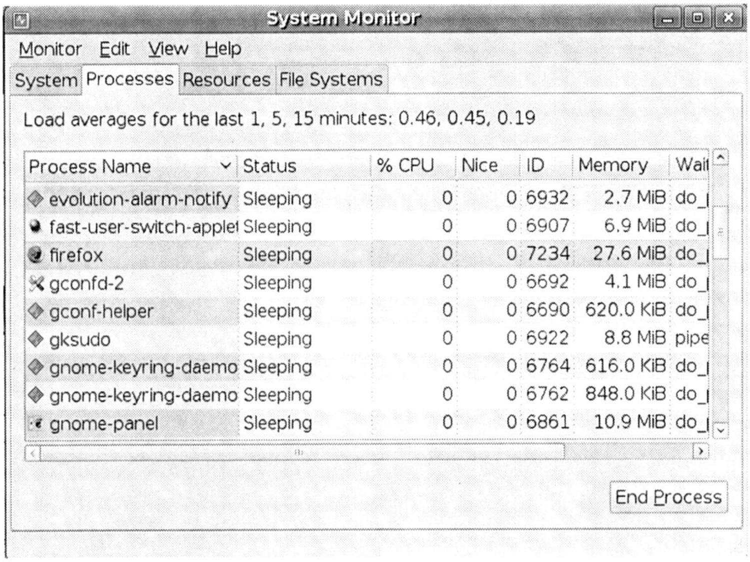

Figure 12-2: GNOME System Monitor: Processes

Terminal Window

The Terminal window allows you to enter Linux commands on a command line (Applications | Accessories | Terminal) . It also provides you with a shell interface for using shell commands instead of your desktop. The command line is editable, allowing you to use the backspace key to erase characters on the line. Pressing any key will insert the key. You can use the left and right arrow keys to move anywhere on the line, and then press keys to insert characters, or use backspace to delete characters (see Figure 12-3). Folders, files, and executable files are color coded: black for files, blue for folders, and green for executable files. Shared folders are displayed with a green background.

Figure 12-3: Terminal Window

The terminal window will remember the previous commands you entered. Use the up and down arrows to have those commands displayed in turn. Press the ENTER key to re-execute the currently displayed command. You can even edit a previous command before running it, allowing you to execute a modified version of a previous command.

The terminal window will display all your previous interactions and commands for that session. Use the scrollbar to see any previous commands you ran and their displayed results.

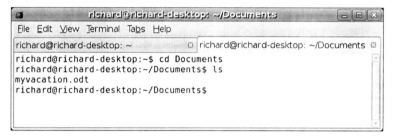

Figure 12-4: Terminal Window with tabs

You can open as many terminal windows as you want, each working in its own shell. Instead of opening a separate window for each new shell you may want, you can open several shells in the same window, using tabbed panels. Select Open Tab from the File menu to open a new tab window, (**Shift-Ctrl-t**). Each tab runs a separate shell, letting you enter different commands in each (see Figure 12-4). You can use the Tabs menu to move to different tabs, or just click on its panel to select it. The Tab menu is displayed on the toolbar only if multiple tabs are open. For a single window, the Tab menu is not displayed (see Figure 12-3).

The terminal window is also supports GNOME desktop cut/copy and paste operations. You can copy a line from a Web page and then paste it to the terminal window (you may have to use the Copy entry on the Terminal window's Edit menu). The command will appear and then you can press ENTER to execute the command. This is useful for command line operations that may be displayed on an instructional Web page. Instead of typing in a complex command yourself, just copy from the Web page directly, and then paste to the Terminal window. Perform any edits if needed.

Login Window

If you want to change the login window, you can use the Login Window Preferences window accessible from Login Window entry in the System | Administration menu. This configures the GNOME Display Manager, which runs your login process.

Here you can set the background image, icons to be displayed, the theme to use, users to list, and even the welcome message (see Figure 12-5).

Login screens can be configured for local or remote users. You can choose between a plain screen, a plain screen with face browser, and a themed screen. The Local tab lets you select what screen to use for local logins, as well as browse among available themes. You can choose from a number of themes. From the Remote tab you can select plain, select plain with browser, or use the same configuration as your local logins. On the Users tab, you can select which users you want displayed when using a face browser. The latest Ubuntu theme is selected by default. You can also opt to have the theme randomly selected.

Figure 12-5: Login Window Themes

On the security panel, you can set up an automatic login, skipping the login screen on startup (see Figure 12-6). You can even set a timed login, automatically logging in a specific user after displaying the login screen for a given amount of time. In the Security segment of the panel you can set security options such as whether to allow root logins or allow TCP (Internet) access, as well as setting the number of allowable logins. Click the Configure X Server button on this panel to open a window for configuring X server access. Check the GNOME Display Manager Reference Manual, accessible with the Help button, for details.

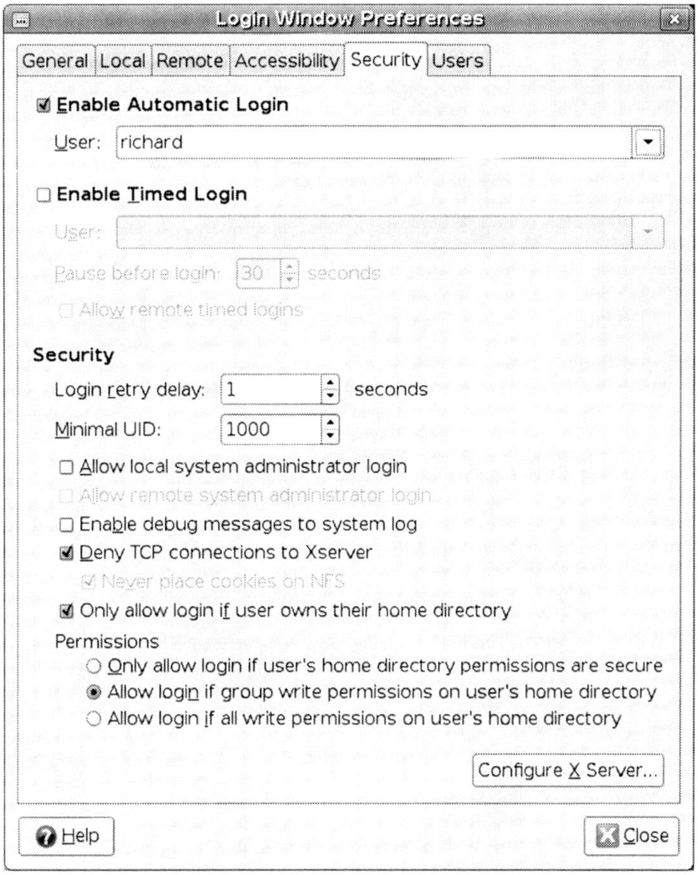

Figure 12-6: Login Window automatic login

Scheduling Tasks

Scheduling regular maintenance tasks, such as backups, is managed by the **cron** service on Linux, and implemented by a **cron** daemon. A daemon is a continually running server that constantly checks for certain actions to take. These tasks are listed in the **crontab** file. The **cron** daemon constantly checks the user's **crontab** file to see if it is time to take these actions. Any user can set up a **crontab** file of their own. The root user can set up a **crontab** file to take system administrative actions, such as backing up files at a certain time each week or month.

Creating cron entries can be a complicated task, using the crontab command to make changes to crontab files in the **/etc/crontab** directory. Instead you can use several GUI cron scheduler tools to easily set up cron actions. Two of the more useful tools are KCron and GNOME Schedule which create an easy to use interface for creating scheduled commands.

GNOME Schedule

GNOME Schedule is a more recent tool that also creates and easy to use interface for managing scheduled tasks (See Figure 12-7). It is currently part of the Universe repository, though part of the GNOME desktop release. Once installed (**gnome-schedule** package) you can access it from the Applications | System Tools menu as Scheduled Tasks.

Figure 12-7: GNOME Schedule

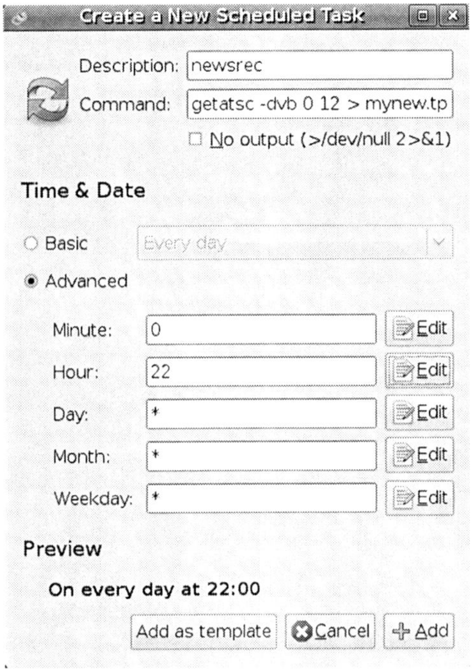

Figure 12-8: Schedule new task

Use the New button to schedule a task. You are first asked if you want to create the task as a recurrent item, one time task, or from a template. The Create a New Scheduled Task window then open where you can specify the time and date, and whether to repeat weekly or monthly (see Figure 12-8). You can use the Basic button to set defaults for Hourly, Daily, Weekly, or Monthly entries. Then click Advanced to specify a time.

The template feature lets you set up a new schedule with information for a previous one, using the same or similar commands but different time. Click the Template button to add a new template. This opens a window similar to the Create task window in Figure 12-8. Once you have created the template you can use it to create scheduled tasks. When creating a task, from the initial menu, choose "A task from a predefined template. This opens the Choose template window (see Figure 12-9). Clicking the Use template button opens the Create task window where you can modify your task.

To delete a task, just select the entry in the Scheduled Tasks window and click the Delete button. To run a task immediately, select and click the Run task button.

On the Scheduled Tasks window you can click the Advanced button to see the actual cron entries created by GNOME Schedule.

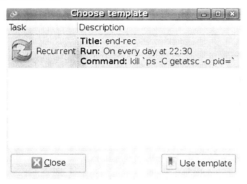

Figure 12-9: Schedule templates

KCron (KDE4)

KCron which creates and easy to use interface for creating scheduled commands. It is part of the Ubuntu main repository and is maintained by Ubuntu. KCron is a KDE desktop tool and will require installation of supporting KDE libraries (selected automatically for you when you install KCron). To run KCron, login to the KDE desktop. Use the New entry in the Edit menu to schedule a command, specifying the time and date, and whether to repeat weekly or monthly.

System Log

Various system logs for tasks performed on your system are stored in the **/var/log** directory. Here you can find logs for mail, news, and all other system operations, such as Web server logs. The **/var/log/messages** file is a log of all system tasks not covered by other logs (see Figure 12-10). This usually includes startup tasks, such as loading drivers and mounting file systems. If a driver for a card failed to load at startup, you find an error message for it here. Logins are also recorded in this file, showing you who attempted to log in to what account. The **/var/log/maillog** file logs mail message transmissions and news transfers. To view these logs you can use the GNOME Log Viewer, System | Administration | Log File Viewer. A side panel lists different logs. Selecting one will display the log on the panel to the right. For **/var/log/messages**, select **messages**. You can also choose to display messages in this file just for a specific date.

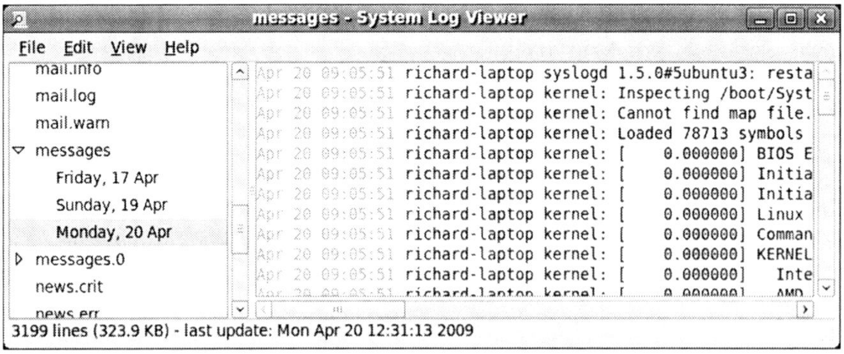

Figure 12-10: Log Viewer

Disk Usage Analyzer

The disk usage analyzer lets you see how much disk space is used and available on all your mounted hard disk partitions (see Figure 12-11), Applications | Accessories | Disk Usage Analyzer. It will also check all LVM and RAID arrays. Usage is shown in simple graph, letting you see how much overall space is available and where it is. You can scan your home directory (Scan Home), your entire file system (Scan Filesystem), a particular folder (Scan Folder), or a remote folder (Scan Remote Folder). When you scan a directory or the file system, disk usage for your directories is analyzed and displayed in the left pane along with a representational graph for the disk usage on the right pane. In the left listing, each files system is first shown with a graph for its usage, as well as its size and number of top-level directories and files. Then the directories are shown, along with their size and contents (files and directories).

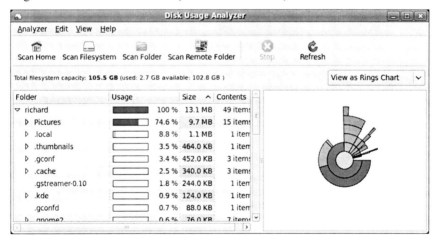

Figure 12-11: Disk Usage Analyzer, Applications | Accessories | Disk Usage Analyzer

On the right pane, the graph can be either a Ring Chart or a Treemap. The Ring Chart is the default. Choose the one you want from the View as drop down menu. For the Ring Chart, directories are show, starting with the top level directories at the center and moving out to the subdirectories. Passing your mouse over a section in the graph will display its directory name and disk usage, as well as all its subdirectories. The Treemap chart shows a box representation, with greater disk usage in larger boxes, and subdirectories encased within directory boxes.

Virus Protection

For virus protection you can use the Linux version of ClamAV, **www.clamav.org**. This Virus scanner is included on the Ubuntu main repository. You will have to download and install it using Synaptic. Choose the clamav, clamav-base, clamav-freshclam, and clamav-data. In addition you may want either ClamTK (clamtk package, GNOME) or Klamav (KDE) front ends. Selecting just clamtk will automatically select the other clamav packages for installation. You can access ClamTK from the Applications | System Tools menu as Virus Scanner. With ClamTK, you can scan specific files and directories, as well as your home directory (see Figure 12-12). Searches can be recursive, including subdirectories. You have the option to also check dot configuration files (Scan hidden). You can also perform quick or recursive scans of your home directory. Infected files are quarantined.

When you first start ClamTK an Antivirus Signatures window open with buttons for choosing how to update the antivirus signatures, either as Single user or System Wide. Then click the Save button to save your preferences.

To update your virus definitions, you need to run **clamtk** with administrative access. Open a terminal window and enter the following. You will be prompted for your user password.

```
gksu clamtk
```

You can then go to the Help menu and select Update Signatures to update your definitions.

You can also install the clam-daemon which works with your email application to detect viruses.

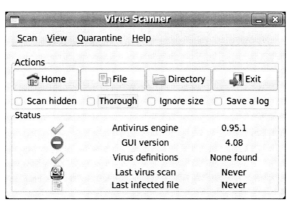

Figure 12-12: The clamtk tool for ClamAV virus protection.

Testing Hardware

Ubuntu provides a hardware testing utility to check your hardware and report any problems. You are encouraged to set up an account at **www.launchpad.net** where you can send your results. From the Applications | System Tools menu, select Hardware Testing. You are first asked how you are using your system: Desktop, Laptop, or Server. Then each major hardware device is tested and you can enter your confirmation or add comments. Devices tested include sound, display, video, mouse, keyboard, network card, and network connection.

Hardware Sensors

Another concern with many users is the temperatures and usage of computer components. The GNOME hardware monitor display detected temperatures for your CPU, system, hard drives, and, if available, for your graphics card, as well as any other sensors your computer may support, like fan speeds. You can also detect the extent your CPU is being used. You install different software packages to enable certain sensors (see Table 12-2).

Sensor application	Description
lm-sensors	Detects and accesses computer (motherboard) sensors like CPU and fan speed. Run **sensors-detect** once to configure.
hddtemp	Detects hard drive temperatures
powernowd	Detects CPU usage
GNOME sensors-applet	GNOME applet to display sensor information for all sensors. Also called **Hardware Sensors Monitor**.
ksenors	KDE sensor applet

Table 12-2: Sensor packages and applications

For CPU, system, fan speeds, and any other motherboard supported sensors, you use the **lm-sensors** service. Download and install the **lm-sensors** package. First you have to configure your sensor detection. In a terminal window enter following and answer yes to the prompts:

```
sudo sensors-detect
```

The CPU temp will be available. If you have a multi-core processor and want the core temperatures for each, then the coretemp module has to be loaded. Edit the **/etc/modules** file and add the module coretemp to the list. The coretemp module will automatically be loaded when your system starts up.

```
gksu gedit /etc/modules
```

This service will detect hardware sensors on your computer. It will run as the Hardware Monitor service in System | Administration | Services.

For hard drive temperature detection you install **hddtemp**. During the installation, you will be prompted to configure the hddtemp service to start automatically.

You can then download and install the **sensors-applet** package, the GNOME applet for displaying sensor information (use KSensors for KDE desktop). Once the applet is installed, you can add it to the panel as the **Hardware Sensors Monitor**. You can right-click the applet icon and open its preferences window, where you can set the temperature scale and display information (see Figure 12-13). You can then use the GNOME sensors applet to display any sensor information (Sensors tab). They will be group by the service providing the sensor access, usually lmsensors, hddtemp, and a graphics driver, in this example, Nvidia. In Figure 12-13, the CPU, System, CPU fan, graphics card, and two hard drives are seleted for display.

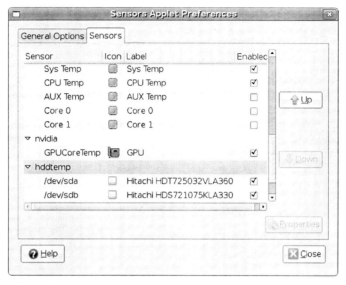

Figure 12-13: GNOME Sensor configuration

The hardware sensor information will then be displayed on the panel. You can configure the sensors applet to use either centigrade or Fahrenheit temperatures. Fan speeds can also be displayed, if your computer detects them. Figure 12-14 shows CPU fan speed, the System temperature, the CPU temperature, the graphics card temperature, and two hard drive temperatures.

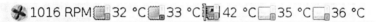

Figure 12-14: Hardware sensor display on GNOME panel

Another useful applet is the CPU Frequency Scaling Monitor, which will display CPU usage (See Figure 12-15). This applet used the **powernowd** service to detect how much of the CPU is being used. Most current CPUs support frequency scaling, which will lower the CPU frequency when it has few tasks to perform. Intel CPUs will scale down to 60 percent and AMD by 50 percent.

Figure 12-15: CPU Frequency Scaling Monitor

Computer Janitor

The Computer Janitor application is designed to detect unused software packages on your system. These are usually packages installed as additional dependent packages that where selected automatically when you installed a particular package. If you later remove a package, not all the dependent packages may also be removed. As your install and remove packages, unused dependent package may pile up, remaining on your system and using space, while no longer needed. Computer Janitor is also useful if you upgrade your system instead of performing a clean install. Computer Janitor will detect the unused packages from the previous release, letting you remove them easily.

Computer janitor will detect unused packages and let you remove them (see Figure 12-16). It will also suggest any configuration changes, fixing configuration files like the GRUB **menu.lst** file. For example, you may have removed old kernels without updating the menu.lst file to remove their entries. Computer Janitor will correctly edit your **menu.lst** file for you, removing the old kernel entries. When editing the **menu.lst** file, Computer Janitor will not edit the default number. If you had previously changed this to make a specific kernel or other operating system your default, you may have to edit your **menu.lst** file to change the default number so that it lines up again, taking into account the kernel entries that Computer Janitor removed for you.

You can access Computer Janitor from System | Administration | Computer Janitor. You will be prompted to enter your password.

The packages detected for removal will be listed. You can un-check the ones you want to keep. All will be selected initially. If you are unsure of a package, uncheck it. Click the Cleanup button to remove the selected packages.

Figure 12-16: Computer Janitor

Before the packages are removed, you are prompted to re-consider, warning you that removing needed packages can break some of your system's capability. Use this tool carefully. If there are not that many unused packages on your system, you may want to leave them alone.

13. System Administration

Ubuntu Administrative Tools

Controlled Administrative Access

Users and Groups

Bluetooth

Managing Services

File System Access

DKMS

Editing Configuration Files Directly

Backup Management: rsync, BackupPC, and Amanda

This chapter reviews a few administrative task and tools you may normally use. Most administrative configurations tasks are now performed for you automatically. Devices like printers, hard drive partitions, and graphics cards are now detected and set up for you automatically. There are cases where you may need to perform tasks manually like adding new users or trouble-shooting your display. Administrative operations can now be performed with user-friendly system tools. This chapter discusses a few system administration operations, and tells where to find out how to perform certain common tasks like adding new users and configured remote printers. Most administration tools can be found in System | Administration and System | Preferences menus.

Ubuntu Administration Menus	Description
System	Administration	Ubuntu menu for accessing administrative tools
System	Preferences	Ubuntu menu for desktop interface configuration like mouse or screen resolution
Applications	System Tools	Ubuntu menu for accessing specialized administrative applications and configuration tools

TIP: If you have difficulties with your system configuration, check the **http://ubuntuforums.org** site for possible solutions. The site offers helpful forums ranging from desktop and install problems to games, browsers, and multimedia solutions. Also check the support link at **www.ubuntu.com** for documentation, live chat, and mailing lists.

Ubuntu Administration Tools	Description
Synaptic Package Manager	Apt Software management using online repositories
Add/Remove Applications	Apt Software management, Add/Remove Applications
Update Manager	Update tool using Apt repositories
Network Manager	Configures your network interfaces (GNOME)
services-admin	Services tool, manages system and network services such as starting and stopping servers. (GNOME)
time-admin	Changes system time and date (GNOME)
users-admin	User and Group configuration tool
system-config-printer	Printer configuration tool (Fedora/Red Hat)
system-config-samba	Configures your Samba server (Fedora/Red Hat). User level authentication support.
gnome-language-selector	Selects a language to use
Gufw	Configures your network firewall
polkit-gnome-authorization	Sets authentication settings for devices and administration tasks, PolicyKit

Table 13-1: Administration Tools on System | Administration

Ubuntu Administrative Tools

On Ubuntu, administration is handled by a set of separate specialized administrative tools, such as those for user management and printer configuration (see Table 13-1). To access the GUI-based administrative tools, you log in as a user that has administrative access. This is the user you created when you first installed Ubuntu. On the GNOME desktop System administrative tools are listed on the System | Administration menu. Here you will find tools to set the time and date, manage users, configure printers, and install software. Users and Groups lets you create and modify users and groups. Printing lets you install and reconfigure printers. All tools provide very intuitive GUI interfaces that are easy to use. In the Administration menu, tools are identified by simple descriptive terms, whereas their actual names normally begin with the terms like admin or system-config. For example, the printer configuration tool is listed as Printing, but its actual name is **system-config-printer**, whereas Users and Groups is **admin-users**. You can separately invoke any tool by entering its name in a terminal window.

Ubuntu uses the GNOME administrative tools, with KDE counterparts, administrative tools adapted from the Fedora distribution supported by Red Hat Linux, and independent tools, like Firestarter for your firewall, PolicyKit for device authorizations, and the Synaptic Package Manager for software installation. The GNOME administrative tools are suffixed with the term **admin**, whereas the Fedora tools have the prefix **system-config**. With Ubuntu 7.10, the Printing administrative tool is Fedora's **system-config-printer**, replacing the GNOME printer-admin tool used in previous Ubuntu releases. A Samba GUI tool is now available for Ubuntu, which is the Fedora **system-config-samba** tool. Some tools will work on Ubuntu, but are not yet supported. The Fedora **system-config-lvm** tool provides a simple and effective way to manage LVM file systems, but is not yet supported directly by Ubuntu. You can, however, download, convert, and install the software package on Ubuntu, and it will work fine. In addition, Virus protection is handled by an entirely separate application like ClamAV.

Note: Many configuration tasks can also be handled on a command line, invoking programs directly. To use the command line, open a terminal window by selecting the Terminal entry in the Applications | Accessories menu. This opens a terminal window with a command line prompt. Commands like sudo and make discussed later will require a terminal window.

Controlled Administrative Access

To access administrative tools, you have to login as a user that have administrative permissions. The user that the created during installation is automatically given administrative permissions. Log in as that user. When you attempt to use an administrative tool to use, like those in the System | Administration menu, you will be prompted in a window to enter your user password. This is the password for the user you logged in as. You can use the Users and Groups tool to grant or deny particular users administrative access.

To perform system administration operations, you must first have access rights enabling you to perform administrative tasks like add new users or set the time. There are several ways to gain such access, each with more refined access controls. In each case you have to login as a user who has been granted administrative access. The access methods are: logging in as the root user, login as a sudo supported user (gksu is the graphical version of sudo), and unlocking an administrative tool for access by a PolicyKit authorized users. PolicyKit is the new preferred access method and is used on most administrative tools. The sudo granted access method was used in previous Ubuntu releases, and is still used for software upgrade and installation tasks (Synaptic and Update Manager). The root user access was and is still discouraged, but provides complete control over the entire system.

- PolicyKit: Provides access only to specific applications and only to users with administrative access for that application. Requires that the specific application be configured for use by PolicyKit.

- **sudo** and **gksu**: Provides access to any application will full root level authorization. Given a time limit to reduce risk. The gsku command is used for graphical administrative tools like Synaptic. You will still need to use sudo to perform any standard Unix commands at the root level like editing configuration files.

- **root** user access, **su**: Provides complete direct control over the entire system. This is the traditional method for accessing administrative tools. Disabled by default on Ubuntu, but can be enabled. The **su** command will allow any user to login as the root user if they know the root user password. Logging in as the root user makes you the superuser.

PolicyKit

PolicyKit will let any user start up an administrative tool, but restrict use to read only access. On the users-admin tool for managing users, you will be able to see the list of users on your system, but not make any changes to them, or even add new users. In effect, you are locked out. For PolicyKit controlled utilities, a Lock button will appear in the lower right of the administrative tool's window. To gain full access, you need to unlock it. Click on the Unlock button to open a window where you can specify the authorized user you want to use, and password for that authorized users (see Figure 13-1). The list of authorized users is selectable from a pop-up menu. The user you created when you installed your system is an authorized user. Authorized users are those user granted administrative access when their account was set up. For single user systems, with just one user, this will default to user you logged in as.

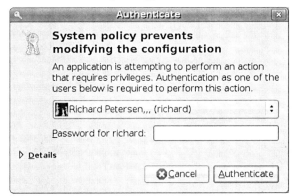

Figure 13-1: PolicyKit authorization window

With PolicyKit, you can login as a user with no administrative access, and then gain access to an administrative tool by selecting a user with that access and entering that user's password. Without PolicyKit, you would first have to login as an administrative user that would be able to access any administration application and be able perform any administrative task. With PolicyKit, you do not have to login as an administrative user, just use that user to access a particular administrative tool.

sudo and gksu

The sudo service provides administrative access to specific users. You have to be a user on the system with a valid username and password that has been authorized by the sudo service for administrative access. This allows other users to perform specific superuser operations without having full administrative level control. You can find more about sudo at **www.sudo.ws**.

gksu

You can use the **gksu** command in place of **sudo** to run graphical applications with administrative access. The **gksu** tool is a front end to sudo that does not require a terminal window (another name for **gksu** is **gksudo**). The gsku tool will prompt you to enter your password, assuming you are logged in as a user that has sudo authorized administrative access (See Figure 13-2).

You can enter the **gksu** command in a terminal window with the application as an argument, or set up an application launcher with **gksu** as the command. The following example will start up the Gedit editor with administrative access, allowing you to directly edit system configuration files (see Figure 13-3).

```
gksu gedit
```

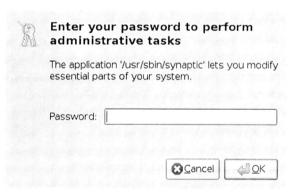

Enter your password to perform administrative tasks

The application '/usr/sbin/synaptic' lets you modify essential parts of your system.

Password: |

Cancel   OK

Figure 13-2: gksu prompt for access to administrative tools

The administrative tools on your desktop actually invoke their applications using gksu, as in **gksu synaptic**. You will see this command in the Launcher panel in the application's properties window. If you run **gksu** directly without any application specified, it will prompt you to enter the application. You could set up a GNOME or KDE application launcher for an application with the gksu command prefixing the application command.

Figure 13-3: Invoking Gedit with gksu command

sudo command

Some administrative operations require access from the command line in the terminal window. For such operations you would use the **sudo** command, run from a terminal window. You can open a terminal window using the Terminal tool accessible from the Applications | Accessories window. For easier access, you can drag the menu entry for the Terminal tool to the desktop to create a desktop Terminal icon for creating a terminal window.

```
sudo
```

To use sudo to run an administrative command, the user precedes the command with the sudo command. The user is then prompted to enter their password. The user is issued a time-restricted ticket to allow access.

```
sudo date 0406145908
password:
```

From the terminal window, you would then enter the sudo command with the administrative program name as an argument. For example, to use Vi to edit system configuration files, you would have start Vi using the **sudo** command in a terminal window, with the vi and the file name as its arguments. This starts up Vi with administrator privileges. The following example will allow you to edit the **/etc/fstab** file to add or edit file system entries for automatic mounting. You will be prompted for your user password.

```
sudo vi /etc/fstab
```

sudo configuration

Access is controlled by the /etc/sudoers file. This file lists users and the commands they can run, along with the password for access. If the NOPASSWD option is set, then users will not need a password. ALL, depending on the context, can refer to all hosts on your network, all root-level commands, or all users. See the Man page for **sudoers** for detailed information on all options.

To make changes or add entries, you have to edit the file with the special sudo editing command visudo. This invokes the Vi editor to edit the **/etc/sudoers** file. Unlike a standard editor, **visudo** will lock the **/etc/sodoers** file and check the syntax of your entries. You are not allowed to save changes unless the syntax is correct. If you want to use a different editor, you can assign it to the EDITOR shell variable.

A sudoers entry has the following syntax:

```
user    host=command
```

The host is a host on your network. You can specify all hosts with the ALL term. The command can be a list of commands, some or all qualified by options such as whether a password is required. To specify all commands, you can also use the ALL term. The following gives the user george full root-level access to all commands on all hosts:

```
george   ALL = ALL
```

To specify a group name, you prefix the group with a **%** sign, as in **%mygroup**. This way, you can give the same access to a group of users. By default sudo will grant access to all users in the **admin** group. These are user granted administrative access. The ALL=(ALL) ALL entry allows access by the root to all hosts as all users to all commands.

```
%admin    ALL=(ALL)    ALL
```

It is possible to allow members of a certain group access without a password. Use the NOPASSWD option. A commented **sudo** group is provided in the **/etc/sudoers** file.

```
%admin    ALL=NOPASSWD    ALL
```

By default sudo will deny access to all users, including the root. For this reason, the default **/etc/sudoers** file sets full access for the root user to all commands. The ALL=(ALL) ALL entry allows access by the root to all hosts as all users to all commands.

```
root    ALL=(ALL)    ALL
```

Though on Ubuntu the sudo file is configured to allow **root** user access, Ubuntu does not create a **root** user password. This prevents you from logging in as the **root** user, rendering the sudo root permission useless.

In addition, you can let a user run as another user on a given host. Such alternate users are placed within parentheses before the commands. For example, if you want to give **george** access to the **beach** host as the user **mydns**, you use the following:

```
george beach = (mydns) ALL
```

To give **robert** access on all hosts to the date command, you would use

```
robert ALL=/usr/bin/system-config-date
```

If a user wants to see what commands he or she can run, that user would use the sudo command with the **-l** option.

```
sudo -l
```

Full Administrative Access: root, su, and superuser

Ubuntu is designed to never let anyone directly access the root user. The **root** user has total control over the entire system. Instead certain users are given administrative access with which they can separately access administrative tools, performing specific administrative tasks. Even though a **root** user exists, a password for the root user is not defined, never allowing access to it.

You can, though, activate the root user by using the **passwd** command to create a root user password. Enter the **passwd** command with the root user name in a sudo operation.

```
sudo passwd root
```

You will be prompted for your administrative password, and then prompted by the **passwd** command to enter a password for the **root** user. You will then be prompted to repeat the password.

```
Enter new UNIX password:
Retype new UNIX password:
passwd: password updated successfully
```

You can then log in with the **su** command as the root user, making you the superuser (you still cannot login as the root user from the GDM login window). Because a superuser has the power to change almost anything on the system, such a password is usually a carefully guarded secret, changed very frequently, and given only to those whose job it is to manage the system. With the correct password, you can log in to the system as a system administrator and configure the system in different ways. You can also add or remove users, add or remove whole file systems, back up and restore files, and even designate the system's name and address.

```
su root
```

The **su** command alone with assume the root username.

```
su
```

The **su** command can actually be used to login to any user, provided you have that user's password.

It is possible to access the root user using the **sudo** command on the **su** command. The **su** command is the superuser command. Superuser is another name for **root** user. A user granted administrative access by **sudo**, could then become the **root** user. The following logs into the root user.

```
sudo su
```

To exit from a **su** login operation, when you are finished on that account, just enter exit.

```
exit
```

Users and Groups

Currently, the easiest and most effective way to add new users is to use the users-admin. tool. You can access it from the GNOME Desktop menu, System | Administration menu | Users and Groups entry. You will be prompted to enter you administrative password. The users-admin tool opens up with a Users Settings window listing users with their full name, login name, and home directory.

When you start up the users-admin application (System | Administration | Users and Groups), only read access is allowed, letting you scroll through the list of users, but not make any changes or add new ones (see Figure 13-4).

Figure 13-4: Users and Groups locked

Read only access is provided to all users, but to use users-admin, you have to unlock it. User entries will be grayed out. Users will be able to see the list of users on your system, but not modify their entries, add new ones, or delete current users. To perform these operations you need administrative access. Administrative access for the users-admin tool is controlled by Policykit. Click the Unlock button at the bottom of the window. This opens a prompt for you to enter your user password (see Figure 13-5). Then click the Authenticate button. User entries will no longer be grayed out.

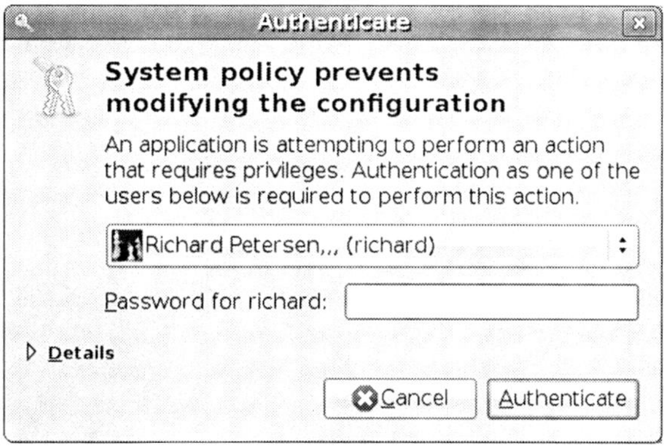

Figure 13-5: Policykit unlock prompt

After you unlock the users-admin, the Unlock button is grayed out, and you can now make changes (see Figure 13-6). The User Settings window will list users according with their icon, full name, and login name. The icon is the image each user chooses with their About Me tool in the System | Preferences menu. To the right are buttons for adding new users, deleting users, editing a user's properties, and managing groups. With administrative access granted, the bottom Unlock button will be grayed out.

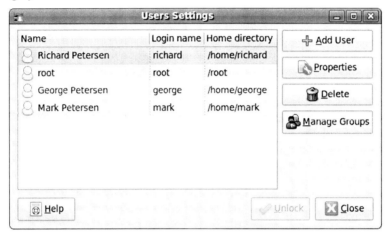

Figure 13-6: Users and Groups unlocked

New Users

To create a new user, click Add User. This opens a New user account window that displays four tabs, Account, Contact, User Privileges, and Advanced (see Figure 13-7). The Account has entries for the Username, Real Name, Profile, and password. The Read Name is the user's full name. The Profile entry is a pop-up menu listing Desktop user, Administrator, and Unprivileged. Administrator will allow the user to perform system wide configuration tasks. These users can use the administration tools and the sudo command to perform system-wide administration tasks. Desktop users do not have any kind of administration access. Unprivileged denies access to most resources, though online access is allowed. If operates much like a dumb terminal.

On the Contacts tab, you can add basic contact information if you wish for an office address, as well as work and home phones.

On the User Privileges tab you can control device access as well as administrative access (see Figure 13-8. Here you can restrict or allow access to CD-ROMs, scanners, and external storage like USB drives. You can also determine if the user can perform administrative tasks. The "Administer the System" entry is left unchecked by default. If you want to allow the user to perform administration tasks, be sure to check this box.

The Advanced tab lets you select a home directory, the shell to use, a main group, and a user ID. Defaults will already be chosen for you. A home directory in the name of the new user will be specified and the shell used will be the BASH shell. Normally you would not want to change these settings, though you might prefer a different shell, like the C-Shell. For the group, the user will have a group with its own user name. In addition, the user will have access to all system resource groups like cdrom, audio, video, and scanner.

Figure 13-7: Users and Groups: Create New User

To later change settings, select the User in the User Settings window and click the Properties button. A four tabbed Account Properties window opens with the same Account, Contact, User Privileges, and Advanced tabs. To delete a user, select it and click the Delete button.

Alternatively, you can use the `useradd` command in a terminal window or command line to add user accounts and the `userdel` command to remove them. The following example adds the user **dylan** to the system:

```
$ useradd Dylan
```

Groups

To manage groups, click on the Manage Groups button. This opens a Group Settings window that lists all groups (see Figure 13-9). To add users to a group, select it and click Properties. In the Properties window, users will be listed and you can select the ones you want to add.

To add a new group, click on the Add Group button to open a New Group window where you can specify the group name, its id, and select users to add to the group.

To later add or remove users to or from a group, click on the group name in the Group settings window and click Properties. You can then check or uncheck users from the Group Members listing.

If you want to remove a user as member, click the check box to remove its check. Click OK to effect your changes. If you want to remove a group, just select its entry in the Groups panel and then click the Delete button.

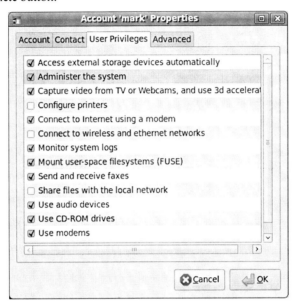

Figure 13-8: Users and Groups: User Privileges

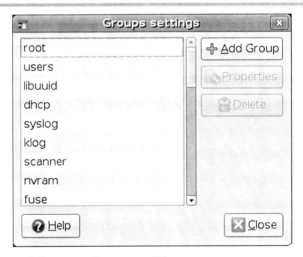

Figure 13-9: Users and Groups: Groups settings

You can also add groups to a user by selecting the user in the Users panel, and opening their Properties window. Then select the Groups panel (see Figure 13-10). Select the groups you wan that user to belong to.

Figure 13-10: Group Properties: Group Users panel

Passwords

One common operation performed from the command line is to change a password. The easiest way to change your password on the GNOME desktop is to use the About Me utility (System | Preferences | Personal | About Me). Click on the Change Password button. A dialog opens up in which you enter your current password, and then the new password twice.

Alternatively you can use the **passwd** command. If you are using GNOME or KDE you first have to open a terminal window (Applications | System Tools | Terminal). Then, at the shell prompt, enter the **passwd** command. The command prompts you for your current password. After entering your current password and pressing ENTER, you are then prompted for your new password. After entering the new password, you are asked to reenter it. This is to make sure you actually entered the password you intended to enter.

```
$ passwd
Old password:
New password:
Retype new password:
$
```

Tip: You can use the system-config-rootpassword tool (Root Password on System | Administration) to change the password for the root user.

Managing Services

Many administrative functions operate as services that need to be turned on. They are daemons, constantly running and checking for requests for their services. When you install a service, its daemon is normally turned on automatically. You can check to see if this is so, using the services-admin tool, System | Administration | Services. This opens the Services Settings window (see Figure 13-11). Services are listed descriptively with the actual name of their daemon in parenthesis.

Figure 13-11: Services: services-admin

Each service will have its own checkbox. When checked the service is run when the system starts up. If unchecked the service is not run. Figure 13-11 shows several commonly use services like Windows file sharing (samba), CPU power management (**powernowd**), and the Graphical Login Manager (**gdm**).

You can also start, start, and restart a service from a terminal window using either the service script directly or the **service** command with the service name. Service scripts are located in the **/etc/init.d/** directory. To restart the Samba file sharing service you could use either of the following commands.

```
sudo /etc/init.d/samba restart
sudo service samba restart
```

File System Access

Various file systems can be accessed on Ubuntu easily. Any additional internal hard drive partitions on your system, both Linux and Windows NTFS, will be automatically detected and can be automatically mounted, providing immediate and direct access from your desktop. In addition you can access remote Windows shared folders and make your own shared folders accessible.

Access Linux File Systems on Internal Drives

Other Linux file systems on internal hard drives will be detect by Ubuntu automatically. Icons for them will be displayed on Computer window. Initially they will not be mounted. You will have to first validate your authorization to mount a disk. To mount a file system for the first time, double click on its icon. A Policykit authorization window will appear similar to that in Figure 13-1. You then enter your user password. The option to Remember authorization is checked, keeping the authorization indefinitely. Whenever you start up your system again, the file system will be mounted for you automatically.

Your file system is then mounted, displaying its icon both in the Computer window and the desktop. The file system will be mounted under the **/media** directory and given folder with the name of the file system label, or, if unlabeled, with the device name like **sda3** for the third partition on the first SATA drive.

Once granted, authentication access will remain in place for a limited time, allowing you to mount other file systems without having to enter your password. These file systems will then be automatically mounted also, provided you had left the Remember Authorization checked in the Authenticate window.

Any user with administrative access on the primary console is authorized to mount file systems. You can use PolicyKit agent to expand or restrict this level of authorization, as well as enabling access for specific users.

In addition, your partitions will automatically be displayed on the desktop and in the computer window as disks. Select Computer from the Places menu.

Access to Windows NTFS File Systems on Internal Drives

If you have installed Ubuntu on a dual-boot system with Windows XP, NT, or 2000, or otherwise need access to NTFS partitions, Linux NTFS file system support is installed automatically. Your NTFS partitions are mounted using FUSE, file system in user space. The same authentication control used for Linux file systems applies to NTFS file systems. Icons for the NTFS partitions will be displayed in the Computer window (Computer in Places menu). The first time you access the file system, you may be asked to provide authorization, as in Figure 13-1. Your NTFS file system is then mounted with icons displayed in the Computer widow and on the desktop. Whenever you start up your system, they will be automatically mounted for you. The partitions will be mounted under the **/media** directory with their labels used as folder names. If they have no labels, then they are given the name **disk**, and then numbered as **disk0**, **disk1**, and so on for additional partitions (unlabeled removable devices may also share these names). The NTFS partitions are mounted using **ntfs-3g** drivers.

Access to Local Network Shared File Systems (Windows)

Shared Windows folders and printers on any of the computers connected to your local network are automatically accessible from your Ubuntu desktop. The DNS discovery service (Ahavi) automatically detects hosts on your home or local network and will let you access directly any of their shared folders.

To access the shared folders, select Network from the Places menu to open the Network Places window (see Figure 13-12). Your connected computers will be listed. If you know the name

402 *Part 4: Administration*

of the Windows computer you want to access, just click on its icon, otherwise, click on the Windows network icon to see just the Windows machines (see Figure 13-13).

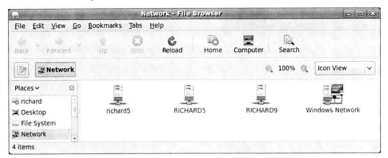

Figure 13-12: Network Places

Once selected, the shared folders will be shown.

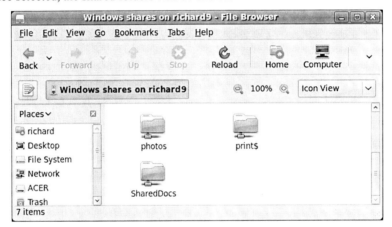

Figure 13-13: Remote shares

Figure 13-14: Mount remote Windows ShareDocs

You can then access a shared folder and it will be automatically mounted on your desktop. The Places sidebar will show an entry for the folder with an Eject button for unmounting it if you wish. You can also right-click on the desktop icon and select unmount volume. Figure 13-14 shows the ShareDocs shared folder on a Windows systems mounted on the Ubuntu desktop.

However, local systems cannot access your shared folders until you install a sharing server, Samba for Windows systems and NFS for Linux/Unix systems. Should you attempt to share a directory; an error notice will be displayed asking you to install Samba or NFS.

Shared Folders for your network

To share a folder on your local network, right-click on it and select Sharing options. This opens a window where you can allow sharing, and whether to permit modifying, adding, or deleting files in the folder (see Figure 13-15). You can also use the Share panel on the file's properties dialog (see Figure 13-17). You can also allow access to anyone who does not also have an account on your system (guest). Once you have made your selections, click the Create Share button. You can later change the sharing options if you wish.

Figure 13-15: Folder Sharing Options

To allow access by other users, permissions on the folder will have to be changed. You will be prompted to allow Nautilus to make these changes for you. Just click the "Add the permissions automatically button" (see Figure 13-16).

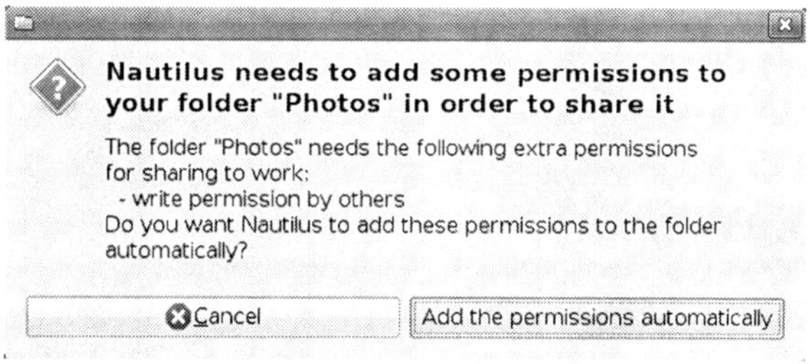

Figure 13-16: Folder Sharing permissions prompt

Folders that are shared will display a sharing emblem next to their icon on a file manager window.

Documents

Figure 13-17: Prompt to install sharing service (Samba and NFS)

Figure 13-18: Folder Share panel

To allow others to access your folders be sure the sharing servers are installed, Samba for Windows systems and NFS for Linux/Unix systems. The serves will be automatically configured for you and run. You will not be able to share folders until these servers are installed. If your sharing servers are not installed, you will be prompted to install them (see Figure 13-17). Click the Install service button. The Samba servers will be downloaded and installed. You are then prompted to restart your GNOME session. Click the Restart session button.

To later change the sharing permissions for a folder, open the folder's Properties window and then select the Share tab. When you make a change, a Modify Share button will be displayed. Click it to make the changes. In Figure 13-18 Guest access is added to the Photos folder.

To share folders (directories) with other Linux systems on your network, you use the NFS service (**nfs-kernelserver**). For Windows systems you use the Samba service (**samba**). It is possible to use the older **system-config-samba** tool to set up access. For more complex Samba configuration you can use SWAT or system-config-samba tools.

Permissions on GNOME

On GNOME, you can set a directory or file permission using the Permissions panel in its Properties window (see Figure 13-19). For Files, right-click the file or directory icon or entry in the file manager window and select Properties. Then select the Permissions panel. Here you will find pop-up menus for read and write permissions, along with rows for Owner, Group, and Other. You can set owner permissions as Read Only or Read And Write. For the group and others, you can also set the None option, denying access. The group name expands to a pop-up menu listing different groups; select one to change the file's group. If you want to execute this as an application (say, a shell script) check the Allow Executing File As Program entry. This has the effect of setting the execute permission

Figure 13-19: File Permissions

The Permissions panel for directories operates much the same way, but it includes two access entries, Folder Access and File Access (see Figure 13-20). The Folder Access entry controls access to the folder with options for List Files Only, Access Files, and Create And Delete Files. These correspond to the read, read and execute, and read/write/execute permissions given to directories. The File Access entry lets you set permissions for all those files in the directory. They are the same as for files: for the owner, Read or Read and Write; for the group and others, the entry adds a None option to deny access. To set the permissions for all the files in the directory accordingly (not just the folder), click the Apply Permissions To Enclosed Files button.

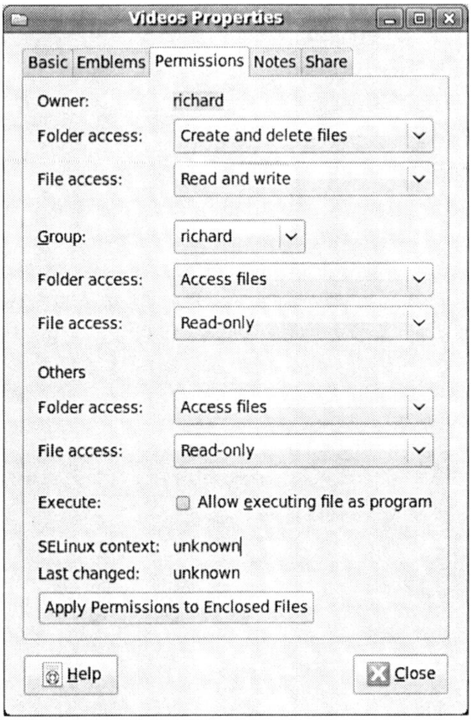

Figure 13-20: Folder Permissions

Automatic file system mounts with /etc/fstab

Though most file systems are automatically mounted for you, there may be instances where you need to have a file system mounted manually. Using the mount command you can do this directly, or you can specify the mount operation in the **/etc/fstab** file to have it mounted automatically. Ubuntu file systems are uniquely identified with their UUID (Universally Unique IDentifier). These are listed in the **/dev/disk/by-id** directory (or with the **sudo blkid** command). In the **/etc/fstab** file, the file system partition devices are listed as a comment, and then followed by the actual file system mount operation using the UUID. The following example mounts the file system on partition /dev/sda3 to the **/media/sda3** directory as an **ext3** file system with default options (**defaults**).

```
# /dev/sda3
UUID=b8c526db-cb60-43f6-b0a3-5c0054f6a64a /media/sda3 ext3 defaults 0 2
```

You can also identify your file system by giving it a label. You can use the **ext2label** command to label a file system. In the following example, the Linux file system labeled **mydata1** is mounted to the **/mydata1** directory as an ext3 file system type.

/etc/fstab

```
# /etc/fstab: static file system information.
#
# <file system> <mount point>    <type>  <options>        <dump>  <pass>
proc            /proc            proc    defaults         0       0
# /dev/sda2
UUID=a179d6e6-b90c-4cc4-982d-a4cfcedea7df / ext3 defaults,errors=remount-ro 0 1
# /dev/sda3
UUID=b8c526db-cb60-43f6-b0a3-5c0054f6a64a /media/sda3  ext3 defaults 0 2
# /dev/sda1
UUID=48b96071-6284-4fe9-b364-503817cefb74  none  swap  sw      0 0
/dev/hdc        /media/cdrom0    udf,iso9660 user,noauto,exec    0 0
/dev/fd0        /media/floppy0   auto        rw,user,noauto,exec 0 0
LABEL=mydata1 /mydata1           ext3        defaults            1 1
```

Should you have to edit your **/etc/fstab** file, you can use the **gksu** command with the **gedit** editor on your desktop. In a terminal window (Applications | Accessories | Terminal) enter the following command. You will be first prompted to enter your password.

```
gksu gedit /etc/fstab
```

To mount manually, use the **mount** command and specify the type with the **-t ext3** option. Use the **-L** option to mount by label. List the file system first and then the directory name to which it will be mounted. For a NTFS partition you would use the type **ntfs**. The mount option has the format:

```
mount -t type  file-system  directory
```

The following example mounts the **mydata1** file system to the **/mydata1** directory

```
mount -t ext3  -L mydata1   /mydata1
```

Bluetooth

Ubuntu Linux now provides Bluetooth support for both serial connections and BlueZ protocol–supported devices. Bluetooth is a wireless connection method for locally connected devices such as keyboards, mice, printers, and even PDAs and Bluetooth-capable cell phones. You can think of it as a small local network dedicated to your peripheral devices, eliminating the needs for wires. Bluetooth devices can be directly connected through your serial ports or through specialized Bluetooth cards connected to USB ports or inserted in a PCI slot. BlueZ is the official Linux Bluetooth protocol and has been integrated into the Linux kernel since version 2.4.6. The BlueZ protocol was developed originally by Qualcomm and is now an open source project, located at **http://bluez.sourceforge.net**. It is included with Ubuntu in the bluez-utils and bluez-libs packages, among others. Check the BlueZ site for a complete list of supported hardware, including adapters, PCMCIA cards, and serial connectors.

If you have Bluetooth devices attached to your system, the Bluetooth applet will be displayed on your panel. Right-click to display options for your bluetooth devices (see Figure 21). The setup new device entry starts the Bluetooth Device Wizard which will detect your connected devices. The Send and Browse files lets you manage files on a Bluetooth device. The Preferences option displays the Bluetooth Preferences window. You can also access Bluetooth Preferences from the System | Preferences | Bluetooth menu.

The Bluetooth Preferences window has a General tab and tabs for any connected Bluetooth adapters (see Figure 22). The General tab has options for the display of the Bluetooth panel icon.

Figure 13-21: Bluetooth applet menu and panel icon

An adapter tab will have the name of the Bluetooth adapter. The default is usually your host name with a number, like richard-desktop-0. You can change it. You can also specify the visibility of the device. To add a device, click the Add button to start up the Bluetooth Device Wizard, detecting a new device.

Figure 13-22: Bluetooth Preferences

Bluetooth headsets are not supported well on Linux. The will be detected, but may not operate. You can try using the **snd-bt-sco** module and running the **btsco** utility to provide support. You will have to install the **bluez-btsco** package (Universe repository). See the BlutoothSkype page for more details.

```
http://help.ubuntu.com/community/BluetoothSkype
```

Note: The Bluetooth Analyzer tool can display bluetooth protocol traces, useful for detecting problems (Applications | System Tools | Bluetooth Analyzer, use System | Preferences | Main Menu to display menu entry)

DKMS

DKMS is the Dynamic Kernel Module Support originally developed by DELL. DKMS enabled device drivers can be automatically generated whenever your kernel is updated. This is helpful for proprietary drivers like the Nvidia and ATI proprietary graphics drivers (the X11 open source drivers, Xorg, are automatically included with the kernel package). In the past, whenever you updated your kernel, you also had to download and install a separate proprietary kernel module complied just for that new kernel. If the module was not ready, then you could not use a proprietary driver. To avoid this problem, DKMS was developed with uses the original proprietary source code to create new kernel modules as they are needed. When you install a new kernel, DKMS then detects the new configuration and compiles a compatible proprietary kernel module for your new kernel. This action is fully automatic and entirely hidden from the user.

On Ubuntu 9.04 both the Nvidia and ATI proprietary graphics drivers are DKMS enable packages that are managed and generated by the DKMS service. The generated kernel modules are placed in the **/lib/modules/***kernel-version***/kernel/updates** directory. When you install either graphics proprietary package, their source code in downloaded and used to create a graphics drivers for use by your kernel. The source code is placed in the **/usr/src** directory.

The DKMS configuration files and build locations for different DKMS enabled software are located in subdirectories in the **/var/lib/dkms** directory. The subdirectories will have the module name like fglrx for the ATI proprietary driver and nvdia for the Nvidia drivers. Within this directory will be version subdirectories for different driver releases like **8.543** for ATI or **177.80** for Nvidia. A source link accesses the source code files in the **/etc/src** directory for that driver version. The **build** subdirectory contains configured source and support files like patches, used to actually generate the kernel module. Both include the **dkms.conf** configuration file for that software package. The compiled module will be located in the version directory and have the extension **.ko**, as in **fglrx.ko**.

DKMS configuration files are located in the **/etc/dkms** directory. The **/etc/dkms/framework.conf** file holds DKMS variable definitions for directories DKMS uses like the source code and kernel module directories. The **/etc/init.d/dkms_autoinstaller** is a script the runs the DKMS operations to generate and install a kernel module. DKMS removal and install directives for kernel updates are maintained in the **/etc/kernel** directory.

Should DKMS fail to install and update automatically, you can perform the update manually using the **dkms** command. The **dkms** command with the **build** action will create the kernel module, and then the **dkms** command with the install action will install module to the appropriate kernel module directory. The **-m** option specifies the module you want to build and the **-k** option is the kernel version (use **uname -r** to display your current kernel version). Drivers like Nvidia and ATI release new versions regularly (ATI every month). You use the **-v** option to specify the driver version you want. See the man page for **dkms** for full details.

```
sudo dkms build -m fglrx -v 8.543 -k 2.6.27-7-generic
sudo dkms install -m fglrx -v 8.543 -k 2.6.27-7-generic
```

Editing Configuration Files Directly

Though the administrative tools will handle all configuration settings for you, there may be times when you will need to make changes by directly editing configuration files. These are usually text files in the **/etc** directory or dot files in a user home directory, like **.bash_profile**. To change any of these files, you will need administrative access, requiring you to first log in as the **root** user.

You can use any standard editor such as Vi or Emacs to edit these files, though one of the easiest ways to edit them is to use the Gedit editor on the GNOME desktop. Select Text Editor from the Accessories menu. This opens a Gedit window. Click Open to open a file browser where you can move through the file system to locate the file you want to edit.

Caution: Be careful when editing your configuration files. Editing mistakes can corrupt your configurations. It is advisable to make a backup of any configuration files you are working on first, before making major changes to the original.

Gedit will let you edit several files at once, opening a tabbed pane for each. You can use Gedit to edit any text file, including ones you create yourself. Three commonly edited configuration files are **.bash_profile**, **/boot/grub/grub.conf**, and **/etc/fstab**. The **.bash_profile** file configures your login shell, **/etc/fstab** file lists all your file systems and how they are mounted, and **/boot/grub/grub.conf** file is the configuration file for your Grub boot loader.

To edit any of the system wide configuration files, like those in the **/etc** directory, you will first need root user access. Either login as the root user and run gedit, or, as any user with administrative access, run **gedit** from a terminal window using the `sudo` command. You will be prompted for the root user password. You could also login as the root user from a terminal window using the `su` command. Then enter the `gedit` command on that terminal line.

```
sudo -u root gedit
```

User configuration files, dot files, can be changed by individual users directly. They do not show up automatically on Gedit. Dot files like **.bash_profile** have to be chosen from the file manager window, not from the Gedit open operation. First configure the file manager to display dot files by opening the Preferences dialog (select Preferences in the Edit menu of any file manager window) and then check the Show Hidden Files entry and close the dialog. This displays the dot files in your file manager window. Double-click to open one in Gedit.

Backup Management: rsync, BackupPC, and Amanda

Backup operations have become an important part of administrative duties. Several backup tools are provided on Linux systems, including Amanda and the traditional dump/restore tools, as well as the `rsync` command for making individual copies. Anaconda provides server-based backups, letting different systems on a network back up to a central server. BackupPC provides network and local backup using configured rsync and tar tools. The dump tools let you refine your backup process, detecting data changed since the last backup. Table 13-2 lists websites for Linux backup tools.

Individual Backups: archive and rsync

You can back up and restore particular files and directories with archive tools like `tar`, restoring the archives later. For backups, `tar` is usually used with a tape device. To automatically schedule backups, you can schedule appropriate `tar` commands with the **cron** utility. The archives can be also compressed for storage savings. You can then copy the compressed archives to any medium, such as a DVD disc, a floppy, or tape. On GNOME you can use File Roller (Archive Manager) to create archives easily (Applications | Accessories | Archive Manager). The Archive

Manager menu entry is not initially displayed, use System | Preferences | Main Menu to have it displayed on the Applications | Accessories menu.

File Roller also supports LZMA compression, a more efficient and faster compression method. On Archive Manager, when creating a new archive, select "Tar compressed with lzma (.tar.lzma)" ad the Archive type. When choosing Create Archive from Nautilus file manager window on selected files. On the Create Archive dialog, choose the **.lzma** file type for just compression, and the **.tar.lzma** type for a compressed archive.

Website	Tools
`http://rsync.samba.org`	rsync remote copy backup
`www.amanda.org`	Amanda network backup
`http://dump.sourceforge.net`	dump and restore tools
`http://backuppc.sourceforge.net`	BackupPC network or local backup using configured rsync and tar tools.

Table 13-2: Backup Resources

If you want to remote-copy a directory or files from one host to another, making a particular backup, you can use **rsync**, which is designed for network backups of particular directories or files, intelligently copying only those files that have been changed, rather than the contents of an entire directory. In archive mode, it can preserve the original ownership and permissions, providing corresponding users exist on the host system. The following example copies the **/home/george/myproject** directory to the **/backup** directory on the host **rabbit**, creating a corresponding **myproject** subdirectory. The **-t** specifies that this is a transfer. The remote host is referenced with an attached colon, **rabbit:**.

```
rsync -t /home/george/myproject   rabbit:/backup
```

If, instead, you wanted to preserve the ownership and permissions of the files, you would use the **-a** (archive) option. Adding a **-z** option will compress the file. The **-v** option provides a verbose mode.

```
rsync -avz /home/george/myproject   rabbit:/backup
```

A trailing slash on the source will copy the contents of the directory, rather than generating a subdirectory of that name. Here the contents of the **myproject** directory are copied to the **george-project** directory.

```
rsync -avz /home/george/myproject/   rabbit:/backup/george-project
```

The **rsync** command is configured to use SSH remote shell by default. You can specify it or an alternate remote shell to use with the **-e** option. For secure transmission you can encrypt the copy operation with ssh. Either use the **-e ssh** option or set the **RSYNC_RSH** variable to ssh.

```
rsync -avz -e ssh /home/george/myproject   rabbit:/backup/myproject
```

As when using **rcp**, you can copy from a remote host to the one you are on.

```
rsync -avz lizard:/home/mark/mypics/   /pic-archice/markpics
```

You can also run rsync as a server daemon. This will allow remote users to sync copies of files on your system with versions on their own, transferring only changed files rather than entire directories. Many mirror and software FTP sites operate as rsync servers, letting you update files without have to download the full versions again. Configuration information for rsync as a server is kept in the **/etc/rsyncd.conf** file. On Ubuntu, rsync as a server is managed through **xinetd**, using the **/etc/xinetd.d/rsync** file, which starts **rsync** with the `--daemon` option. In the **/etc/services** file, it is listed to run on port 873. It is off by default, but you can enable it with system-config-services On Demand Services panel or `chkconfig`.

```
chkconfig rsync on
```

Tip: Though it is designed for copying between hosts, you can also use **rsync** to make copies within your own system, usually to a directory in another partition or hard drive. In fact there are eight different ways of using **rsync**. Check the **rsync** Man page for detailed descriptions of each.

BackupPC

BackupPC provides an easily managed local or network backup of your system or hosts on a system using configured rsync or tar tools. There is no client application to install, just configuration files. BackupPC can back up hosts on a network, including servers, or just a single system. Data can be backed up to local hard disks or to network storage such as shared partitions or storage servers. You can configure BackupPC using your Web page configuration interface. This is the host name of your computer with the /backuppc name attached, like **http://rabbit.turtle.com/backuppc**. Detailed documentation is installed at **/usr/share/doc/BackupPC**. You can find out more about BackupPC at **http://backuppc.sourceforge.net**.

BackupPC uses both compression and detection of identical files to significantly reduce the size of the backup, allowing several hosts to be backed up in limited space. Once an initial backup is performed, BackupPC will only back up changed files, reducing the time of the backup significantly.

BackupPC has its own service script with which you start the BackupPC service, **/etc/init.d/backuppc**. Configuration files are located at **/etc/BackupPC**. The **config.pl** file holds BackupPC configuration options and the hosts file lists hosts to be backed up.

Amanda

To back up hosts connected to a network, you can use the Advanced Maryland Automatic Network Disk Archiver (Amanda) to archive hosts. Amanda uses tar tools to back up all hosts to a single host operating as a backup server. Backup data is sent by each host to the host operating as the Amanda server, where they are written out to a backup medium such as tape. With an Amanda server, the backup operations for all hosts become centralized in one server, instead of each host having to perform its backup. Any host that needs to restore data simply requests it from the Amanda server, specifying the file system, date, and filenames. Backup data is copied to the server's holding disk and from there to tapes. Detailed documentation and updates are provided at **www.amanda.org**. For the server, be sure to install the Amanda-server package, and for clients you use the amanda-clients package.

Amanda is designed for automatic backups of hosts that may have very different configurations, as well as operating systems. You can back up any host that supports GNU tools, including Mac OS X and Windows systems connected through Samba.

14. Network Connections

Ubuntu will automatically detect and configure your network connections with Network Manager. Should the automatic configuration either fail or be incomplete for some reason, you can also use Network Manager to perform a manual configuration. On GNOME, NetworkManager is accessed using a GNOME applet or from the System | Preferences | Network Configuration menu entry. On KDE you use KNetworkManager. In addition your network will also need a firewall. UFW (with the Gufw interface) or Firestarter is recommended. You may also connect to a network with Windows computer. To access them you use the Samba server. To access shared directories and printers on other Linux and UNIX computers on your network, you can use the NFS. For dial-up service, you can use NetworkManager, If you are working from a command line interface, you can use WvDial. Table 14-1 lists several different network configuration tools.

Network Information: Dynamic and Static

If you are on a network, you may need to obtain certain information to configure your interface. Most networks now support dynamic configuration using either the older Dynamic Host Configuration Protocol (DHCP) or the new IPv6 Protocol and its automatic address configuration. In this case, you need only check the DHCP entry in most network configuration tools. If your network does not support DHCP or IPv6 automatic addressing, you will have to provide detailed information about your connection. Such connections are known as static connections, whereas DCHP and IPv6 connections are dynamic. In a static connection, you need to manually enter your connection information such as your IP address and DNS servers, whereas in a dynamic connection this information is automatically provided to your system by a DHCP server or generated by IPv6 when you connect to the network. For DHCP, a DHCP client on each host will obtain the information from a DHCP server serving that network. IPv6 generates its addresses directly from the device and router information such as the device hardware MAC address.

Network Configuration Tool	Description
Network Manager	Automates wireless and standard network connection, selection, and notification (System | Preferences | Network Connections). Used for all network connections including LAN, wireless, broadband, VPN, and DSL.
network-manager-kde	KDE version of NetworkManager
gnome-network-admin	Older GNOME network configuration tool (Universe repository).
ufw	Sets up a network firewall.
Gufw	GNOME interface for UFW firewall
Firestarter	Sets up a network firewall.
wvdial	PPP modem connection, enter on a command line.
pand	Implements the Bluetooth Personal Network.

Table 14-1: Ubuntu Network Configuration Tools

In addition, if you are using a DSL dynamic, ISDN, or modem connection, you will also have to supply provider, login, and password information, whether your system is dynamic or static. You may also need to supply specialized information such as DSL or modem compression methods, dialup number, or wireless channels to select.

You can obtain most of your static network information from your network administrator or from your ISP (Internet service provider). You would need the following information:

The device name for your network interface   For LAN and wireless connections, this is usually an Ethernet card with the name **eth0** or **eth1**. For a modem, DSL, or ISDN connection, this is a PPP device named **ppp0** (**ippp0** for ISDN). Virtual private network (VPN) connections are also supported.

Hostname   Your computer will be identified by this name on the Internet. Do not use localhost; that name is reserved for special use by your system. The name of the host should be a simple word, which can include numbers, but not punctuation such as periods and backslashes. The hostname includes both the name of the host and its domain. For example, a hostname for a machine could be **turtle**, whose domain is **mytrek.com**, giving it a hostname of **turtle.mytrek.com**.

Domain name   This is the name of your network.

The Internet Protocol (IP) address assigned to your machine   This is needed only for static Internet connections. Dynamic connections use the DHCP protocol to automatically assign an IP address for you. Every host on the Internet is assigned an IP address. Traditionally, this address used an IPv4 format consisting of a set of four numbers, separated by periods, which uniquely identifies a single location on the Internet, allowing information from other locations to reach that computer. Networks are now converting to the new IP protocol version 6, IPv6, which uses a new format with a much more complex numbering sequence.

Your network IP address   Static connections only. This address is usually similar to the IP address, but with one or more zeros at the end.

The netmask   Static connections only. This is usually 255.255.255.0 for most networks. If, however, you are part of a large network, check with your network administrator or ISP.

The broadcast address for your network, if available (optional)   Static connections only. Usually, your broadcast address is the same as your IP address with the number 255 added at the end.

The IP address of your network's gateway computer   Static connections only. This is the computer that connects your local network to a larger one like the Internet.

Name servers   Static connections only. The IP address of the name servers your network uses. These enable the use of URLs.

NIS domain and IP address for an NIS server   Necessary if your network uses an NIS server (optional).

User login and password information   Needed for dynamic DSL, ISDN, and modem connections.

Network Manager

Network Manager will automatically detect your network connections, both wired and wireless. Network Manager makes use the automatic device detection capabilities of udev and HAL to configure your connections. Should you instead need to configure your network connections manually, you still use Network Manager, selecting the manual options and entering the required network connection information. Network Manager operates as a daemon with the name NetworkManager. It will automatically scan for both wired and wireless connections.

Ubuntu 9.04 uses an enhanced version of Network Manager which can also manually configure any network connection, replacing GNOME's network-admin. Ubuntu uses Network Manager to configure all your network connections. This includes wired, wireless, and all manual connections. The network-admin tool has been dropped. Network Interface Connection (NIC cards) hardware is detected using HAL. Information provided by Network Manager is made available to other applications over D-Bus.

Network Manager is designed to work in the background, providing status information for your connection and switching from one configured connection to another as needed. For initial configuration, it detects as much information as possible about the new connection. It operates as a GNOME Panel applet, monitoring your connection, and can work on any Linux distribution.

Network Manager is user specific. When a user logs in, sets up the network connection preferred by that user, though wired connections will be started automatically. The user preferred wireless connections will be start up.

Network Manager applet and options menu

Basic network connection operations are discussed in Chapter 3.

Network Manager will display a Network applet icon to the right on the top panel. The Network Manager applet icon will vary according to the type of connection. An Ethernet (wired) connection will display two computer monitors, one in front of the other. A wireless connection will display a staggered bar graph (see Figure 14-1). If the connection is not active, a red x will appear on the icon. When Network Manager is detecting possible wireless connections, it will display a rotating connection image. If you have both a wired and wireless connection, and the wired connection is active, the wired connection image (double monitor) will be used.

Figure 14-1: Network Manager wired, wireless, and detection icons.

Figure 14-2: Network Manager options

Right-click to have the option of editing your connection, shutting off your connection (Enable Networking and Enable Wireless), or to see information about the connection (see Figure 14-2). A computer with both wired and wireless connections will have entries to Enable Networking and Enable Wireless. Selecting Enable Wireless will disconnected only the wireless connections, leaving the wired connection active. The Enable Wireless checkbox will be come unchecked and a message will be displayed telling you that your wireless connection is disconnected.   Selecting Enable Networking will disable your wired connection, along with any wireless connections. Do this to work offline, without any network access.

A computer with only a wired network device (no wireless) will only show an Enable Networking entry, as shown here. Selecting it sill disconnect you from any network access, allowing you to work offline.

Network Manager manual configuration for all network connections

For any wired network connection that Network Manager automatically connects to, a configuration entry will be placed for it in the Network Connections Wired tab. The Auto eth0 connection in this example will have an Auto eth0 entry in the Network Connections window Wired tab. Clicking on it displays an "Editing Wired Connection" window that holds all the configuration information for that network connection.

When you connect to a wireless network for the first time, a configuration entry will be made for the wireless connection in the Wireless tab of the Network Connections tool.

Should you need to edit any network connection, wired or wireless, you right-click on the Network Manager icon and select Edit Network Connections (see Figure 14-2). You can also select System | Preferences | Network Connections. This opens Network Manager's Network Connections window as shown in Figure 14-3. Established connections will be listed, with Add, Edit, and Delete buttons for adding, editing, and removing network connections. Your current network connections should already be listed, having been automatically detected by udev and HAL. In the Figure 14-3 a wired Ethernet connection referred to as **Auto eth0** is listed, the first Ethernet connection. This is an automatic configuration set up by Network Manager when it automatically connected to the wired network.

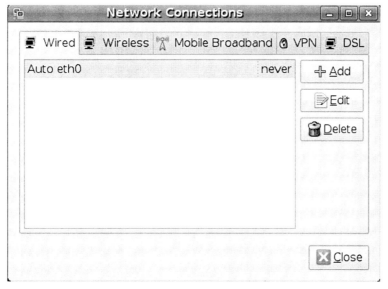

Figure 14-3: Network configuration

Figure 14-4: DHCP Wired Configuration

On the Network Connections window there are three tabs: Wired, Wireless, Mobile Broadband, VPN, and DSL.

> **Wired**: The wired connection is used for the standard IPv4 and IPv6 Ethernet connections, featuring support for DHCP and manual Ethernet settings.

> **Wireless**: The Wireless tab is where you enter in wireless configuration data like your ESSID, password, and encryption method.

> **Mobile Broadband**: The mobile broadband tab is the wireless 3G configuration, with selection for the service you are using.

> **VPN**: The VPN tab lets you specify a virtual private network. Be sure VPN support is installed on your system.

> **DSL**: The DSL tab lets you set up a direct DSL connection.

Each tab will list their configured network connections. Click on the ADD or EDIT buttons to configure a new network connection of that type, or edit an existing one.

All configuration dialogs will display an option at the bottom of the dialog to allow you to make your configuration available to all users (this replaces the "System setting" option use in previous versions). In effect, this option implements a system wide network connection configuration.

Figure 14-5: Manual Wired Configuration

Wired Configuration

To edit a wired connection, select the connection and click the EDIT buttons on the Wired tab. This opens an Editing window as shown in Figure 14-4.

The ADD button is used to add a new connection and opens a similar window, with no settings. The Wired tab lists the MAC hardware address and the MTU. The MTU is usually set to automatic. Figure 14-4 shows the standard default configuration for a wired Ethernet connection using DHCP. Connect automatically will set up the connection when the system starts up.

There are three tabs, Wired, 8.02.1x Security, and IPv4 Settings.

The IPv4 Setting tab lets you select the kind of wired connection you have. The options are:

➢ **Automatic (DHCP)**: DHCP connection. Address information is blocked out.

➢ **Automatic (DHCP) addresses only**: DHCP that lets you specify your DNS server addresses.

➢ **Manual**: Enter your IP, network, and gateway addresses along with your DNS server addresses and your network domain name.

> ➢ **Link-local only**: IPv6 private local network (like IPv4 192.18.0 addresses). All address entries are blocked out.

> ➢ **Shared to other computers**: All address entries are blocked out.

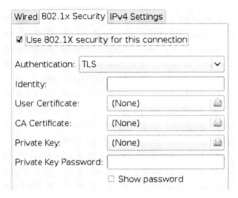

Figure 14-6: 802.1 Security Configuration

Figure 14-7: Wireless configuration

Figure 14-5 shows the manual configuration entries for a wired Ethernet connection. Click the Add button to enter the IP address, network mask, and gateway address. Then enter the address for the DNS servers and your network search domains.

The Routes button will open a window where you can manually enter any network routes.

The 802.1 tab allows you to configure 802.1 security, if your network supports it (see Figure 14-6).

Wireless Configuration

For wireless connections, you click ADD or EDIT on the Network Connections window's Wireless tab. The Editing Wireless connection window opens with tabs for your wireless information, security, and IPv4 settings (See Figure 14-7). On the Wireless tab you specify your SSID, along with your Mode and MAC address.

Figure 14-8: Wireless Security: WEP and WPA

On the Wireless Security tab you enter your wireless connection security method (see Figure 14-8). The commonly used method, WEP, is supported, along with WPA personal. The WPA personal method only requires a password. More secure connections like Dynamic WEP and Enterprise WPA are also supported. These will require much more configuration information like authentication methods, certificates, and keys.

On the IPv4 Settings tab you enter your wireless connection's network address settings. This tab is the same as the IPv4 Setting on the Wired connection (see Figures 14-5 and 14-6). You have the same options: DHCP, DHCP with DNS addresses, Manual, Link-local only, and Shared.

DSL Configuration

For a direct DSL connection, you click ADD or EDIT on the Network Connections window's DSL tab. The DSL connection window will open, showing tabs for DSL configuration and for wired, PPP, and IPv4 network connections. On the DSL tab you enter your DSL user name, service provider, and password (see Figure 14-9). A wired connection only requires a MAC address and MTU byte amount. The PPP tab is the same as that used for Mobile Broadband, and IPv4 is the same as that used for Wired, Wireless, and Mobile Broadband.

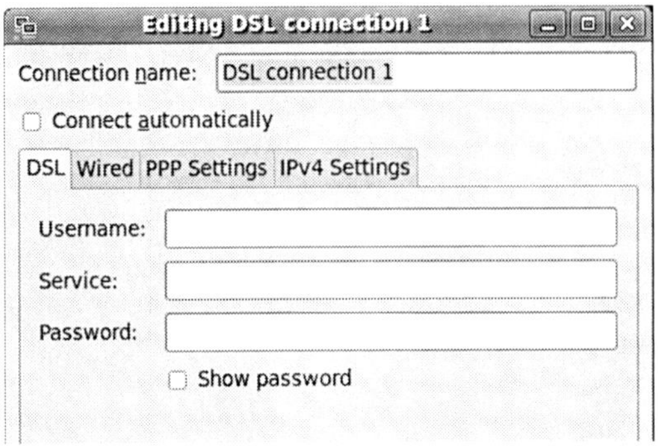

Figure 14-9: DSL manual configuration

Mobile Broadband: 3G Support

To set up a Mobile Broadband 3G connections, you select the Mobile Broadband tab in the Network Connections window, and click the ADD or EDIT button. A 3G wizard will start up to help you set up the appropriate configuration for your particular 3G service (see Figure 14-10).

The 3G wizard thin displays a Service Provider window with possible 3G service providers (see Figure 14-11).

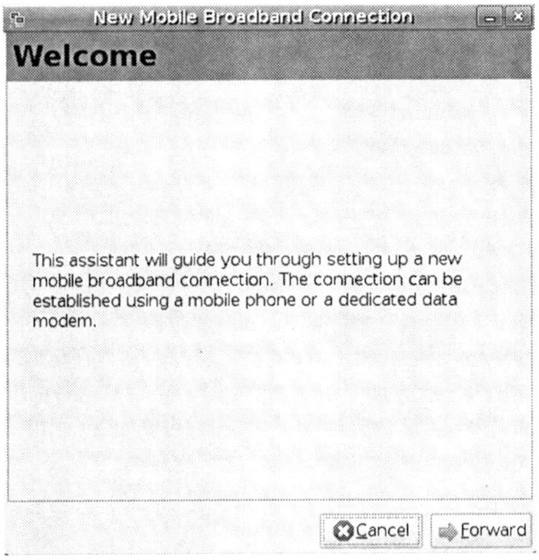

Figure 14-10: 3G Wizard

The providers are organized by country, with the country you selected for your time zone initially displayed.

To see other countries, click on the expand arrow. A Country list will be displayed.

Figure 14-11: 3G Provider Listings

As you select a country, its available 3G services are displayed in the Provider listing (see Figure 14-12).Once you have made your selection, you are asked to verify it. You can give the selection label a different name if you wish (see Figure 14-13).

Figure 14-12: 3G Country listing

Once a service is selected, you can further edit the configuration by clicking its entry in the Mobile Broadband tab and clicking the EDIT button. The Editing window opens with tabs for Mobile Broadband, PPP, IPv4 settings. On the Mobile Broadband panel you can enter your number, user name, and password. Advance options including the APN, Network, type, PIN, and PUK (see Figure 14-14). The APN should already be entered.

Figure 14-13: 3G provider verification

Figure 14-14: 3G configuration

PPP Configuration

For either Wireless Broadband or DSL connections you can also specify PPP information. The PPP tab is the same for both (See Figure 14-15). There are sections Authentication, Compression, and the Echo options. Check what features are supported by your particular PPP connection. For Authentication, click the Configure button to open a dialog listing possible authentication methods. Check the ones you connection supports.

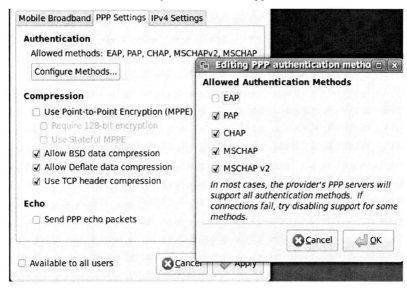

Figure 14-15: PPP Configuration

Network Manager VPN

The VPN Connection entry submenu will list configured VPN connection for easy access. The Configure VPN entry will open Network Manager to the VPN tab where you can then add, edit, or delete VPN connections. The Disconnect VPN entry will end the current active VPN connection. The VPN tab will not be active until you first install VPN software, like **openvpn**.

Network Manager wireless router, using your wireless connection as a wireless router.

You can also set up your wireless connection as a wireless router for your own wireless network. The "Create New Wireless Network" entry will open a dialog letting you set up your computer as a wireless router that other computers can connect to (see Figure 14-16). Enter a Network name, select the kind of wireless security you want to use, and enter a password for accessing the network. You will be prompted to enter your keyring password.

The wireless network you created will not perform any SSID broadcasting. You access it through the "Connect to Hidden Wireless network" entry on the Network Manager menu. This opens the "Hidden wireless network" window (see Figure 14-16). Your new wireless network will be listed in the Connection drop-down menu. When you select it, the network name and security information is displayed.

Figure 14-16: Create New Wireless Network and connect as Hidden network

Command Line PPP Access: wvdial

If, for some reason, you have been unable to set up a modem connection on your Desktop, you may have to set it up from the command line interface. For a dial-up PPP connection, you can use the wvdial dialer, which is an intelligent dialer that not only dials up an ISP service but also performs login operations, supplying your username and password.

The wvdial program first loads its configuration from the **/etc/wvdial.conf** file. In here, you can place modem and account information, including modem speed and serial device, as well as ISP phone number, username, and password. The **wvdial.conf** file is organized into sections, beginning with a section label enclosed in brackets. A section holds variables for different parameters that are assigned values, such as `username = chris`. The default section holds default values inherited by other sections, so you needn't repeat them. Table 14-2 lists the wvdial variables.

You can use the wvdialconf utility to create a default **wvdial.conf** file for you automatically; wvdialconf will detect your modem and set default values for basic features. You can then edit the **wvdial.conf** file and modify the Phone, Username, and Password entries with your

ISP dial-up information. Remove the preceding semicolon (;) to unquote the entry. Any line beginning with a semicolon is ignored as a comment.

```
$ wvdialconf
```

Variable	Description
Inherits	Explicitly inherits from the specified section. By default, sections inherit from the [Dialer Defaults] section.
Modem	The device wvdial should use as your modem. The default is **/dev/modem.**
Baud	The speed at which wvdial communicates with your modem. The default is 57,600 baud.
Init1...Init9	Specifies the initialization strings to be used by your modem; wvdial can use up to 9. The default is "ATZ" for Init1.
Phone	The phone number you want wvdial to dial.
Area Code	Specifies the area code, if any.
Dial Prefix	Specifies any needed dialing prefix—for example, 70 to disable call waiting or 9 for an outside line.
Dial Command	Specifies the dial operation. The default is "ATDT".
Login	Specifies the username you use at your ISP.
Login Prompt	If your ISP has an unusual login prompt, you can specify it here.
Password	Specifies the password you use at your ISP.
Password Prompt	If your ISP has an unusual password prompt, you can specify it here.
Force Address	Specifies a static IP address to use (for ISPs that provide static IP addresses to users).
Auto Reconnect	If enabled, wvdial attempts to reestablish a connection automatically if you are randomly disconnected by the other side. This option is on by default.

Table 14-2: Variables for wvdial

You can also create a named dialer. This is helpful if you have different ISPs you log in to. The following example shows the **/etc/wvdial.conf** file:

To start wvdial, enter the command **wvdial**, which then reads the connection configuration information from the **/etc/wvdial.conf** file; wvdial dials the ISP and initiates the PPP connection, providing your username and password when requested.

```
$ wvdial
```

You can set up connection configurations for any number of connections in the **/etc/wvdial.conf** file. To select one, enter its label as an argument to the **wvdial** command, as shown here:

```
$ wvdial myisp
```

Command Line Manual Wireless Configuration

NetworkManager will automatically detect and configure your wireless connections. However, you can manually configure your connections with wireless tools like Network Manager (wireless properties), Kwifimanager, and ifwconfig. Wireless configuration using system-config-network was discussed in the previous section.

Wireless configuration makes use of the same set of Wireless Extensions. The Wireless Tools package is a set of network configuration and reporting tools for wireless devices installed on a Linux system. They are currently supported and developed as part of the Linux Wireless Extension and Wireless Tools Project, an open source project maintained by Hewlett-Packard.

Wireless Tools consists of the configuration and report tools listed here:

Tool	Description
iwconfig	Sets the wireless configuration options basic to most wireless devices.
iwlist	Displays current status information of a device.
iwspy	Sets the list of IP addresses in a wireless network and checks the quality of their connections.
iwpriv	Accesses configuration options specific to a particular device.

The wireless LAN device will have an Ethernet name just like an Ethernet card. The appropriate modules will automatically be loaded, listing their aliases in the **/etc/modprobe.conf** file.

iwconfig

The `iwconfig` command works much like `ifconfig`, configuring a network connection. It is the tool used by the Internet Connection Wizard and by system-config-network to configure a wireless card. Alternatively, you can run `iwconfig` directly on a command line, specifying certain parameters. Added parameters let you set wireless-specific features such as the network name (nwid), the frequency or channel the card uses (freq or channel), and the bit rate for transmissions (rate). See the `iwconfig` Man page for a complete listing of accepted parameters. Some of the commonly used parameters are listed in Table 14-3.

For example, to set the channel used for the wireless device installed as the first Ethernet device, you would use the following, setting the channel to 2:

```
iwconfig eth0 channel 2
```

You can also use `iwconfig` to display statistics for your wireless devices, just as `ifconfig` does. Enter the `iwconfig` command with no arguments or with the name of the device. Information such as the name, frequency, sensitivity, and bit rate is listed. Check also **/proc/net/wireless** for statistics.

Instead of using `iwconfig` directly to set parameters, you can specify them in the wireless device's configuration file. The wireless device configuration file will be located in the **/etc/sysconfig/network-scripts** directory and given a name like **ifcfg-eth1**, depending on the name of the device. This file will already contain many `iwconfig` settings. Any further setting can be set by assigning `iwconfig` values to the IWCONFIG parameter as shown here.

```
IWCONFIG="rate 11M"
```

Parameter	Description
essid	A network name
freq	The frequency of the connection
channel	The channel used
nwid or domain	The network ID or domain
mode	The operating mode used for the device, such as Ad Hoc, Managed, or Auto. Ad Hoc = one cell with no access point, Managed = network with several access points and supports roaming, Master = the node is an access point, Repeater = node forwards packets to other nodes, Secondary = backup master or repeater, Monitor = only receives packets
sens	The sensitivity, the lowest signal level at which data can be received
key or enc	The encryption key used
frag	Cut packets into smaller fragments to increase better transmission
bit or rate	Speed at which bits are transmitted. The auto option automatically falls back to lower rates for noisy channels
ap	Specify a specific access point
power	Power management for wakeup and sleep operations

Table 14-3: Commonly Used Parameters

iwpriv

The iwpriv command works in conjunction with iwconfig, allowing you set options specific to a particular kind of wireless device. With iwpriv, you can also turn on roaming or select the port to use. You use the *private-command* parameter to enter the device-specific options. The following example sets roaming on:

```
iwpriv eth0 roam on
```

iwspy

Your wireless device can check its connection to another wireless device it is receiving data from, reporting the quality, signal strength, and noise level of the transmissions. Your device can maintain a list of addresses for different devices it may receive data from. You use the iwspy tool to set or add the addresses that you want checked. You can list either IP addresses or the hardware versions. A + sign will add the address, instead of replacing the entire list:

```
iwspy eth0 +192.168.2.5
```

To display the quality, signal, and noise levels for your connections, you use the iwspy command with just the device name:

```
iwspy eth0
```

iwlist

To obtain more detailed information about your wireless device, such as all the frequencies or channels available, you use the `iwlist` tool. Using the device name with a particular parameter, you can obtain specific information about a device, including the frequency, access points, rate, power features, retry limits, and encryption keys used. You can use iwlist to obtain information about faulty connections. The following example will list the frequencies used on the **eth0** wireless device.

```
iwlist eth0 freq
```

Firewalls

Like all Linux systems, Ubuntu implements its firewall using IPTables. You can choose from several different popular firewall management tools. Ubuntu now provides its own firewall management tool called the Uncomplicated Firewall (ufw). IPtables and ufw are on the Ubuntu main repository; all others are in the Universe repository. You can also choose to use other popular management tools like Firestarter or Fwbuilder. Firestarter provides a desktop interface whereas ufw is command line only. Both ufw and Firestarter are covered in this chapter, along with the underlying IPTables firewall application. Search Synaptic Package Manager for firewall to see a more complete listing.

Important Firewall Ports

Commonly used services like Linux and Windows file sharing, remote printer access, and Secure SHell remote access, use certain network connection ports on your system (see Table 14-4). A default firewall configuration will block these ports. Your will have to configure your firewall to allow access to the ports these services use before those services will work.

Port number	Service
137	Samba
139	Netbios-ssn
22	Secure SHell, ssh
2049	NFS, Linux and Unix shares
631	IPP, Internet Printing Protocol, access to remote Linux/Unix printers
21	FTP
25	SMTP, forward mail
110	POP3, receive mail
143	IMAP, receive mail

Table 14-4: Service ports

To access a Windows share, you not only have to have the Samba service running, but also have to configure your firewall to allow access on port 137, the port Samba services use to connect to Windows systems. In particular, to also allow direct access to the detected shares on your system (Ahavi), you have to also allow access on port 139. Most can be selected easily as preconfigured items in firewall configuration tools, like Gufw and Firestarter. Some, though, may not be listed. Gufw may not have a preconfigured entry for Samba, 137.

Setting up a firewall with ufw

The Uncomplicated Firewall, ufw, is now the official firewall application for Ubuntu. It provides a simple firewall that can be managed with a few command-line operations. Like all firewall applications, ufw uses IPTables to define rules and run the firewall. The ufw application is just a management interface for IPTables. Default IPtables rules are kept in before and after files, with added rules in user files. The IPtables rule files are held in the **/etc/ufw** directory. Firewall configuration for certain packages will be placed in the **/usr/share/ufw.d** directory. The ufw firewall is started up at boot using the **/etc/init.d/ufw** script. You can find out more about ufw at the Ubuntu Firewall site at **http://wiki.ubuntu.com/UbuntuFirewall** and at the Ubuntu firewall section in the Ubuntu Server Guide at **http://doc.ubuntu.com**. The Server Guide also shows information on how to implement IP Masquerading on ufw.

You can now manage the ufw firewall with either the standard ufw command or using the new Gufw configuration tool. You can quickly enable or disable the firewall by right-clicking on the Gufw icon and selecting Enable/Disable Firewall.

Gufw

Gufw provides an easy to use GNOME interface for managing your ufw firewall. A simple interface lets you add rules, both custom and standard. Help entry in the Gufw Help menu will open the Gufw manual, which provides a very detailed explanation of Gufw features and use, including screenshots and examples.

Figure 14-17: Gufw

Gufw is in the Ubuntu Universe repository, currently given Ubuntu development support. You will have to install it with Synaptic, System Administration (Universe). Once installed, you can access Gufw from the System | Administration | Firewall configuration menu entry. Gufw preferences will let you display the Gufw icon on the panel, letting you easily access the Gufw interface.

Gufw will initially open with the firewall disabled with no ports configured. All components, except the check box labeled Firewall enabled. That check box will be empty. Above the checkbox a large Disabled label will be displayed. To enable the firewall, just click the Enabled check box. The Disabled label will be replaced by a green Enabled label. Figure 14-17 shows the firewall enabled, as well as the SSH port configured (22).

Gufw has three sections, Current Configuration, Add a new rule, and Rules. The Current Configuration has two options, Deny or Allow incoming traffic. By default, incoming traffic will be denied. Rules will make exceptions, allowing only certain traffic in. Should you select the Allow incoming traffic option, the firewall, though active, becomes ineffective, allowing all connections.

Figure 14-18: Gufw Preconfigured rules

Gufw has three tabs for managing rules in the Add a new rules section: Simple, Preconfigured, and Advanced. On the Simple tab you can specify a port to allow. The Preconfigure tab provides a pop-up menu listing services by name for which Gufw will enter the port for you. To allow connection for trusted services like SSH or NFS, you just select their entry from the pop-up menu and then click the Add button. A port entry will then appear in the Rules segment. In Figure 14-18 the netbios-ssn discovery service has been selected and then added, showing up in the Rules section as "139/tcp ALLOW Anywhere". There is a corresponding rule for the udp protocol. Also in the Rules section is the SSH entry for port 22.

Services can also be blocked. To prevent FTP service, you could select the FTP entry, but then changed the Allow entry to Deny.

Figure 14-19: Gufw Simple rules

Besides Allow and Deny, you can also choose a Limit option. The Limit option will enable connection rate limiting, restricting connections to no more than 6 every 30 seconds for a given port. This is meant to protect against brute force attacks.

Should there be no preconfigured entry, you can use the Simple tab to allow access to a port. Currently, you have to do this to allow Samba access, port 137. You may also have to do this to allow access on BitTorrent ports for BitTorrent applications. In Figure 14-19 Samba access is allowed by adding a rule for port 137.

On the Advanced tab you can enter more complex rules. You can set up allow or deny rules for tcp or udp protocols, and specify the host and port (see Figure 14-20).

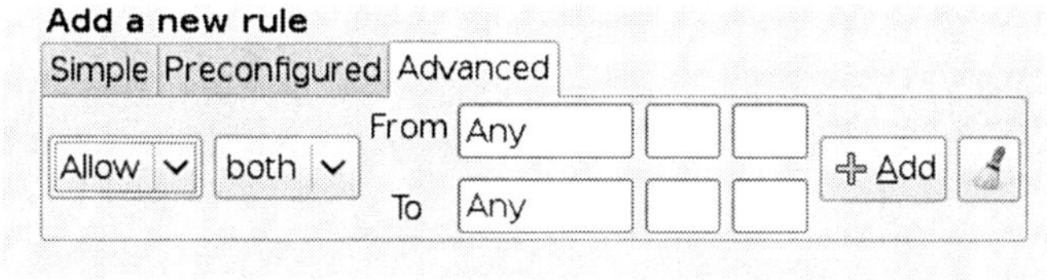

Figure 14-20: Gufw Advanced rules

If you should want to remove a rule, select it in the Rules section and then click the Remove button. To clear out all rules, click the Select all button and then the Remove button.

ufw commands

IPtables firewall rules are set up using **ufw** commands entered on a command line in a Terminal window. Most users may only need to use **ufw** commands to allow or deny access by services like the Web server or Samba server. To check the current firewall status, listing those services allowed or blocked, use the status command.

```
sudo ufw status
```

If the firewall is not enabled, you will have to first enable it with the enable command.

```
sudo ufw enable
```

You can restart the firewall, reloading your rules, using the /etc/init.d/ufw command.

```
sudo /etc/init.d/ufw restart
```

You can then add rules using allow and deny commands and their options as listed in Table 14-5. To allow a service, use the allow command and the service name. This is the name for the service listed in the /etc/services file. The following allows the ftp service.

```
sudo ufw allow ftp
```

If the service you want is not listed in /etc/services, and you know the port and protocol it uses, can specify the port and protocol directly. For example, the Samba service uses port 137 and protocol tcp.

```
sudo ufw allow 137/tcp
```

The status operation will then show what services are allowed.

```
sudo ufw status
To                  Action          From
21:tcp              ALLOW           Anywhere
21:udp              ALLOW           Anywhere
137:tcp             ALLOW           Anywhere
```

To remove a rule, prefix it with the **delete** command.

```
sudo ufw delete allow 137/tcp
```

More detailed rules can be specified using address, port, and protocol commands. These are very similar to the actual IPTables commands. Packets to and from particular networks, hosts, and ports can be controlled. The following denies ssh access (port 22) from host 192.168.03.

```
sudo ufw deny proto tcp from 192.168.03 to any port 22
```

UFW also supports connection rate limiting. Use the **limit** option in place of **allow**. With **limit**, connections are limited to 6 per 30 seconds on the specified port. It is meant to protect against brute force attacks.

The rules you add are placed in the **/var/lib/ufw/user.rules** file as IPTables rules. ufw is just a front end for **iptables-restore** which will read this file and set up the firewall using **iptables** commands. **ufw** will also have **iptables-restore** read the **before.rules** and **after.rules** files in the

/etc/ufw directory. These files are considered administrative files that include needed supporting rules for your IPTables firewall. Administrators can add their own IPTables rules to these files for system specific features like IP Masquerading.

Commands	Description
enable | disable	Turn the firewall on or off
status	Display status along with services allowed or denied.
logging on | off	Turn logging on or off
default allow | deny	Set the default policy, allow is open, whereas deny is restrictive
allow *service*	Allow access by a service. Services are defined in **/etc/services** which specify the ports for that service.
allow *port-number/protocol*	Allow access on a particular port using specified protocol. The protocol is optional.
deny *service*	Deny access by a service
delete *rule*	Delete an installed rule, use **allow**, **deny**, or **limit** and include rule specifics.
proto *protocol*	Specify protocol in **allow**, **deny**, or **limit** rule
from *address*	Specify source address in **allow**, **deny**, or **limit** rule
to *address*	Specify destination address in **allow**, **deny**, or **limit** rule
port *port*	Specify port in **allow**, **deny**, or **limit** rule for **from** and **to** address operations

Table 14-5: UFW firewall operations

The **before.rules** file will specify a table with the * symbol, as in ***filter** for the netfilter table. For the NAT table you would use ***nat**. At the end of each table segment, a COMMIT command is needed to instruct ufw to apply the rules. Rules use **-A** for allow and **-D** for deny, assuming the **iptables** command. The following would implement IP Forwarding when placed at the end of the **before.rules** file (see Ubuntu firewall server documentation). This particular rule works on the first Ethernet device (eth0) for a local network (192.168.0.0/24).

```
# nat Table rules
*nat
:POSTROUTING ACCEPT [0:0]
# Forward traffic from eth1 through eth0.
-A POSTROUTING -s 192.168.0.0/24 -o eth0 -j MASQUERADE
# don't delete the 'COMMIT' line or these nat table rules won't be processed
COMMIT
```

Default settings for ufw are placed in **/etc/defaults/ufw**. Here you will find the default INPUT, OUTPUT, and FORWARD policies. A **default deny** command will set the default INPUT to DROP and OUTPUT to ACCEPT, whereas a **default allow** will set both INPUT and OUTPUT defaults to ACCEPT. FORWARD will always be drop. To allow IP Masquerading, FORWARD would have to be set to ACCEPT. Any user rules you have set up would not be affected. You would have to change these manually.

Setting Up Your Firewall with Firestarter

Ubuntu also provides the Firestarter firewall configuration tool with which you can set up your firewall. Firestarter, though popular, is located in the Universe repository. You should use either Gufw or Firestarter, but not both at the same time.

To access Firestarter select Firestarter from the System | Administration menu. The first time you start up Firestarter the Firewall Wizard starts up which will prompt you for your network device and Internet connection sharing information (see Figure 14-21). Much of the configuration is automatic. If you are using a local home or work network, you may have to add rules for services like Samba Windows network access or the network address of your local network. After the Welcome screen, the Network device setup panel lets you select your network device, like an Ethernet connection or modem, as well as whether to use DHCP to detect your address information

Figure 14-21: Firestarter setup wizard

The Internet connection sharing setup panel is rarely used. You will most likely just skip it. It is used only for local networks where your computer is being used as a gateway to the Internet, letting other computer on your local network to access the Internet through your computer. There is usually a second Ethernet device connected to the local network as well as a local DHCP server controlling local network addressing. Again, this is rarely used, as most Internet gateways are now handled by dedicated routers, not computers. A final screen prompts you to start the firewall now, with a button to save your configuration. Click the SAVE button.

Firestarter will then start up with a window titled with your computer name. There are three panels: Status, Events, and Policy (see Figure 14-22). The toolbar entries will change with each panel selected. The Status panel lets you start and stop your firewall using the Stop/Start Firewall button in the toolbar. Its status is shown as a play or stop icon in the Status segment of the Status panel. The Events segment of this panel shows inbound and outbound traffic, and the Network segment lists your network devices along with device information like the number of packets received, sent, and average activity. Usually there will be only one device listed (a computer functioning as a gateway will have several). An expansion list will show Active connections. Here you can see what kind of connection is active, like Samba or Internet connections.

The Events panel will list any rejected connections, Blocked Connections. The Save, Clear, and Reload buttons on the toolbar let you save the event log, clear it, or reload to see the latest events.

The Policy panel shows rules for allowing host and service connections (see Figure 14-23). A pop-up menu lets you show Inbound traffic or Outbound traffic policies. On this panel you can add your own simplified rules for inbound or outbound hosts. The toolbar shows Add Rule, Remove Rule, Edit Rule, and Apply Rule buttons.

Figure 14-22: Firestarter Firewall

For Inbound Traffic, when you can set up rules for connections, services, or forwarding. There will be segments for each. Click on the segment first, and then click on the Add Rule button. The dialog is different depending on the type of rule you are setting up. For a connection, the Add Rule dialog will let you enter the host, IP address, or network from which you can receive connections.

For a service, you can select the service to allow from a pop-up menu, along with the port, as well as whether to allow access by anyone or from a specific host or network (see Figure 14-24). By default all inbound traffic is denied, unless explicitly allowed by a rule. If you are setting up a firewall for just your personal computer connected to a network, you would enter a rule for the local network address. You could also set up rules to allow access by services like Samba or BitTorrent. Though Firestarter does have a preconfigured entry for Samba, it does not have a separate one for Netbios-ssn, port 139. You would have to add one manually.

The Outbound Traffic is more complex. Here you can set either a permissive or restrictive policy. There are entries for each to select which. The permissive is selected by default. The permissive entry will still reject blacklisted hosts and services, and the restrictive entry will allow white listed hosts and services. Each has both a connection and service segment, just like the Inbound connections, with the same options.

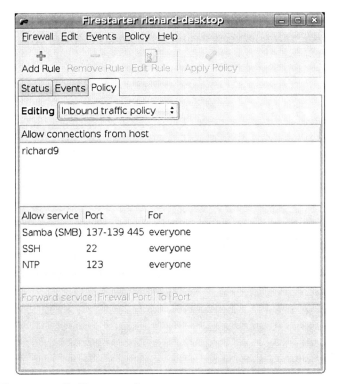

Figure 14-23: Firestarter Policy panel

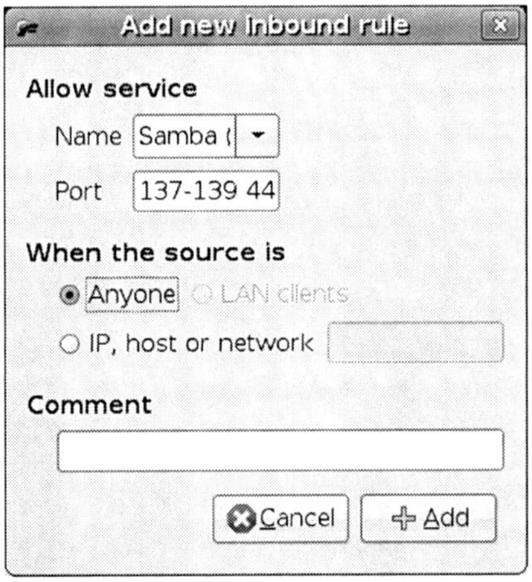

Figure 14-24: Firestarter, choosing a service to permit

If permissive is selected, you will allow all outbound traffic, except those you specifically deny. For this configuration, you can create Deny rules for certain hosts and services. When setting up a Deny rule for a service you can choose a service from a pop-up menu, and specify its port. You can then reject either anyone using this service, or specify a particular host or network. For a connection, you simply specify the host, IP address, or network that can connect. The connection rules act like your own blacklist, listing hosts or network you will not allow yourself or others on your network to connect to.

If restrictive, you deny all outbound traffic, except those you specifically allow. In this case, you can set up Allow rules to allow connections by certain hosts and services, rejecting everything else. The restrictive option is not normally used, as it would cut off any connections from your computer to the Internet, unless you added a rule to permit the connection.

To configure your Firestarter firewall, click on the Preferences button. This opens a Preference window where you can set either Interface or Firewall settings.

For the Interface settings you can set either the Events logged or the Policy. The Events panel lets you eliminate logging of unwanted events, like redundant events or events from specific hosts or ports. The Policy panel has an option to let you apply changes immediately.

For Firewall Settings, you have panels for Network Settings, ICMP Filtering, ToS Filtering, and Advanced Options. Network Settings just selects your network device. Here you could change your network device between Ethernet, wireless, or modem. The ICMP filtering panel blocks ICMP packet attacks. Options allow certain ICMP packets through, like Unreachable to notify you of an unknown site. The Type of Service panel lets you prioritize your packets by both the kind of service and maximized efficiency. For the kind of service you can choose either workstations, servers, or the X Window System. For maximized efficiency you can choose reliability, throughput, or interactivity. Workstations and throughput are selected by default.

The Advanced options panel lets you select the drop method (silent or error reported), the Broadcast traffic rejection policy for internal and external connections (External broadcasts are blocked by default), and traffic validation block reserved addresses

GNOME Network Tools: gnome-nettool

For the GNOME desktop, the **gnome-nettool** utility provides a GNOME interface for entering the `ping` and `traceroute` commands as well as Finger, Whois, and Lookup for querying users and hosts on the network (see Figure 14-25). The **gnome-nettool** utility is installed by default and is accessible from System | Administration | Network Tools. Whois will provide domain name information about a particular domain, and Lookup will provide both domain name and IP addresses. It also includes network status tools such as **netstat** and **portscan**. The first panel, Devices, describes your connected network devices, including configuration and transmission information about each device, such as the hardware address and bytes transmitted. Both IPv4 and IPv6 host IP addresses will be listed.

Network Information: ping, finger, traceroute, and host

You can use the `ping`, `finger`, `traceroute`, and `host` commands to find out status information about systems and users on your network. The `ping` command is used to check if a remote system is up and running. You use `finger` to find out information about other users on your network, seeing if they are logged in or if they have received mail; `host` displays address information about a system on your network, giving you a system's IP and domain name addresses; and `traceroute` can be used to track the sequence of computer networks and systems your message passed through on its way to you. Table 14-6 lists various network information tools.

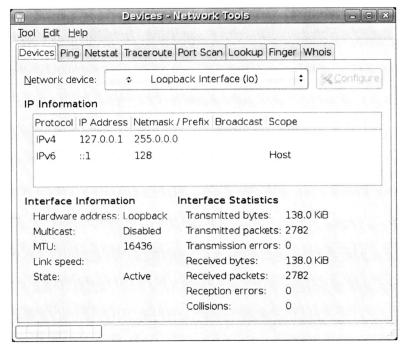

Figure 14-25: Gnome network tool

Network Information Tools	Description
ping	Detects whether a system is connected to the network.
finger	Obtains information about users on the network.
who	Checks what users are currently online.
whois	Obtains domain information.
host	Obtains network address information about a remote host.
traceroute	Tracks the sequence of computer networks and hosts your message passes through.
ethereal	Protocol analyzer to examine network traffic.
gnome-nettool	GNOME interface for various network tools including ping, finger, and traceroute.
mtr and xmtr	My traceroute combines both ping and traceroute operations (Traceroute on System Tools menu).

Table 14-6: Network Tools

ping

The `ping` command detects whether a system is up and running. `ping` takes as its argument the name of the system you want to check. If the system you want to check is down, `ping` issues a timeout message indicating a connection could not be made. The next example checks to see if **www.redhat.com** is up and connected to the network:

```
# ping www.redhat.com
PING www.redhat.com (209.132.177.50) 56(84) bytes of data.
64 bytes from www.redhat.com (209.132.177.50):icmp_seq=1 ttl=118 time=36.7ms
64 bytes from www.redhat.com (209.132.177.50):icmp_seq=2 ttl=118 time=36.9ms
--- www.redhat.com ping statistics ---
4 packets transmitted, 3 received, 25% packet loss, time 3000ms
rtt min/avg/max/mdev = 36.752/37.046/37.476/0.348 ms
```

You can also use `ping` with an IP address instead of a domain name. With an IP address, `ping` can try to detect the remote system directly without having to go through a domain name server to translate the domain name to an IP address. This can be helpful for situations where your network's domain name server may be temporarily down and you want to check if a particular remote host on your network is connected.

```
# ping 209.132.177.50
```

Note: A `ping` operation could also fail if `ping` access is denied by a network's firewall.

finger and who

You can use the `finger` command to obtain information about other users on your network and the `who` command to see what users are currently online on your system. The `who` and `w` commands lists all users currently connected, along with when, how long, and where they logged in. The `w` command provides more detailed information. It has several options for specifying the level of detail. The `who` command is meant to operate on a local system or network; `finger` can operate on large networks, including the Internet, though most systems block it for security reasons.

Note: Ethereal is a protocol analyzer that can capture network packets and display detailed information about them. You can detect what kind of information is being transmitted on your network as well as its source and destination. Ethereal is used primarily for network and server administration.

host

With the `host` command, you can find network address information about a remote system connected to your network. This information usually consists of a system's IP address, domain name address, domain name nicknames, and mail server. This information is obtained from your network's domain name server. For the Internet, this includes all systems you can connect to over the Internet.

The `host` command is an effective way to determine a remote site's IP address or URL. If you have only the IP address of a site, you can use `host` to find out its domain name. For network administration, an IP address can be helpful for making your own domain name entries in your **/etc/host** file. That way, you needn't rely on a remote domain name server (DNS) for locating a site.

```
# host gnomefiles.org
gnomefiles.org has address 67.18.254.188
gnomefiles.org mail is handled by 10 mx.zayda.net.
```

```
# host 67.18.254.188
188.254.18.67.in-addr.arpa domain name pointer gnomefiles.org.
```

traceroute

Internet connections are made through various routes, traveling through a series of interconnected gateway hosts. The path from one system to another could take different routes, some of which may be faster than others. For a slow connection, you can use **traceroute** to check the route through which you are connected to a host, monitoring the speed and the number of intervening gateway connections a route takes. The **traceroute** command takes as its argument the hostname or IP addresses for the system whose route you want to check. Options are available for specifying parameters like the type of service (-t) or the source host (-s). The **traceroute** command will return a list of hosts the route traverses, along with the times for three probes sent to each gateway. Times greater than five seconds are displayed with an asterisk, *.

```
traceroute rabbit.mytrek.com
```

You can also use the mtr or xmtr tools to perform both ping and traces (Traceroute on the System Tools menu).

15. Printing

Editing Printer Configuration

Printer Classes

Adding New Printers Manually

Remote Printers

Ubuntu Printers remotely accessed from Windows

This chapter covers the new version of the Printing configuration tool, system-config-printer, now used in Ubuntu 9.04. The configuration panes are similar to Ubuntu 8.04 with several important exceptions. When you select a printer driver, you can now choose to download it from the OpenPrinting repository. A separate dialog is now used to select both system-wide and personal default printers. In general, the configuration and management interface is organized into separate windows, instead of using a single window with selectable servers and printers.

Automatic printer detection

Whenever you first attach a local printer, like a USB printer, you will be asked to perform basic configuration such as confirming the make and model. Removable local printers are managed by udev and HAL, tools designed to automatically detect and configure removable devices. A message will appear as soon as you connect your USB printer.

If a driver is available for your printer, it will be selected automatically for you. Should you want to use a different driver, or printer is being detected incorrectly, you can click on the Find diver button to select the driver. A Change Driver window opens up where you can enter in the printer configuration information.

If the driver is not available, a Missing printer driver notification will be displayed.

Figure 15-1: Printer detection notification

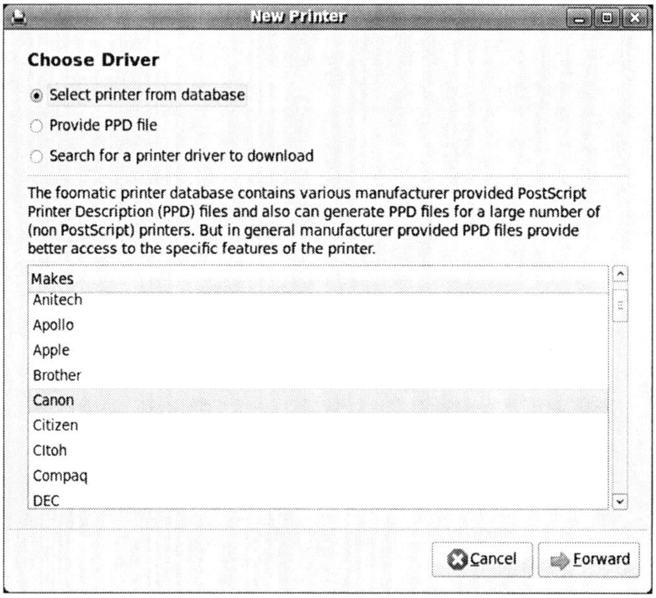

Figure 15-2: Choose Printer driver for missing driver

A New Printer dialog opens where you can choose how to locate your driver (see Figure 15-2).

system-config-printer

To later change your configuration or to add a remote printer, you can use the printer configuration tool, system-config-printer. This utility enables you to select the appropriate driver for your printer, as well as set print options such as paper size and print resolutions. You can configure a printer connected directly to your local computer or a printer on a remote system on your network. You can start system-config-printer by selecting the Printing entry in the System | Administration menu.

Figure 15-3: system-config-printer tool

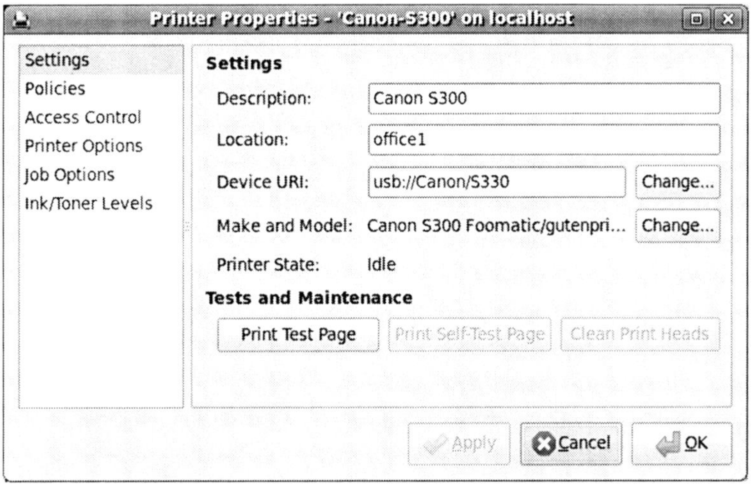

Figure 15-4: Printer properties window

The Printer configuration window displays icons for installed printers (see Figure 15-3). The menu bar has menus for Server configuration and selection, Printer features like its properties and the print queue, printer groups, and viewing printers by group and discovered printers. A toolbar has buttons for adding new printers manually and refreshing print configuration. A Filter search box lets you display only printers matching a search pattern. Click on the broom icon in the search box to clear the pattern. Clicking on the Looking glass icon in the File search box will display a pop-up menu that will let you search on Name, Description, Location, and Manufacturer/Model. You can save searches as a search group. You can also use the search results to create a printer group.

To see the printer settings such as printer and job options, access controls, and policies, double-click on the printer icon or right-click and select Properties. The Printer Properties window opens up with five panes: Settings, Policies, Access Control, Printer Options, and Job Options (see Figure 15-4). These are the same as those used in Ubuntu 8.04.

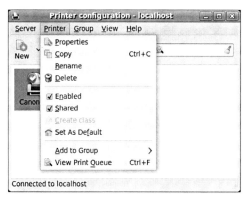

Figure 15-5: Printer configuration window Printer menu

Figure 15-6: Printer icon menu

The Printer configuration window Printer menu lets you rename the printer, enable or disable it, and make it a shared printer. Select the printer icon and then click the Printer menu (see Figure 15-5). The Delete entry will remove a printer configuration. Use the Set As Default entry to make the printer a system-wide or personal default printer.

The Printer icon menu is accesses by right-clicking on the printer icon (see Figure 15-6). It adds entries for accessing the printer properties and viewing the print queue. If the printer is already a default, there is no Set As Default entry. The properties entry opens the printer properties window for that printer.

The View Print Queue entry opens the Document print status window listing jobs for that printer. You can change the queue position as well as stop or delete jobs (see Figure 15-7). From the job menu you can cancel, hold (stop), release (restart), or reprint a print job. Reprint is only available if you have set the preserve jobs option in the printer settings Advanced dialog. You can also authenticate a job. From the View menu you can choose to display just printed jobs and refresh the queue.

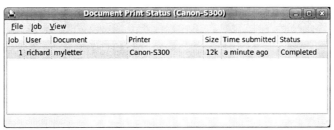

Figure 15-7: Printer queue

To check the server settings, select Settings from the Server menu. This opens a new window showing the CUPS printer server settings (see Figure 15-8). The Advanced button opens a window for job history and browser server options. If you want to allow reprinting, then select the "Preserve job files (allow reprinting)" option.

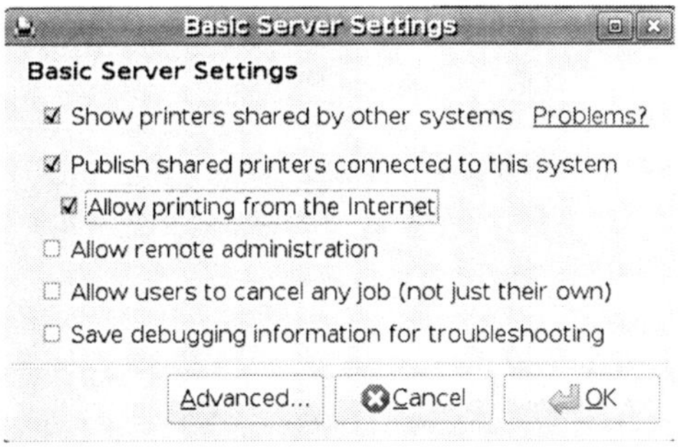

Figure 15-8: Server Settings

Figure 15-9: Selecting a CUPS server

To select a particular CUPS server, select the Connect entry in the Server menu. This opens a "Connect to CUPS Server" window with a drop down menu listing all current CUPS servers from which to choose (see Figure 15-9).

Editing Printer Configuration

To edit an installed printer, double click its icon in the Printer configuration window, or right-click and select the Properties entry. This opens a Printer Properties window for that printer. A sidebar lists configuration panes. Click on one to display that pane. There are configuration entries for Settings, Policies, Access Control, Printer Options, and Job Control (see Figure 15-10).

Once you have made your changes, you can click Apply to save your changes and restart the printer daemon. You can test your printer with a PostScript, A4, or ASCII test sheet selected from the Test menu.

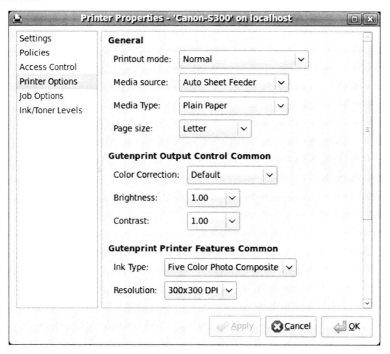

Figure 15-10: Printer Options pane

On the Settings pane you can change configuration settings like the driver and the printer name, enable or disable the printer, or specify whether to share it or not (see Figure 15-4). Should you need to change the selected driver, click on the Change button next to the Make and Model entry. This will open printer model and driver windows like those described in the Add new printer manually section. There you can specify the model and driver you want to use, even loading your own driver.

The Policies pane lets you specify a start and end banner, as well as an error policy which specifies whether to retry or abort the print job, or stop the printer should an error occur. The Access Control pane allows you to deny access to certain users.

The Printer Options pane is where you set particular printing features like paper size and type, print quality, and the input tray to use (see Figure 15-11).

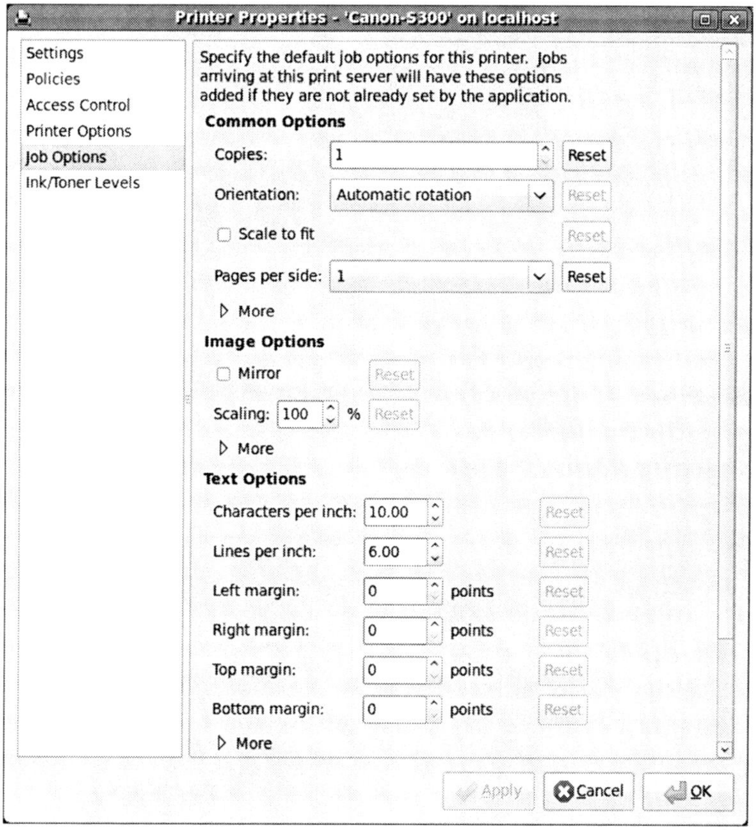

Figure 15-11: Jobs Options pane

On the Job Options pane you can select default printing features (see Figure 15-8). A pop-up menu provides a list of printing feature categories to choose from. You then click the Add button to add the category, selecting a particular feature from a pop-up menu. You can set such features as the number of copies (copies); letter, glossy, or A4-sized paper (media); the kind of document, for instance, text, PDF, PostScript, or image (document format); and single- or double-sided printing (sides).

The Ink/Toner Levels pane will display Ink or Toner levels for supported printers, along with status messages.

Default System-wide and Personal Printers

To make printer the default printer, either right-click on the printer icon and select "Set As Default", or single click on the printer icon and then from the Printer configuration window's Printer menu select the "Set As Default" entry (see Figure 15-5 and 15-6). A Set Default Printer dialog open with options for setting the system-wide default or setting the personal default (see Figure 15-12). The system-wide default printer is the default for your entire network served by your CUPS server, not just your local system.

Figure 15-12: Set Default Printer dialog

The system-wide default printer will have a green check mark emblem on its printer icon in the Printer configuration window.

Should you wish to use a different printer yourself as your default printer, you can designate it as your personal default. To make a printer your personal default, select the entry "Set as my personal default printer" in the Set Default Printer dialog. A personal emblem, a heart, will appear on the printer's icon in the Printer configuration window. In Figure 15-13, the S300-windows printer is the system-wide default, whereas the S330 printer is the personal default.

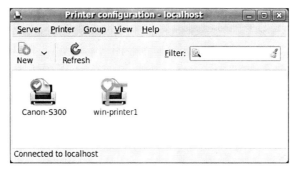

Figure 15-13: System-wide and personal default printers

If you have more than one printer on your system, you can make one the default by clicking Make Default Printer button in the printer's properties Settings pane.

Printer Classes

The Class entry in the New menu lets you create a printer class. You can access the New menu from the Server menu or from the New button. This feature lets you select a group of printers to print a job instead of selecting just one. That way, if one printer is busy or down, another printer can be automatically selected to perform the job. Installed printers can be assigned to different classes. When you click the Class entry in the New menu, a New Class window opens. Here you can enter the name for the class, any comments, and the location (your host name is entered by default). The next screen lists available printers on right side (Other printers) and the printers you assigned to the class on the left side (Printers in this class). Use the arrow button to add or remove printers to the class. Click Apply when finished. The class will appear under the Local Classes heading on the main system-config-printer window. Panes for a selected class are much the same as for a printer, with a members pane instead of a print control pane. In the Members pane you can change what printers belong to the class

Adding New Printers Manually

Printers are normally detected automatically, though in the case of older printers and network printers, you may need to add the printer manually. In this case click the New button and select Printer. A New Printer window opens up displaying series of dialog boxes where you select the connection, model, drivers, and printer name with location.

On the Select Device screen, you select the appropriate printer connection information. Connected local printer brands will already be listed by name, such as Canon. For remote printers you specify the type of network connection, like Windows printers via Samba for printers connected to a Windows system, AppSocket/HP Direct for HP printers connected directly to your network. The Internet Printing Protocol (ipp) for printers on Linux and Unix systems on your network. These connections are displayed under the Network Printer heading. Click the pointer to display them.

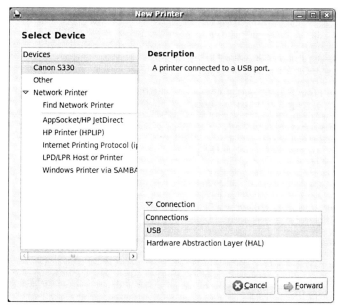

Figure 15-14: Selecting a new printer connection

For most connected printers, your connection is usually determined by the device hotplug services udev and HAL, which now manage all devices. Printers connected to your local system will be first entries on the list. A USB printer will simply be described as a USB printer, using the usb URI designation (see Figure 15-14 and 15-4).

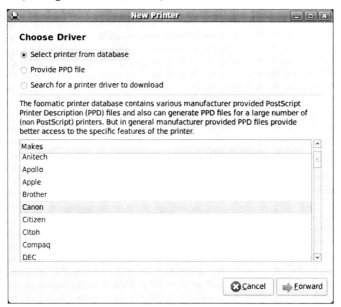

Figure 15-15: Printer manufacturer for new printers

For an older local printer, you will need to choose the port the printer is connected to, such as LPT1 for the first parallel port used for older parallel printers, or Serial Port #1 for a printer connected to the first serial port. For this example an older parallel printer will be set up, LPT #1.

A search will then be conducted for the appropriate driver, including downloadable drivers. If the driver is found, the Choose Driver screen is then displayed with the appropriate driver manufacturer already selected for you. You need only click the forward button. On the next screen, also labeled Choose Driver, the printer models and drivers files will be listed and the appropriate one already selected for you. Just click the Forward button. The Describe Printer screen is then displayed where you can enter the Printer Name, Description, and Location. These are ways you can personally identify a printer. Then click Apply.

If you printer driver is not detected or detected incorrectly, then, on the Choose Driver screen you have the options to choose the driver yourself from the database, from a PPD driver file of your own, or from your own search of the OpenPrinting online repository. The selection display will change according to which option you choose.

The database option will list possible manufacturers. Use your mouse to select the one you want.

The search option will display a search box for make and model. Enter both the make (printer manufacturer) and part of the model name (See figure 3-15). The search results will be available in the Printer model drop down menu. Select the one you want.

The PPD file option simply displays a file location button that when clicked, open a Select file dialog you can use to locate your PPD file on your system.

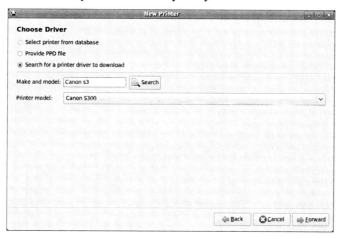

Figure 15-16: Searching for a printer driver from the OpenPrinting repository

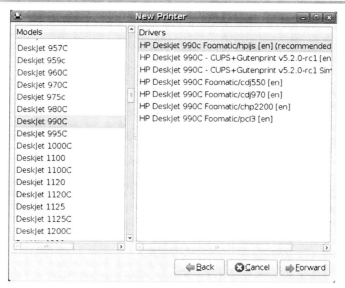

Figure 15-17: Printer Model and driver for new printers using local database

Instead of manually selecting the driver, you can try to search for it on OpenPrinting repository (see Figure 15-16). Click the Search for a printer driver to download entry. Enter the printer name and model and click the Search button. From the pop up menu labeled Printer model, select the driver for your printer. Then click Forward.

If you are selecting a printer from the database, then, on the next screen you select that manufacturer's model along with its driver (see Figure 15-17). For some older printer, though the driver can be located on the online repository, you will still choose it from the local database (the drivers are the same). The selected drivers for your printer will be listed. You can find out more about the printer and driver by clicking the Printer and Driver buttons at the bottom of the screen. Then click the Forward button.

You then enter in your printer name and location (see Figure 15-18). These will be entered for you using the printer model and your system's host name. You can change the printer name to anything you want. When ready, click Apply.

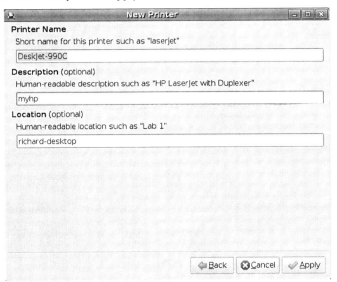

Figure 15-18: Printer Name and Location for new printers

You then see an icon for your printer displayed in the Printer configuration window. You are now ready to print.

Remote Printers

To install a remote printer that is attached to a Windows system or another Linux system running CUPS, you specify its location using special URI protocols. For a locally attached USB printer, the USB URI is uses, **usb**. For another CUPS printer on a remote host, the protocol used is **ipp**, for Internet Printing Protocol, whereas for a Windows printer, it would be **smb**. Older UNIX or Linux systems using LPRng would use the **lpd** protocol.

You can also use system-config-printer to set up a remote printer on Linux, UNIX, or Windows networks. When you add a new printer or edit one, the New Printer/Select Connection dialog will list possible remote connection types. When you select a remote connection entry, a pane will be displayed where you can enter configuration information.

For a remote Linux or UNIX printer, select either Internet Printing Protocol (ipp), which is used for newer systems, or LPD/LPR Host or Printer, which is used for older systems. Both panes display entries for the Host name and the Printer name. For the Host name, enter the hostname for the system that controls the printer. For the Printer name, enter the device name on that host for the printer. The LPD/LPR dialog also has a probe button for detecting the printer.

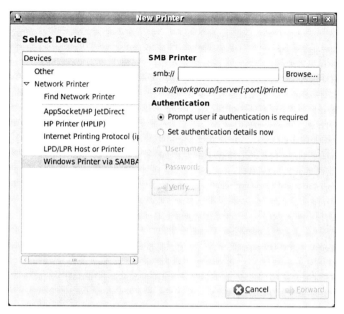

Figure 15-19: Selecting a Windows printer

For an Apple or HP jet direct printer on your network, select the AppSocket/HP jetDirect entry. You are prompted to enter the IP address and printer name.

A "Windows printer via Samba" is one located on a Windows network (see Figure 15-19). You need to specify the Windows server (host name or IP address), the name of the share, the name of the printer's workgroup, and the username and password. The format of the printer SMB URL is shown on the SMP Printer pane. The share is the hostname and printer name in the **smb** URI format *//workgroup/hostname/printername*. The workgroup is the windows network workgroup that the printer belongs to. On small networks there is usually only one. The hostname is the computer where the printer is located. The username and password can be for the printer resource itself, or for access by a particular user. The pane will display a box at the top where you can enter the share host and printer name as a **smb** URI.

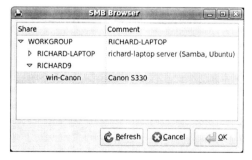

Figure 15-20: SMB Browser, selecting a remote windows printer

You can click the Browse button to open a SMB Browser window, where you can select the printer from a listing of Windows hosts on your network (see Figure 15-20). For example, if your Windows network is WORKGROUP, then the entry WORKGROUP will be shown, which you can then expand to list all the Windows hosts on that network (if your network is MSHOME, then that is what will be listed).

When you make your selection, the corresponding URL will show up in the **smb://** box (See Figure 15-21). If you are using the Firestarter firewall, be sure to turn it off before browsing a Windows workgroup for a printer, unless already configured to allow Samba access. Also on the pane, you can enter in any needed Samba authentication, if required, like user name or password. Check "Authentication required" to allow you to enter the Samba Username and Password.

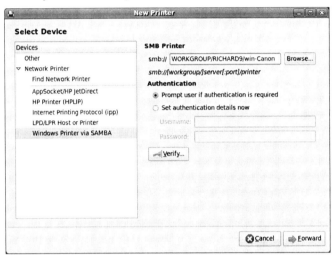

Figure 15-21: Remote windows printer connection configuration

You then continue with install screens for the printer model, driver, and name. Once installed, you can then access the printer properties just as you would any printer (see Figure 15-22).

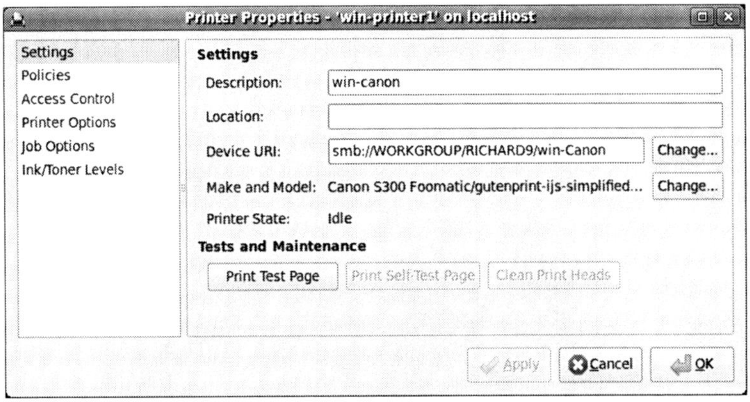

Figure 15-22: Remote Windows printer Settings

To access an SMB shared remote printer, you need to install Samba and have the Server Message Block services enabled using the smb and nmb daemons. The Samba service will be enabled by default. The service is enabled by checking the Windows Folders entry in the Gnome Services tool (System | Administration | Services). Printer sharing must, in turn, be enabled on the Windows network.

Ubuntu Printers remotely accessed from Windows

On a Windows system, like Windows XP, you can use the Add Printer Wizard to locate a shared printer on a Linux system (see Figure 15-23). Locate the Ubuntu system, click on it, and the shared printers on the Ubuntu system will be listed.

Tip: If the Windows driver for your printer on your Windows system should fail, you could just attach printer to an Ubuntu system and use the Linux drivers, even remotely accessing the printer from your Windows system.

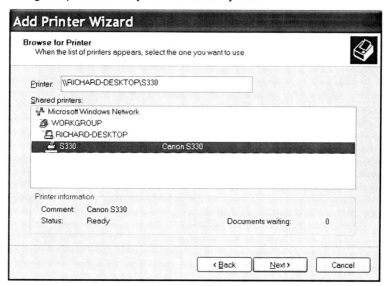

Figure 15-23: Remote Linux printer selection on Windows

Appendix A: Getting Ubuntu

The Ubuntu Linux distribution installs a professional-level and very stable Linux system along with the KDE and GNOME GUI interfaces, flexible and easy-to-use system configuration tools, an extensive set of Internet servers, a variety of different multimedia applications, and thousands of Linux applications of all kinds. You can find recent information about Ubuntu at **www.ubuntu.com**.

Most Ubuntu software is available for download from the Ubuntu repository. Install disks are available also, either as smaller desktop only installs, or larger server installs. You normally use the Ubuntu Desktop Live CD to install Ubuntu. Ubuntu distribution strategy relies on install disks with a selected collection of software that can be later updated and enhanced from the very large collection of software on the Ubuntu repository. This means that the collection of software in an initial installation can be relatively small. Software on the Ubuntu repository is also continually updated, so any installation will likely have to undergo extensive updates from the repository.

With smaller install disks, you can quickly download and burn an Ubuntu install image. The Desktop Live CD is available from the GetUbuntu page on the Ubuntu Web site. There are 32 bit and 64 bit versions for all current releases. The release covered in this book is the 9.04 release, Jaunty Jackalope.

`www.ubuntu.com/getubuntu`

In addition, there are Server and Alternate versions as well as an Install DVD. These you can download ISO images for all versions directly from the following site.

`http://releases.ubuntu.com/jaunty`

This site also includes the torrents for the versions, letting you use a BitTorrent client to download the CD or DVD image. Torrents are also listed at:

`http://torrent.ubuntu.com`

You can also use Jigdo to download an image from various mirrors at once, switching to the fastest as their access loads change.

Also, there are several editions of Ubuntu that you can download from the respective edition Web site. Edubuntu and Kubuntu are available at **http://releases.ubuntu.com**. The others can be downloaded from **http://cdimages.ubuntu.com**.

➢ **www.edubuntu.org**   Educational version

➢ **www.xubuntu.org**   Xfce desktop version

➢ **www.kubuntu.org**   KDE desktop version

➢ **http://wiki.ubuntu.com/Gobuntu**   Open Source only version

The Ubuntu Network Remix image (UNR) is a USB image designed for use on netbook PCs. The UNR can operate like a Live USB image. It is designed for netbook PCs with up to 10 inch screens and a minimum 256MB RAM. The image file is named **ubuntu-9.04-netbook-remix-i386.img**. The UNR is available at **http://releases.ubuntu.com/jaunty** and at **http://www.ubuntu.com/getubuntu/download-netbook**. You use USB Imagewriter (**usb-imagewriter** package) to burn it on Ubuntu. For details see:

```
https://help.ubuntu.com/community/Installation/FromImgFiles
```

Install/Live DVD and MID USB images

The Install/Live DVD and MID USB file images are available either as a torrent files or full image files at **http://cdimages.ubuntu.com** under the **releases/jaunty/release** directory.

```
http://cdimages.ubuntu.com/releases/jaunty/release/
```

The Install/Live DVD image file is a large file, about 4.3 GB.

Ubuntu also provides a Low-Power Intel Architecture MID USB image for handheld devices using the Intel Atom and A1xx processors. This is a Live CD image that can be burned to a USB drive, which can then be run on the handheld directly from the USB drive. The MID USB image is available from **http://releases.ubuntu.com** as **ubuntu-9.04-mid-lpia.img**.

Additional editions

Additional community supported editions are also available like Kubuntu-4 with KDE release 4, mythbuntu for MythTV, and UbuntuStudio with image development software. You can download these, along with the other editions from

```
http://cdimages.ubuntu.com
```

Once you have the install image, you will need to burn it to a DVD or CD disk, which you can then use to install your system.

If you are a first time user, you may want to first run the Live CD to see how Ubuntu operates, before you decide to install. The Live-CD can run from system memory.

```
http://help.ubuntu.com
```

Using BitTorrent

You can use any FTP or Web client, such as gFTP or Firefox, to download the CD image files. The DVD image, though, is a very large file that can take a long time to download, especially if the FTP site is very busy or if your have a slow Internet connection. An alternative for such very large files is to use BitTorrent. BitTorrent is a safe distributed download operation that is ideal for large files, letting many participants download and upload the same file, building a torrent that can run very fast for all participants. The BitTorrent files are located both at **http://releases.ubuntu.com**.

You will first need to install the BitTorrent client. Transmission is the default BitTorrent client installed on GNOME by Ubuntu (Applications | Internet | Transmission). For KUbuntu you can use Ktorrent. There are other several BitTorrent clients available such as **azureus**, **rtorrent**, and the original **bittorrent**.

Jigdo

The preferred method for downloading large DVD ISO images is Jigdo (Jigsaw Download). Jigdo combines the best of both direct downloads and BitTorrent, while maximizing use of the download data for constructing various spins. In effect, Jigdo sets up a bittorrent download operation using just the Ubuntu mirror sites (no uploading). Jigdo automatically detects the mirror sites that currently provide the fastest download speeds and downloads your image file from them. Mirror sites accessed are switched as download speeds change. If you previously downloaded directly from mirrors, with Jigdo you no longer have to go searching for a fast download mirror site. Jigdo finds them for you.

See the Jigdo Download Howto page at **http://help.ubuntu.com** for more details.

```
https://help.ubuntu.com/community/JigdoDownloadHowto
```

Jigdo is available for the server and alternate CD/DVDs. It is not used for the desktop versions (32 or 64 bit).

For jigdo, first install the **jigdo-file** package and then run the **jigdo-lite** command in a terminal window. You will be prompted for a **.jigdo** file. You can provide the URL for the .jigdo file for the ISO image you want, or download the **.jigdo** file first and provide its path name. At the **http://releases.ubuntu.com** site you will find jigdo files for each ISO image, along with **.torrent** and **.iso** files. The jigdo file for an i386 server is:

```
ubuntu-9.04-server-i386.jigdo
```

Its full URL would be:

```
http://releases.ubuntu.com/releases/9.04/ubuntu-9.04-server-i386.jigdo
```

Jigdo organizes the download into central repository that can be combined into different spins. If you download the Ubuntu desktop CD, and then later the server CD, the data already downloaded for the desktop CD can be used to build the server CD, reducing the actual downloaded data significantly. You will be prompted to provide the location of any mounted CD or CD image.

You can also use jigdo, which provides a GNOME interface for using jigdo. Install the **jigdo** package and run the **jigdo** command in a terminal window.

Appendix B: XFce4 Desktop

Several editions of Ubuntu like XUbuntu use the XFce desktop instead of either GNOME or KDE. XFce is designed as a stripped down desktop with very little resource overhead, ideal for laptops or systems dedicated to single tasks.

Figure B-1: XFce desktop

The XFce4 desktop is a lightweight desktop designed to run fast without the kind of overhead required for full featured desktops like KDE and GNOME. You can think of it as a window manager with desktop functionality. It includes its own file manager and panel, but the emphasis is on modularity and simplicity. Like GNOME, XFce4 is based on GTK+ GUI tools. The desktop consists of a collection of modules like the thunar file manager, xfce4-panel panel, and the xfwm4 window manager. Keeping with its focus on simplicity, XFce4 features only a few common applets on its panel. It small scale makes it appropriate for laptops or dedicated systems, that have no need for complex overhead found in other desktops.

XFce is used primarily on XUbuntu and Mythbuntu, though you can install it on any Ubuntu desktop system. With Synaptic use the **xfce4** metapackage in the Universe repository (Miscellaneous - Graphical section).

XFce is useful for desktop designed for just a few tasks, like multimedia desktops. The desktop displays icons for your Home directory, file system, and trash. The bottom panel holds a menu button on the left side with the image of mouse. From the menu you can access any Ubuntu software applications along with Ubuntu administration tools. The administration tools are listed on the Settings submenu. To configure the XFCE4 interface, you use the Xfce 4 Settings Manager, accessible from the XFce4 menu at Settings | Xfce 4 Settings Manager. This opens the Settings window which shows icons for your desktop, display, panel, user interface, among others (see Figure B-1). Use the Appearance tool to select themes, icons, and toolbar styles (Settings). The Panel tool lets you add new panels and control features like fixed for freely movable and horizontally or vertically positioned.

To configure the desktop, select the Desktop icon on the Settings window or right-click on the desktop and select Desktop Settings from the pop-up menu. This opens the Desktop window where you can select the background image, control d menu behavior, and set icon sizes.

Note: You can also access applications as well as the Settings Manager and Desktop Settings by right-clicking on the desktop background to display the desktop menu. The Settings Manager is accessible from Applications | Settings | Xfce 4 Settings Manager, and the Desktop Settings is listed on the initial menu.

Initially, in a new install of XFce4, there is a bottom panel with buttons for an applications menu, terminal window, file manager, Web browser, network connections (Network Manager), workspace switcher, hide/show desktop, time and date, and quit (running person). The panel also holds a taskbar for open windows. You can add more items by clicking on the panel and selecting Add new items. This opens a window with several applets like the clock and workspace switcher, as well as Xfce Menu and Launcher applets. The launcher applet will let you specify an application to start and choose an icon image for it. To move an applet, right-click on it and choose Move from the pop-up menu. Your mouse becomes hand that you can use to move the applet on the panel.

The file manager lists entries for not just for your home directory, but also your file system, desktop, and trash contents. The File menu lets you perform folder operations like creating new directories. From the Edit menu you can perform tasks on a selected file like renaming the file or creating a link for it.

Table Listing

Figure Listing

Index

Printed in the United States
221413BV00002BA/1/P